WINNING ON APPEAL

Better Briefs and Oral Argument

WINNING ON APPEAL

Better Briefs and Oral Argument

by Ruggero J. Aldisert

Senior United States Circuit Judge
The United States Court of Appeals
for the Third Circuit

Second Edition

National Institute for Trial Advocacy

Aldisert, Ruggero J.,*Winning on Appeal: Better Briefs and
Oral Advocacy, Second Edition* (NITA, 2003).

ISBN 1-55681-824-6

About the Author

Ruggero J. Aldisert, Senior United States Circuit Judge, is Chief Judge Emeritus of the United States Court of Appeals for the Third Circuit. Prior to his appointment to the federal appellate bench in 1968, Judge Aldisert had extensive experience in Pittsburgh as a trial lawyer and as a judge on the Pennsylvania Court of Common Pleas. Since taking senior status in 1987, Judge Aldisert has continued to sit regularly with the Third Circuit, and by designation, with other courts of appeals.

Judge Aldisert is a prominent author and leader of seminars for new United States Circuit Judges. In addition to his prior books on the law, the judge has written for numerous legal journals in the United States and Europe. He has published over thirty articles on jurisprudence, civil procedure, federal jurisdiction, federal-state relations, the doctrine of precedent, antitrust law, comparative law, logic for lawyers and judges, the judicial process, the role of the courts in a democratic society, and other topics.

Judge Aldisert served for twenty years as an adjunct professor at the University of Pittsburgh Law School and was a highly respected leader of seminars for newly elected United States Circuit judges and state supreme court justices. He has lectured at law schools and before bar, judicial, and academic groups in eight countries, including countries in Eastern Europe, on subjects ranging from constitutional law to comparative judicial process.

The judge lives in Santa Barbara, California, with his wife Agatha. The Aldiserts have three grown children, Lisa M. Aldisert, of New York City, Robert L. Aldisert, Esq., of Portland Oregon, and Gregory J. Aldisert, Esq., of Los Angeles, California. The Aldiserts have five grandchildren.

For my sons

Robert L. Aldisert, Esq. and Gregory J. Aldisert, Esq.

Summary of Contents

Table of Contents

PART ONE
THE THEORY AND CRITICISMS OF WRITTEN AND ORAL ADVOCACY

PART TWO
TECHNICAL REQUIREMENTS FOR BRIEFS
Chapter 4.   Jurisdiction

Chapter 5. Issue Preservation and Standards of Review

PART THREE
THE NUTS AND BOLTS OF BRIEF WRITING

Chapter 6. Getting Started: Requirements for Briefs, Records and Appendices

PART FOUR
THE NUTS AND BOLTS OF PREPARING AND
DELIVERING ORAL ARGUMENT

Chapter 22. Preparing for Oral Argument

Chapter 23. How Top-Flight Appellate Lawyers Prepare

Chapter 24. Delivering the Argument

PART FIVE
CHECKLISTS

APPENDICES

Foreword

For thirty-one years Ruggero J. Aldisert—"Rugi" as he is affectionately known by his many friends, in high places and low, all around the world—has served with distinction as a judge. He had seven years as a state trial judge in Allegheny County and since 1968 has been judge, then chief judge, and now senior judge of the United States Court of Appeals for the Third Circuit. As a senior judge he is anything but retired. He sits regularly with federal appellate courts around the country and finds time to write books such as this one.

In a Foreword to one of the earlier books, Justice Harry A. Blackmun of the Supreme Court of the United States said about Judge Aldisert:

> He loves the law. He yearns to know its history and its character or, to use the word he has employed effectively in this volume, its anatomy. He has a persistent but most refreshing curiosity about the law. He wants to know what it is, why it is, and how all of us who labor in its vineyards use or misuse it.

It is not enough, however, for him to learn about the law. Like Chaucer's Clerk, "gladly he would lerne and gladly teche." He has been a fine judge, but not very well-hidden behind the austere judicial robes is the heart and the mind of a teacher. For more than twenty of the years he was serving on the state and federal bench he was also an adjunct professor at the University of Pittsburgh Law School. He has taught antitrust law at the University of Augsburg (Bavaria) and he came and taught for a summer at the University of Texas Law School, to the great benefit of our students and to the delight of our faculty. For years he played an active part in the Senior Appellate Judges Seminar at New York University School of Law, and time out of mind he has been a speaker or on a panel at a judicial conference, a law school, or a seminar for newly appointed judges.

This is his fourth book. It follows *The Judicial Process* (1976), *Logic for Lawyers: A Guide to Clear Legal Thinking* (1988), and *Opinion Writing* (1990). The titles of those books, and this, show he has distilled the lessons he has learned from his service as a judge and set them out for the instruction of his colleagues on the bench and of the lawyers who appear before the judges. He is trying to teach us the things his experience tells him we ought to do.

This is a wonderfully instructive book. The writing is clear and vigorous. Comments from state chief justices, federal chief justices, and from law clerks add a broader perspective to what Judge Aldisert has himself observed. Although the instruction this book provides will be particularly valuable to the neophyte at the bar, even the most experienced veteran will find things here worth pondering.

Does this mean I agree with every piece of advice Judge Aldisert offers? Of course not—any more than I agree on all aspects of constitutional law with my four faculty colleagues who also offer the basic course in that subject. In § 22.8, for example, Judge Aldisert writes about "the mandatory rehearsal" before oral argument. I would not dream of rehearsing an argument. Indeed I refuse even to discuss a case in the period leading up to when I am going to argue it. At least for my style of argument, freshness and spontaneity are vitally important. I think long and hard about what may be said at oral argument, but I do not put words on paper nor do I discuss the case with others.

This is only to say that there is more than one way to write a brief and prepare for oral argument. With most of the advice Judge Aldisert offers here, I agree. And even when, as with rehearsing an argument, I do not agree, I recognize that his recommendations have much force and that many lawyers will benefit from following the methods he suggests.

There is a sense in which appellate advocacy cannot be taught. Ultimately it is the lawyer, all alone at the lectern, who must count on his or her instinct and sense of the situation—perhaps even genius—to carry the day. But that lawyer is far more likely to succeed if he or she is well schooled in the fundamentals. These are splendidly taught here by Judge Aldisert. The wise lawyer will master the methods recommended in this book before striking out on a different and individual path.

Charles Alan Wright
Wlliam B. Bates Chair for
the Administration of Justice
The University of Texas Law School

Austin, Texas
November, 1992

Professor Charles Alan Wright died in Austin, Texas on July 7, 2000. He was a dear friend. At the American Law Institute's Memorial Tributes to him in London, England on July 17, 2000, Professor Gareth Jones described him as I knew him so well:

Charlie was a big man in every sense of that adjective, a formidable frame, a powerful intellect. His legal memory, constant recall, never ceased to astonish me. He was a courageous parent and citizen who believed passionately in a United States which should be free of ethnic discrimination. It was typical of the man that he took away his daughter from a school which refused to admit black students.

What are my personal memories of Charlie? He was first and foremost a companion whom one always looked forward to meeting, constantly challenging, never aggressively so, a correct but not pedantic grammarian who respected the proper use of the English language, a person who enjoyed material comfort, had an engaged sense of humor, and was a most hospitable host.

Preface to the First Edition

I wrote this book for one purpose: to suggest methods of improving appellate written and oral advocacy.

I wrote it from the perspective of one who has been reading briefs and listening to arguments since 1961, both in a state trial court and in many federal appellate courts. I wrote it also from the perspective of one who has long been active in state and federal judicial education programs; in programs where the quality of written and oral presentations by lawyers constantly commanded our attention.

The book is for lawyers. I call it *Winning on Appeal*, because that is what lawyers want to do and should want to do. But we cannot promise that what follows in these pages will do just that. More often than not, hefty, hearty precedents and facts embedded in concrete will control the outcome. But in a certain percentage of cases—in which the rule of law, and therefore, the decision, could go either way—how and where the axe will fall may depend upon the quality of appellate advocacy.

It is here where what is said in these pages may produce a difference. And it is here where I will make a guarantee: if you follow the advice contained in these pages, you will create the maximum impression on the judges who will hear your case; your written and oral presentation will generate maximum effectiveness in convincing the court to your point of view. Certainly, you will not always prevail; only one party wins on appeal. Factual findings, controlling legal precepts, or previously stated policy concerns of the court often run counter to propositions that you advance. But if you follow the proffered advice, you will be discharging the high responsibility of an officer of the court—to assist judges in achieving a completely informed, totally rational and probably correct decision.

I am a senior United States circuit judge now living in California, although my home court is still the Court of Appeals for the Third Circuit in Philadelphia. One of the privileges of senior judge status is the opportunity to sit by designation in other United States Courts of Appeals. Thus I have had the unique experience of working with judges and lawyers in a wide geographic area. I have become a circuit rider. No saddle bags or horse here, just a jet plane.

In my own third circuit, lawyers from Pennsylvania, New Jersey, Delaware, and the Virgin Islands have appeared before me by brief or oral argument for many years. I have learned that the phrase, "a Philadelphia lawyer," may indeed mean the best, but alas, less often than not. I have been designated to sit on the eleventh circuit and learned to respect members of the bar from Florida, Alabama, and Georgia; and the fine professionals from Texas, Louisiana, and Mississippi when I sat with the fifth circuit in New Orleans. When sitting on the tenth circuit on many occasions, I learned something about some very competent lawyers from Wyoming, Utah, Kansas, Colorado, New Mexico, and Oklahoma. Because I now am a California resident, I regularly sit on the ninth circuit and have a fair exposure to some excellent advocates from Montana, Idaho, Nevada, Arizona, Washington, Oregon, California, Alaska, Hawaii, Guam, and the Marianas Islands.

I have heard the best, "in every clime and place," as in the Marines Hymn, and I probably have heard the worst. After all these years, however, I have not become jaded. The juices still run swiftly when a brief truly inspires and oral argument "ceases to be an episode in the affairs of a client and becomes a stone in the edifice of the law," as once described by Supreme Court Justice Robert H. Jackson:

> To participate as advocate in supplying the basis for decisional law-making calls for the vision of the prophet, as well as a profound appreciation of the continuity between the law of today and that of the past. He will be sharing the task of reworking decisional law by which every generation seeks to preserve its essential character and at the same time to adapt it to contemporary needs. At such a moment the lawyer's case ceases to be an episode in the affairs of a client and becomes a stone in the edifice of the law.

Now a few words about the book. It is designed to be a desk reference, not as an essay to be read from cover to cover (although it would not be a bad idea for neophytes to the appellate process to do just this). Read Part One (chapters 1–3) to learn what judges expect from lawyers; learn also to avoid the stated criticisms of written and oral arguments. Part Three (chapters 6–21) and Part Four (chapters 22–24) are required reading; they address the nuts and bolts on how to improve your written and oral skills.

The table of contents is all-important. It is your road map to this book. Totally familiarize yourself with it. Immerse yourself in it so you will know exactly where to go when you need particular assistance. Although placed near the rear of the book, checklists for briefs and oral argument, contained in chapter 25, are all-important. Photocopy them. Keep them handy as you prepare and implement your appellate strategy.

I am indebted to many. Over thirty chiefs of our states' highest courts (as well as a number of their colleagues) responded to my request for advice on how to improve briefs and arguments. Their wise counsel appears throughout the text as well as in tables set forth in §§ [9.7.1, 21.2, 22.3]. The chief judges of the United States courts of appeals kindly offered suggestions to a difficult situation that often faces lawyers at argument when a single judge embarks on an irrelevant, intellectual frolic. Their guidance has been summarized and appears in tables at §§ [9.7.2, 21.3, 22.4, 24.6.3.2].

I am grateful for the insights received from many United States circuit judges and state supreme court justices who attended the Senior Appellate Judges Seminars of the Institute of Judicial Administration in New York during the many years when I served as a faculty discussion leader and associate director. I acknowledge the contributions contained in many articles written by judges to which references are made with appreciation.

An appellate judge soon learns that the quality of the judicial process is often commensurate with the quality of appellate advocacy, and though we judges may tell lawyers what improvements we want and why we want them, it is for successful appellate lawyers to tell us how they do it. I have researched many thoughtful articles and make generous references and attributions to them, especially Stephen M. Shapiro, of Mayer, Brown & Platt, Chicago, and Jordan B. Cherrick of [Thompson Coburn], St. Louis.

I acknowledge the contributions of Kenneth Starr, the [former] United States Solicitor General; James D. Crawford of Schnader, Harrison, Segal & Lewis, and Edward F. Mannino, Philadelphia; John H. Bingler, Jr., of Thorp, Reed & Armstrong, Pittsburgh; and Bobby R. Burchfield of Covington and Burling, Washington, D.C.; Michael T. Reagan of Ottawa, Illinois, and Nancy J. Arnold of Chicago graciously invited me to present some of this material at 1991 and 1992 workshops of the Appellate Lawyers Association of Illinois, which I found stimulating and most helpful.

Several knowledgeable colleagues in appellate advocacy read the manuscript, or parts thereof, and provided thoughtful commentary that greatly enhanced the finished text. These reviewers included Senior Judges Max Rosenn, Joseph F. Weis, Jr., and Leonard I. Garth, my longtime colleagues on the third circuit; also three distinguished former law clerks, United States District Judge Robert J. Cindrich of the Western District of Pennsylvania (Pittsburgh), and [Dean] David W. Burcham of Loyola of Los Angeles Law School, and Margaret D. McGaughey,

Assistant United States Attorney for the District of Maine. They expended much valuable time in this endeavor and I thank them for many perceptive observations. I thank Anne Marie Finch, Susan Simmons Seemiller, Linda Schneider, Glenn J. Dickinson, and Kathleen M. Vanderziel for research and editorial assistance.

There now have been three generations of Aldiserts in the law (I do not exclude my father John S. Aldisert, who though not formally trained, became a self-taught medico-legal specialist in his thirty-three years as Chief Deputy Coroner of Allegheny County [Pittsburgh], Pennsylvania, supervising investigations and presiding at inquests). In preparing this book, I turned to the third generation for advice and counsel. An appreciative father is gratified to have available the wisdom of his sons, Robert L. Aldisert, of Perkins Coie, Portland, Oregon, and Gregory J. Aldisert of Kinsella, Boesch, Fujikawa and Towle, Los Angeles.

Most of all, I am profoundly grateful to my wife, Agatha, for her understanding, inspiration, and love, and for graciously permitting so many intrusions into our "retirement" time.

Ruggero J. Aldisert
Santa Barbara, California

November 1992

Preface to the Revised First Edition

This book on appellate advocacy is more than a style manual on how to write for and speak to an appellate tribunal. It is a practical guide about how to avoid pitfalls that often prevent your written or oral argument from being considered on the merits. In particular, we emphasize that success in preserving arguments on the merits comes only through a complete understanding of conditions precedent to being heard by the court.

We explain the importance of demonstrating that the appellate court has jurisdiction to hear your appeal. We underscore the necessity of preserving the points for review; this means presenting for consideration at the trial level those arguments which you intend to present to the appellate court. We emphasize the distinctions among the various standards of review, critical factors that determine the power of the magnifying lens adjusted by appellate courts to examine your various arguments.

But much more emerges from these pages. We discuss the theory and criticisms of written and oral advocacy, the technical requirements for briefs, the nuts and bolts of brief writing as well as preparing for the delivering of oral argument. We have created practical checklists to be used in every case. All of this reflects my firm conviction (and that espoused by the many appellate judges who contributed to these pages) that preparation for appellate advocacy begins at trial. Appellate strategy is an important aspect of trial advocacy. A sure approach for getting nowhere on appeal is to wait until the adverse verdict or ruling has been made and then attempt to flyspeck the record to fashion points for appeal. It is therefore most fitting that this edition be published under the auspices of the National Institute for Trial Advocacy (NITA), because effective appellate performance begins with good trial advocacy. I am proud to be associated with NITA, universally recognized by lawyers and law schools as the premier force in advocacy training.

I am gratified that this book has been extremely well received by judges and lawyers since it first appeared in the hardcover edition. One of my favorite comments came from Senior Circuit Judge John C. Godbold of Montgomery, Alabama, who served variously as chief judge of the United States Court of Appeals for both the Fifth and Eleventh Circuits, as well as Director of the Federal Judicial Center:

> If you know a young lawyer who wants to be a litigator, give him a copy of this book for Christmas. If you know an

old lawyer who engages in litigation and fancies himself an expert, give him a copy without waiting for Christmas.

Ruggero J. Aldisert
Santa Barbara, California

May 1996

Preface to the Second Edition

Although we call this book the Second Edition, it is really the third version. In 1996, we called the second version the "Revised First Edition" because the only changes were statistical updates—reversals on appeals in the federal courts, the frequency of oral argument and the granting of certiorari petitions in the United States Supreme Court.

With over a decade experience subsequent to the original text, we know now that, in addition to being adopted by many law schools as the text for appellate advocacy courses, the book has become a popular desk reference on how to write an effective brief and deliver a persuasive oral argument. Because it has evolved into a "how-to" manual, I have made the text more reader-friendly by overhauling the format for maximum efficiency.

This edition is a fundamental makeover. For the most part, it is more a new book, than a tweaking of the earlier versions. Without lengthening it, we now have twenty-five chapters, in place of the previous seventeen.

Part One, "The Theory and Criticisms of Written and Oral Appellate Advocacy," retains the same format, except that the tables of statistics represent the most up-to-date information available, instead of 1990 or 1995. The book continues to be unique in consolidating current empirical data on the odds of prevailing on appeal, or having a case orally argued. The tables reveal a trend of fewer published opinions, fewer reversals, and less oral argument in the appellate courts. References to appellate rules have been updated to track amendments since 1990.

Major revisions appear in Part Three, "Nuts and Bolts of Brief Writing" and Part Four, "Nuts and Bolts of Preparing and Delivering Oral Argument." Chapters have been designed to identify discrete requirements for an effective brief or argument, and to advise how to meet these prerequisites. To be sure, most of the suggestions are from personal judicial experience of more than forty years, first as a Pennsylvania state trial judge beginning in 1961, and then as a United States circuit judge since 1968. From the time the first version of this book appeared, I have continued to regularly sit with my own third circuit, both on merits panels as well as panels considering motions and pro se cases. In addition I have sat with the fifth, seventh, ninth, tenth, and eleventh circuits, and still continue to visit with some of them. These travels have given me a unique experience of reading briefs and hearing arguments of lawyers from Atlanta, Georgia to Seattle, Washington.

As in the previous editions, however, there is more than one judge offering advice in these pages. Nineteen current chief justices of state courts, nine chief judges of United States courts of appeals, more than a score of other United States circuit judges and other state appellate judges have graciously offered excellent suggestions which I set forth to improve your appellate advocacy. On many issues—too numerous to detail here—the views of these distinguished appellate judges totally corroborate my advice. Thus, the success of this book has been that what we say here reflects not merely "one man's opinion," but rather a broad-based consensus that exclaims, "This is what you should not do," and "This is what we judges look for when reading your brief and listening to your argument."

A great new dimension also appears in this edition. It is one thing for us judges to tell you what we desire from oral argument; it is quite another to tell you how to prepare for us. This advice must come from the great lawyers. For this reason, I turned to a number of the nation's outstanding appellate lawyers, true masters in oral advocacy, and I have devoted the whole of chapter 23 to set forth their advice. Three lawyers are from Philadelphia, two from Washington, D.C. (one a former United States Solicitor General), two from Illinois, and one each from St. Petersburg, Florida; Pittsburgh, and Los Angeles. This new chapter augments suggestions from other appellate lawyers interspersed in previous chapters on various subjects.

I am gratified that this book has been so well received by both the practicing bar and law students, and I am grateful to the many judges, scholars, and practitioners who have contributed to the present edition. In the text of pages that follow, I attribute law review sources for many references. I now thank the following authors for quoted material that appears in the tables on various subject areas: David O. Boehm, *Clarity and Candor are Vital in Appellate Advocacy*, N.Y. St. B.J., Sept./Oct. 1999, at 52; Joel F. Dubina, *How to Litigate Successfully in the United States Court of Appeals for the Eleventh Circuit*, 29 Cumb. L. Rev. 1 (1998); Henry D. Gabriel, *Preparation and Delivery of Oral Argument in Appellate Courts*, 22 Am. J. Trial Advoc. 571 (1999); Thomas R. Haggard, *Writing the Reply Brief*, Scrivener, Mar./Apr. 2001; Mark R. Kravitz, *Oral Argument Before the Second Circuit*, 71 Conn. B.J. 204 (1997); Marcia L. McCormick, *Selecting and Framing the Issues on Appeal: A Powerful Persuasive Tool*, 90 Ill. B.J. 203 (2002); Gary L. Sasso, *Anatomy of the Written Argument*, 15 Litig. 30 (1989); *Appellate Oral Argument*, 20 Litig. 27 (1994); Jacques Weiner, Jr., *Ruminations From the Bench: Brief Writing and Oral Argument in the Fifth Circuit*, 70 Tul. L. Rev. 187 (1995); Karen Williams, *Help Us Help You: A Fourth*

Circuit Primer on Effective Appellate Oral Arguments, 50. S.C.L. Rev. 591 (1999); Patricia M. Wald, *Tips from 19 Years on the Appellate Bench*, 1 J. App. Prac. & Proc. 7 (1999).

I also thank the many state appellate judges and the judges of the United States courts of appeals who graciously responded to my requests for their advice. I thank all lawyers who have written briefs and argued before me over the years; those judges of the U.S. Court of Appeals for the Third and Tenth Circuits who responded to my specific request on how lawyers may more effectively persuade appellate judges; the various state court administrators who answered my request for specific court statistics; and Professor J. Thomas Sullivan, of William H. Bowen School of Law, University of Arkansas at Little Rock, for supplying me with all back issues of his excellent new publication, *The Journal of Appellate Practice and Procedure.*

I want to thank the folks at the National Institute of Trial Advocacy (NITA), my publisher. They are an exceptionally talented cadre of dedicated and efficient professionals. It is an honor to be associated with them.

I extend my appreciation to Mimi Hildbrand for her loyalty and devotion to this project. I am especially indebted to Michael A. Mugmon, Esq. and Robert K. Simonds, Esq. for profound editorial, analytical, and research assistance.

But most of all, I thank my wife of over fifty years, Agatha, who patiently endured many weekends while I was closeted in the den preparing this new edition and infringing upon our personal time. I publicly acknowledge her constant inspiration and loving support, and the many acts of kindness and assistance, including the authorship of its title, as I wrote the several editions of this book.

Ruggero J. Aldisert
Santa Barbara, California

July 2003

PART ONE
THE THEORY AND CRITICISMS OF
WRITTEN AND ORAL APPELLATE ADVOCACY

Chapter 1

APPELLATE REVIEW: A PANORAMA

§ 1.1 Overview

This book is for lawyers. It is for a special breed of lawyers—the men and women who write briefs and argue appeals before state and federal appellate courts. It is also for those who aspire to be appellate lawyers, either as members of the bar or as law students.

Moreover, the book looks in one direction—from the bench to the bar. It is a vista that perceives written and oral argument from the viewpoint of those to whom arguments are addressed. In 1940, John W. Davis, one of the nation's great appellate advocates, drew an interesting analogy:

> [S]upposing fishes had the gift of speech, who would listen to a fisherman's weary discourse on flycasting, the shape and color of the fly, the size of the tackle, the length of the line, the merit of different rod makers and all the other tiresome stuff that fisherman talk about, if the fish himself could be induced to give his views on the most effective methods of approach? For after all it is the fish that the angler is after and all his recondite learning is but the hopeful means to that end.[1]

In this book, the fish are giving the advice. Judicial fish are explaining to lawyer anglers how to catch them.

This book recognizes that there are different types of skilled anglers. Many are great trial lawyers, but their well-honed skills in familiar lakes do not necessarily translate to unpredictable, swift-moving rivers.

Appellate advocacy is specialized work. It draws upon talents and skills that are far different from those utilized in other facets of practicing law. Being a good trial lawyer does not mean that you are also a qualified appellate advocate. The consummate trial lawyer knows how to open to a jury, examine witnesses, protect the trial record with objections and motions, and how to close during summation. He or she knows how to prepare a succinct trial memorandum that has the capacity to persuade the harried trial judge who is chained to the bench, a prisoner to an overloaded calendar.

---

1. John W. Davis, *The Argument of an Appeal*, 26 A.B.A.J. 895, 895 (1940).

The successful trial lawyer is really a successful salesperson—successful in the sense of persuading the fact finder to select from the mass of testimony and evidence those adjudicative facts that favor the lawyer's client. To persuade is to sell effectively. I think of good trial lawyers as able salespersons, a function they do not always recognize and one that many of them probably would deny. There comes to mind the rebuke flung in the face of Willy Loman in the play, *Death of a Salesman* "The only thing you got in this world is what you can sell. The funny thing is that you're a salesman, and you don't know that."[2]

But salespersons have different customers, dissimilar audiences, disparate objectives, and diverse time frames. At trial the major objective is to persuade the fact finder, often a panel of lay jurors, that credibility lies on the side of your witnesses, and to show that the evidence, although controverted, favors your client.

For the most part, trial lawyers work within a framework of existing legal precepts. Out of a congeries of conflicting evidence presented, they seek but one objective: to persuade the fact finder to accept a version of the dispute favoring their client. Trial lawyers ascertain the factual strengths and weaknesses of both sides of their cases and then sift, select, and evaluate the evidence to be presented.

The best of this stellar breed carve a convincing argument from an amorphous mass of testimony and create an aura of righteousness around the client and the cause. This is not to say that trial lawyers need only know how to manage the facts. To protect the record and to guard against both improper and unfavorable rulings, they must know and be prepared to argue the legal precepts that will control the precise shade of fact finding that is sought.

The trial courtroom is where the great stars of the legal galaxy shine. But trial courts and appellate courts are constellations far apart in that galaxy. The two settings demand different skills, knowledge, and tools. Those lawyers who perform as both trial and appellate advocates must learn to adjust their techniques to match the demands of each court. The appellate lawyer deals primarily with law, not facts, and only with professional judges, not lay juries.

A trial lawyer may take days or even weeks to persuade a trial judge or jury; an appellate lawyer has time dribbled out to the minute. In the United States Courts of Appeals (and other "hot" courts where

---

2. Arthur Miller, *Death of a Salesman* 97 (1949)

the judges have studied the briefs prior to oral argument), much of the time is devoted to answering questions from members of the bench.

Then, too, the trial environment honors the oral tradition. Persuasion takes place by speech, rather than by written word. Rhetorical skills, in the effective use of words to influence or persuade, may properly shape the argument before a lay body, but be totally unacceptable when arguing points of law to a court. Thus, although arguments of distraction are fair tactics to sway or arouse the jury in a trial court, they are not acceptable in an appellate court.

The trial advocate is not limited to reasoned argument and may speak of many things, including irrelevant, somewhat irrational, or shamelessly emotional matters. These are ploys, but ploys that are used everywhere, every day. They are used in advertising and political campaigns, and by essay writers, columnists, editorial writers, and television commentators. They are of such ancient lineage that many bear Latin names: *argumentum ad misericordiam* (appeal to pity), *ad verecundiam* (appeal to prestige), *ad hominem* (appeal to ridicule), *ad populum* (appeal to popular opinion), *ad antiquitam* (appeal to tradition), *ad terrorem* (appeal to fear), *ad superbium* (appeal to snobbery or pride), *ad superstitionem* (appeal to credulity). And if the wind is right and the sail is full, the trial advocate can hoist a little *dicto simpliciter* (applying the general rule to exceptional circumstances) or some hasty generalization, or tie on a *non sequitur* or *post hoc ergo propter hoc* (fallacy of false cause) or *ignoratio elenchi* (fallacy of irrelevance, an argument that has nothing to do with the point at issue).

But do not carry this stuff upstairs to the appellate court. Check this baggage after you finish your closing summation. You are still a salesperson when you appear before the multijudge court, but it is a different audience, requiring different rhetorical skills. The oral tradition of the trial court gives way to a mixture of writing and speaking, but the proportions are not fifty/fifty; it is heavily weighted on the writing side, with perhaps a 3:1 mix. The oral tradition where trials are often measured in weeks gives way to enforced page limits in briefs, and, when the appellate court votes to hear oral argument, the time is doled out in minutes. In the United States Courts of Appeals, fifteen or twenty minutes per side is the norm.

The appellate lawyer is still a salesperson, but the lawyer carries a different sample case. Principally, the law is argued, and the tools of argument—the rhetoric, if you please—must be adjusted accordingly.

Too many lawyers fail to make this adjustment. Indeed, too many lawyers do not even realize that it requires an adjustment.

All of which leads to the question I am often asked: "What is the quality of appellate advocacy today?" There is no quick answer. Certainly, most advocacy by brief or by oral argument cannot be rated as "good," let alone "excellent." A substantial amount of "poor" advocacy hangs out there, too much for judges to be lackadaisical about, and too pervasive for the American Bar Association or state bars to do much about, because many of the firms represented by national and state bar leaders are themselves guilty of sloppy appellate practices. I am reluctant to assign percentages in the form of a general evaluation, but suffice it to say that there is a vast wasteland of mediocrity out there. At the very least, the quality quotient is not commensurate with the fees being charged for appellate brief writing and oral argument. The problem is extensive enough to stimulate my writing this book.

I do not think that I suffer from forensic fatigue as a result of reading thousands of appellate briefs since 1968. I deliberately want to discount a crankiness factor that may set in after many years of service. I am sure of this, because I have held these views since my very first days as an appellate judge. I can still remember the shock of reading appellate briefs when I first came to the court of appeals after having served as a Pennsylvania state trial judge. I expected that the quality of these written arguments would be vastly, if not astronomically, superior to the trial memoranda to which I had been accustomed. But that was not the case then, and it is not the case now.

Then, too, is the reaction, and it has been universal, of the many bright law clerks who have come to me as top honor students from our great law schools. When working on their first assignments in chambers, they immediately note the poor quality of many briefs, even those from prestigious law firms with which they had summered or interviewed. Even today, the clerks, having worked assiduously on the briefs and having come to tentative conclusions in favor of one side, will witness the oral argument performance of the lawyer for that side and moan, "That guy is ruining my case!"

In a 1982 law review article, after witnessing the civil law systems in force on the European continent, I expressed these concerns:

> Because I trust the American system and its reliance on
> pragmatic, strident and vigorous advocate lawyers more
> than I trust a system of relying on judges ensconced in
> ivory towers with their law clerk acolytes, I believe that

professional competence of lawyers is essential. Because I
see so many dangerously incompetent appellate lawyers,
I would like to see an immediate emphasis on improving
professional competence so that we do not slip by default
into an ivory tower law system. . . . I believe that the thrust
and parry of opposing appellate briefs is the best instrument to refine the law and to achieve justice.[3]

§ 1.2 The Avalanche of Appeals

Look for a moment at the paper storm that has descended on the
West Publishing Company. The 27,527 published opinions that West
received in 1929 represented approximately the same number it
received in 1964—some thirty-five years later. Yet by 1981, the volume had almost doubled to 54,104. By 1991, the number of published
opinions peaked at 65,333. Although the number of published opinions
has progressively dropped since then to a twenty-year low of 54,059 in
2001, this reduction is deceptive. With the rise in unpublished opinions over that same time, the total number of opinions—published and
unpublished—has continued to increase.[4]

Is case law churning and developing at the rate reflected by the
increasing number of published and unpublished opinions? Of course
not. Our common law tradition requires unity of law throughout a
jurisdiction and requires also the flexibility to incorporate legal precepts as they develop. Within this tradition is the concept of gradual
change, with case law that creeps from point to point, testing each step,
in a system built by accretion from the resolution of specific problems.
Nevertheless, no one, not even the most fervent supporter of publication in every case, can seriously suggest that every one of these cases
submitted for publication refines or defines the law or has precedential
or institutional value. The reason for the avalanche is not only the
expansion of trial and appellate litigation, but also because today there
is no institutional inhibition against the paper storm.

Reasons why there was no such deluge of appeals as recently as
forty years ago are easily identifiable. To be sure, we must recognize
the general litigation increase attributed to the growth of population,
commerce, industry, and the explosive effect of civil rights, environmental

---

3. Ruggero J. Aldisert, *The Appellate Bar: Professional Responsibility and Professional
Competence—A View from the Jaundiced Eye of One Appellate Judge*, 11 Cap. U.L. Rev.
444, 455 (1982) (footnote omitted).

4. Letter from Kate MacEachern, Manager, West Group, to Ruggero J. Aldisert 1 (Nov.
15, 2002).

and securities regulation, products liability, the expanded concepts of torts, and the relatively untested realm of the Internet. But there are other reasons. At one time, most state and federal courts had a specialized appellate bar—experts in evaluating the prospects of relief on appeal. No such bar exists today, even at the level of the United States Supreme Court. Most lawyers now believe that they are competent to pursue and to win an appeal. However, even though you may be a good trial lawyer and know the rocky terrain of trial courtrooms, your expertise does not guarantee that you will successfully scale the slippery slopes of appellate advocacy. Experienced appellate judges despair when they examine the superficial preparation by some lawyers whose cases unreasonably crowd their dockets.

Moreover, we have seen a profound change in the lawyer-client relationship. Many lawyers are no longer able to control, or even to moderate, the demands of emotion-laden clients. Often, professional advice and wisdom are insufficient to curb the excesses of losing parties in lawsuits. Persons who would never dare to instruct a cardiovascular specialist on heart surgery have no qualms about instructing their lawyers when and how to prosecute appeals of highly technical cases.

Such persons are everywhere. They are not restricted to any economic or social class. Appellants are rich or poor; from the east, west, north, and south; scarred by adverse jury verdicts or angered by judicial rulings. They are chief executive officers of multinational corporations who direct prestigious law firms on when to move and when not to move. They are impecunious defendants in criminal cases represented by court-appointed counsel who have nothing to lose by cluttering appellate dockets. Some appellants rationalize their actions thus: "I got a raw deal. Hey, it's just a crapshoot and maybe I will be lucky." Most people think cases are retried on appeal *de novo*. They simply cannot recognize that courts of appeals have limited review powers.

§ 1.2.1   The Decision to Appeal

Then there are the lawyers. Some accede to demands for appeal because they fear they may lose clients and earn reputations as "no-guts" lawyers. Others frankly and vulgarly resort to a self-interested, protective maneuver, taking appeals as calculated defenses against possible malpractice suits by clients for failure to exhaust all remedies. Others, unfortunately, take appeals to keep the fee meter running.[5]

Another very important factor is economics. Until recently, taking an appeal required a substantial cash outlay. When I came to the bar, all appellate briefs and the entire record had to be commercially printed. This was a major expense that discouraged some unnecessary appeals. Now appeals are available at discount prices. New court rules no longer require professional printing, which means that the office photocopy machine may grind out briefs at a fraction of the former cost. The rules also allow the appellant to select those parts of the record necessary to support the brief. Appeal costs that formerly ran to substantial pre-inflation dollars are now reduced, in most cases, to a few hundred bucks. In addition, what does an appellant stand to lose if the appeal costs are assessed against him or her? In the majority of cases, the only expense is to pay minimal court costs and the opponent's costs in photocopying the brief and some pages from the record.

The high cost of delivering legal services at trial also has a direct bearing on the increase of appeals. Once a litigant has invested a substantial amount of money at trial, the additional expenses of taking an appeal do not appear extremely formidable. Unlike trial costs, where additional witnesses and depositions and prolonged court days make the legal costs an open-ended affair, there are discrete steps of processing an appeal that can be calculated with specificity in advance.

Even in the most borderline case, if the losing party has already invested $100,000 or $125,000 to present or defend a claim at trial, the costs of taking an appeal, by comparison, do not appear prohibitive. For another $10,000 to $20,000 investment, a respectable appeal may often be lodged and carried to fruition. Comparatively speaking, the appeal expenses are not high because your counsel can take the trial brief, cut and paste it for appellate court consumption, examine the record already prepared for post-trial argument, select parts for inclusion in the appendix or excerpts of record, and have it reproduced in-house or at the photocopy shop. Counsel can then take a few hours to prepare for

---

5. Roger J. Miner, *Professional Responsibility in Appellate Practice: A View from the Bench*, 19 Pace L. Rev. 323, 326 (1999).

oral argument, travel to the city (coach class) where the appellate court sits, deliver the fifteen-minute argument, and return home.

To be sure, these shortcuts do not produce the most desirable or effective advocacy—as is suggested in the chapters that immediately follow—but taking an appeal today is relatively cost-effective when compared to massive trial expenses. And if you lose on appeal, unless the case involves a fee-shifting statute, generally speaking, as stated before, you only have to pay the minimal court costs and expenses your opponent incurred in photocopying its brief. Thus, the sheer cost-effectiveness at the appeal level when compared to the astronomical costs at trial is probably a major factor causing the dramatic recent increase of appellate filings. It is the exact opposite of the old adage, "In for a penny, in for a pound."

I emphasize these particular circumstances because the increase of appeals has not been directly related to the increase of trial court filings. Proportionately, the increase in appeals has been much higher. When I first became a United States circuit judge, in the fiscal year ending in 1969, the district courts terminated 73,354 cases. By 2002, this figure had increased to 248,886 or an increase of 339 percent. By comparison, the appeals terminated in 1969 numbered 9,014; in fiscal 2002 there were 57,555 appeals, or an increase of 639 percent.[6] Although the raw numbers are smaller, the rate of appeals increased much more drastically.

§ 1.3 The Odds of Winning an Appeal

I often have wondered how an attorney responds to the client when asked: "If I take an appeal, what are my chances of winning?" The statistics are there to make a book. For example, if you take a direct appeal as of right to the United States Court of Appeals, the odds of getting a reversal are as follows:

---

6. Statistics on federal court filings and dispositions are published annually by the Administrative Office of the United States Courts. To access all figures, visit the Administrative Office's comprehensive Web site at http://www.uscourts.gov/ statisticalreports.html. Administrative Office of the United States Courts, *U.S. Court of Appeals–Judicial Caseload Profile*, at http://www.uscourts.gov/cgi-bin/cmsa2002.pl.

United States Court of Appeals—National Average of Reversals (%)[7]

Nature of Proceeding	1998	1999	2000	2001	2002
ALL APPEALS	10.4%	9.2%	9.5%	9.1%	9.5%
Criminal	6.5	5.4	6.3	5.7	5.6
U.S. Prisoner Petitions	10.3	11.3	11.1	10.7	9.5
Other U.S. Civil Cases	11.0	11.8	11.8	10.8	11.0
Private Prisoner Petitions	7.5	10.1	9.1	9.5	9.9
Other Private Civil Cases	12.7	15.2	11.4	11.8	12.2
Bankruptcy	14.4	13.6	14.7	12.2	13.9
Administrative Appeals	6.6	6.6	7.0	8.4	12.3

From this, we conclude that the reversal rates from 1998 to 2002 for all appeals averaged 9.54 percent. Expressed otherwise, here are your odds of reversing the district court:

- All appeals: 1 in 10

- Criminal cases: 1 in 18

- Private civil actions: 1 in 9

---

7. Administrative Office of the United States Courts, *U.S. Court of Appeals – Appeals Terminated on the Merits, by Circuit, During the 12-Month Period Ending March 31, 2002*, Table B.5, at http://www.uscourts.gov/caseload2002/tables/b05mar02.pdf.

What are the odds of reversal in the state appellate court? Unfortunately, very few courts keep these statistics. The following table reflects activity in the intermediate courts of some jurisdictions:

State Intermediate Courts[8]

State	Reversal percentage
California	10.0 %
Connecticut	14.3 %
Idaho	12.16 %
Indiana	23.1 %
New York	9.3 %
Pennsylvania (Superior Court)	14.1 %
Texas	6.2 %
Virginia	15.3 %
Wisconsin (civil)	27.0 %
(criminal)	12.0 %

Certiorari Appellate Courts

When the highest court of the jurisdiction grants a petition for review (also known as a petition for writ of certiorari), the odds of prevailing generally increase. The real trick is to get the court to grant your petition. During the 2001–2002 court term, the United States Supreme Court granted only ninety-six, or 1.5 percent of the 6,343 petitions it received from litigants attempting to appeal from judgments of the various United States Courts of Appeals.[9]

---

8. The state court statistics in this section were obtained directly from the administrative offices of the individual state courts. Some states maintain published reports, whereas others conducted original research for this study. The percentages represent reversal rates for 2001 or 2002.

9. Director of the Administrative Office of the United States Courts, *2002 Annual Report of the Director*, Table B-2, at http://www.uscourts.gov/judbus2002/appendicesb02sep02.pdf.

The following table reflects the chances of having a petition for review granted by the highest court of several representative states, if applicable, as well as the odds for obtaining a reversal. The statistics represent figures from 2001 or 2002:

State Highest Courts

State	Discretionary Petitions Considered	Number Granted	Percentage Granted	Cases Decided	Percentage Reversed
Alaska	——	——	——	271	18.4%
Delaware*	——	——	——	598	7.4%
District of Columbia*	——	——	——	1768	3.2%
Florida	1327	131	10.0%	——	——
Georgia**	577	31	5.37%	3313	——
Georgia	328	7	1.02%	——	——
Hawaii	69	29	42.02%	778	——
Idaho	168	12	0.07%	125	16.8%
Illinois	1881	98	5.2%	——	——
Indiana	685	95	13.86%	——	——
Montana*#	315	81	25.7%	——	——
Nevada*	——	——	——	925	9.0%
New Jersey	1447	126	8.7%	205	37.6%
New York	——	——	——	176	35.2%
North Dakota*	——	——	——	340	10.0%
Ohio	2112	131	6.2%	——	——
Pennsylvania	1749	111	6.3%	108	29.6%
Rhode Island*	60	5	8.3%	661	9.0%
South Carolina	559	141	25.2%	——	——
Tennessee	995	69	6.9%	——	——
(Court of Appeals)	125	84	67.2%	——	——
(Criminal Appeals)	70	60	85.7%	——	——
Texas					
(Supreme Court)	1001	97	9.6%	112	97.3%
(Criminal Appeals)	2017	146	7.2%	146	34.2%
Vermont*	——	——	——	68	20.5%
Virginia	——	——	——	——	——
(Supreme Court)	2901	308	10.6%	150	46.0%
(Court of Appeals)	2711	365	16.1%	641	15.3%
West Virginia*	3237	1365	42.17%	——	——
Wisconsin	1038	69	6.64%	249	7.2%

*This state and the Court of Appeals for D.C. have no intermediate court.

**Georgia differentiates between discretionary appeals and habeas corpus applications.

#Writs only.

§ 1.4 The Odds of Being Granted Oral Argument

When I was appointed to the United States Court of Appeals for the Third Circuit in 1968, the court permitted oral argument in every case. When, later in the year, we reduced the length of argument from forty-five minutes a side to thirty minutes, the Philadelphia bar moaned and wailed as if it would be the end of the advocacy world. One generation later, the customary allotted time allowance is fifteen minutes, and oral argument is now the exception, not the rule. In the United States courts of appeals, the advocate's major tool is the written brief, not oral presentation. Notwithstanding protestations to the contrary, I think that the trend is irreversible. I do not believe that justice suffers as a result.

Federal Appellate Courts

My experience in riding the circuits has taught me that if an appeal presents an issue of institutional or precedential significance, oral argument will be granted by the court. Various courts have different procedures through which this decision is reached, but by and large, the judges seem to err on the side of granting oral argument in unworthy cases, rather than denying the opportunity in deserving cases.

What then are the odds that the judges will grant oral argument in your case? The following records of the United States courts of appeals provide some indication:[10]

---

10. Director of the Administrative Office of the United States Courts, *2002 Annual Report of the Director*, Table B-5, at http://www.uscourts.gov/judbus2002/appendicesb05sep02.pdf.

Circuit	Percentage Argued in 1990	Percentage Argued in 2002
ALL CIRCUITS	44.8%	32.9%
D.C.	56.5%	47.8%
First	66.8%	54.1%
Second	76.4%	54.5%
Third	25.8%	25.0%
Fourth	31.9%	18.1%
Fifth	27.9%	26.0%
Sixth	48.1%	34.7%
Seventh	56.2%	50.6%
Eighth	44.1%	32.5%
Ninth	51.6%	38.7%
Tenth	41.1%	30.0%
Eleventh	45.7%	22.4%

The comparison of these two years illustrates a significant development in the judicial process during the span of a decade: a nationwide decline of 11.9 percent in cases being argued. Only one appeal in three, 32.9 percent to be precise, will be listed for argument. I am also informed by my own experience: judges will no longer vote for oral argument where the law is clear and the application of facts to the law equally plain. Another facet of this phenomenon is the increase of non-precedential opinions being written in cases that have no precedential or institutional value in lieu of opinions to be published in the *Federal Reporter*.

This should be a signal to lawyers that today, more than ever, the appellant's brief takes on a vital and decisive role. You must not only write to persuade the court to reverse the judgment of the district court, but you must meet a threshold burden of demonstrating in your brief that, on the basis of the proper standard of review, a serious reversible error was committed in the trial court. A serious and arguable question of law must be presented.

State Appellate Courts

The chances of obtaining oral argument in the state appellate courts vary widely from state to state. For example, the Oklahoma Supreme Court accords oral argument in civil appeals only under very rare circumstances. Because most states do not maintain published statistics on the percentage of oral arguments granted, it is difficult to determine if there is a national trend in the states favoring or disfavoring oral argument. Recent statistics from the highest courts of several representative states suggest that oral argument is frequently allowed in those cases submitted on the merits. The statistics represent percentages from 2001 or 2002:

State	Percent Argued
Iowa	49.5%
Mississippi	69.3%
New York	97.7%
North Carolina	98.9%
Oregon	95.5%
Pennsylvania	89.0%
Rhode Island	14.5%
Texas Supreme Court	74.5%
Vermont	66.8%

§ 1.5 Summary

The reality is that a large majority of cases stand or fall at the intermediate appellate level. As shown in § 1.3, the chances of winning are small. Why then are more cases appealed than ever before? The cause, at least in part, can be found in the forces described above: the litigious temperament of our American society and the attitudes of many lawyers. It should be noted that this thesis does not apply to the many advocates of ability and integrity who practice before the appellate courts of this country—attorneys distinguished not only by the appeals they present, but also by those they do not.

I will not devote much space in this book to the process of deciding which cases to appeal. But a basic premise underlying the entire discussion is that altogether too many cases are sent up, or rather dragged up willy-nilly, before appellate courts. Honing cases along the lines suggested in the pages that follow will cause some to disappear entirely. What will remain, I should hope, will be a solid core of substantial questions, adequately explored and clearly presented. The judicial system would benefit from this result, certainly, and lawyers could conserve their resources and use their time more effectively.

This is a book about bringing effective appeals. It is a book for lawyers—and lawyers like to win. I do not guarantee to the reader greater successes than the merits of the cases warrant. I do believe, however, that cases with merit will find their way into the minds of the deciding judges.

Over the years, many state chief justices graciously furnished me with advice for appellate lawyers for inclusion in this book. In concluding his suggestions, former New Jersey Chief Justice Robert N. Wilentz wrote:

> The foregoing has nothing to do with the effectiveness of the art of advocacy in the sense of trying to help lawyers with their cases. It has to do only with the effectiveness of briefs and oral argument in helping the court arrive at a totally rational, totally informed, and probably correct decision.

Chief Justice Wilentz recognized a distinction here, and so do I. I also see appellate justice at its best as a cooperative effort between the court and counsel. Excellence on either side is infectious. We should hold each other, and ourselves, to the highest standards. My hope is that this book will serve that important and honorable endeavor.

Chapter 2

THE PURPOSE OF BRIEF WRITING

§ 2.1 Overview

An appellate brief may be defined as a written, reasoned elaboration that justifies a conclusion. It is a demonstration of written, reflective thinking expressed in a logical argument designed to educate and to persuade. In a practical sense, it is a written statement of reasons explaining why an appellate court should reverse, vacate, or affirm the judgment or final order of the tribunal from which the appeal is taken.

Briefs are written for one audience and one audience only—judges and their law clerks. They have the most limited readership of any professional writing. You write to persuade a court, not to impress a client. You write to persuade a court to your point of view; at a minimum, you write to convince the court to grant oral argument in your case. The key word is "persuasion." If a brief does not persuade, it fails. Every brief writer must understand this and never forget it. As you write, prop a sign, literally or figuratively, on your desk that asks, "Will this brief persuade the reader?"

Persuasion is the only test that counts. Literary style, massive displays of scholarship, citations that thunder from the ages, and catchy phrases are uniformly pointless if the writing does not persuade.

Authorities may differ as to a precise definition of "persuasion." Kenneth Andersen describes it as "a communication process in which the communicator seeks to elicit a desired response from his receiver."[1] Erwin Bettinghaus is more specific: "As a minimal condition, to be labeled as persuasive, a communication situation must involve a conscious attempt by one individual to change the attitudes, beliefs, or behavior of another individual or group of individuals through the transmission of some message."[2]

Although both these definitions effectively express a general concept, what Bettinghaus says has a special relevance to counsel for the appellant, who has the burden of persuading the appellate court that the trial judge committed reversible error. Although not usually stated as a traditional burden of proof, in actual practice, the presumption of correctness lies with the trial tribunal. Evidence of this

---

1. Kenneth E. Andersen, *Persuasion: Theory and Practice* 6 (1971).
2. Erwin P. Bettinghaus, *Persuasive Communication* 4 (3d ed. 1980).

presumption is the jurisprudential axiom: when an appellate court is equally divided, the judgment of the trial court must be affirmed.

The appellant is required to rebut this presumption of correctness. To do this, the appellant must challenge the attitudes or beliefs expressed by the trial court and presumably endorsed by the appellate court; the appellee's task is to reinforce these attitudes or beliefs.

When considering persuasion in the abstract, however, Professor Nicholas M. Cripe reminds us that persuasion in an appellate court "differs from the common persuasive [writing or] speaking situation such as political speeches, protest rallies, legislative debates, revival meetings, jury trials, and especially commercial advertising and selling."[3] Appellate advocates must tackle rhetorical problems rarely encountered by other persuasive writers or speakers. They are limited to a small number of available relevant arguments. They must carefully select and present these contentions in a setting where the atmosphere and traditions render ineffectual or inappropriate techniques commonly used in other types of persuasive writing and speaking.

The audience is a concise grouping of "highly trained, intelligent, frequently articulate judges who likely will react unfavorably" to anything but the formal style of authoritative persuasion.[4] Moreover, unlike most literature of scholarly persuasion, appellate briefs are not read at a leisurely pace and their contents savored and digested in a contemplative environment. Rather, briefs must compete with other demands on an appellate judge, as described in § 2.5, "The Brief-Reading Environment." For now, it is enough to say that astronomical caseloads require judges to read large numbers of briefs while simultaneously performing other judicial functions demanding equal priority.

§ 2.2 Elements of the Argument

In law, as in formal logic, the word "argument" takes on a special meaning. An argument is a group of propositions of which one is claimed to follow from the others, which are regarded as support or grounds for the truth of that one. An argument is not a loose collection of propositions; it has a formal structure that one trained in the law recognizes.

The *conclusion*, or "therefore" statement of an argument—the precise relief sought in the brief—is a proposition that is affirmed on

---

3. Nicholas M. Cripe, *Fundamentals of Persuasive Oral Argument*, 20 Forum 342, 345 (1985).

4. *Id.*

the basis of the other propositions of the argument. Logicians call these *premises*; lawyers call them points, or issues, in the brief. These points are designed to serve one purpose and one purpose only: they supply evidence or reasons for supporting the desired conclusion.[5]

Reasoning is the process of reaching a conclusion through a series of propositions in argument form. Reasoning is reflective thinking. In a brief, we reason from something we know—the statute, procedural rule, or case law—to something that we did not know prior to our reasoning—the conclusion. Reasons, as distinguished from reasoning, are the considerations set forth in the terms and propositions in the premises "which have weight in reaching the conclusion as to what is to be done, or which we employed to justify it when it is questioned."[6]

The conclusion in a brief is not just the major thing; it is the only thing. Indeed, it is the only game in town. The purpose of a brief is to convince the court to accept your conclusion—to reverse, vacate, or affirm the lower court's judgment. The only purpose of the brief's contents that precede the conclusion—statements of jurisdiction, standards of review, issues, facts, and the discussion of legal precepts—is to set the stage for logical premises to justify the suggested conclusion.

Unlike an opinion of the court, a law review article or a professional treatise, a brief sells only its conclusion. Remember, the brief writer is a persuader. The lawyer is selling something, and that something is the conclusion.

Your brief is nothing more nor less than an expanded categorical syllogism containing premises (propositions). The conclusion you urge in your brief can only be true when (1) the other propositions (premises) are true, and (2) these propositions imply the conclusion; in other words, the conclusion is inferred from these premises.[7]

The argument is designed to educate the court by setting forth solid reasons which, if accepted, may be incorporated into the court's opinion. The reasons must be logical, but until they appear in a judicial opinion, they are not "performative utterances" that possess the strong bite of precedent. Reasons in a brief have no life of their own. They are tools of education and persuasion only. Their role in an appellate brief differs from a law review article or legal treatise, where the focus is

---

5. Ruggero J. Aldisert, *Logic for Lawyers: A Guide to Clear Legal Thinking* 28 (3d ed. 1997).

6. John Dewey, *How We Think* 17 (2d ed. 1933).

7. *See* chapter 16 for a complete definition and discussion of "The Logical Form" and effective "syllogisms."

information and comprehensiveness. Reasons in an appellate brief are designed to do one thing: to convince a court to accept your conclusion. The only measure of their success is the extent to which they persuade the judge to accept the brief's conclusion.

The written brief always has played an important role in the American appellate court system. By contrast, the English appellate system relies entirely on oral argument.[8] Oral argument in an American appellate court is a fleeting moment; a written brief is a permanent formality. The court relies on the written brief prior to oral argument, in the decision-making process afterward, and in the post-argument decision-justifying process—the preparation of the opinion.

Moreover, the astronomical increase in appellate court caseloads has emphasized the importance of briefs and diminished the importance of oral arguments. Crushing caseloads have imposed severe restrictions on the time available for oral argument and the length of time allotted. From 1961 to 1987 for example, the total number of filings in the United States courts of appeals increased from 4,204 to 35,176, or *737 percent*;[9] and from 1987 to 2002 the increase was another 64 percent resulting in a current case load of 57,555.[10]

Notwithstanding many exhortations about the importance of oral argument, in today's appellate environment you must write to win. Do not depend solely on your powers of speech, regardless of how great they may be. Your hopes hang on the written argument; the oral argument is only a safety net.

§ 2.3 Gaining and Maintaining Attention

Pioneer psychologist William James once said, "That which holds the attention determines the action." To the brief writer, this means two things: (1) you must gain the attention of the reading judge, and (2) you must maintain it. Attention is a necessary condition for persuasion.

When you start to plan your brief, place yourself in the judge's shoes. The judge will pull down from the shelf the set of briefs—typically, blue for the appellant, red for the appellee, gray for the reply,

---

8. For an excellent description of the English appellate system, *see* Robert J. Martineau, *Appellate Justice in England and the United States: A Comparative Analysis* (1990).

9. *Id.* at 155.

10. Administrative Office of the United States Courts, *United States Court of Appeals–Judicial Caseload Profile*, at http://www.uscourts.gov/cgi-bin/cmsa2002.pl.

and green for the amicus curiae. (Mine will have been tied together with "tape, red," noted in the Judiciary Act of 1789; traditions persist long and hard in my chambers.) The judge then will open the briefs and ask, "Now, what is the excuse for this appeal?" This is not an indication that the judge is prejudging the merits; it is only the presumption of trial court correctness at work.

The appellant always must be conscious of this presumption and remember that the odds of reversal favor the appellee. Keep in mind the track records set forth in chapter 1: between 1997 and 2001, the appellant's odds of prevailing were one in ten in the United States courts of appeals.

Whether appellant or appellee, you must plan your brief to gain the immediate attention of the judge. You do this by:

- Leading from strength; hitting the reader between the eyes with your strongest argument.

- Expressing a message that the reader will understand.

- Structuring a presentation within the framework of the reader's knowledge, beliefs, and attitude.

John W. Davis once wrote:

[Judges] are anxiously waiting to be supplied with what Mr. Justice Holmes called the "implements of decision." These by your presence you profess yourself ready to furnish. If the places were reversed and you sat where they do, think what it is you would want first to know about the case. How and in what order would you want the story told? How would you want the skein unraveled? What would make easier your approach to the true solution?[11]

To gain the attention of the judge, the writing must be simple and clear. Here you may benefit from the advice of professors of speech and debate at the undergraduate level. Robert Huber at the University of Vermont taught his debate students a simple argument pattern designed to keep the argument clear, which brief writers can adopt to gain and maintain the judges' attention. The schematic is N-E-P-C: NAME IT, EXPLAIN IT, PROVE IT, CONCLUDE IT. Although devised for oral argument, this design works equally well for written briefs. Professor Cripe says, "If outlined, NAME IT would be a Roman

---

11. John W. Davis, *The Argument of an Appeal*, 26 A.B.A.J. 895, 896 (1940).

numeral, EXPLAIN IT the capital letters, PROVE IT the Arabic numbers and small letters under the EXPLAIN IT sections, CONCLUDE IT probably a capital *D* or *E* tying up the point."[12]

The first principle of gaining and maintaining attention is to write for the person who will read your brief. You do not write for publication. You do not write to show your colleagues how smart you are, how well you know the subject matter, or how stupid you believe the judges to be. All this may well be true. But the name of the game is "persuade the judge." You don't score points for anything else.

The second principle is subsumed in the first. To gain the judge's attention, you must immediately establish your credibility as a brief writer. Without credibility you may possibly gain the judge's attention, but you will never maintain it. Unless you maintain it, you will never induce the judge to accept your conclusion. And unless you persuade the judge to accept your conclusion, the brief is not worth the paper it is written on. Getting the judge to accept your conclusion is to appellate advocacy what the bottom line is to business.

So much for this short exposition on brief writing theory. I now pause to survey the problems that many appellate judges see in brief writing.

§ 2.4   Criticisms of Briefs

Before we address the criticisms of briefs that judges lodge against lawyers, certain things must be said. First, writing an appellate brief is not easy. It may be the most difficult task of advocacy. What you write, in most cases, is your client's last opportunity to claim or defend. Before we criticize, let us put certain things in perspective.

On a scale of difficulty, writing a brief is much more arduous, calls for much more research, and requires much more intellectual choice and judgment than does writing a judicial opinion. It is easier for a judge to write an opinion than for a lawyer to write a brief from scratch; the judge has the advantage of both parties' work product. The brief writer has to narrow the issues; this part of the judge's task already is performed. The brief writer has to select the precedents and supply the authorities; the judge examines them, confirms their authenticity and, via independent research, ascertains their continued vitality. In so doing, the opinion writer has a distinct advantage over the brief writer,

---

12. *Cripe, supra* note 3, at 350.

because it can be assumed that the cited authorities already have been cross-checked by opposing counsel in answering briefs.

Second, many of the criticisms leveled against briefs also may be directed against judicial opinions.[13] There is sufficient criticism to go around to all hands—to those on the bench as well as to those at the bar. Both have much room for improvement.

But the similarity stops there. A litigant does not lose a case because a judge's opinion fails to convince. Judges' tenures seldom are affected if their work product is sloppy, turgid, rambling, repetitious and, at times, incomprehensible. But the quality of professional legal writing directly affects the persuasive powers of briefs, and, indirectly, the reputation of the lawyer in the professional community and personal standing in the law firm.

Examine, if you will, the following criticisms and decide if you are guilty of any of the practices. Remember the bottom line. For writing a convincing brief, you do not get Brownie points or a pat on the head. You win the case. For writing a bad brief, you are not directed to sit in the corner. You probably will lose the case. It is that simple.

What then are the criticisms generally expressed by judges against lawyers' briefs today? Here are some:

- Too long. Too long. Too long.

- Too many issues or points.

- Rudderless; no central theme(s).

- Failure to disclose the equitable heart of the appeal and the legal problem involved.

- Lack of focus.

- Absence of organization.

- Cluttering the logical progression with excessive citations and verbiage.

- Uninteresting and irrelevant fact statements.

- Misrepresented facts and case holdings.

- Failure to mention or properly cite cases against you.

---

13. Ruggero J. Aldisert, *Opinion Writing* 6–7 (1990).

- Failure to state proper jurisdiction (appellate and trial court).

- Failure to set forth the proper standard of review for each point presented.

- Failure to apply the standard of review properly.

- Failure to prepare an accurate table of contents.

- Failure to prepare an accurate table of authorities with page references to the brief.

- Failure to set forth a summary of argument before proceeding into a discussion of each point.

- Unclear, incomprehensible, irrelevant statements of reasons.

- When applicable, failure to state that a point is an independent reason that may support the brief's conclusion, regardless of how the court rules on other issues.

- Misrepresenting or exaggerating the adversary's arguments.

- Inaccurate or incomplete citations.

- Citing cases that have been overruled.

- Discussing unnecessary details of precedents and compared cases.

- Failure to show similarity or dissimilarity of material facts in compared cases.

- Failure to cite to the record when necessary.

- Citing to a record not contained in the appendix or excerpts of record.

- Failure to support the brief with a sufficient appendix or excerpts of record.

- Failure to complete the brief with a terse summation demonstrating why the reader should agree with the conclusion.

- Failure to state the relief requested.

- Typos, misspellings, and grammatical mistakes.

- Failure to observe the court's appellate rules.

- Failure to observe color codes on brief covers when required by court rules.

§ 2.5 The Brief-Reading Environment

Lawyers should understand the environment in which briefs are read. The general public and the legal profession generally are familiar with the working environment of trial judges—the courtroom and the chambers. But they are typically unfamiliar with where and when appellate judges do their thing. Briefs are sometimes, but not very often, read in a cloistered setting—a quiet, library-like room where the only sound may be a softly ticking clock. Briefs usually must compete with a number of other demands on the judge's time and attention. The telephone rings. The daily mail arrives with motions and petitions clamoring for immediate review. The chamber's e-mail account spits out an urgent message or another judge's draft opinion, the reviewing of which is given a higher priority than drafting your own opinions. The Clerk's office sends a fax with an emergency motion. The air courier arrives with an overnight delivery. The law clerks buzz you on the intercom because they have hit a snag in a case. So the deathless prose that you have been reading in the blue or red-covered brief must await another moment. Or another hour. Or another day.

So the briefs are wrapped up and taken home, where they are to be looked at after the nightly news but before your favorite evening television show. In the meantime, your spouse wants to talk with you, or the kids clamor for attention, or friends telephone. The briefs are rewrapped and set aside for another time. Or they are read in airport waiting rooms, or aboard a plane with the person in the next seat glancing across and speculating, "Gee, I suppose you're a lawyer. Let me ask you about this lawsuit I want to bring." Or the briefs are read late at night in hotel rooms with poor lighting, thus inviting soporific consequences.

Look at the numbers. When I first became an appellate judge in 1968, each active judge on the court was required to hear ninety appeals a year, which amounted to six sittings a year and fifteen sets of briefs per sitting. Each active judge on the court now has to decide approximately 485 appeals a year,[14] participate in standing panels for *pro se* cases and motions, and sit in approximately seven scheduled sittings a year. This means that each judge must read approximately

---

14. Administrative Office of the United States Courts, *U.S. Court of Appeals – Judicial Caseload Profile*, at http://www.uscourts.gov/cgi-bin/cmsa2002.pl.

1,000 briefs a year written by lawyers, plus at least fifty briefs written by *pro se* litigants and a like number of counseled responses, and frequently many reply briefs. In many of the state intermediate courts, the caseload is even more formidable.

I have described in detail the brief-reading environment for one purpose only: to emphasize that the written brief can be an effective instrument of persuasion only if it is concise, clear, accurate, and logical.

Chapter 3

THE PURPOSE OF ORAL ARGUMENT

§ 3.1 Overview

We have said that the purpose of the written brief is to educate the court and to persuade it to accept a conclusion. We have said also that most appellate courts today are "hot," in the sense that prior to oral argument, the judges have read the briefs. What then is the purpose of oral argument? Why is it necessary? These are good questions, and lawyers who understand the proper answers are well on their way to becoming effective appellate advocates.

Chief Justice William H. Rehnquist suggests that the brief may be compared to the entire motion picture show, and the oral argument to the previews. "[T]he preview selects the dramatic and interesting scenes that are apt to catch the interest of the viewer and make [the viewer] want to see the entire movie."[1] On the other hand, Judge Frank Coffin of the First Circuit explains his perceived differentiation:

> The challenge in planning and making an oral argument differs significantly from that in writing a brief. In constructing an effective brief, the writer may rely on felicity and grace to ease the burden of reading, but his purpose remains to convince the reader through what must largely be an intellectual effort. The purpose of oral argument, on the other hand, is to appeal to all the springs of motivation, to persuade.[2]

I can agree with Chief Justice Rehnquist that there are limited circumstances when the oral argument is but a preview, and the brief is the picture show that follows. Probably, this is true in the U.S. Supreme Court, where the justices grant certiorari on one issue, perhaps two, and by the time oral argument rolls around, they have had the benefit of the written argument supporting the petition for certiorari and can delay serious consideration of the brief-in-chief until after argument. I think, however, that this is the exception to the "hot" court practice. All U.S. circuit judges and most judges of the states' highest courts have a comprehensive understanding of the written briefs before listening to the argument. I also agree that the oral argument can be considered the "preview" in the cold courts, where the drill is to hear arguments

---

1. William H. Rehnquist, *Oral Advocacy*, 27 S. Tex. L.J. 289, 299 (1986).

2. Frank M. Coffin, *The Ways of a Judge: Reflections from the Federal Appellate Bench* 109 (1980).

first and to read briefs later. But in the vast majority of appellate courts today, the differences in the purposes of written and oral argument are far more pervasive.

The written brief is designed to educate and inform. Ostensibly, the brief has been written by a specialist in a particular field of law—one who has become thoroughly familiar with the issues and law over a long period of time and who has spent more than a year narrowing the legal issues. Ideally, this specialist has proceeded through the pretrial motion skirmishes and a possible trial or hearing, decided upon a strategy to upset the trial court's determination, and performed detailed legal research for appellate consumption and then summarizing the relevant law for presentation before a group of judicial generalists— appellate judges who are regularly exposed to the entire gamut of legal issues. The specialist lawyer then prepares for the benefit of the generalist judge a detailed segment of a small portion (or what purports to be a detailed segment of a small portion) of the grand mosaic of the law. The brief is a comprehensive presentation of relevant law concerning a tiny corner of the legal world.

By the time oral argument comes around, the generalist judge, having examined and studied the briefs, is no longer a stranger to the relevant substantive law. The court has been furnished with a lens through which to examine the intricate pattern of that tiny portion of the grand legal mosaic. Oral argument gives the lawyer an opportunity to furnish the court with a magnifying power to the lens, to focus on how the relevant segments of the grand mosaic fit together. Oral argument must not be considered as the first glimpse of the scene, nor a reconnaissance, nor even an exploration of the territory to be covered. The brief is designed to do this. Oral argument is neither preparatory artillery nor a preliminary probe to determine soft or hard spots. Oral argument takes judges by the hand and directs them through the maps previously supplied them. It merely supplements and reinforces what has gone before and directs the judges to a desired objective in the forensic battle by opening wide the pathways that were previously identified as possible routes in the written brief.

The judges already know your battle plan. They have read your written submission. At oral argument, this plan of yours is put to the test; as Holmes would say, it will be washed in cynical acid.

§ 3.2 The Judges' View

Reduced to its essence, the purpose of oral argument is to clarify and emphasize what has been written. Lawyers must understand that the clarification process must be viewed not only from the perspective of the lawyer, but also from that of the judge.

Consider what judges expect oral argument to accomplish:

To clarify issues. The judges want you to help them isolate the issues they must decide and to assist them in resolving any collateral issues—such as jurisdiction, standing, or mootness—that might not have been briefed but now stand in the way of reaching the merits of the stated argument. The judges may insist on a further explanation of the claims or defenses asserted in the briefs. Notwithstanding the best efforts of writers, ambiguity does exist. The judges use oral argument to ask what counsel is actually contending.

To clarify the record. Many, if not most, of the questions asked by judges refer to the record. The judges may ask you to substantiate factual claims by reference to the record. They may ask you to bring into better focus important record facts, details of pleadings, findings of the tribunal, and evidentiary support. They may ask you to clarify confusing legal contentions by referring to precise quotations in the precedents cited. They may ask for information as to the party's specific position in the trial court. They may ask what steps were taken at trial to preserve points for review.

To clarify the scope of claims or defenses. The judges always are interested in knowing how far the requested legal precept will carry. This is where hypothetical questions come into play, and lawyers must be ready for them. Because every holding is a potential precedent, the judges must know how wide a swath in the law is being cut.

To examine the practical impact of claims and defenses. The judges may inquire as to the potential burdens imposed on the individual or on society, the effects on employer-employee relations, the implications as to freedoms of private citizens and effective law enforcement, and possible hindrances on commercial transactions or on the use of private property. That is, the judges want to know whether acceptance of an argument will produce impractical or nonsensical results.

To examine the logic of claims or defenses. The judges will test the logical order of your argument by probing for fallacies. They may inquire as to the premises you have asserted by generalizing from other cases to your own. When analogies are offered by counsel, they may request that you list resemblances and differences in the material facts.

To cut through the underbrush. The judges use oral argument to ascertain what issues are not preserved or abandoned as well as those issues that the court does not have to decide.

To lobby for or against particular positions. Having read the briefs, and having some intimate knowledge of their colleagues' inclinations, judges may use oral argument as a form of internal advocacy. They may stake out tentative positions in advance of the decision conference. The problem for the lawyer, however, is that he or she often does not know if the judge is staking out a position or playing devil's advocate.

§ 3.3 The Lawyers' View

Lawyers have different goals in the oral argument process:

To face the decision makers eye to eye. Oral argument is one of two occasions when the judges get together to consider a case (the other is the decision conference), but it is the only opportunity for the lawyer to face the court eyeball to eyeball without "filtering" by the law clerks who figure greatly in the brief-reading and bench memorandum-writing process. Here the lawyer has the opportunity of conveying to the court that quality that Aristotle called ethos—the personal character of the speaker. Other aspects of Aristotle's *The Rhetoric* may emerge from the written brief: pathos, the proper attitude in the recipient of the argument, and logos—arguments which demonstrate the truth, real or apparent.[3] But oral argument is the only opportunity the lawyer has to personally motivate the judges by force of his or her personality, and to convey what Bettinghaus described as three factors that people use in judging a speaker's credibility—trustworthiness, qualifications and personal characteristics.[4]

To emphasize and simplify the pivotal or gut issues of the brief. Here, the lawyer distills from usually a fifty-page brief two or three pivotal issues (no more please) that will make or break the case. The lawyer truly must strike for the jugular and give the court what Holmes called the "implements of decision."

To come to grips with real questions that trouble the court. Early in the argument, you will learn from the judges' questions any misgivings, concerns, or doubts about the arguments presented in the brief. This

---

3. Nicholas M. Cripe, *Fundamentals of Persuasive Oral Argument*, 20 Forum 342, 357 (1984).

4. Erwin P. Bettinghaus, *Persuasive Communication* 95 (3d ed. 1980).

is the only opportunity to lay these to rest. Put aside any prepared remarks and immediately respond to the court's invitation to dispel the uncertainty. Essentially, this is counsel's opportunity to participate in the judges' decision conference.[5]

To correct misimpressions of fact or law. Be alert to any misimpressions the judges may have about the case. Be alert to any signs that the judges are proceeding on erroneous assumptions of fact or law, and take the opportunity to correct such errors.

To demonstrate the logical soundness of your position. Show the court that your argument hangs together under fire. Stephen M. Shapiro—a former Deputy Solicitor General and an appellate specialist with Mayer, Brown, Rowe & Maw—offers this perspective:

> Oral argument is the anvil on which a solid position is hammered out and confirmed—or shattered entirely by repeated blows. Effective advocates use oral argument to dramatically demonstrate that [their] position is sound. Thus, despite difficult questions and criticisms, there always is a logical response and the argument hangs together in a coherent way. There are, in short, no hidden defects, gaps in reasoning, or unanticipated consequences. Some arguments fall apart entirely under the pressure of argument. Other arguments, which have been carefully honed in advance, are strengthened and confirmed by the process of debate.[6]

Arguing a case before an appellate court is not easy today. Judges know this and lawyers must understand this. It takes a special kind of litigator, and top-flight litigators are hard to come by on both the trial and appellate levels. Most so-called litigators are deposition takers. They learn bad habits by taking and defending depositions in an unnecessarily confrontational atmosphere in which ad hominem attacks on opposing counsel are more the rule than the exception. But even when litigators get before a trial judge, their performance is more fact-specific than law-oriented. When they do get to argue questions of law—usually at summary judgment or at post-trial j.n.o.v. or new trial motions—there is usually a heavy factual overlay to the presentation before a very busy state or federal trial judge or magistrate judge. Lawyers often "wing it" in arguing legal questions on the trial court level.

---

5. Stephen M. Shapiro, *Oral Argument in the United States Supreme Court*, 33 Cath. U.L. Rev. 529, 531-32 (1984).

6. *Id.* at 532.

Unless you are a prosecutor, a public defender, or a municipal, county, state, or federal agency lawyer, you do not get to an appellate court very often. And when you get there, in only five of the federal judicial circuits would you get even a fifty-fifty chance of appearing in person to argue the case.

Therefore, arguing a case is difficult because the average lawyer does not have the necessary experience (1) to understand what is expected, (2) to comprehend the shorthand expressions used by the judges in firing questions and (3) to avoid being jittery, high-strung, agitated and tense during the presentation. Appearing before an appellate court is to revisit whatever ogre of a professor you had in law school. In the "hot" courts, the Socratic method comes storming back at you with a ferocity that you have not experienced in years. The snide remarks and sarcasm of trial judges in evidence rulings are love taps by comparison. The captious, quibbling carping of your law office superiors pale into insignificance, because at least there you believed that you knew more about the case than they did.

But here, in the majesty of the huge appellate courtroom, you suddenly are faced with an unrelenting attack on your brief. You are bombarded with hypotheticals of which you never dreamed. You may find yourself the target of an unyielding, obdurate, and unrelenting line of questioning from one of the judges inexorably committed to an idiosyncratic frolic, or you may find yourself caught in the cross fire among the various members of the bench totally immersed in intra-court judicial advocacy. In such circumstances, how do you perform as a competent, persuasive appellate advocate?

The short answer is that you must prepare, prepare, prepare. You must master the subject matter of your case—yes, I said the subject matter of which your case is only a part, not merely the limited factual and legal perimeters of your case itself—so that you will know as much as possible about the ramifications of a decision and its capacity to expand or contract the law. You must master the record completely and devise means to effect instant entry to particular passages when requested by the judges. Justice Robert H. Jackson has supplied appellate advocates with these inspiring words: "If the day of one's making an oral argument is not one of the great days in a lawyer's life, he should not make the argument."[7] Justice William O. Douglas's experience suggests that many lawyers were not moved by this spirit: "Few

---

7. Myron H. Bright, *The Ten Commandments of Oral Argument*, 67 A.B.A.J. 1136, 1136 (1981) (citation omitted).

truly good advocates appeared before the Court. In my time 40 percent were incompetent. Only a few were excellent."[8]

§ 3.4 Criticisms of Oral Argument

You must prepare, prepare, prepare. You must learn to avoid the following litany of complaints the judges lodge against the quality of oral argument today.

§ 3.4.1 General Criticisms

- Inadequate preparation.

  — Failure to master the facts.

  — Failure to master the internal trial court history of the case.

  — Failure to master the relevant law.

- Failure to psych out the court (or panel) in advance to learn what really triggers their decisions.

- Ineptitude in answering the court's questions.

- Repeating excerpts from the written brief instead of designing a hard-hitting oral presentation.

- Failure to cash in on questions from obviously sympathetic judges.

- Talking too much.

  — If you have made your point, sit down. Do not exhaust every minute of allotted time. You might open a door and get into trouble.

  — If it is obvious that the court understands your argument on a point, then stop and move to another.

  — Rebut, do not repeat.

- Getting sidetracked on minor, not controlling, points simply because one of the judges on the bench opened the door.

---

8. *Id.*

§ 3.4.2   Specific Criticisms

- Leading off the argument with a weak point or an unnecessarily provocative contention that generates friction on the bench at the outset. When you see frowns on the judges' faces or heads shaking, play your next highest card immediately.

- Sticking inflexibly to a prepared speech when the judges express interest in other areas.

- Mangling the facts.

  — Do not reargue evidentiary matters that have been resolved adversely by the fact-finder.

  — Do not use hyperbole, overstatement, or exaggeration in describing record facts.

- Failing to communicate verbally.

  — Do not mumble and mutter. All is lost unless the judges can hear you.

  — Do not use emotional rhetoric, high-flown oratory, or irrelevant lines of argument intended to incite emotional responses instead of logical conclusions.

  — Do not speak in monotone.

  — Do not lose eye contact with the judges by reading at length from the text of an oral argument script or from legislative history, opinions, statutes, regulations, or the trial record.

- Failing to relate the appropriate standard of review to the particular issue.

- Failing to come to grips with the plain language of case holdings or statutory or constitutional provisions; bluffing about a statute or trial transcript.

- Failing to marshal valuable time allotted you.

  — Do not waste time on trivial matters or on issues already discussed adequately. Recognize when everything has been said and move on.

— Do not continue to talk after the red light has flashed on or the presiding judge has called time, unless the court wishes argument to continue.

- Failing to accept or acknowledge helpful observations or reformulations of argument suggested by a judge.

§ 3.4.3 Inept Handling of Questions

Many of the criticisms of oral argument lodged by judges concern the manner with which lawyers answer questions from the court. Whatever had been the custom of judges in yesteryear, most appellate arguments take the form of a colloquy between the bench and the bar. Carefully read the comments of the state chief justices set forth in the text that follows and in the tables titled "The Chief Justices Speak" and "The Chief Judges Speak." Avoid these faults:

- Failing to listen carefully to a question from the bench and answering some other question that the judge has not asked.

- Evading questions by stating "That's a different case . . ." or by failing to give a direct, simple, and comprehensible answer.

- Refusing to give a yes or no answer when the judge requests one and when it is possible to do so.

- Attempting to postpone answers to questions, or promising to cover matters that are never covered adequately later.

- Giving long-winded, multiple-paragraph answers to straight-forward questions, or relying on complex and incomprehensible factual descriptions in responding to questions.

- Giving timorous responses to questions that seem overbearing, or displaying disappointment when questioning is hostile.

- Attempting to answer questions by propounding other questions back to the court.[9]

---

9. Although the foregoing are my own observations and those of my state and federal colleagues, I am indebted to the concise summary offered by veteran lawyers in the Solicitor General's office set forth in Shapiro, *supra* note 5.

§ 3.4.4   The Law Clerks Speak

Having listed the complaints expressed by veteran judges and appellate lawyers, I now turn to observations generally shared by law clerks, who witness oral argument after having done important preparatory work. Where a judge may have spent hours examining the briefs and records, the law clerks have spent days studying and analyzing the briefs in depth and performing original research on the legal issues involved. They are a special breed of professional observers; they know enough about the issues and the record to follow the oral argument precisely. Their comments reflect many of the same criticisms offered by judges and lawyers:

- Attorneys too often do not answer the questions put to them, or try to bluff when they do not know the answer, or simply lie and misrepresent. They often show a defensive attitude to questions, instead of considering oral argument as their opportunity to participate in the judges' decision conference.

- They spend too much time repeating what has already been said in the brief, instead of letting the brief speak for itself.

- They do not know when to sit down. ("If you have said all you planned to say, ask the judges if they have any questions. If they don't, sit down. The best oral advocates do.")

- They attempt to retry the evidence in the case before the appellate court. Attorneys often fail to recognize the difference between effective trial advocacy before a jury and effective appellate advocacy before an appellate court.

- They become too attached to one argument, instead of moving to other points. No matter how intrinsically interesting an issue may be, it has no place in oral argument unless it is likely to persuade the court to accept the advocate's point of view.

- Attorneys often are not adequately prepared. They do not know the facts or the law.

§ 3.5 The Purpose of Oral Argument: A Summary

We will later offer detailed suggestions on how to avoid pitfalls that have led to these criticisms. These will appear in chapters 22 and 24 on preparing for and delivering the argument.

We conclude our discussion on the purpose of oral argument at this juncture by emphasizing again that because most judges in most appellate courts read briefs prior to argument, the oral argument should not be a scissors-and-paste job of excerpts from the written brief. Extensive preparation is necessary, and it must range far from that required for writing the brief. You must be prepared for an onslaught of questions from the bench that not only test the logical premises of the written submission, but may extend to outer perimeters of the subject matter of which your case is but an isolated part. The questions often take the form of hypotheticals seeking assistance from you as to where the lines should be drawn to expand or contract the specific legal precept you are urging upon the court. To argue effectively, then, familiarity with your brief is not enough. You must know the extensive perimeters of the law and know precisely where your case fits in that larger landscape. Demonstrate a comprehensive familiarity with the entire subject matter of substantive law of which your case is but a part.

What Justice Robert H. Jackson once said of his experiences as solicitor general summarizes the joys and pitfalls of any lawyer arguing before any court:

> The order and progression of an argument are important to its ready comprehension, but in the Supreme Court these are not wholly within the lawyer's control. It is difficult to please nine different minds, and it is a common experience that questions upset the plan of argument before the lawyer has fairly started. I used to say that, as Solicitor General, I made three arguments of every case. First came the one that I planned—as I thought, logical, coherent, complete. Second was the one actually presented—interrupted, incoherent, disjointed, disappointing. The third was the utterly devastating argument that I thought of after going to bed that night.[10]

Your goal to achieve the purpose of the oral presentation is to make "the utterly devastating argument" that Solicitor General Jackson thought of after going to bed on the night following his court appearance.

As a *sine qua non*, every appellate lawyer must recognize the fundamentals of persuasion—how the case, with all its warts and blemishes,

---

10. Robert H. Jackson, Advocacy *Before the United States Supreme Court*, 37 Cornell L.Q. 1, 6 (1951).

looks to the court. What do the judges know about the case? How do the judges feel about what they know or do not know? Your strategy will determine how to order your arguments; how much time to allow each part; how to word and support your arguments; but first and foremost, you must be satisfied that the arguments you select are the arguments the court will most likely accept.

Cicero summarized it well when he advised would-be orators centuries ago:

> Be clear, so the audience understands what is being said.

> Be interesting, so the audience will want to listen to what is being said.

> Be persuasive, so the audience will agree with what is being said.[11]

---

11. *Cripe, supra* note 3, at 357 (quoting Cicero).

PART TWO

TECHNICAL REQUIREMENTS FOR BRIEFS

Chapter 4

JURISDICTION

§ 4.1 Overview

A few years ago, a senior partner in one of the nation's prestigious law firms, stood before three circuit judges in the United States Courthouse in Philadelphia and announced his name as attorney for the appellant. He got no further. My colleague, then Judge John J. Gibbons interrupted: "Counsel, I don't think this court has jurisdiction. This looks like a Rule 54(b) situation because certain claims are still open below."

The very urbane practitioner, who for years had played a dominant role in the American Bar Association, paused for a moment and then folded up his notes and said, "I apologize for taking up the court's time. There is no jurisdiction. May I have the court's permission to withdraw the appeal?" His embarrassment was equaled by the chagrin of partners in the two opposing law firms, equally renowned, who likewise had failed to consider the question of appellate jurisdiction and had failed to raise the issue in their briefs.

Do you have jurisdiction to bring the appeal? Not a word in a federal appellate court brief should be written on the substantive merits of a case until you answer this question in the affirmative. Similarly, ascertain fully the various state court jurisdictional requirements. Indeed, even though time constraints may require you to file a notice of appeal, no serious discussions with your client as to the advisability of pursuing the appeal should go forward until you are absolutely confident that the appellate court has jurisdiction *at this time*. Likewise, the appellee's first chore is to determine whether the appellant has the right to file the appeal *at this time*.

If you are an appellate lawyer in a federal court, you have an additional burden. You must also decide if the federal district trial court had jurisdiction to entertain the case. The jurisdiction of federal courts is more limited than that of their state counterparts. The federal courts may hear cases based only on diversity of citizenship (with the requisite amount in controversy) or federal questions, statutory or constitutional. Unlike other appellate issues placed in contention, which must be preserved by objection or by the plain error doctrine, the question of jurisdiction may be raised at any time on any appellate level either by the court *sua sponte* or by one of the parties.

§ 4.2 Subject Matter Jurisdiction Checklist

1. *Federal courts*—In the federal system, jurisdiction must have been proper in the district court or administrative agency.

2. *Jurisdiction in original proceedings.*

3. *Interlocutory orders*—Appeal may be permitted by rule or statute, e.g., 28 U.S.C. § 1292(a), which permits appeal from "[i]nterlocutory orders of the district courts . . . granting, continuing, modifying, refusing or dissolving injunctions, or refusing to dissolve or modify injunctions. . . ." and 28 U.S.C. §1292(b) (special certifications of questions by both district and circuit judges).

4. *Final judgments.*

5. *Multiple claims or parties*—In those courts adhering to a rule such as Federal Rule of Civil Procedure 54(b), Judgment Upon Multiple Claims or Involving Multiple Parties, be certain to count the number of parties and claims below to determine whether the trial court disposed of *all claims of all parties*. Otherwise, there is no final judgment, unless the trial court has made an express determination that there is no just reason for delay and has made an express direction for the entry of judgment.

6. *Collateral orders.*

7. *Mandamus.*

§ 4.3 Appealability in the Federal System

Rule 12(h)(3) of the Federal Rules of Civil Procedure provides that "[w]henever it appears by suggestion of the parties or otherwise that the court lacks jurisdiction of the subject matter, the court shall dismiss the action." The lawyer, and the court before which you bring your appeal, have a duty to inquire into jurisdiction—both jurisdiction as to the appeal and jurisdiction as to the original action. The Supreme Court has stated that "[a]n appellate federal court must satisfy itself not only of its own jurisdiction, but also of that of the lower courts in a cause under review."[1] The advocate also must do as much.

To begin your examination of federal appellate jurisdiction, consider that every appeal from a district court presents at least three jurisdic-

---

1. *Mitchell v. Maurer*, 293 U.S. 237, 244 (1934).

tional issues: (1) whether the district court order or judgment is appealable immediately, either under the final judgment rule or a recognized exception; (2) whether the notice of appeal is sufficient, and (3) whether the notice of appeal was timely filed. You must satisfy yourself that you have qualified under these three sections before you can begin to convince an appellate court that you have.

§ 4.3.1 Final Orders

Do you have a final decision? Under 28 U.S.C. § 1291, "[t]he courts of appeals shall have jurisdiction of appeals from all final decisions of the district courts . . . except where a direct review may be had in the Supreme Court." (Cases of direct review to that court are rare and are specifically delineated by statute.) Parties may appeal certain interlocutory orders by right,[2] and others by permission,[3] but generally, the courts of appeals have the power to review only final decisions.[4]

A final decision is one which "ends litigation on the merits and leaves nothing for the court to do but execute the judgment."[5] The finality requirement of 28 U.S.C. § 1291 is to be given its practical rather than its technical construction. A court will consider the balance between "the inconvenience and costs of piecemeal review" and "the danger of denying justice by delay."[6] If it appears that you lack finality, argue the justice side. If it appears that your opponent has prematurely brought an appeal, argue the inconvenience and costs of piecemeal review side.[7]

The final judgment rule furthers four goals: (1) deference to the district courts,[8] (2) efficient use of judicial resources, (3) the prevention of harassment and the avoidance of a costly, and (4) dilatory succession of separate appeals.[9] The result is that some erroneous trial court

---

2. 28 U.S.C. § 1292(a).

3. 28 U.S.C. § 1292(b).

4. *United States v. MacDonald*, 435 U.S. 850, 857–58 n.6 (1978).

5. *Van Cauwenberghe v. Biard*, 486 U.S. 517, 521–22 (1988) (quoting *Catlin v. United States*, 324 U.S. 229, 253 (1945)).

6. *Dickinson v. Petroleum Conversion Corp.*, 338 U.S. 507, 511 (1950) (footnote omitted).

7. *See also Cobbledick v. United States*, 309 U.S. 323, 324–25 (1940) ("Finality as a condition of review is an historic characteristic of federal appellate procedure. It was written into the first Judiciary Act and has been departed from only when observance of it would practically defeat the right to any review at all. . . . To be effective, judicial administration must not be leaden-footed.").

8. *Flanagan v. United States*, 465 U.S. 259 (1984); *Firestone Tire & Rubber Co. v. Risjord*, 449 U.S. 368 (1981).

9. *Cobbledick*, 309 U.S. at 324–25.

rulings go uncorrected until the appeal of the final decision, but this is preferable to a rule that would permit piecemeal appellate review to disrupt litigation in the trial court. The rule can either help or hinder you depending upon which side of the courtroom you stand.

a. Examples of appealable "final orders"

   1. Grant of a motion to dismiss[10]

   2. Imposition of sentence in a criminal case[11]

   3. Order compelling arbitration in a suit under section 301 of the Labor Management Relations Act[12]

   4. Stay in exercise of Pullman abstention[13]

b. Examples of orders that are not "final" and are not immediately appealable

   1. Denial of a motion to dismiss[14]

   2. Denial of a motion to disqualify counsel in a civil trial[15]

   3. Denial of a motion for judgment on the pleadings[16]

   4. Denial of summary judgment[17]

   5. Grant of partial summary judgment[18]

Some of these non-final matters, however, may be reviewable under exceptions to the final judgment rule established by statute, rule, or case law.

---

10. *Rosenberg Bros. & Co. v. Curtis Brown Co.*, 260 U.S. 516 (1923).

11. *Flynt v. Ohio*, 451 U.S. 619, 620 (1981) (per curiam); *Berman v. United States*, 302 U.S. 211, 212-13 (1937).

12. *Goodall-Sanford v. United Textile Workers of Am.*, 353 U.S. 550 (1957).

13. *Moses H. Cone Mem. Hosp. v. Mercury Constr. Corp.*, 460 U.S. 1 (1983).

14. *Catlin*, 324 U.S. at 229.

15. *Firestone Tire*, 449 U.S. at 368.

16. *Sinclair Refining Co. v. Stevens*, 123 F.2d 186 (8th Cir. 1941), *cert. denied*, 315 U.S. 804 (1942).

17. *Pacific Union Conference of Seventh Day Adventists v. Marshall*, 434 U.S. 1305 (1977).

18. *Brooks v. Fitch*, 642 F.2d 46 (1981).

§ 4.3.2   Finality under Rule 54(b)

What do you do if you have a case involving multiple claims and parties and you want to appeal only as to one or a few? Fed. R. Civ. P. 54(b) governs the entry of final judgment in civil cases involving multiple claims and parties. If an order or decision adjudicates fewer than all claims or determines the claims of fewer than all parties, Rule 54 provides that such order or decision "shall not terminate the action as to any of the claims or parties" and such an order is therefore not appealable until the entire action is decided. However, you may request that the district court enter final judgment under Rule 54(b) as to fewer than all the claims or parties after an express determination that there is no just reason for delay.

The purpose of Rule 54(b) is to avoid the possible injustice of a delay in entering judgment (and thus delay of appeal) on distinctly separate claims and to reduce the risk that a litigant will inadvertently forfeit his or her right to appeal.[19] The decision whether to certify an order for immediate appeal is within the district court's sole discretion.[20]

To qualify for certification under Rule 54(b), the order must be final as defined by 28 U.S.C. §1291,[21] it must involve multiple claims[22] or parties, and there must be an express determination that there is "no just reason for delay." In addition, a majority of courts of appeals require that the district court's certification should be accompanied by a reasoned explanation, however brief, of its conclusion.[23]

§ 4.3.3 Collateral Orders

If you do not have a final judgment on the merits, do not despair completely. There is a chance, a small chance to be sure, but nevertheless a slight opening does exist. In some circumstances, an order may qualify as a "final decision" under §1291 absent an entry of final judgment. The Supreme Court created this common-law exception to the final judgment rule in *Cohen v. Beneficial Industrial Loan Corp.*, 337 U.S. 541 (1949). "To come within the 'small class' of decisions excepted from the final judgment rule by *Cohen*, the order must conclusively

---

19. *Dickinson*, 338 U.S. at 512.

20. *Curtiss-Wright Corp. v. Gen. Elec. Corp.*, 446 U.S. 1 (1980).

21. *Sears Roebuck & Co. v. Mackey*, 351 U.S. 427 (1956).

22. *Liberty Mutual Ins. Co. v. Wetzel*, 424 U.S. 737 (1976).

23. *Cullen v. Margiotta*, 811 F.2d 698, 711 (2d Cir.), *cert. denied*, 483 U.S. 1021 (1987).

determine the disputed question, resolve an important issue complete-ly separate from the merits of the action, and be effectively unreview-able on appeal from a final judgment."[24]

Under the Cohen doctrine, where rights will "be irretrievably lost in the absence of immediate appeal," collateral review is available.[25] The Supreme Court has strictly construed this requirement and refused to convert the limited exception carved out in *Cohen* into a license for broad disregard of the finality rule imposed by Congress in 28 U.S.C. § 1291.[26]

a. Examples of appealable collateral orders

    1. Denial of a motion to dismiss on the basis of qualified immunity from suit[27]

    2. Denial of bail[28]

    3. Order requiring defendants to pay 90 percent of the costs of notice to prospective class members in class action[29]

    4. Denial of dismissal based on double jeopardy[30]

    5. Denial of dismissal of a criminal case against a person entitled to protection under the speech or debate clause of the Article I of the Constitution[31]

b. Examples of orders that are not appealable

    1. Denial of motion to stay or dismiss an action based on *Colorado River* doctrine[32]

    2. Denial of motion to dismiss on grounds of forum non conviens[33]

---

24. *Coopers & Lybrand v. Livesay*, 437 U.S. 463, 468 (1978) (footnote and citations omitted).

25. *Richardson-Merrell, Inc. v. Koller*, 472 U.S. 424, 430–31 (1985).

26. *Firestone Tire*, 449 U.S. at 368.

27. *Mitchell v. Forsyth*, 472 U.S. 511, 528 (1985).

28. *Stack v. Boyle*, 342 U.S. 1 (1951) (now codified in 18 U.S.C. §§ 3145(c) and 3731).

29. *Eisen v. Carlisle & Jacquelin*, 417 U.S. 156 (1974).

30. *Abney v. United States*, 431 U.S. 651 (1977).

31. *Helstoski v. Meanor*, 442 U.S. 500 (1979).

32. *Gulfstream Aerospace Corp. v. Mayacamas Corp.*, 485 U.S. 271 (1988) (overruling *Enelow-Ettleson* doctrine).

33. *Van Cauwenberghe*, 486 U.S. at 517.

3. Discovery orders[34]

4. Denial of a petition to disqualify an attorney[35]

5. Denial of a motion to dismiss based on vindictive prosecution[36]

If you can demonstrate irreparable harm from one of these usually non-appealable orders, you might be entitled to seek certification under 28 U.S.C. § 1292(b) or relief by mandamus.

§ 4.3.4   Nonfinal appealable orders

§ 4.3.4.1   Interlocutory Appealable Orders Under 28 U.S.C. § 1292(a)

Title 28 U.S.C. §1292(a) provides:

> Except as provided in subsection (c) and (d) of this section, the courts of appeals shall have jurisdiction of appeals from:
>
> (1) Interlocutory orders of the district courts of the United States . . . or of the judges thereof, granting, continuing, modifying, refusing or dissolving injunctions, or refusing to dissolve or modify injunctions, except where a direct review may be had in the Supreme Court;
>
> (2) Interlocutory orders appointing receivers, or refusing orders to wind up receiverships or to take steps to accomplish the purposes thereof, such as directing sales or other disposal of property;
>
> (3) Interlocutory decrees of such district courts or the judges thereof determining the rights and liabilities of the parties to admiralty cases in which appeals from final decrees are allowed.[37]

---

34. *Borden Co. v. Sylk*, 410 F.2d 843 (3d Cir. 1969).

35. *Firestone*, 449 U.S. at 368.

36. *United States v. Hollywood Motor Car Co.*, 458 U.S. 263 (1982).

37. 28 U.S.C. § 1292(a).

Under section 1292(a)(1), you may confront the situation where a district court enters an order not technically granting or denying an injunction, but having the same effect.[38] When a district court order does not expressly deny an injunction, but has the ultimate effect of so doing, you must "show that the interlocutory order of the district court might have a 'serious, perhaps irreparable consequence,' and that the order can be 'effectively challenged' only by immediate appeal."[39]

§ 4.3.4.2   Certification Under 28 U.S.C. § 1292(b)

You are in the midst of litigation. You have experts ready to testify, exhibits prepared and labeled, associates scurrying around researching issues and a host of support staff ready for the fight. The district court decides an important and controversial issue of law prior to trial which does not finally dispose of any claim or party, but which has substantial consequences on the outcome of the case. In this circumstance, you may wish to seek certification under section 1292(b) so that the order is immediately appealable. Unlike a Rule 54(b) certification, however, the court of appeals may decline jurisdiction under section 1292(b) and thereby deny the certification of the interlocutory appeal. The scope of appellate jurisdiction extends only to questions of law raised by the order certified by the district court.[40] However, if it is your only shot, you should go for it.

How do you get an appeal under section 1292(b)? Permissive appeals under this section are sought by filing a petition for permission to appeal with the clerk of the court of appeals within ten days of the entry of the district court order.[41] Under section 1292(b), the district court will certify the order for appeal only on a showing that: (1) the order raises a controlling question of law, the determination of which will end the action in the district court;[42] (2) there is a substantial ground for difference of opinion on the question; (3) the interlocutory appeal will materially advance the ultimate termination of the litigation; and (4) the order involves an actual, not hypothetical, question of law. Certification is

---

38. *Stringfellow v. Concerned Neighbors in Action*, 480 U.S. 370, 378–79 (1987); *Gulfstream Aerospace Corp. v. Mayacamas Corp.*, 485 U.S. 271 (1988); *Carson v. American Brands, Inc.*, 450 U.S. 79, 83–84 (1981). *But see Hershey Foods Corp. v. Hershey Creamery Co.*, 945 F.2d 1272 (3d Cir. 1991).

39. *Carson v. American Brands, Inc.*, 450 U.S. 79, 84 (1981).

40. *United States v. Stanley*, 483 U.S. 669 (1987).

41. Fed. R. App. P. 5(a).

42. James Wm. Moore, Walter J. Taggart & Jeremy C. Wicker, 9 *Moore's Federal Practice* ¶ 110.22 [2], at 259 (2d ed. 1989).

not easy to obtain, but if the issue has a serious impact on your case or even on your trial strategy, do not disregard it as an option.

§ 4.4 Appealability in State Systems

States range across the board in their treatment of appealability. On one extreme is New York, which allows appellate review to the appellate division of the Supreme Court (trial) as of right to virtually every judgment and order. On the other extreme is Wisconsin, which strictly limits appellate review to final judgments and orders. The remainder of the states fall somewhere in between. Most follow the federal model in large part.

§ 4.5 A Word of Caution

A word of caution is warranted: be sure that you understand your local rules, be they state or federal. This book is not intended to be an authority on these important rules. Rules change and so do the ways that the courts interpret them, so be on top of your reading in this crucial area.

§ 4.6 The Notice of Appeal

On a more basic level, you begin with the notice of appeal. In most states, and in the federal system, the notice of appeal is filed with the clerk of the trial court, not the appellate court.

The courts tend to be generous in ruling on the adequacy of the document itself. Fed. R. App. P. 3(c), for example, provides that an appeal "shall not be dismissed for informality of form or title of the notice of appeal."[43]

On one point, however, the Supreme Court has taken a hard line. A notice of appeal must specifically name all of the parties to the appeal.[44] An "etc." or an "et al." will not do. Parties not named in the appeal must be dismissed.[45] This draconian penalty for a ministerial defect can lead to substantial liability in malpractice.

---

43. A document intended to serve as an appellate brief may qualify as the notice of appeal required by Rule 3. *Smith v. Barry*, 502 U.S. 244 (1992).

44. *Torres v. Oakland Scavenger Co.*, 487 U.S. 312, 318 (1988).

45. *Id.*

§ 4.7 Mandatory Timely Filing

Your notice of appeal must be filed within the period prescribed. The jurisdiction of the appellate court depends on it. If you fail to comply with this requirement, the court must dismiss the appeal.[46] This can be a potent litigation tool if you represent the appellee and something to be carefully watched and adhered to should you represent the appellant. You do not want to be a day late, or you may find yourself more than a dollar short.

Fed. R. App. P. 4(a) sets out the time limits for an appeal of right in a civil case. The notice of appeal must be filed within thirty days after the date of entry of the judgment or order appealed. A cross-appeal is timely if filed within fourteen days of the filing of the notice of appeal or within the original appeal period.[47] If "the United States or an officer or agency thereof" is a party, however, any appellant has sixty days in which to appeal.[48]

A criminal defendant has ten days from the entry of judgment to file a notice of appeal;[49] the government may file an appeal within thirty days.[50]

The time period begins to run under Rule 4(a)(1) from the date of entry of judgment or order appealed from, not from the date of the order.[51] This may give you some extra time should the district court delay entering judgment until several days or even weeks after it has issued an order. Always remember the "separate document rule" and use it to your advantage. As required by Rule 58, the time period begins to run from the date on which a judgment has been set forth in a separate document. The purpose of this requirement is to avoid "uncertainties as to the date on which the appeal period begins."[52] However, a separate document is neither a jurisdictional requirement nor cast in stone; an appeal may be allowed in its absence.[53]

---

46. *Budinich v. Becton Dickinson & Co.*, 486 U.S. 196, 203 (1988).

47. Fed. R. App. P. 4(a)(3).

48. Fed. R. App. P. 4(a)(1).

49. Fed. R. App. P. 4(b).

50. 18 U.S.C. § 3731.

51. *United States v. Indrelunas*, 411 U.S. 216, 221 (1973) (per curiam); *but see FirsTier Mortg. Co. v. Investors Mortg. Ins. Co.*, 498 U.S. 269 (1991) (notice of appeal filed after order but before judgment is effective if the order would have been appealable if immediately followed by the entry of judgment).

52. *Indrelunas*, 411 at 221–22.

53. *Bankers Trust Co. v. Mallis*, 435 U.S. 381 (1978) (per curiam). *See also FirsTier*, 498 U.S. at 269.

The time period in federal criminal appeals begins to run from the date of the entry of the judgment or order appealed from. If the government files a notice of appeal, the defendant then has ten days to file an appeal.

The computation of time for the filing of a notice of appeal is governed by Rule 26(a). The basic rules are: (1) do not include the day of entry of judgment or order in the computation; (2) if Saturday, Sunday, or a legal holiday is the last day of the period, the period ends on the next day which is not a Saturday, Sunday, or legal holiday; and (3) the notice of appeal is filed when it is received by the clerk of the district court. Courts give extra consideration to the difficulty encountered by pro se prisoners in filing a notice of appeal and hold that the delivery to prison officials for mailing of a notice of appeal by a prisoner, rather than its receipt by the clerk of the district court, constitutes the time of its filing.[54]

What do you do if you completely miss the filing date? Do not panic and do not give up. If you have failed to file a notice of appeal within the thirty or sixty days after entry of judgment, you may still have a chance to appeal. There are two ways in which you can extend the time for taking an appeal: the tolling doctrine and a motion under Rule 4(a)(5) for extension due to excusable neglect.

§ 4.7.1   Tolling

Under Fed. R. App. P. 4(a), the appeal period is tolled for all parties if one of these motions under the Federal Rules of Civil Procedure is timely filed:

1. a motion for judgment as a matter of law under Rule 50(b);

2. a motion to amend or make additional findings of fact under Rule 52(b);

3. a motion to alter or amend the judgment under Rule 59;

4. a motion for a new trial under Rule 59.

In accordance with each of the rules under which these motions are filed, the motions must either be filed or served within ten days of the district court's entry of judgment.[55] Therefore, if you filed one of these

---

54. *Houston v. Lack*, 487 U.S. 266 (1988).

55. Fed. R. Civ. P. 50(b), 52(b), 59(b), and 59(e).

motions, you may have saved your practice, your client's respect, and possibly, the case.

Even so, remember that a motion filed under Rule 60(b) (for stated reasons including mistake, fraud, and newly discovered evidence) does not toll the appeal period. Frequently, a party will file a post-judgment motion within ten days of the entry of judgment without indicating which rule is being invoked. The court must then construe the motion to determine whether it tolls the time for taking an appeal. The court usually must choose between Rules 52(b) or 59 and 60(b). All three cover post-judgment requests for relief from judgment, but Rule 60(b) is not restricted by a ten-day time limit. As a trade-off, however, it does not toll the time for appeal from, or affect the finality of, the original judgment.[56] Therefore, identify which alternative is best for you and argue it.

Under Rule 4(a)(4), once the district court has decided the motion which tolls the appeal period, the appeal period begins again from the date of entry of the decision on the motion.

§ 4.7.2   Extension of Time Under Rule 4(a)(5)

A second way you can enlarge the appeal period is by obtaining an extension from the district court. The court of appeals is without power to waive the time requirement for appeal,[57] but the district court may extend the time for appeal under Rule 4(a)(5). In a civil case, if you file a motion before the expiration of the appeal period provided in Rule 4(a), the district court, on a showing of excusable neglect or good cause, can extend the period to file for up to thirty days past the prescribed time or ten days from the date of the order granting the motion, whichever occurs later.

---

56. *Browder v. Director, Dept. of Corrections of Illinois*, 434 U.S. 257, 263 n.7 (1978).

57. *United States v. Robinson*, 361 U.S. 220, 224 (1960).

Chapter 5

ISSUE PRESERVATION AND STANDARDS OF REVIEW

§ 5.1 Issue Preservation for Review

A mainstay of the common law tradition is that the trial court must decide all matters in the first instance. Questions and objections must be presented in that forum and your adversary permitted to respond. This ensures that issues appealed have actually been decided by the trial court.

Appellate determination of reversible error is based on the presence of three interrelated circumstances:

- specific rulings, acts, or omissions by the trial tribunal constituting trial error;

- which follow an objection by counsel or the grant or denial of an oral or written motion or submission;

- accompanied by a proper and appropriate course of action recommended by the appellant that was rejected by the tribunal.

When all three elements are present, the issue has been properly preserved for review.

The necessity of preserving the issue is the short answer to the question: when does one start to prepare for an appeal? The textbook response is: the earlier the better. At a very minimum, you must have one eye cocked on the appellate court during all pretrial, trial, and post-trial proceedings. If and when an adverse ruling is made against you, be certain that your objection is on the record. Unless the trial transcript discloses it or a pretrial or post-trial colloquy or ruling has been transcribed or appears in a filed motion and order, appellate review will not be available—or, at best, under strict plain error restrictions.

Preserve the issue at all costs. Do not be content with "informal" rulings made at sidebar or in chambers with no court reporter present. Always request that the trial court's ruling and your objection be entered on the record. Have this done immediately after the "informal" ruling is made, no matter how inconsequential it may appear at the time. Do not depend on "resurrecting" or "reconstructing" the record on appeal. Your adversary invariably will have a different recollection of what was said in chambers or in other off-the-record discussions, and you cannot depend upon the trial judge's memory for assistance.

Generally speaking, if the issue was not first presented to the trial judge or administrative agency, the reviewing court will not consider it. There are, of course, exceptional cases in particular circumstances that will prompt a reviewing appellate court to consider questions of law, even though these questions were not pressed upon the court or administrative agency below. A ruling by the appellate court in the first instance may be appropriate where blatant injustice might otherwise result. Such cases, however, are very rare and come under the category of "plain error" or the notion of basic and fundamental error. Justice Hugo Black explained the purpose of the general rule:

> Ordinarily an appellate court does not give consideration to issues not raised below. For our procedural scheme contemplates that parties shall come to issue in the trial forum vested with authority to determine questions of fact. This is essential in order that parties may have the opportunity to offer all the evidence they believe relevant to the issues which the trial tribunal alone is competent to decide; it is equally essential in order that litigants may not be surprised on appeal by final decision there of issues upon which they have had no opportunity to introduce evidence. And the basic reasons which support this general principle applicable to trial courts make it equally desirable that parties should have an opportunity to offer evidence on the general issues involved in the less formal proceedings before administrative agencies entrusted with the responsibility of fact finding.[1]

Argue plain error if you must—if your jurisdiction allows it—but do not rely on it.

The bottom line: preserve the issue for appeal by making the proper contemporaneous objection or motion at pretrial, trial, or post-trial and be certain that the record reflects that the objection or motion had been made and that the trial court adversely ruled on it.

§ 5.2 Standards of Review

Standards of review are critically important in effective advocacy. In large part, they determine the power of the lens through which the appellate court may examine a particular issue in a case. The error

---

1. *Hormel v. Helvering*, 312 U.S. 552, 556 (1941); *see also Newark Morning Ledger Co. v. United States*, 539 F.2d 929, 932 (3d Cir. 1976).

that may be a ground for reversal under one standard of review may be insignificant under another. It does not matter what you ask the court to do on appeal if the court cannot jump the hurdle posed by the standard of review. You must craft your brief on appeal to reflect the proper standard and to show why, under that standard, your client deserves to win. If your appeal raises more than one issue, then you should state the standard of review for each point.[2]

The appellate process generally reduces to limited types of review: fact-finding by judges under the clearly erroneous rule or by the administrative agency under the substantial evidence rule; review of the trial court's exercise of discretion; and plenary review of the choice, interpretation, and application of the controlling legal precepts. The competent advocate will have a clear understanding of the scope of review pertaining to each point in his or her brief. The Federal Rules of Appellate Procedure now require a statement of the review standard for each issue presented in the briefs.[3]

I elevate the necessity of correctly stating the review standard to a question of minimum professional conduct. I say this because I have seen otherwise competent lawyers completely falter when asked to state the standard of review. A psychological block seems to crush those who refuse to recognize that trial tribunals' fact-finding processes can fast-freeze evidence into rigid and unchangeable facts. It makes no sense for lawyers to take a closing speech to a jury and dress it up as a brief to an appellate court. The closing summarizes the litigant's best *evidence*; appellate courts address findings of *fact*. This is a key distinction.

§ 5.3 The Import of your "Day in Court"

Everyone is entitled to his or her "day in court." Access to tiers of appellate review notwithstanding, this typically means only one day: the proceeding in which the fact-finder determines the facts from evidence or where a judge exercises discretion or makes rulings of law. Where facts are not in dispute, the court decides the matter without live witnesses and often on papers with oral argument—the most popular today being summary judgment. These initial determinations for the most part are final and binding, difficult to surmount even by impressive appellate briefs, thick volumes of records, or eloquent argument. The truth—lost upon most lay persons, and unfortunately, upon

---

2. Throughout this book, I will use "issue" and "point" interchangeably to refer to each major contention raised in an appeal.

3. Fed. R. App. P. 28(a)(9)(B).

many lawyers—is that most trial court decisions are set in quick-hardening jurisprudential cement and will be subject to an extremely limited scope of appellate review.

Where the controversy is one of *fact*, findings ordinarily are permanent. Practical and philosophical impediments prevent an appellate court from displacing the fact-finder's resolution of conflicting evidence. When a *legal* determination is challenged, a popular misconception is that reversal may be easily obtainable. Although reviewable, a legal ruling, even though erroneous, may not be sufficient grounds for reversing. When the trial court is left with the right to exercise discretion, the appellate court may not properly substitute its views for those of the trial court. Here, the appellate court's function is limited to discovering and defining the parameters of allowable discretion and interfering only when convinced that the use of discretion below has exceeded those limitations. The reviewing court calls such a transgression an "abuse," or more accurately, a "misuse" of the exercise of proper discretion.

"A defendant is entitled to a fair trial but not a perfect one."[4] Although the trial court may err in some of its rulings, the determination as to whether the judgment should be reversed turns on whether the error is "reversible." To recognize these distinctions and to accommodate this precise awareness to the cause at hand is the hallmark of an expert appellate advocate.

For a proper understanding of the fact-finding procedures, it is necessary to separate the distinct concepts involved in the review of judicial findings. The difference in these concepts—basic facts (both direct and inferred) and ultimate facts (mixed facts and law)—is fundamental in the review process.

§ 5.4 Three Categories of Facts.

Fact-finding is the province of the trial tribunal, be it a court or administrative agency. The skill of a trial advocate is measured by an ability to persuade the factfinder to convert a congeries of testimony and evidence into adjucative facts. The fact-finder may be a jury, a judge, an arbitrator, a hearing examiner or an administrative law judge, or the board to which he or she reports. Trial advocacy, which deals with fact-based persuasion, calls for skills completely different from the appellate advocacy of legal persuasion on questions of law.

---

4. *Lutwak v. United States*, 344 U.S. 604, 619 (1953)

The fact-finder is the sole judge of credibility and is free to accept or reject even uncontradicted oral testimony.[5] Without regard to the number of rungs an appellant may climb up the appellate ladder, the American tradition—in most cases—does not permit a reviewing court to disturb findings of credibility. *See* § 5.5.1 *infra*.

For a proper understanding of the jurisprudence of fact-finding review, it is necessary to segregate three distinct and fundamental concepts: basic facts, inferred facts, and ultimate facts. The importance of distinguishing these three types is reflected in the various standards of judicial review. When the court, sitting as a fact finder, identifies the basic facts and facts permissibly inferred therefrom, neither may be disturbed on review unless they are deemed clearly erroneous.[6] "A review of ultimate facts," on the other hand, "entails an examination for legal error of the legal components of those findings.[7]

§ 5.4.1 Basic and Inferred Facts

Although writers and judges are not uniform in the labels placed on various types of facts, "basic facts" are best understood as historical and narrative accounts elicited from the evidence presented by witnesses at trial, or admitted by stipulation and not denied in responsive pleadings. In 1937, Justice Butler described these as "primary, evidentiary or circumstantial facts."[8]

Evidence that is inferred from witness testimony or documentary evidence, rather than being direct, is often called circumstantial. Inferences of facts are permitted only when, and to the extent that, logic and human experience indicate a probability that certain consequences can and do follow from the basic events or conditions.[9] No legal precept is implicated in drawing permissible factual inferences.

---

5. *Nanty Glo v. Am. Surety Co.*, 309 Pa. 236 (1932); *see also Sartor v. Arkansas Natural Gas Corp.*, 321 U.S. 620 (1944); *NBO Indust. Treadway Cos. v. Brunswick Corp.*, 523 F.2d 262 (3d Cir. 1975), *cert. denied*, 429 U.S. 1090 (1977); *Rhoades, Inc. v. United Air Lines, Inc.*, 340 F.2d 481, 486 (3d Cir. 1965).

6. Fed. R. Civ. P. 52(a); *see United States v. United States Gypsum Co.*, 333 U.S. 364, 394 (1948).

7. *Smith v. Harris*, 644 F.2d 985, 990 (3d Cir. 1981); *see also Universal Minerals, Inc. v. C.A. Hughes & Co.*, 669 F.2d 98, 102–103 (3d Cir. 1981) (discussing the distinction between the review of basic and inferred facts on the one hand and of ultimate facts on the other).

8. *Helvering v. Tex-Penn Oil Co.*, 300 U.S. 481, 491 (1937).

9. *See, e.g., Edward J. Sweeney & Sons, Inc. v. Texaco, Inc.*, 637 F.2d 105, 116 (3d Cir. 1980), *cert. denied*, 451 U.S. 911 (1981).

The inferences that the court permits the jury to adduce in a courtroom do not differ significantly from the inference that you reach daily in informally accepting a probability or arriving at a conclusion when presented with some basic evidence. A court permits the jury to draw the inference because of shared experiences in human endeavors. Perhaps the only distinction between extracting these factual conclusions from daily life and from the courtroom is that a jury's act of drawing or not drawing an inference is preceded by a judge's instruction. The instruction serves to guide the jury through some process of ordered consideration. The court informs the jury that it must weigh the narrative or historical evidence presented, make credibility findings when appropriate, and then draw only those inferences that are reasonable in reaching a verdict.

§ 5.4.2   Ultimate Facts: Mixed Questions of Law and Fact

Notwithstanding what I have said above, we must distinguish an inferred fact from an "ultimate fact." So conceived, an ultimate fact is a mixture of fact and legal precept.

We usually express an ultimate fact in the language of a standard enunciated by case law or by statute. For example, we say that an actor's conduct was negligent, or the injury occurred in the course of employment, or the rate is reasonable, or the company has refused to bargain collectively. "The ultimate finding is a conclusion of law or at least a determination of a mixed question of law and fact."[10]

It is always the responsibility of the fact-finder—jury, judge, or administrative agency—to find the narrative or historical facts and to draw proper inferences therefrom. Often the fact-finder must go further and determine the ultimate facts as well, based on the court's instruction in a jury case or on a proper application of a legal precept in a nonjury trial or agency hearing. The fact-finder always operates within the acknowledged limitations of any judicial process.

Narrative or historical data are, at best, imperfect re-creations of the actual events. They are constructed from the perceptions of witnesses. The most we can hope for is that the witnesses will be not only honest but reasonably accurate in both perception and recollection, and that the fact-finder will also be intelligent and fair in evaluating the evidence presented. The appellate advocate must work within a

---

10. *Helvering*, 300 U.S. at 491 (1937).

time-tested mechanism designed to fashion a courtroom reconstruction of what actually occurred. It does not produce perfection in all cases, but it does serve as a reasonable facsimile in most cases.

Once basic facts have been found, they are seldom dislodged. Therefore, it is important to understand the different roles a trial and an appellate lawyer play vis-à-vis the facts. The trial lawyer's skill is measured by the ability to persuade the fact finder of basic facts. The skill of the appellate lawyer, however, is often measured by the ability to convince the court that a given "fact" is not a "basic" fact but an "ultimate" fact, thus giving the court more leeway to review the precise issue.

Where the ultimate fact has been found by a judge, the reviewing court may not disturb, except for clear error, the basic fact component in the mixed question of law and fact, but the appellate court is free to review the "law" segment of the ultimate fact *de novo*.[11] This means that review is available when there is insufficient evidence to sustain the requirements of the legal precept upon which the ultimate fact is premised. For example, in a review of a finding of negligence in an automobile case, the evidence of speed, the location of vehicles and direction of travel is historical or narrative. This is the "basic" fact component of the "ultimate" fact of negligence. It is not reviewable in jury trials, and it is subject to extremely limited review in bench trials.

Consider *Universal Minerals, Inc. v. C.A. Hughes & Co.*,[12] which presented the question of whether there had been an "abandonment" of a pile of culm (refuse from a coal mine). The court explained that "abandonment" is not a question of narrative or historical fact, but an ultimate fact—a legal concept with a factual component—that is a conclusion of law or at least a determination of a mixed question of law and fact. The court explained:

> In reviewing the ultimate determination of abandonment, as an appellate court, we are therefore not limited by the "clearly erroneous" standard, . . . but must employ a mixed standard of review. We must accept the trial court's findings of historical or narrative facts unless they are clearly erroneous, but we must exercise a plenary review of the

---

11. *But see* Adam Hoffman, Note, *Corralling Constitutional Fact: De Novo Fact Review in the Federal Appellate Courts*, 50 Duke L.J. 1427 (2001), and Evan Tsen Lee, *Principled Decision Making and the Proper Role of Federal Appellate Courts: The Mixed Questions Conflict*, 64 S. Cal. L. Rev. 235 (1991), for discussions of possible conflicts in the circuits as to what portion of a mixed question should be subject to plenary review.

12. 669 F.2d 98 (3d Cir. 1981).

trial court's choice and interpretation of legal precepts and its application of those precepts to the historical facts . . . Thus we separate the distinct factual and legal elements of the trial court's determination of an ultimate fact and apply the appropriate standard to each component.[13]

An appellate court uses the same approach when we review a jury's findings on a mixed question, but the distinction is more easily understood in that context because of the strict allocation of competence between the jury and the trial court and because of the intercession of the Seventh Amendment. If, for example, a jury finds that a party has abandoned an interest in property, we review the court's jury instructions to determine whether the court erred in its explanation of the law; if we find no error we examine the record to determine whether the evidence was sufficient to justify someone of reasonable mind in drawing the factual inferences underlying the conclusion.

Legislative facts—facts that have been authoritatively found by an extralegal body—also figure in the judicial process at both levels, trial and appellate. Use of such facts is not only permissible, but extremely helpful in deciding the interpretation or applicability of a given legal precept. When a court arrogates to itself the role of the legislative fact-finder, without supporting data in the record, its action is at best, questionable.

§ 5.5 Who Found the Facts?

The first inquiry in reviewing findings of fact is whether the facts were found by a judge, jury, or administrative agency. The nature of the fact-finder will determine the scope of the appellate court's scrutiny and guide the launching of your attack.

§ 5.5.1 Fact-finding: Judicial Proceedings

The Seventh Amendment has controlling force in federal jury cases: "In Suits at common law, where the value in controversy shall exceed twenty dollars, the right of trial by jury shall be preserved, and no fact tried by a jury shall be otherwise re-examined in any Court of the United States, than according to the rules of the common law." Most state constitutions have similar provisions.[14] So long as there is some

---

13. *Id.* at 103.

14. *See, e.g.,* Pa. Const. art. I, § 6; N.J. Const. art. I, § 9; Del. Const. art. I, § 4.

evidence from which the jury could arrive at the finding by a process of reasoning, the jury's findings of fact, especially those resolving conflicts in testimony, will not be disturbed. This, of course, is a different issue than the quantum of evidence necessary to sustain the various burdens of proof in civil and criminal cases.[15]

Facts found by a judge alone need a stronger evidentiary base. The findings, under the federal rules and in those states adhering to the substance of Fed. R. Civ. P. 52(a) shall not be set aside "unless clearly erroneous, and due regard shall be given to the opportunity of the trial court to judge of the credibility of the witnesses." "Clearly erroneous" has been interpreted to mean that a reviewing court can upset a finding of fact, even when supported by some evidence, but only if the court has "the definite and firm conviction that a mistake has been committed."[16] This has been construed by one United States court of appeals to mean that the appellate court must accept the factual determination of the fact finder unless that determination "either (1) is completely devoid of minimum evidentiary support displaying some hue of credibility, or (2) bears no rational relationship to the supportive evidentiary data."[17]

Because only the factfinder has an opportunity to observe the demeanor of witnesses, it is generally the rule "that a fact finder's determination of credibility is not subject to appellate review."[18] Conversely, in cases in which the trial judge decides a fact issue on written or documentary evidence, some reviewing courts previously adopted the view that "we are as able as [the judge] to determine credibility, and so we may disregard his finding."[19] Many courts and thoughtful commentators, however, thought otherwise.[20] Congress finally resolved the question by approving an amendment to Rule 52(a) suggested by the Federal Advisory Committee on Civil Rules. The rule now reads, "Findings of fact, whether based on oral or documentary evidence, shall not be set aside unless clearly erroneous, and due regard shall be given to the opportunity of the trial court to judge the credibility of the witnesses."

---

15. *See, e.g., Jackson v. Virginia,* 443 U.S. 307 (1979).

16. *United States Gypsum,* 333 U.S. at 395.

17. *Krasnov v. Dinan,* 465 F.2d 1298, 1302 (3d Cir. 1972).

18. *Government of the Virgin Islands v. Gereau,* 502 F.2d 914, 921 (3d Cir. 1974), *cert. denied,* 424 U.S. 917 (1976).

19. *Orvis v. Higgins,* 180 F.2d 537, 539 (2d Cir. 1950).

20. *Lundgren v. Freeman,* 307 F.2d 104 (9th Cir. 1962); Charles Alan Wright, *The Doubtful Omniscience of Appellate Courts,* 41 Minn. L. Rev. 751 (1957).

In some state systems, it is necessary to inquire about and understand the stability given to facts found by a chancellor in equity. Historically, these facts were subject to a broad review in equity, but some jurisdictions, like Pennsylvania, give the same effect to a chancellor's findings as to a jury verdict when considering a post-trial motion.[21] In the past, Pennsylvania had an unusual practice in which exceptions to a chancellor's decree nisi as to both findings of fact and conclusions of law had to be considered by a multi-judge en banc panel before a final decree was entered. Under that practice, the facts found by the chancellor approved by the en banc court had the efficacy of a jury verdict.

§ 5.5.2   Fact-Finding: Administrative Agencies

The reviewing court may not set aside the findings of administrative agencies unless they are "unsupported by substantial evidence" in light of the whole record.[22] What, however, is substantial evidence? For some time recourse has been made to a Supreme Court statement by Chief Justice Hughes: "Substantial evidence is more than a mere scintilla. It means such relevant evidence as a reasonable mind might accept as adequate to support a conclusion." Justice Stone gave further clarification: substantial evidence "means evidence which is substantial, that is, affording a substantial basis of fact from which the fact in issue can be reasonably inferred. . . . [I]t must be enough to justify, if the trial were to a jury, a refusal to direct a verdict when the conclusion sought to be drawn from it is one of fact for the jury."[23] By 1988, the Supreme Court was prepared to state:

> We are not, however, dealing with a field of law that provides no guidance in this matter. Judicial review of agency action, the field at issue here, regularly proceeds under the rubric of "substantial evidence" set forth in the Administrative Procedure Act, 5 U.S.C. § 706(2)(E). That phrase does not mean a large or considerable amount of evidence, but rather "such relevant evidence as a reasonable mind might accept as adequate to support a conclusion."[24]

---

21. *Schwartz v. Urban Redevelopment Auth.*, 206 A.2d 789 (Pa. 1965).

22. 5 U.S.C. § 706(2)(E); *see Beth Israel Hospital v. NLRB*, 437 U.S. 483 (1978); *Universal Camera Corp. v. NLRB*, 340 U.S. 474 (1951); 4 K. Davis, *Administrative Law* chs. 29–30 (1958 & Supp. 1970).

23. *NLRB v. Columbian Enameling & Stamping Co.*, 306 U.S. 292, 299–300 (1939).

24. *Pierce v. Underwood*, 487 U.S. 552, 564–65 (1988).

In the review of administrative agency proceedings, as in the review of judicial factfinding, the question of credibility is for the administrative law judge to determine.[25] When the agency does not accept the ALJ's findings, substantial evidence is not found so readily.[26]

§ 5.6 A Comparison: Common Law and Civil Law Traditions

The nonreviewability of facts found by a court of the first instance or an administrative agency is peculiar to the common law tradition. Civil law tradition permits review of facts through the courts of the second instance. Thus, new evidence can be taken and the evidence below reexamined in the various appeals courts—for example, the French *cour d'appel*, the German *Oberlandesgerichthof*, and the Italian *corte d'appello*. Beyond the court of the second instance, the appeal to the final court is restricted to matters of law only—in France, a *pourvoi en cassation*; in Germany a *Revision*, and in Italy, a *ricorso in cassazione*.[27] Similarly, there is generous review of facts in appeals from administrative agencies to the specialized courts. In civil cases in Louisiana,

---

25. Thus, in *NLRB v. Lewisburg Chair & Furniture Co.*, 230 F.2d 155, 157 (3d Cir. 1956): "Questions of credibility of witnesses have to be resolved in litigation but in labor cases this court is not the place where such resolving takes place." Under the substantial evidence standard, a reviewing court does not re-weigh the evidence, resolve testimonial conflicts or "displace the Board's choice between two fairly conflicting views, even though the court would justifiably have made a different choice had the matter been before it *de novo*." *Universal Camera Corp. v. NLRB*, 340 U.S. 474, 488 (1951). The Court does not pass on the credibility of the witnesses, reweigh the evidence or reject reasonable Board inferences simply because other inferences might also reasonably be drawn. *See NLRB v. Walton Mfg. Co.*, 369 U.S. 404, 405 (1962).

26. *Eastern Engineering & Elevator Co. v. NLRB*, 637 F.2d 191, 197 (3d Cir. 1980):

> In our review of the Board's order, the statute furnishes our basic direction: the reviewing court treats as conclusive the factual determinations in a Board decision if they are 'supported by substantial evidence on the record considered as a whole.' 29 U.S.C. § 160(f). That the responsibility of fact finding is placed on the Board and not on the hearing judge, however, does not end our inquiry. The Supreme Court has directed us to recognize that an administrative law judge's findings of fact constitute a vital part of the whole record that the court must review. These findings 'are to be considered along with the consistency and inherent probability of testimony. The significance of his report . . . depends largely on the importance of credibility in the particular case.' *Universal Camera Corp. v. NLRB*, 340 U.S. 474, 496 (1951). We must 'recognize that evidence supporting a conclusion may be less substantial when an impartial, experienced examiner who has observed the witnesses and lived with the case has drawn conclusions different from the Board's than when he has reached the same conclusion.'

27. Ruggero J. Aldisert, *Rambling Through Continental Legal Systems*, 42 U. Pitt. L. Rev. 935 (1982).

the sole civil law jurisdiction in the United States, the state's courts of appeal (the courts of second instance) may review facts.[28]

§ 5.7 Discretion

One who blindly challenges on appeal the exercise of discretion might do better to take a leisurely stroll through an uncharted minefield. If the issue implicates lower tribunal discretion, the appellate lawyer who fails to recognize this, in my charitable and understated view, misses by light years the minimum standards of competence. To try to beguile the appellate court to review discretionary actions de novo is simply a waste of the lawyer's abilities, the client's money, and the court's time.

Bouvier's Law Dictionary defines "discretion" as:

> That part of the judicial function which decides questions arising in the trial of a cause, according to the particular circumstances of each case, and as to which the judgment of the court is uncontrolled by fixed rules of law.

---

28. The Louisiana Constitution of 1974 provides:

> Art. 10(B). Scope of Review. Except as limited to questions of law by this constitution, or as provided by law in the review of administrative agency determinations, appellate jurisdiction of a court of appeal extends to law and facts.

In *Brown v. Avondale Shipyards Inc.*, 413 So. 2d 183, 184 (La. Ct. App. 1982), the court observed:

> [W]e point out that our constitution, Article V Section 10(B), provides that the scope of appellate review extends to both law and facts. The case of *Arceneaux v. Domingue*, 365 So. 2d 1330 (La. 1978), requires us to examine the entire record in our appellate review.

In *Arceneaux*, the Louisiana Supreme Court explained:

> "Manifestly erroneous" in its simplest terms means "clearly wrong.". . . Therefore, the appellate review of facts is not completed by reading so much of the record as will reveal a reasonable factual basis for the finding of the trial court; there must be a further determination that the record establishes that the finding is not clearly wrong.

365 So. 2d at 1333.

Yet, generally speaking, in Louisiana, the trial court's findings of fact, particularly when they are dependent upon credibility of witnesses, are entitled to great weight and will not be disturbed on appeal in absence of manifest error. *See, e.g., Echizenya v. Armenio*, 354 So. 2d 682, *writ refused*, 356 So. 2d 1006 (La. Ct. App. 1978).

The power exercised by courts to determine questions to which no strict rule of law is applicable but which, from their nature, and the circumstances of the case, are controlled by the personal judgment of the court.[29]

Hart and Sacks define certain other types of discretion as "the power to choose between two or more courses of action each of which is thought of as permissible."[30]

As a jural concept, discretion admits of some lack of precision, and formal definitions of the concept mark only the beginning of understanding. I agree with Professor Ronald Dworkin that discretion, like the hole in the doughnut, does not exist except as an area left open by a ring of restriction.[31] Legislative or judicial authorities should guide both the exerciser and the reviewer by defining with some specificity the outer limits of the discretion. The Court of Appeals of the Third Circuit has noted:

The mere statement that a decision lies within the discretion of the trial court does little to shed light on its reviewability. It means merely that the decision is uncontrolled by fixed principles or rules of law. . . . In our judicial system, a wide variety of decisions covering a broad range of subject matters, both procedural and substantive, is left to the discretion of the trial court. The justifications for committing decisions to the discretion of the court are not uniform, and may vary with the specific type of decisions. Although the standard of review in such instances is generally framed as "abuse of discretion," in fact the scope of review will be directly related to the reason why that category or type of decision is committed to the trial court's discretion in the first instance.[32]

Often appellate lawyers fail to recognize discretionary decisions and argue as if plenary review applies. One can guide down the street a horse bearing a sign that reads, "I am a cow," but no one will be deceived. By the same token, one cannot urge de novo review of a trial court's exercise of discretion. Minimal competence demands at least

---

29. 1 J. Bouvier, *Bouvier's Law Dictionary* 884 (Rawle ed. 1914).

30. Henry M. Hart & Albert Sacks, *The Legal Process* 162 (tent. ed. 1958). An example of this type of discretion, described as a power of continuing discretion, is the power of the President of the United States to fill a vacancy on the federal bench.

31. Ronald Dworkin, *Taking Rights Seriously* 31 (1977).

32. *United States v. Criden*, 648 F.2d 814, 817 (3d Cir. 1981) (footnote omitted).

a recognition that certain decisions are committed to lower tribunal discretion and will not be set aside absent a showing of abuse—more properly, misuse—of that discretion.

Many of us inside and outside the judicial world are dissatisfied, on the one hand, with the exercise of discretion by trial courts, administrative agencies, and representatives of the executive branch of government, and on the other hand, with appellate review of discretionary actions. This dissatisfaction probably motivates recent sophisticated analyses of the discretion concept. The dissatisfaction may be justified, because courts and legislative bodies have been content with the generic words "discretion" and "discretionary power" without defining the contours of the exercise, other than occasionally attaching the adjective "broad."[33] Knowing simply that one is invested with discretion does not tell much. The crucial inquiry, necessarily, is the extent of the discretionary power conferred. Thus, although the recent commentators have outlined sophisticated nuances, it remains for the courts to calibrate its full measure and for attorneys to feel the brunt of it.

Dworkin delineates two "weak" senses of discretion and one "stronger sense."[34] At one end of the scale is discretion conferred because "for some reason the standards an official must apply cannot be applied mechanically but demand use of judgment." At the same end is discretion conferred because "some official has final authority to make a decision and cannot be reviewed and reversed by any other official." Dworkin calls both of these senses "weak" and distinguished them from a discretion in which the official "is simply not bound by standards set by the authority in question."

Consider the differences among the following: (a) The sergeant is to pick his five best people to go on foot patrol. (b) The sergeant is told to pick his five fastest runners to go on patrol. (c) The sergeant is told to pick any five people to go on patrol. Can you see the difference in the degree of discretion granted?

Professor Maurice Rosenberg has explained that:

> probably the most pointed and helpful [reason] for bestowing discretion on the trial judge as to many matters is, paradoxically, the superiority of his nether position. It is not that he knows more than his loftier brothers; rather,

---

33. The Supreme Court has agreed that although a district court had discretion under the old doctrine of *forum non conveniens*, it "had a broader discretion in the application of the [change of venue] statute [28 U.S.C.A. § 1404]." *Norwood v. Kirkpatrick*, 349 U.S. 29, 30 (1955).

34. Ronald Dworkin, *The Model of Rules*, 35 U. Chi. L. Rev. 14, 32–33 (1967).

he sees more and senses more. In the dialogue between the appellate judges and the trial judge, the former often seem to be saying: "You were there. We do not think we would have done what you did, but we were not present and we may be unaware of significant matters, for the record does not adequately convey to us all that went on at the trial. Therefore, we defer to you."[35]

In 1957, Judge Stanley Barnes echoed this preference for direct observation:

> The trial judge saw and heard the plaintiff; saw his twitch-ings, what they were and what they were not, as did the jury. He saw or heard the other matters relied on by appel-lant; he felt the "climate" of the trial. The trial judge found no fraud nor misrepresentation. . . . The Court of Appeals should not and will not substitute its judgment for that of the trial court, nor reverse the lower court's determination save for an abuse of discretion.[36]

If one starts with an understanding of discretion as encompass-ing the power of choice among several courses of action, each of which is considered permissible, it would seem difficult, if not conceptually impossible, to disturb discretionary choice on review. Nonetheless, appellate courts continue to do so, couching their actions in language which disclaims a substitution of choices for those of the trial courts. This type of review generates tension between trial and appellate courts. When it results in reversal, the litigant who prevailed below is justifiably surprised and irate. Notwithstanding lengthy opinions with detailed evaluations of facts, the core reasons supporting reversals, in the guise of finding an improper use of discretion, are generally unsat-isfactory.

What then can we say to the lawyer who either finds fault with or defends the trial court's exercise of discretion? I can come up with no neat answer. But where the trial court has been invested with "broad discretion," the ninth circuit came up with a fairly workable formula-tion in 1942:

---

35. Maurice Rosenberg, *Judicial Discretion of the Trial Court, Viewed from Above*, 22 Syracuse L. Rev. 635, 663 (1971).

36. *Atchison, Topeka & Santa Fe Ry. Co. v. Barrett*, 246 F.2d 846, 849 (9th Cir. 1957) (citation omitted).

Discretion, in this sense, is abused when the judicial action is arbitrary, fanciful or unreasonable, which is another way of saying that discretion is abused only where no reasonable man would take the view adopted by the trial court. If reasonable men could differ as to the propriety of the action taken by the trial court, then it cannot be said that the trial court abused its discretion.[37]

But what is "broad discretion?" I go back to the sergeant who had been ordered to pick five persons for the patrol. The exercise of discretion depends upon the discretionary power:

Conferred Power	*Discretionary extent*
Pick any five persons.	Very broad, totally unfettered.
Pick any five men.	Broad, but constrained by gender.
Pick the five best.	Somewhat constrained: What is meant by "best?"
Pick the five fastest runners	Moderate, constrained by running ability.
Pick the five strongest	Moderate, constrained by muscle strength.
Pick the five youngest or oldest	Very limited.
Pick the tallest or shortest	Very limited.

How do we convert these illustrations to appellate review of trial court discretion? Professor Rosenberg has given us some excellent examples showing a range of gradations beginning with what he calls Grade *A*, where discretion is extremely broad and virtually impervious to appellate assault, and running to Grade *E*, where discretion is almost certainly reviewable.[38]

The lesson from this is that there are degrees of discretion. An able appellate lawyer will analyze the extent of the discretionary power available and the policy behind it, and then demonstrate whether the lower tribunal was endowed with broad, limited or very little prerogative.

---

37. *Delno v. Market St. Ry. Co.*, 124 F.2d 965, 967 (9th Cir. 1942).

38. Maurice Rosenberg, *Appellate Review of Trial Court Discretion*, Federal Judicial Center publication FJC-ETS-77-3 (1975).

Review of discretion is somewhat broader than the very narrow range that governs fact finding, but its scope has stated limitations. Appellate lawyers must understand, however, that our metaphorical minefield is not an impassable barrier and that careful testing can identify safe pathways forward to the desired objective. Appellate lawyers must understand also that the exercise of discretion by the tribunal of the first instance has its limits and they must be able to articulate where those limits are. The competent lawyer carefully sets forth the boundaries of a permissible exercise of discretion and then demonstrates how those boundaries were transgressed. The outstanding appellate lawyer persuades the court to expand or narrow its review of discretion on the basis of the policies underlying the grant of discretion.

§ 5.8 Questions of Law

When it comes to the review of the trial court's determination of the law, the appellate courts are given the freest of reins. The review of fact finding is at the nadir of the appellate function; the examination of the trial court selection, interpretation, and application of legal precepts is the zenith.

On a question of law, the appellate court is not restricted by the division of judicial labors which protect findings of fact in the common law tradition or under the constitutions of the various sovereignties or the limited review of discretion. Generally speaking, the appellate court is free to examine *de novo* all aspects of legal precepts: the choice by the tribunal of the controlling legal precept, the interpretation of it, and the application of the precept as chosen and interpreted to the findings of fact.

A reviewing court's function is to determine whether a trial court committed a mistake of law of sufficient magnitude to require that its judgment be reversed or vacated. Putting aside those jurisdictions in which appellate courts must search the record for error, the reviewing court's role is inexorably entwined with the performance of the advocates. An appellate court may, under circumstances, consider matters *sua sponte* but, generally, when an appellate court considers questions raised by an appellate alleging error of law, it relies upon the issues and legal arguments set forth by the advocate.

In 1877, a reviewing court stated: "The court erred in some of the legal propositions announced to the jury; but all the errors were harmless. Wrong directions which do not put the traveler out of his way furnish no reasons for repeating the journey."[39] Roger J. Traynor regarded this as a literary epigram but not as a legal precept, for the question of whether wrong directions do or do not put the traveler out of his way is a troublesome one. The difficult question is to decide whether the trial error becomes reversible error. Working under the assumption that one is not entitled to a perfect trial, but only to a fair one, it becomes necessary to fashion a method of ascertaining the circumstances under which the results of an admittedly imperfect trial will be disturbed.

We cannot draw any line in the sand to determine when any run-of-the-will trial mistakes transform themselves into reversible error. The line to reversible error is crossed when the mistake seriously infected the truth finding process, or when the final judgment has been rendered on uncontroverted facts and the party against whom the ruling was made could possibly have been entitled to relief.

§ 5.9 Examples of Standards of Review: *See* Appendix *A*

§ 5.10 Summary

I cannot overstate the importance of recognizing that not all judicial review is plenary, that the scope of review is extremely narrow when it comes to fact-finding, that review of the exercise of discretion is somewhat broader but still severely circumscribed, and that the broadest review is employed to determine *de novo* error in the choice, interpretation, or application of a legal precept.

Appellate courts are now requiring appellate briefs to contain proper statements of trial and appellate court jurisdiction and to set forth the precise scope of review for each point asserted on appeal. I am convinced that briefs and oral argument would be more effective—in turn, producing better judicial decisions—if counsel would identify the standard of review for each point.

More precise in content, stripped of surplusage, opposing briefs could hit the issues head-on instead of glancing off. Presented with more accurate and efficient arguments, the courts will be able to upgrade the product of their work, and judge-made law would in the words of Professor Harry W. Jones, "contribute[ ] to the establishment and preservation of a social environment in which the quality of human life can be spirited, improving, and unimpaired."[40]

---

39. *Cherry v. Davis*, 59 Ga. 454, 455 (1877).
40. Harry W. Jones, *An Invitation to Jurisprudence*, 74 Colum. L. Rev. 1023, 1030 (1974).

PART THREE

NUTS AND BOLTS OF BRIEF WRITING

Chapter 6

GETTING STARTED: REQUIREMENTS FOR BRIEFS, RECORDS, AND APPENDICES

§ 6.1 Overview

Because requirements for briefs and supporting records, or excerpts thereof, vary throughout the country, I do not intend to present a compendium. My purpose is merely to touch on some features of United States courts of appeals and state systems. I do this to emphasize that differences do exist, even among the federal circuits, and that lawyers must be aware of them. I also do this to emphasize that you diminish the efficacy of your brief when you do not follow a court's briefing rules. Because of the extraordinary caseloads in appellate courts, judges are understandably disturbed when they turn to a particular section of a brief for information and find it wanting because the rules have not been observed. Nor are they pleased when parts of the briefs arrive in dribs and drabs after counsel discover they have omitted something. When these arrive after the judge has already read the brief, lawyers run the risk that they will never be read.

Do not consider what we set forth about rules to be definitive; this book should not be cited as authoritative. It is not even intended as a secondary source. Only the latest edition of the Federal Rules of Appellate Procedure, the circuit rules, or the state rules should be consulted in preparing an appeal. My purpose is only to point out the principal peaks and alert you that differences exist in rules and practice, state by state, circuit by circuit.

The federal system will be discussed in detail because it affords some, if not complete, uniformity throughout the country. Rules in the state systems differ from jurisdiction to jurisdiction. Although it is difficult to generalize, I can offer a number of suggestions to alert you to problems relating to briefing rules. I begin with some commandments:

United States Courts of Appeals. Do not, I repeat, do not rely exclusively on the Federal Rules of Appellate Procedure. They are only the starting point. You must always examine the rules of the individual circuits for local idiosyncracies. If a difference does exist between the federal rules and the circuit rules, the circuit rules control to the extent that they are "not inconsistent with" the federal rules. You may obtain these rules from the clerk of the court of each circuit. You also can find them in Title 28 of the United States Code.

State Appellate Courts. Each state appellate court may have its own rules. Thus, do not assume that the rules of the state's highest court govern practice in the intermediate appellate court. If in doubt, ask the clerk of court.

Nomenclature. Throughout these pages, I typically refer to the party bringing the appeal as the *appellant*, although in some states, in appeals from federal administrative agencies, and in the United States Supreme Court, the moving party is known as the *petitioner.* I will refer to the opposing party as the *appellee*, although in these same courts the answering party is known as the *respondent.* In most jurisdictions, the appellate proceeding is known as an *appeal*, although appeals from administrative agencies generally are termed *petitions for review.* Federal legislation has made most of the Supreme Court's jurisdiction discretionary, thus reducing direct appeals in favor of *petitions for certiorari* either to a United States court of appeals or to a state appellate court. Accordingly, when I use the terms *appellant* and *appellee*, you may wish to read them as *petitioner* and *respondent.*

§ 6.2 Requirements for Briefs: Federal Court

The general requirements for briefs filed in federal appellate courts are set forth in Fed. R. App. P. 28. The federal rules outline these components in some detail, and most state courts follow a similar pattern.

The federal rules require the appellants to include the following elements, under appropriate headings and in the order indicated:

Provision of Rule 28(a)	Comment
A corporate disclosure statement if required by Rule 26.1	*A relatively new requirement designed to permit judges to recuse (or disqualify) themselves if they have a financial interest in any party, or in a parent or subsidary company of party.*

A table of contents, with page references; and a table of authorities—cases (alphabetically arranged), statutes and other authorities—with references to the pages of the brief where they are cited.	*Generally required in all state appellate courts.*
A jurisdictional statement, including: (A) the basis for the district court's or agency's subject matter jurisdiction, with citations to applicable statutory provisions and with reference to the relevant facts establishing jurisdiction; (B) the basis for the court of appeals' jurisdiction, with citations to applicable statutory provisions and with reference to the relevant facts to establish such jurisdiction; (C) the filing dates establishing the timeliness of the appeal or petition for review; and (D) an assertion that the appeal is from a final order or a final judgment that disposes of all parties' claims, or inforion establishing the court of appeals' jurisdiction on some other basis.	*In federal appeals, make certain that you also state the basis for subject matter jurisdiction in the agency or district court.*
A statement of the issues presented for review.	
A statement of the case briefly indicating the nature of the case, the course of proceedings, and the disposition below.	

A statement of the facts relevant to the issues submitted for review with appropriate references to the record. *The references to the record should be done in accordance with Rule 28(e).*

A summary of the argument, which must contain a succinct, clear, and accurate statement of the arguments made in the body of the brief, and which must not merely repeat the argument headings.

The argument, which must contain: (A) the appellant's contentions and the reasons for them, with citations to the authorities, statutes, and parts of the record relied on; and (B) for each issue, a concise statement of the applicable standard of review (which may appear in the discussion of the issue or under a separate heading placed before the discussion on the issues).

A short conclusion. State the precise relief sought.. *Make it clear.*

A certificate of compliance, if required by Rule 32(a)(7)

Appellees must conform to these requirements as well, except that they may omit statements of jurisdiction, of the issues, or of the case if they are satisfied with those of the appellants.

An appellant may file a reply to the appellee's brief; if the appellee has cross-appealed, the appellant may respond. Where the appellant has responded, the appellee as cross-appellant may reply. This is the *only* time an appellee is permitted to respond to a reply brief. All reply briefs must contain a table of contents and a table of authorities.[1]

Where appropriate, briefs should refer to the relevant portions of the record, which typically are reproduced as an appendix.[2] Lawyers should understand that, both in theory and in actual use, an appendix is precisely what the word denotes—a supplement that adds supporting details to what was said in the text. An appropriate appendix should do no more and no less.

If a determination of the issues requires the court to examine particular statutes, rules, or regulations, court rules permit brief writers to place the relevant text of these sources in either the brief or an addendum to the brief. Where these sources are critical to understanding the argument, I prefer to see the relevant portion—the heart of the issue —placed in the text, with the full source either footnoted or placed in the addendum. Requirements for the appendix are discussed in §§ 6.6 and 6.7 below.

§ 6.3 Special Rules of the United States Courts of Appeals

Each of the courts of appeals has promulgated local rules either supplementing or modifying the provisions of Rule 28. A lawyer appearing before these courts should carefully examine the court's current local rules, which can be found in Title 28 of United States Code.

The following is an indication of *some* additions or modifications to the general requirements of Rule 28, adopted by the various circuits: statement of related cases; designation in the table of authorities of authorities principally relied on; request for (or waiver of) oral argument; copy of any unpublished disposition cited; copy of the judgment or order appealed from; relevant portions of any jury instructions; preliminary statement giving the name of the judge or agency officer who rendered the decision below and the citation of the decision or opinion, if reported.

If the court dispenses with the requirement of an appendix, the appellant must append these items to the brief: the relevant docket entries in the court below; the judgment or order appealed from, including any accompanying memorandum or opinion; the notice of appeal; certificate of interested persons; references to the record where appropriate; and fact sheets for certain appeals (Social Security, Title VII, and habeas corpus appeals under §§ 2254 and 2255).

---

1. Fed. R. App. P. 28(c).

2. *Id.* at Rule 28(e).

§ 6.4 Clerical Rules

In addition to the requirements for the contents of briefs, parties to an appeal must observe certain clerical rules regarding the form of the briefs, such as the print and paper size, the number of pages allowed,[3] the binding method required, the color and content of the front cover, and the number of copies to file. In the United States courts of appeals, the appellant's brief must be blue; the appellee's brief, red; the reply brief, gray; and the intervenor or amicus brief, green.[4] The front cover generally shall contain the name of the court and case number, the title of the case, the nature of the appellate proceeding, the name of the lower court, the title of the document, and the names and addresses of counsel filing the brief.[5] It bears repeating that each appellate court—state or federal—is very exacting regarding these requirements. Examine the rules every time you prepare a brief to ensure that each requirement of the court is met.

§ 6.5 Requirements for Briefs: State Courts

Unlike the federal appellate courts, the state courts do not follow a uniform briefing system. Requirements for briefs in state courts are as many and as varied as the states themselves. Generally speaking, all states require the following: table of contents, table of authorities, statement of the case, statement of issues, statement of facts, and the argument and conclusion stating the precise relief sought. Some require a summary of argument, copies of relevant statutes, rules and regulations, a statement of jurisdiction, and specific references to the record. The length of briefs varies from thirty pages to seventy-five pages (if typewritten) with fifty pages being about the norm. California has an unique rule: each point must be set off with a concise heading that generally describes the subject matter covered. Failure to comply can result in dismissal.[6]

§ 6.6 Requirements for the Record and Appendix: Federal Court

The record in federal appeals consists of all papers and exhibits filed in the district court, any transcript of proceedings, and a copy of

---

3. Fed. R. App. P. 32 (a)(7) provides that principal briefs shall not exceed thirty pages or 14,000 words, and reply briefs shall not exceed fifteen pages.

4. Fed. R. App. P. 32(a)(2).

5. *Id.*

6. *Superior Sand Co. v. Smith*, 64 P.2d 1149 (Cal. Ct. App. 1937).

the docket sheet.[7] Within ten days after filing a notice of appeal, the appellant must order from the court reporter a transcript of those portions of the proceedings relevant to the appeal.[8] Once the district clerk has received the transcript and the record on appeal is complete, the clerk generally has a duty to transmit the entire record to the clerk of the court of appeals.[9] However, a lawyer appearing before a particular court of appeals should ensure that the circuit's local rules do not modify these general rules.

The appellant must also prepare and file an appendix to the briefs containing: "(1) the relevant docket entries in the proceeding below; (2) any relevant portions of the pleadings, charge, findings or opinion; (3) the judgment, order or decision in question; and (4) any other parts of the record to which the parties wish to direct the particular attention of the court."[10] If the parties do not agree on the contents of the appendix, the appellee can compel the appellant to include items.[11]

Rule 30(f) allows courts of appeals to dispense with the requirement of an appendix. The ninth and eleventh circuits take a moderate approach, requiring excerpts of the record in lieu of a full-blown appendix.[12]

Some courts of appeals require both an appendix and an addendum to the briefs. The first circuit, for example, requires the appellant to include at the end of the brief a copy of the judgment or order appealed from, any relevant jury instructions, and pertinent portions of any documents relevant to the issues on appeal.[13]

Many courts will excuse an appellant from filing an appendix for good cause shown.[14] Thus, if you have a good reason to omit the appendix, such as when the record is short or the appeal is expedited, you should consider filing a motion to dispense with the appendix. The court also may excuse the appendix requirement if the appellant is proceeding in forma pauperis.

The most important lesson to be learned is that the local rules in the various courts of appeals do vary. An attorney appearing before one of these courts must study the local briefing rules carefully and follow

---

7. Fed. R. App. P. 10(a).

8. Fed. R. App. P. 10(b)(1).

9. Fed. R. App. P. 11(b).

10. Fed. R. App. P. 30(a).

11. Fed. R. App. P. 30(b).

12. 9th Cir. R. 30-1; 11th Cir. R. 30-1.

13. 1st Cir. R. 28(a).

14. D.C. Cir. R. 30(f).

them to the letter. A well-presented brief and appendix that adhere to the court's requirements will not only assist the court, but will ensure that the court does not sanction the client or the attorney for noncompliance, as some local rules permit.[15] It also will present a professional image to the court.

§ 6.6.1 Some Personal Advice

Permit me to offer some advice on the basis of my own experience sitting by designation with those courts of appeals that discourage the filing of appendices. Notwithstanding the local rules, I would file as an excerpt of record or as an addendum to the brief copies of (1) any opinion written by the district court; (2) if the issue relates to a jury instruction, the entire jury charge, the transcript of any jury instruction conference conducted under Fed. R. Civ. P. 51 or Fed. R. Crim. P. 30, and if relevant, a transcript of testimony supporting your requested instruction; and (3) a rather detailed transcript of the proceedings when the issue is insufficiency of the evidence. I also urge you to include copies of any unpublished opinions cited in your brief. Even though the rules may not require it, *always* paginate the appendix and include an accurate, detailed table of contents.

By following these recommendations, you will give each member of the panel the opportunity to examine these materials before, during, and after oral argument. Personally, I prefer to study them before argument and certainly before the panel's decisionmaking conference. I do not accept the notion advanced by some judges that these materials are beneficial only to the opinion-writing judge. That they are in the record and readily available to the circuit judge stationed at the seat of the court where the record is stored also is not sufficient. The good appellate lawyer will ensure that every member of the panel has easy access to them.

§ 6.7 Requirements for the Record and Appendix: State Court

When appearing before a state appellate court, you must familiarize yourself with that court's rules, if any, regarding transmission of the record on appeal and preparation of an appendix for the court. Some states require both the record and an appendix; others require one or the other. Generally speaking, you must file a copy of the judgment

---

15. 3d Cir. R. 30.5(a) (providing that the court may impose sanctions "upon finding that any party has unreasonably and vexatiously caused the inclusion of materials in an appendix that are unnecessary for the determination of the issues presented on appeal").

appealed from, the notice of appeal and the entire trial court record. Requirements for appendices vary: some require a table of contents, relevant docket entries, the judgment of the trial court or any intermediate court of appeals, the trial court opinion, the jury instructions and other pertinent portions of the pleadings and transcript. In some cases the parties may file a joint appendix or the appellee is given the option of filing a separate one.

§ 6.8 A Wrap-Up on Briefs and Records Rules

I cannot overemphasize the necessity of knowing and observing the rules governing briefs and the supporting record (whether by way of appendix, addendum, excerpt of record or the entire transcript). Failure to respect these rules may not cause your case to be dismissed, but it may get you off on the wrong foot. The best you can hope for in an appeal is a sympathetic court; at the very least, you want a neutral tribunal, not one that is hostile. You certainly do not want to face a court that has formed the impression: "This lawyer is complaining that the trial judge did not follow the rules of the game, but in taking this appeal, this character isn't following ours!"

Philosopher Henry Habberly Price has emphasized the importance of first impressions. He has explained that a sort of mental occurrence takes place when we are in the process of acquiring a favorable or unfavorable initial impression, and that such a disposition is not necessarily a very long-lived one; it may last only a few seconds.[16] But the advice is clear: do not make an initial bad impression by filing a sloppy brief that fails to follow the court's requirements.

In some instances, failure to follow the rules may result in more drastic consequences. In *Kushner v. Winterthur Swiss Ins. Co.*,[17] my court dismissed an appeal for failure to file a brief and appendix conforming to the local rules. The appellant's brief failed to set forth the names and addresses of counsel, and the appendix omitted the relevant trial court docket entries and notice of appeal and was not paginated. The court stated:

> We have explained the practical reasons for our action. [Much valuable time had to be expended by three judges and personnel of the clerk's office repairing the incomplete brief and appendix.] There is jurisprudential justification

---

16. Henry Habberly Price, *Belief and Will*, in 28 Proceedings of the Aristotelian Society 15–16 (1954).

17. 620 F.2d 404 (3d Cir. 1980)

for our decision as well. Each appellant in this court must of necessity allege that the district court violated some rule of substantive or procedural law relating to the finding of facts, the exercise of discretion, the choice of proper legal precept, the interpretation of the precept chosen, or its application to the facts as found. The litigant, then, who charges that the rules were not followed in the district court should himself follow the rules when he applies for relief in this court. Sauce for the goose is sauce for the gander.[18]

Failure to follow briefing rules also may result in lesser sanctions, such as the striking of briefs[19] or monetary sanctions against counsel.[20]

§ 6.9 Cover Page, Table of Contents, and Table of Authorities

§ 6.9.1 Overview

The table of contents and table of authorities are important to judges. Take care to ensure that they are complete and accurate. How well you do this depends on when you do them. These tables comprise the first pages of most briefs but should not be completed until the brief is in its final stages.

Judges constantly refer to these tables. They look to the table of contents to sense an overview of the case and for speedy references. They become frustrated when the tables omit crucial information or cite to incorrect page numbers or contain errors in citation. You want judges to be happy customers. They are not happy when your tables lead them astray.

Although the cover page may be prepared at any time, for administrative ease I suggest preparing the cover at the same time you prepare the tables of contents and authorities.

---

18. *Id.* at 407. Subsequent courts have dismissed appeals for failure to follow local rules. *See, e.g., Haugen v. Sutherlin,* 804 F.2d 490, 491 (8th Cir. 1986) (violation of "all the rules in the Federal Rules of Appellate Procedure and [the] local Eighth Circuit rules pertaining to form for briefs and record"); *Connecticut Gen. Life Ins. Co. v. Chicago Title & Trust Co.,* 690 F.2d 115, 116 (7th Cir. 1982) (failure to following briefing schedule), cert. denied, 464 U.S. 999 (1983).

19. *See, e.g., McGoldrick Oil Co. v. Campbell, Athey & Zukowski,* 793 F.2d 649, 653 (5th Cir. 1986).

20. *See, e.g., Westinghouse Elec. Corp.* v. NLRB, 809 F.2d 419, 425 (7th Cir. 1987).

§ 6.9.2 Cover Page

The cover page is used by the clerk's office and the court to identify the brief. Thus, it is important to set forth correctly on the cover page the court in which the brief is being filed, the docket number, the case caption, the court below, the party filing the brief and the attorneys on the brief. Fed. R. App. P. 32(a) specifically provides:

> . . . The front covers of the briefs . . . shall contain: (1) the name of the court and the number of the case;(2) the title of the case (see Rule 12(a)); (3) the nature of the proceeding in the court (e.g., Appeal, Petition for Review) and the name of the court, agency, or board below;(4) the title of the document (e.g. Brief for Appellant, Appendix); and (5) the names and addresses of counsel representing the party for whom the brief is filed.

State rules follow the same general requirements. You should arrange the required information in the form suggested or mandated by the court, but the most important factor is accuracy. A brief containing an incorrect docket number or case caption could be misfiled or lost.

You also must ensure that the cover page is printed in the proper color. As stated before, the federal rules require that the appellant's brief be blue; the appellee's brief, red; the reply brief, gray; and any intervenor or amicus brief, green.[21] The cover of the appendix, if separately printed, should be white.[22] This color code may not be important to lawyers, but it is critically important to judges because of the time pressures under which they study the briefs. It enables them to quickly flick from one brief to another in a given case. You must keep in mind that often a judge will read a point in the appellant's brief and immediately examine the appellee's response.

A valuable suggestion, often unheeded in appeals involving multiple parties or cases that are consolidated, is to set forth the name of the appellant or the appellee on the cover page. Instead of merely stating "Brief for Appellee," you should state "Brief for Appellee John J. Jones." This will allow the judge to identify immediately the party submitting the brief.

---

21. Fed. R. App. P. 32(a).

22. *Id.*

The following is an example of a typical cover page filed in the United States Court of Appeals for the Third Circuit. Because it is an appellee's brief, it should be printed on red paper.

UNITED STATES COURT OF APPEALS

FOR THE THIRD CIRCUIT

No. 91-1023

UNITED STATES OF AMERICA,
Plaintiff-Appellee,

v.

RAYMOND TORRES,
Defendant-Appellant.

APPEAL FROM THE DENIAL OF A MOTION TO VACATE,
SET ASIDE OR CORRECT SENTENCE PURSUANT TO
28 U.S.C. § 2255 ENTERED BY THE U.S. DISTRICT COURT
FOR THE EASTERN DISTRICT OF PENNSYLVANIA AT
CRIMINAL NOS. 89-0211 and 89-0302

BRIEF FOR APPELLEE

MICHAEL M. BAYLSON
United States Attorney Attorney

Walter S. Batty, Jr.
Assistant U.S. Attorney
Chief of Appeals

Jeffrey M. Lindy
Assistant U.S. Attorney
U.S. Courthouse
601 Market Street
Philadelphia, PA 19106

---

§ 6.9.3 Table of Contents

A good table of contents is very simple to prepare because it follows the logical pattern of your brief. In most instances, the task can be handled by an experienced legal secretary or paralegal, perhaps even by your wordprocessing program. The key is neatness and accuracy. Because many judges scan the table of contents to get a preview of coming attractions, a neat, accurate and complete table of contents can help create a good first impression. Conversely, a sloppy, incomplete table can give the reader a negative impression of the entire brief. Carefully draft the table "to be consistent with the quality demonstrated throughout the remainder of your brief."[23] Consider these comments by the former Chief Justice of the Idaho Supreme Court, Robert E. Bakes:

> [A]n opening table of contents spelling out each of the portions of the brief and the pages on which they are contained helps a judge immediately get into a case. This opening table of contents should break down the sections of the argument portion of the brief by issues, with page references, so that the judge can go quickly to a particular part of a brief. . . . A good table of contents saves a great deal of time.

The table of contents should list by page each component of the brief.[24] Each issue and subissue should be included under the "Argument" heading. As recommended in chapter 10, if the court's rules permit, the issues should be stated in declarative form, not posed as an interrogatory or as a sentence beginning with "whether." If the rules permit, you should frame each issue so that it becomes the heading in the argument portion of the brief. Your objective: cast the issue in language that the court can accept completely and adopt as a topic sentence in its opinion.

Consider form as well as substance. When the brief is not professionally printed with a variety of typefaces and fonts for emphasis, you should use care in selecting the characters used on your word processor. Because your purpose is to communicate, you should understand that a sentence typed in all capital letters is not as easy to read as one presented in caps and lower case. Moreover, reading is even more complicated when a single-spaced, all-caps sentence is underlined. Stating

---

23. S. Eric Ottensen, *Effective Brief-Writing for California Appellate Courts*, 21 San Diego L. Rev. 371, 375 (1984).

24. Fed. R. App. P. 28(a)(1).

the issue is not the same as giving the title of a book or a play. Unless the court rules require otherwise, you need only capitalize the first word in the issue sentence and any proper names. Capitalizing the first letter in every word in a sentence interferes with smooth reading.

A caveat: Save enough time to prepare an accurate table of contents. The table should be prepared while the argument is being drafted. The last-minute additions should be only the final page numbers.

I consider the following a model table of contents:

TABLE OF CONTENTS

_____

This table of contents is particularly effective because the reader's
eye is not distracted by unnecessary capitalization, underlining, or
boldface print. The table also serves as a map of the entire brief; it succinctly tells the reader what the issues are and where each required
element of the brief can be found. An effective alternative form utilizes
all capital letters in the main point and lower case in the subpoints:

_____

_____

Consider the following examples of less effective tables of contents:

TABLE OF CONTENTS

(*Author's Comment:* The use of underlining makes this table much more difficult to read than the first model above.)

TABLE OF CONTENTS

(*Author's Comment:* Does this table of contents tell the reader anything about the appeal? Does the eye quickly follow to the precise page number without the dotted line?)

TABLE OF CONTENTS

(*Author's Comment*: Once again, the reader is kept in the dark regarding the nature of the appeal except that it involves two arguments.)

§ 6.9.3.1 Cross-Reference Indexing

I strongly recommend that the arguments in the appellee's brief track those set forth by the appellant. Thus, by looking at the table of contents, the reader can readily ascertain where the appellee has responded to a particular argument posed by the appellant. Former Florida First District Court of Appeal Chief Judge Larry G. Smith has remarked:

> [A]side from the usual problems associated with lack of adequate research and care in preparation [of briefs], perhaps the most glaring (and, I might add, judge-infuriating) problem is the practice followed by some attorneys in the restating and argument of the issues in a sequence and under a heading different than that used by the appellant, without proper indexing, and without explanation of where the response to specific points raised by the appellant may be found.[25]

If it is necessary for an appellant to place the various arguments in a different sequence than the appellee, the appellant should provide the court with a cross-reference index. The United States Court of Appeals for the Third Circuit, for example, requires the appellee to provide a cross-reference index when filing a single brief in response to consolidated appeals by several appellants.[26] The following is an example of an effective cross reference index which appeared in a brief responding to two consolidated petitions for a writ of mandamus:

CROSS-REFERENCE INDEX

Petitioners' Contentions	*Respondents' Answering Contentions*
1. Writ of mandamus should issue because district court abused its discretion and acted arbitrarily (Celotex brief 10–13; Eagle-Picher brief 8–11).	Requirements for writ are not met; district court did not act arbitrarily nor did it usurp power (Respondents' brief 8–11).

---

25. Morris, *Oral Arguments and Written Briefs—DCA Judges Comment*, 62 Fla. B.J. 23, 24 (1988) (quoting Chief Judge Larry G. Smith).

26. 3d Cir. R. 28.2. This rule provides, in relevant part:

> The brief of an appellee who has been permitted to file one brief in consolidated appeals shall contain an appropriate cross-reference index that clearly identifies and relates appellee's answering contentions to the specific contentions of the various appellants.

2. Circumstances have changed since Third Circuit upheld class certification in 1986 (Celotex brief 13–30; Eagle-Picher brief 18–28).	Petitioners have shown no change in circumstances sufficient to justify issuance of the writ (Respondents' brief 11–13).
3. District court's denial of class in Davenport v. Gerber Baby Products shows arbitrariness of its refusal to decertify the class in this case (Celotex brief 33–36).	District court properly distinguished Davenport (Respondents' brief 10).
4. The litigation is "unsettleable" (Celotex brief 36–39).	Several defendants have already settled; another settlement is being completed (Respondents' brief 13).

§ 6.9.4 Table of Authorities

Unless you have a word processing program that automatically assembles tables of authorities, putting such a table together can be quite time-consuming. Once again, the key is neatness and accuracy. Judges often use this table to refer to the place or places in a brief where a particular case, statute, or constitutional provision is discussed, or to quickly find the citation to a specific authority. It bears repeating that judges become disturbed when citations are incorrect or page references inaccurate. Carefully proofread the citations and verify the page numbers after the brief is in final form to ensure that any last-minute changes are incorporated in the table of authorities.

Rule 28(a)(1) requires that the table list "cases (arranged alphabetically), statutes and other authorities cited, with references to the pages of the brief where they are cited." The citation to each authority should be complete and in *Bluebook* form.

If you must gather the information for the table of authorities manually, I suggest that you or someone on your staff make a separate 3-by-5-inch index card for each authority. After the complete citation for each authority has been placed on a card, arrange the cards in alphabetical order according to the type of authority. In most instances, you will have three separate piles of cards: one for cases, one for constitutions, statutes, and rules, and one for miscellaneous sources.

Once you cast the brief in final form and are reasonably certain that the page numbers will not change, have someone mark on each index card the pages on which that particular authority appears. Your secretary or typist then can prepare the table of authorities simply by taking the information off the stacks of index cards. Before you undertake this rather arduous task, however, you should check to see if your wordprocessing program is capable of preparing the table automatically. Not only will this save time, but it is likely to produce more accurate results.

Remember to begin working on the table of contents while you are writing the brief. Do not wait until the night before the deadline to start composing it in a frantic burst of overtime madness. Elements of the table should be assembled at the same time drafts of the argument are being prepared. Judges rely on your table in the decision-making process as well as the process of writing an opinion. The table must be complete and accurate. Save enough time to do it right—it is one of the most important parts of the brief.

You also should be aware that some courts, such as the eleventh circuit, require that the table indicate those authorities principally relied on.[27] If this is required, you should place an asterisk in the left-hand margin next to those authorities and note at the bottom of the first page of the table: "Authorities chiefly relied upon are marked with an asterisk."

Consider the following example of a model table of authorities:

TABLE OF AUTHORITIES

Cases: Page

Ashford v. State, 603 P.2d 1162 (Okla. Crim. App. 1987) 15

Brooks v. Tennessee, 406 U.S. 605 (1972) 24

Burgett v. Texas, 389 U.S. 109 (1967). 12

Carrizales v. Wainwright, 699 F.2d 1053 (11th Cir. 1983). 21

Commonwealth v. Rogers, 364 Pa. Super. 477,
    528 A.2d610 (1987) 25

Dowling v. United States, 110 S. Ct. 668 (1990). 12

Henderson v. Kibbe, 431 U.S. 145 (1977). 25

Lisenba v. California, 314 U.S. 219 (1941) 13, 14

---

27. 11th Cir. R. 28-1(e).

Chapter 7

RESEARCH AND USE OF AUTHORITIES

§ 7.1 Research

Insofar as legal research on appeal is concerned, you do not bake the cake from scratch. You already have had a trial or pretrial proceeding. You have preserved the point by making an objection or filing the appropriate motion and receiving an adverse ruling either on the record or by written order. You have asserted some legal propositions in the form of cases, statutes, constitutional provisions or rules that support your position. Ideally, you or the lawyer who appeared before the trial court, already had prepared and submitted a pretrial memorandum, trial brief, or memorandum in support of any post-trial motion. Now that the case has been lost at the trial level, and a notice of appeal has been filed, it is time for additional research.

If you were the trial lawyer, you should go back to the books to find out if there is anything new. Ask yourself whether there is anything else you can look for that may be more convincing than what you already have found. You must Shepardize your authorities to ascertain their present vitality. You must check the latest advance sheets, or even the slip opinions if a substantial lag exists between the announcement of a court's decision and its appearance in the advance sheets. Automated research systems, such as Westlaw and Lexis, are particularly helpful here.

If you are brought in as fresh counsel for the appeal, my advice is to start your research anew. You should not rely solely on the efforts of your predecessor. In either event, your research should be complete and current at the time the brief is written. Although court rules typically allow parties to file supplemental authorities, you should use them only to bring to the court's attention cases that have been handed down since the brief was filed. Sitting with various courts throughout the country, I often receive shortly before oral argument or even after argument "supplemental authorities" that predate the filing of the brief. My immediate reaction: "a sloppy lawyer."

Attorney James D. Crawford of Philadelphia[1] offers this useful brief writing advice to the junior partners and associates in his firm:

---

1. Mr. Crawford, senior counsel at Schnader, Harrison, Segal & Lewis, is a long-time leading appellate lawyer. He was chief appellate counsel in the Philadelphia District Attorney's office during the late 1960s and early 1970s, a period when federal courts were developing new concepts of Fourteenth Amendment protections. He served as chief assistant to then District Attorney Arlen Specter.

- Organize your research before you write. A major brief may involve days or even weeks of research, usually done by more than one person. If the accumulated research is to be used effectively in the brief, you must have some way to find the right cases or statutes to support each point you wish to make when you want to make it.

- It does not matter what technique you choose. Some lawyers find file cards useful. Others make photocopies of cases, mark important passages with a highlighter, and make notes at the head of each case of the propositions for which it stands or the ways in which it can be used. Still others scribble notes meaningful only to themselves on scraps of yellow pads. None, on the other hand, relies primarily on memoranda prepared by others. An author of a brief based on secondary sources alone is not an author or even an editor; he or she is at best a compiler, and appellate practice has a great ability to expose compilers.

- What is important is that you find some way of retrieving the cases you have found in the course of your research. Few things are more frustrating than knowing you have read a controlling case directly on point but cannot find it.

- Know and follow the rules of court. Once you have mastered the facts and the law and are ready to write the brief you have outlined, it is time to turn to the applicable rules of court. These rules will answer many of your questions concerning the form and content of your brief, and failure to follow them—in their current version—invites hostility or even literal rejection by the court. Only a good lawyer can write a really fine brief. But any competent lawyer can write a brief that complies with the applicable rules. What is more, whereas a court will not reject a brief for lack of brilliance, it has the right—exercised with increasing frequency—to reject a brief that does not comport with the rules and will, almost inevitably, think less of arguments presented in a non-complying brief. At oral argument it may take counsel to task for his noncompliance, to his discomfort and at a time when he would like to be arguing his case.

§ 7.2 Study the Record and the Trial Court's Opinion

Before you start writing the brief, it is absolutely essential that you review the trial record, including all documents and exhibits. You must study the record carefully and not just mechanically flick through the pages. You also must read the entire record, not just the portions that favor you. My advice: do not look at the record through rose-colored glasses, seeing only that which you wish to see; examine it with all its warts and blemishes.

You should do all this even if you were trial counsel. If you were not trial counsel, you have no choice. You simply must become familiar with every page of the record. I elevate this requirement to a standard of professional responsibility. We judges too often hear at oral argument, "I'm sorry, your honors, I can't answer that question. I was not trial counsel." Keep in mind that when you assume an appeal, you are taking over from a lawyer who has lost the case. Ask yourself: "Should I start from scratch or start by receiving advice from someone who already has lost? Can I trust the loser's memory?" Indeed, even if you were trial counsel, you cannot trust your own memory. Recollections of what took place do not matter; what does matter is what appears in the record in black and white.

Once you thoroughly understand the record, do not put it aside. As you compose your brief, you must decide, depending on the court rules, what portions of the record to include in the appendix or excerpts of record accompanying the brief. As to what you should include, my advice is to err on the side of completeness. Often an excerpt from the record covering testimony of a witness under questioning may be the most effective and dramatic way of getting a point across. An appellate judge wants to be able to refer immediately to critical parts of the record as the case is studied prior to oral argument. The judge resents having to call the clerk's office, sometimes hundreds of miles away, and ask to borrow the record.[2]

---

2. My view puts me on collision course with my colleagues of the ninth and eleventh circuits who prefer truncated excerpts of record. Because I frequently sit with various circuits, I am able to compare their practice with that of my home court, the third circuit, which generally requires comprehensive appendices. To me, it is not a question of what pleases the judges, or "the advantages [the practice] offers in terms of reducing cost." Fed. R. App. P. 30(f), advisory committee's note (1967). The objectives on appeal are justice for the litigants and preservation of institutional and precedential case law integrity. These concerns clearly outweigh a few more pounds of photocopied record excerpts or a few more dollars in photocopying expenses.

The trial court's opinion (or that of the administrative agency or intermediate appellate court) is a crucial part of this record. Appellate judges study these opinions very carefully, often before reading the briefs. The lawyers for both parties must read the trial court's opinion and understand it thoroughly. The appellant's brief should carefully address both the trial court's rulings on the points presented for appeal and also the reasoning given by the court for each ruling. Even if the appellee disagrees with the reasoning, the better practice is for the appellee at least to set it forth in the brief and then proceed to offer an alternative basis for support.

I emphasize again that you must study the entire record before the brief is written; indeed, you should become totally familiar with it before you complete your legal research. Even a splendid legal argument will not succeed if it is based on facts that do not appear in the record. The strategy of "have brief, need facts" will not work on appeal. There is also no point in preparing a crackerjack legal argument on an issue that was not raised and preserved below. The strategy of "have great point, need record" is equally ineffective.

§ 7.3   Evaluate Your Authorities

When it comes to verifying or authenticating statements in your brief, be aware of a feeling shared by many experienced judges: "I don't trust you. I won't take your word for any statement. Your credibility level is in the negative numbers, and your reputation for veracity is even lower." These are harsh statements, to be sure, but too many judges have been burned too many times not to recognize that statements in a brief must be checked and double-checked. When you authenticate a statement with a citation, the strongest bite of authority is a short verbatim quote with a pinpoint page cite. This gives your argument the greatest credibility, negating the suspicion that you are putting a special interpretation on the citation or are crafting an impermissible paraphrase.

To be sure, all authorities are not currency of equal value. At one extreme is precedent of the sharpest bite—a decision of the jurisdiction's highest court in which the material facts are identical to those in your case, or if you are before an intermediate court, a similar decision of that court. At the other extreme is the least persuasive authority—a conclusory statement contained in a student law review note.

The mix most often seen in briefs is somewhere in between, usually at the higher end of the scale, consisting of decisions of the appellate court that hears the appeal or a decision of the jurisdiction's highest court in which the material facts, although not identical, are similar. Here you must apply the rules of logical analogy.[3] The mix also includes analogous decisions from courts of coordinate authority, or courts lower in the judicial hierarchy or from other jurisdictions; plurality or concurring opinions of the highest court; and legal encyclopedias, law review articles, A.L.R. digests, and the Restatements.

What authorities should you use? I suppose the best answer is, "Anything that will help." But keep in mind that all authorities do not have equal weight. An excellent authority often not used by the appellee is a reference to the trial court's opinion. Another effective authority often overlooked in appeals to the jurisdiction's highest court is a persuasive dissenting opinion of an intermediate appellate court judge.

An informal checklist could be used by appellate lawyers:

- Statutes. Always examine the pocket parts for any amendments to a statute.

- Cases. Always examine the latest advance sheets and slip opinions, particularly if a substantial lag exists between the filing of opinions and their appearance in the advance sheets.

- Furnish the court with the text of all unreported or not easily accessible cases.

- Always Shepardize authorities.

- Go directly to the cases. Do not rely on digests, headnotes (except in jurisdictions, such as Ohio, in which the headnote, and not the text, is precedent), or encyclopedias.

- Use citation forms recommended by the *Bluebook*.

When citing cases and other authorities, you must understand the difference between mandatory and persuasive authorities. Mandatory authorities are those the court must follow as recognized precedent. They include cases from the court's highest jurisdiction which are directly on point, as well as unambiguous statutory language. Persuasive authorities, on the other hand, do not bind the court; they are cited for their persuasive value only. A good example of persuasive authority is a case from another jurisdiction that is directly on point. Your task is

---

3. Ruggero J. Aldisert, *Logic for Lawyers: A Guide to Clear Legal Thinking* 89–100, 227–29 (1989); *see also* chapters 16 and 20, *infra*.

to convince the court to adopt the case holding and the reasons supporting it.

You also should recognize the difference between string citations and multiple citations. String citations typically set forth a list of authorities from the same jurisdiction supporting a single proposition. Not only are such citations unnecessary, but they also tend to distract the reader from the thrust of the argument. It is far more effective to cite to the single, most recent case supporting the proposition.

Multiple citations, however, are very helpful when used to support a proposition that has not been addressed by the court hearing your appeal. In such an instance, you may properly set forth a list of multiple authorities demonstrating the proposition's acceptance in coordinate jurisdictions. This will give your court the opportunity to consider how other jurisdictions have handled the same issue.

Furthermore, you must avoid "trampling on graves." This phrase was coined by Judge William H. Hastie of the third circuit to describe a citation that fails to support the proposition as represented.[4] There is no quicker way to lose credibility with an appellate court than to employ this form of citation. If you cannot find an authority to support your proposition, you must reject the proposition or acknowledge that it is presently unsupported. Do not attempt to twist an available authority to suit your needs; the court will not buy it. You may, however, analogize. It is entirely proper—indeed, it is effective advocacy—to explain to the court that although a compared case is not precisely on point, there are sufficient resemblances to employ the process of analogy.

You can avoid "trampling on graves" by using full quotations from cases. By full quotation, I do not mean setting forth large portions of the text in order to fill up your brief or to avoid having to select the critical text. I mean taking a significant sentence or short paragraph and inserting it as a direct quote to inform the court exactly what the case stands for. This will help lend authoritative quality to your argument. Another highly effective tool, if not overused, is to add explanatory parentheticals to case citations in your brief. The parentheticals can be a descriptive phrase or a short quote describing the facts, reasoning, or holding of the cited case. For a detailed discussion of the use of parentheticals *see* § 19.3.1.

---

4. *United States v. Gibbs*, 813 F.2d 596, 605 (3d Cir. 1987) (Aldisert, J., dissenting).

§ 7.4 Citation Evaluation Chart

I have developed the following chart to evaluate the persuasive weight and usefulness of common legal research materials:

Authority	*Persuasive Value*
Applicable statutes.	Strongest possible authority if statutory provision is invoked.
Direct quote from a case from the highest court in the jurisdiction with *identical* material facts.	Strongest possible authority. Royal straight flush.
Paraphrased holding from a case from the highest court in the jurisdiction with *identical* material facts.	Strongest possible authority without a direct quote.
Case from the court hearing your appeal with *identical* material facts.	Almost as strong as above.
Legislative history, if applicable.	Can be dreadfully overworked, but very persuasive if the statutory language is ambiguous. Committee and conference committee reports reflect more consensus than isolated statements of individual legislators. Be aware of the fallacy of hasty generalization.
Case from the highest court in the jurisdiction with *similar* material facts.	Must analogize to prove that the material facts are similar.
Case from the court in which you appear with *similar* material facts.	Must prove that the material facts are similar.

Case from the highest court in the jurisdiction or the court hearing the appeal with identical or similar facts but with a strong dissent.	Precedential value slightly weakened.
Plurality opinion from the highest court in the jurisdiction or the court hearing the appeal.	Persuasive argument, but reasoning is not controlling precedent.
Case from a coordinate jurisdiction completely supporting your position.	Must show that it is good law and demonstrate, with good reasons, that it is in accordance with the weight of authority. Must also show why this majority rule should be adopted. Multiple citations may be impressive.
Citing and quoting directly from the trial court opinion in your case.	Very persuasive, as evidenced by the frequency with which trial court opinions are quoted in appellate opinions.
If the question is an open one in your jurisdiction, a case from the jurisdiction's trial court completely supporting your position.	Must show that it is good law and demonstrate, with good reasons, that it is in accordance with the weight of authority.
If the question is an open one in your jurisdiction, cases from coordinate jurisdictions that recognize a split with a pronounced majority view.	Numbers help, but the bottom line is the soundness of the reasons supporting the view. Multiple citations probably are necessary.
Case from the highest court in the jurisdiction or the court in which you appear where the material facts are not identical or similar.	Admit the flaw or lack of completeness, but argue that the facts in your case are nevertheless sufficient to support the same holding.

Controlling (mandatory) authorities are against your position. (You should note that the rules of professional responsibility of many jurisdictions require parties to disclose controlling authorities against their position.)

Retired Missouri Judge and Law Professor Charles Blackmar acknowledges, "You have a problem. One possibility is to try to distinguish them. But beware of labored distinctions. You may simply have to argue that the cases which confront you should be overruled, or not followed. Be frank with the court. It is entirely proper to argue that the case is distinguishable, but that if the court feels that the distinction is not sound then the case should be overruled. You are not entitled to ask the Court of Appeals to overrule a Supreme Court case. So you argue distinction."

A controlling (mandatory) case is dead set against you and the panel of the intermediate appellate court lacks the power to overrule the decision of the previous panel.

Concede as much to the panel but try to persuade it to recommend that the case be reheard by the court en banc.

Restatements and Comments

Controlling only if the jurisdiction has adopted a particular section. Otherwise, simply very persuasive authority

Treatises and texts

Persuasive, with degree of persuasion depending upon the reputation of author and the degree of technical sophistication of the subject.

Legal encyclopedias, such as *Corpus Juris Secundum* and *American Jurisprudence.*

Secondary sources only. Should be cited only in the following manner: "*See* cases collected at . . . ."

Law review articles.

May be excellent research tools for finding primary authorities. Conclusions may be persuasive in furnishing reasons to support a proposition. The article should stand on its substance and not on the reputation of the law school.

Chapter 8

FINDING THE ARGUMENT THAT WILL WIN

§ 8.1 Overview

You are now ready to write your argument. But before you start, you should get a couple of things straight: (1) what is the purpose of your brief? and (2) why are you writing it?

Think about these questions for a moment and you will realize that you are doing it for one reason. If you are the appellant, you want the judges to starting thinking of a two-syllable word—"reverse." If you are the appellee, it is spelled another way—"affirm."

The only reason for your brief is to convince the appellate court to reverse or to affirm. Forget about how you spotted and discussed all those issues on your law school exams. Forget about how you wrote that law review article setting a new world record for footnotes per paragraph. And forget the memo you wrote to the firm's senior partner outlining your brilliance with regard to some tiny corner of the law. You are not writing to get tenure on the law school faculty or to persuade the American Law Institute to accept your view in a new Restatement.

If you are the appellant, you know that the statistics are against you. You know you have to beat the odds. In the United States courts of appeals, you want to be that one appeal in ten that reverses the trial court; or if it is a criminal appeal, it is that one case in seventeen.

To do this you have to grab the judges' interest immediately and never let go. You have to tell the judges what the trial court did, why it found in appellee's favor, and why such a finding constituted *reversible* error. Not only a run-of-the-mill error, mind you, but such a departure from propriety that it is highly probable that the breach affected the outcome of the case. Note the nicety here: "highly probable," not "more probable than not." Remember, you were not entitled to a perfect hearing, only a fair one. Not every mistake is reversible error. Many of the trial judges's decisions were within the realm of his or her discretion and to argue an abuse of this discretion is a daunting task.

So, before you write one word, sit down and ask yourself: what's the overriding message I want to send to the appellate court? How do I convince the appellate judges that this is that one out of ten cases that merits reversal?

When you are thinking of the message you want to send, do not start to write your argument unless you have already mastered the record. Do not play the "have-theory-need-facts" game. You know what I mean—picking and choosing tiny tidbits of evidence from the transcript that favor your case but are contrary to those facts found by the factfinder. You tried that before a jury and *it did not work*. Once the appellate judge examines the district court opinion—and most of us read these before we read your argument—we will see the gaping hole in your argument through which the appellee will drive his big rig.

The cornerstone of your argument on appeal is anchored on the facts found by the fact finder, and here we follow the common law tradition. Recall the jurisprudential cement that was fixed by facts found by the jury—they rarely can be disturbed. Facts found by a judge are subject to the clear error standard of review; and we do not disturb administrative agency findings if they are supported by substantial evidence.

What you must do is construct your argument from these facts. You should scour the law for a precedent in your favor and use the facts found to show that the trial judge ignored or interpreted improperly the law. That is always your best shot on appeal. But be certain to distinguish binding precedent from mere argument.

§ 8.2 Precedent: What It Is and What It Is not

"A judicial precedent attaches a specific legal consequence to a detailed set of facts in an adjudged case or judicial decision, which is then considered as furnishing the rule for the determination of a subsequent case involving identical or similar material facts and arising in the same court or a lower court in the judicial hierarchy."[1]

The definition seems simple enough. And you will probably have no problem in deciding what are "identical" facts; but what delivers the real drama on appeal is the fight over which facts are materially similar. It is now that the process of analogy comes center stage. Analogy does not seek proof of identity of one thing with another, but only a comparison of resemblances. In analogies the degree of similarity is always the crucial inquiry.

This analytical process involves several steps: (1) you establish the holding of your chosen case to understand the legal consequences attached to the specific set of facts; (2) you exclude any dictum from the decision; and (3) you determine whether the holding is a binding precedent for a succeeding case containing prima facie similar facts. This last step then involves a double analysis. First, you must state

---

1. *Allegheny Cty. Gen. Hosp. v. NLRB*, 608 F. 2d 865, 969–970 (3d Cir. 1979)

the material facts in the putative precedent and then attempt to find those which are material in the compared case. If the facts are identical or materially similar, then the first case is binding precedent for the second and the court's conclusions should be the same. If the first case lacks any fact deemed material in the second case, or contains any material fact not found in the second, then it is not a bulletproof precedent. Here, the skill of the advocate will often be the determining factor. The plaintiff's lawyer may argue that the historical event or entity in the putative precedent bears many resemblances to the case at bar, wheras the opponent will argue that, although the facts are similar in some respects, those similarities are not material.[2]

The art of advocacy resolves itself into convincing the court which facts in previous cases are indeed positive analogies and which are not. The judge is required to draw this distinction. The successful lawyer is one who is able to convince the judge to draw the distinction in the manner most favorable to his or her client. The problem: seldom are there perfectly identical experiences in human affairs.

The judges know this. What we look for is a reasonable comparison. What is "reasonable" in determining analogies may permit endless differences of opinion. And this is how it should be. The existence of varying views in multi-judge courts is one of the most vitalizing traditions animating the growth of the common law.

§ 8.3 What Facts Are Material

No individual test of materiality may succeed unless there is first a complete understanding of the relevant substantive law precepts and why they came to be.

I suggest these tests with some trepidation and advance them not as truths, not even as probabilities, but only as, to use the weaseliest of terms, "possible possibilities."

- All facts which the court specifically stated to be material must be considered material.

- All facts which the court specifically stated to be immaterial must be considered immaterial.

- All facts which the court impliedly treats as immaterial must be considered immaterial.

---

2. *See* Ruggero J. Aldisert, *Logic for Lawyers: A Guide to Clear Legal Thinking* 89–100, 227–29 (1989); *see also* § 12.8 and chapters 16, 20.

- All facts of person, place, time, kind, and amount are immaterial unless stated to be material.

- If the opinion omits a fact that appears in the record this may be due to (a) oversight, or (b) an implied finding that the fact is immaterial. (Option (b) will be assumed to be the case in the absence of other evidence.)

- If the opinion does not distinguish between material and immaterial facts, then all the facts set forth must be considered material.

- A conclusion based on a hypothetical set of facts is dictum.

This is not to say that these are the only tests of what facts are material—and therefore important—and what facts are merely interesting. There are, no doubt, others. Whatever the test, the process requires patience, care, and thoroughness.

Ultimately, law is reduced, in the case of the judge, to the art of drawing distinctions, and, in the case of the lawyer, to the art of anticipating the distinctions the judge is likely to draw. To be sure, "[i]n a system bound by precedent such distinctions may often be in the nature of hairsplitting, this being the only instrument to hand for avoiding the consequences of an earlier decision which the court considers unreasonable, or as laying down a principle which is 'not to be extended.'"[3] As an art, both the study and practice of law consist of problem solving. Because of the doctrine of *stare decisis*, however, problem solving must not be performed on an ad hoc basis. We must respect the overarching consideration that like cases be decided alike. The real question, as you now understand, is deciding what is a "like case."

§ 8.4 How Far Can You Persuade the Court to Extend or Compress the Law

So the precedent is hanging out there. It is staring at you with its beady eyes, and you do not think you can tame it in order to show that your facts are "similar material facts." You want the chosen case to support your theory, but you also want to be candid with the court. Therefore, you must tell the court that to agree with you might require the formation of new law. Is it possible to convince the court to agree? It depends.

---

3. Dennis Lloyd, *Reason and Logic in the Common Law*, 64 Law Q. Rev. 468, 482 (1948).

§ 8.4.1 Jurisprudential Temperament

It is here where the lawyer must become familiar with the members of the court before the brief is written. You have to examine the opinions the judges have written in the area of the law where your case fits.

You examine these cases not only for the holding and reasoning, but also for insight into the opinion writer's jurisprudential temperament. This temperament is a major determinant of whether the case is controlled by precedent or settled law, or whether judges must, in certain cases, resort to penumbral areas.

Some judges have lower thresholds than others and are more inclined to find solace in shades and fringes rather than the black letter law. But when they so function, it means that they have exhausted the guidance that hefty, hearty precedents can give and they feel that they must turn to other resources. These resources are found in the body of first or supereminent principles, legal or moral, concepts of desirable public policy that form the body of legal philosophy.

But to understand jurisprudential temperament is to recognize that the judge's initial reaction as to whether a case is controlled by precedent (or by unambiguous statutory language) or comes within what is called the penumbral area, is, itself, a gauge of that temperament. We judges have different thresholds, or, as Ralph Waldo Emerson said, "We boil at different degrees." What makes a case controversial or difficult at times is precisely this judicial difference. These judicial reactions are not mechanical, as the label tossers of "liberal" and "conservative" would have us believe; nor are they entirely unpredictable. Our legal system is both a system and a history of reasons—reasons that judges have given for past determinations and reasons that embody many conceptions of human nature. The judge's matured decision is informed by this history. His or her own determination of benefit and harm will be informed by consulting the justifications offered by other judges in other relevant opinions.

This inflow from the cumulative experience of the judiciary also mixes with what is already in the judge's mind. What is already there is an accumulation of personal experience including tendencies, prejudices, and maybe even biases. I do not mean conscious biases, but the unconscious ones that any person may have and which the judge cannot eradicate because he does not know they exist. One of these may be a bias in favor of the justice or equity of the particular case and against any precedent or law that seems to deny it. This is an example of temperament. When such a feeling dominates, the judge's mental notes

111

may emphasize those facts that he or she deems to be significant; the insignificant, being omitted, will disappear from memory. The facts will be molded to fit the justice of the case, and the law will be stretched. Meanwhile, another judge may possess the same intensity of justice for the case, but will refuse to stretch the law and instead state: "We are constrained to hold . . ." In these two circumstances, the feelings of justice are the same, but disparate jurisprudential temperaments command different results.

So, get to know the court. You want to learn what Walter Schaefer, a great Illinois common law judge, once wrote:

> If I were to attempt to generalize, as indeed I should not, I should say that most depends upon the judge's unspoken notion as to the function of his court. If he views the role of the court as a passive one, he will be willing to delegate the responsibility for change, and he will not greatly care whether the delegated authority is exercised or not. If he views the court as an instrument of society designed to reflect in its decisions the morality of the community, he will be more likely to look precedent in the teeth and to measure it against the ideals and the aspirations of his time.[4]

But that is only for openers. You have to be conscious of the limitations of changing the law, even if the judge is inclined to do so.

§ 8.4.2   How Far a Judge May Go

To be sure, Roscoe Pound, Oliver Wendell Holmes, and Benjamin Cardozo were instrumental in changing our approach to decisionmaking and rejecting what the Maryland Court of Appeals said in 1895: "Obviously a principle, if sound, ought to be applied wherever it logically leads, without reference to ulterior results."[5] To Cardozo, filling in the gaps of the law in addressing novel legal questions law was the social welfare, defined as "public policy, the good of the collective body" or "the social gain that is wright by adherence to the standard of right conduct, which find expression in the mores of the community."[6]

---

4. Walter V. Schaefer, *Precedent and Policy*, 34 U. Chi. L. Rev 3 (1966).

5. *Gluck v. Mayor of Baltimore*, 32 A. 515, 517 (Md. 1895).

6. Benjamin Cardozo, *The Nature of the Judicial Process* 71–72 (1921).

In *The Path of the Law*, Holmes gently admonished:

> I think that the judges themselves have failed adequately
> to recognize their duty of weighing considerations of social
> advantage. The duty is inevitable, and the result of the often
> proclaimed judicial aversion to deal with such consider-
> ations is simply to leave the very ground and foundation of
> judgments inarticulate, and often unconscious.[7]

Within a decade, Roscoe Pound was trumpeting the same theme:
"The most important and most constant cause of dissatisfaction with
all law at all times is to be found in the necessarily mechanical operation of legal rules."[8] Critics labeled this blind adherence to precedents,
or to the rules and principles derived therefrom, "mechanical jurisprudence" and "slot machine justice." Pound called for a new look at
what he described as "pragmatism as a philosophy of law," and stated
vigorously: "The nadir of mechanical jurisprudence is reached when
conceptions are used, not as premises from which to reason, but as
ultimate solutions. So used, they cease to be conceptions and become
empty words."[9] He is famous for the epigram: "The law must be stable,
and yet it cannot stand still."[10]

This historical recital is important for two reasons. First, it demonstrates that public policy justifications are legitimate reasons for
supporting an appellate argument. As Justice Schaefer put it, "I suppose whether a precedent will be modified depends upon whether the
policies which underlie the proposed rule are strong enough to outweigh both the policies which support the existing rule and the disad-
vantages of making a change."[11]

---

7. Oliver Wendell Holmes, *The Path of the Law*, 10 Harv. L. Rev. 457, 467 (1897).

8. Roscoe Pound, *The Causes of Popular Dissatisfaction with the Administration of Justice*, in T*he Pound Conference: Perspectives on Justice in the Future* 337, 339 (A. Leo Levin & Russell R. Wheeler, eds. 1979).

9. Roscoe Pound, *Mechanical Jurisprudence*, 8 Colum. L. Rev. 605, 620 (1908).

10. Roscoe Pound, *Interpretations of Legal History* 1 (1923). Lord Denning, a British cousin, tells us exactly where his temperament stands on the gauge:

> What is the argument on the other side? Only this, that no case has been
> found in which it has been done before. That argument does not appeal
> to me in the least. If we never do anything which is not done before, we
> shall never get anywhere. The law will stand still whilst the rest of the
> world goes on, and that will be bad for both.

Packer v. Packer, 2 All E.R. 127, 129 (1953).

11. *Schaefer, supra* note 4.

Second, these masters of the American legal tradition emphasized that there are limitations to judicial lawmaking. There are and should be limits. In 1917, Holmes counseled:

> I recognize without hesitation that judges do and must legislate, but they can do so only interstitially; they are confined from molar to molecular motions. A common law judge could not say I think the doctrine of consideration an act of historical nonsense and shall not enforce it in my court. No more could a judge exercising the limited jurisdiction of admiralty say I think well of the common law rules of master and servant and propose to introduce them here en bloc.[12]

Cardozo limited judicial law making to gap-filling. Although the precise limits of judicial law making have not been staked out, do not expect any court to make radical changes in a single case. To be sure, judicial lawmaking often has exceeded the function of "filling interstices"—the judicially created doctrine of products liability comes to mind in the state courts, and *Brown v. Board of Education, Miranda v. Arizona,* and *Roe v. Wade* in federal constitutional law—but these are rare, pushing-the-envelope cases. You will have better luck remembering that changing the law in the common law tradition is based on gradualness.

Ultimately, the test of judge-made law, as with any law, is its effect on social welfare and its acceptance by society. It behooves the judge who makes law, therefore, to focus openly on policy considerations as he or she seeks to keep the law in tune with changing societal values.

It may be argued that this approach pays mere lip service to the doctrine of separation of powers. The obvious response is that the federal and state constitutions must be read against the backdrop of the common law tradition—a tradition which has given to the courts the authority to interpret rules enacted by the legislature, and to fashion the aggregate of legal precepts that govern society. Further, if legislative authority disagrees with the judicial action, it can overrule that action by statute. So the question is, how can a lawyer persuade the court to overrule a precedent?

---

12. *S. Pac. Co. v. Jensen*, 244 U.S. 205, 211 (1917) (Holmes, J., dissenting)

§ 8.4.3 Precedential Vitality

Stare decisis is the policy of the courts to stand by precedent.[13] The expression "stare decisis" is but an abbreviation of *stare decisis et non quieta movere* (to stand by or adhere to decisions and not disturb that which is settled). *Decisis* means literally and legally: "the decision." A case is important only for what it decides, for the detailed legal consequence following a detailed set of facts. *Stare decisis* serves to preserve what the court *did*, not what it *said*.

Why do we adhere to precedent? To a considerable extent, rules are grounded in factors of habit, tradition, historical accident, and sheer intellectual inertia. We can also go back to the predictability factor in law, recalling Holmes' definition, "[t]he prophecies of what the courts will do in fact, and nothing more pretentious, are what I mean by the law."[14] In addition to these social and psychological roots, precedent also appears to rest in the following values, as spelled out by Thomas Currier in a 1965 law journal article.[15]

- *Stability*. It is socially desirable that social relations have a reasonable degree of continuity and cohesion held together by a framework of reasonably stable institutional arrangements.

- *Protection of Reliance*. The protection of persons who have ordered their affairs in reliance upon contemporaneously announced law [is a value to be safe guarded].

- *Efficiency in the Administration of Justice*. If every case coming before the courts had to be decided as an original proposition, without reference to precedent, the judicial work-load would obviously be intolerable. Judges must be able to ease this burden [of the judicial workload] by seeking guidance from what other judges have done in similar cases.

- *Equality*. [Persons similarly situated should be equally treated.] It is a fundamental ethical requirement that like cases should receive like treatment, that there should be no discrimination between one litigant and another except by reference to some relevant differentiating factor.

---

13. For a more through discussion of this subject, *see* Ruggero J. Aldisert, *Precedent: What It Is and What It Isn't; When Do We Kiss It and When Do We Kill It?*, 17 Pepp. L. Rev. 605 (1990).

14. *Holmes, supra* note 7 at 461.

15. Thomas S. Currier, *Time and Change in Judge-Made Law: Prospective Overruling*, 51 Va. L. Rev. 201, 235–37 (1965).

- *The Image of Justice.* [This phrase does] not mean that any judicial decision ought to be made on the basis of its likely impact upon the court's public relations, in the Madison Avenue sense, but merely that it is important not only that the court provide equal treatment to persons similarly situated, but that, insofar as possible, the court should appear to do so.

In 1970, Justice Harlan set forth similar values:

> Very weighty considerations underlie the principle that courts should not lightly overrule past decisions. Among these are the desirability that the law furnish a clear guide for the conduct of individuals, to enable them to plan their affairs with assurance against untoward surprise; the importance of furthering fair and expeditious adjudication by eliminating the need to relitigate every relevant proposition in every case; and the necessity of maintaining public faith in the judiciary as a source of impersonal and reasoned judgments. The reasons for rejecting any established rule must always be weighed against these factors.[16]

When do we overrule? No black letter guidelines determine when to follow precedent. Although the foregoing weighty considerations underlie the precept that courts should not lightly overrule past decisions, the Supreme Court has set forth a body of concepts that should give a lawyer some guidance when making the frontal assault on the viability of a precedent. In the state courts, the place for relief, of course, is in the state supreme court. But in the federal courts, where the courts of appeals have internal operating procedures preventing a panel from overruling a previous panel's decision, the avenue of relief lies in the petition for en banc rehearing. It is perfectly legitimate to argue to the panel that a given case is ripe for overruling, and urge the panel to so recommend to the full court.

Here are some of the Supreme Court's observations culled from the cases.[17]

- Stare decisis is a principle of policy and not a mechanical formula of adherence to the latest decision, however recent and questionable, when such adherence involves collision with a prior

---

16. *Moragne v. States Marine Lines*, 398 U.S. 375, 403 (1970).

17. *See, e.g., Helvering v. Hallock*, 309 U.S. 106, 119 (1940); *Boys Markets, Inc. v Retail Clerks*, 398 U.S. 235 (1970); *Patterson v. McLean Credit Union*, 491 U.S. 164 (1989); *Payne v. Tennessee*, 501 U.S. 808 (1991) (Marshall & Blackmun, JJ, dissenting).

doctrine more embracing in its scope, intrinsically sounder, and verified by experience.

- We have held that any departure from the doctrine of stare decisis demands special justification.

- Such justifications include the advent of subsequent changes or development in the law that undermine a decision's rationale.

- We have said also that the burden borne by the party advocating the abandonment of an established precedent is greater where the court is asked to overrule a point of statutory construction. Considerations of stare decisis have special force in the area of statutory interpretation, for here, unlike in the context of constitutional interpretation, the legislative power is implicated, and Congress remains free to alter what we have done.

- The need to bring a decision into agreement with experience and with facts newly ascertained.

- A showing that a particular precedent has become a detriment to coherence and consistency in the law.

- Considerations in favor of stare decisis are at their acme in cases involving property and contract rights, where reliance interests are involved. The opposite is true in cases involving procedural and evidentiary rules.

- Cases decided by the narrowest of margins over spirited dissents and thereafter questioned by members of the court.

§ 8.5 Advice from Judges and Lawyers: Writing to Win

Deanell Reece Tacha,
Chief Judge,
United States Court of
Appeals, Tenth Circuit

It seems to me that before ever writing a brief, and certainly before oral argument, counsel should have a very candid discussion with himself or herself about what precisely the issues are that will result in a favorable decision on appeal. By that I mean in the typical case there are usually only one or two outcome-determinative issues. Whether one is appellant or appellee, the question is to be answered precisely is: "What is it that the court must decide to decide in my favor?" If counsel honestly and analytically answers this question, the brief and the oral argument are very clearly targeted to reaching the brief and the oral argument are very clearly targeted to reaching that answer. For example, the appellant must answer in a focused manner: What issue or issues will require the appellate court to reverse the judgment of the court below, and what cases and/or facts precisely address that issue? For appellee, the question is perhaps even more straightforward: What issue requires that the appellate court affirm the district court, and what facts or cases support that result? As I have worked with advocacy classes, I have been struck by the difficulty that advocates have in answering those questions precisely. Either because of a lack of focus or the difficulty of honing a case to that particularity, lawyers seem to have an exceedingly difficult time answering directly these pivotal questions.

Fred I. Parker,
Circuit Judge,
United States Court of
Appeals, Second Circuit

If I read an appellant's brief that, clearly and accurately, sets out the facts, tells me what the district court did, explains why the district court found in appellee's favor and then goes on to explain why that decision was in error, I get engaged in a case and stay with that brief. Such a brief is a joy to read because it allows me to understand the entire case without wasting any time. If the brief has also made me think that the equities or the law suggest reversal, then it has been truly successful. On the other hand, if it leaves me wondering what happened other than that the district court ruled in a way that upset the appellant, it has accomplished nothing.

Bobby R. Burchfield,
Litigation Group
Co-Chair, Covington &
Burling, Washington,
D.C.

Work hard to find the winning argument. To be in this business, we almost have to believe that every case is winnable if only we can find the right argument and make it effectively. Sometimes the winning argument will be unconventional, but if a candid evaluation of the available arguments leads to the conclusion that the conventional arguments cannot succeed, a more creative approach may be necessary. Believe in your position. Critique your own argument mercilessly, and take account of its weaknesses.

James D. Crawford,
Senior Counsel,
Schnader, Harrison,
Segal & Lewis,
Philadelphia, Pa.

Make sure your legal argument is sound, convincing and concise. Clarity and inevitability are the two watch words of a good argument. The court must be able to understand exactly where you are going. More important, the court should be convinced that, on the basis of precedent and reason, there is nowhere else it would want to go.

Henry Deeb Gabriel, *Professor of Law, Loyola University School of Law, New Orleans, Louisiana. (former Department of Justice appellate litigator)*

You should take the opportunity to go beyond the technical, legal points of your case and give the court a common sense, simple reason why all the technical stuff in your brief makes sense. Also remember that only the major concept or theme from your argument will likely be retained by the writing judge when she sits down and starts to draft the opinion. This theme, if possible, should be grounded in broad equitable reasons.

Paul J. Brysh *Assistant United States Attorney, Western District of Pennsylvania, Pittsburgh, Pennsylvania*

I am a firm believer in the value of first impressions. Appellate judges do not tend to make snap judgments, but their first impression of a case may color their thinking at every stage of the appellate process. My objective is therefore, not only to create an impression of the case that is favorable to my position, but also to do so early. For that reason, I often begin my statement of facts with a one-paragraph to one-page overview that reflects how I would like the judges to view the case. The summary of the argument is also a good place to present a favorable view of the legal issues in the appeal. Finally, at the beginning of each argument, I like to begin with a fact, characterization, or legal point that is especially favorable to my position. If, for example, the issue is whether the trial court abused its discretion in denying a request for a continuance by the opposing party, who had already received two continuances, I would probably mention the prior continuances in the first sentence of my argument.

Patricia M. Ward,
Chief Judge Emeritus,
United States Court
of Appeals for the D.C.
Circuit

Visualize the whole before you begin. What overriding message is the document going to convey? What facts are essential to the argument? How does the argument take off from the facts? How do different arguments blend together? Better still, visualize how the judge's opinion should read if it goes your way. (Too many briefs read as if the paralegal summed up all conceivable relevant facts, and then the lawyer took over with the legal arguments, and never the twain doth meet.)

Chapter 9

THE BRIEF: HOW MANY ISSUES?

§ 9.1 Overview: The Appellate Process

We have done housekeeping thus far: jurisdiction, issue preservation, standards of review, requirements for briefs and appendices, and research tools. We must now decide what to say and the first step is to flush out the specific issues of appeal.

Your brief-writing process should be informed by a detailed strategy. Attorney Jordan B. Cherrick of the St. Louis law firm of Thompson Coburn, is credited with the acronym "PASS"—Preparation, Anticipation, Selectivity, and Style.[1] He fashions these elements the keys to successful appellate advocacy:

Preparation: An attorney's mastery of the record, the law, and the rules of the appellate court.

Anticipation: A brief writer's effort to determine how to frame the issues and develop appellate strategy in a way that will best influence the judges who decide the case.

Selectivity: Choosing the facts, events, and legal arguments likely to control the outcome.

Style: The ability to persuade by writing and thinking well.

The previous chapters have dealt with preparation. We now come to *Anticipation*, the decision as to what issues or points (I use the words interchangeably.) will be discussed in the brief. This requires an intelligent, extremely careful consideration of both the *quantity* and *quality* of the issues. Considerations of *quantity* will determine the size of the brief, and the determination of *quality* will you give you the all-important theme or focus for the argument. At the very beginning, therefore, before you set down on paper any of the issues, you must keep these objectives in mind.

---

1. Jordan B. Cherrick, *Issues, Facts, and Appellate Strategy*, 16 Litig. 15 (1990).

§ 9.2 Choosing the Issues: The Lawyer's Decision

Your first chore is to decide what issues you want to discuss. An issue is a separate and discrete question of law or fact, or a combination of the two, set forth in the brief as a reason for reversing or affirming the trial court or agency. It should be a succinct description of the alleged error committed by judge.

It is the lawyer, not the client, who has the ultimate responsibility for deciding what issues will be discussed on appeal. This postulate may be relaxed in a criminal appeal, but lawyers must keep in mind that *their* names go on the briefs and with their names ride their reputations with the judges. On appeal, judges confront lawyers, not litigants. If lawyers present extravagant and bizarre claims over their signatures, they alone are admonished on appeal, not the clients.

What then does the lawyer do in the direct or post-conviction criminal appeal when the client insists on presenting improvident, unreasonable, or even downright outrageous contentions? I suggest two options:

> (1) You can furnish an addendum to your brief arguing the additional issues and indicating that they have been specifically urged by the litigant. At his or her insistence, you are offering them and the accompanying discussion for consideration by the court.

> (2) You can recommend that your client file a pro se brief as permitted in *Anders v. California*, 386 U.S. 738 (1967), and include in your brief a statement that your client plans to do so.

§ 9.3 Narrowing Down the Issues: Step One

The first step is to make an informal list of the issues that possibly may be presented. Do not worry about writing style. This listing is only an inventory. You merely want to know only what issues are available, so do not start winnowing out the losers yet. Catalog every conceivable argument, and set out the complete case in all its unrefined potentiality. University of Texas English Department Professor Betty Flowers devised a method that dramatizes the writing process. She suggests that each of us possesses "a character" or personality that we all have within us. Variously, these are the madman, the architect, the carpenter, and the judge. The madman "is full of ideas, writes crazily, and perhaps rather sloppily, gets carried away by enthusiasm and desires, and if really let loose, could turn out ten pages an hour."[2]

In step one, the brief writer should let the madman takeover. List *every* possible legal point that you can conjure up. This list is only the beginning point, and it will be over-inclusive. Unfortunately, too many brief writers consider it the ending point as well. They dump this gross listing on the laps of appellate judges instead of performing the crucial next step: making a critical judgment as to which issues will probably influence the court.

§ 9.4 Narrowing Down the Issues: Step Two

The second step is weeding out those issues that do not have a reasonable probability of prevailing in the appellate court. This may be the most difficult decision you make. It is certainly the most important one, because what you exclude is as important as what you include. Here is a test you may use:

> Limit the selection of issues to those will most likely attract the interest and generate serious consideration of the appellate judges before whom you appear.

Here you must trade places with the judge, the person you seek to persuade. You must be dispassionate, detached, and imperturbable. You also must be intellectually objective, in the sense that you must put aside emotions and passions that you certainly possess as a result of having lost a case before the trial tribunal.

Having lost, you are understandably disturbed. Not only are you disappointed, but you are angry—a normal reaction. You want to vent your feelings by throwing in not only the kitchen sink, but the plumbing, and street sewers as well. If you do this, and many lawyers do, you make a devastating mistake. Cool it. Calm down. Act like a lawyer, not like a client. Analyze carefully to ascertain where there is an arguable question of trial court error, not simply an imaginable one.

Appellate judges are not law professors. They have different responsibilities. They do not give high grades to lawyers who can spot all the issues. More is not better in appellate advocacy. Judges are interested only in arguable points. The key here is selectivity, not fertility. You should be interested only in case-dispositive issues and arguments that may carry the day.

---

2. Bryan A. Garner, *The Winning Brief* 4–5 (1999).

During trial proceedings you can mix the good with the bad. In your closing speech to a jury you can toss in arguments designed for emotional or populist purposes or even one or two that solicit prejudice and superstition. In examining or cross-examining a witness you can permit extraneous matters to slip in and still avoid harm's way.

The rules of the game change at the appellate level. You cannot afford to dilute, or shall I say, pollute, your brief with superfluous contentions—such futile arguments infect your advocacy. Transfer yourself figuratively to the environment in which your brief will be read by the court. Judges spend hours or maybe days with a brief that took weeks, even months, for you and your colleagues to prepare. Active United States circuit judges were swamped with an average annual caseload of 485 cases per judge during the 2002 court year.[3] Briefs must be read within a period of five or six weeks, while judges simultaneously write opinions from previous sittings, examine pro se briefs and counseled responses, wade through hundreds of motions, and keep abreast of contemporary opinions, and attending a host of judicial conferences and committee meetings. This brief-reading cycle is repeated approximately seven to nine times a year.[4] In many state appellate courts, the cycle is even more onerous. "Given such a demanding work load," writes Judge Harry Pregerson of the ninth circuit, "it is not difficult to imagine our frustration when we are required to trudge through a

3. According to the 2002 Federal Court Management Statistics from the Administrative Office of the United States Courts, federal appeals court judges terminated 27,758 cases on the merits in the twelve-month period ending September 30, 2002—an average of 485 per judge. Administrative Office of the United States Courts, United States Court of Appeals—Judicial Caseload Profile, at http://www.uscourts.gov/cgi-bin/cmsa2002.pl.

4. The practices vary a little among the U.nited States courts of appeals, but the annual caseload per judge is about the same. Judge Harry Pregerson offers this perspective from the United States Court of Appeals for the Ninth Circuit:

> [P]lease bear in mind that each circuit judge hears and prepares for twenty to thirty appellate cases each month and winds up with the job of writing about one-third of the dispositions. This means that each judge is called upon to read sixty to ninety briefs each month. Each judge must also read excerpts of record, pertinent case authority, and portions of the reporter's transcripts.

> But this is just the beginning. Each judge also devotes considerable time to reviewing proposed dispositions circulated by other judges in cases previously argued and submitted and to reading innumerable petitions for rehearings and requests for hearings en banc. In addition, judges spend a significant amount of time dealing with civil and criminal motions.

Harry Pregerson, *The Seven Sins of Appellate Brief Writing and Other Transgressions*, 34 UCLA L. Rev. 431, 433–34 (1986).

fifty-page brief that could have presented its points effectively in fewer than twenty-five pages."[5]

James L. Robertson, a former Justice on the Mississippi Supreme Court, wrote:

> Before putting the first words on paper, try to think like a judge. But not just any judge. Crawl into the minds of the judges who will hear and decide your appeal. Ted Williams always got into the pitcher's mind, not just hours, but days before the game; you must do the same with your judge. Ask yourself, "If I were Judges Nasty, Brutish, and Short, of the Court of Appeals, how would I view these facts and this law?"[6]

When you change places, you should realize at least three things: (1) in the judge's day, many matters other than your brief compete for attention; (2) you never get a second chance to make an initial good impression; and (3) on the appellate court you do not have the luxury of time that you had in the trial tribunal.

§ 9.4.1 Put Your Best Foot Forward—and Only Your Best

Start with your most important point—the killer issue. Never lead off with something weaker. Meritless issues should never survive your final edit. As an appellate judge once wrote me, "Arguing meritless issues is bankrupt advocacy."

Judge Roger Miner of the Second Circuit, reiterates this point:

> I could go on and on describing briefs and oral arguments that fall below professional norms, but time does not permit such a wide-ranging discussion of incompetent performances. Deputy Solicitor General Lawrence Wallace, who has argued more cases before the Supreme Court than any other lawyer in recent times has said: "If you can't answer the question, 'What are the strongest points to be made for the other side?' you're not really prepared to argue the case." I say that too many appellate lawyers cannot describe the strongest point on either side.[7]

---

5. *Id.* at 434.

6. James L. Robertson, *From the Bench: Reality on Appeal*, 17 Litig. 3, 5 (1990).

7. Roger J. Miner, *Professional Responsibility in Appellate Practice: A View from the Bench*, 19 Pace L. Rev. 323, 337 (1999).

Circuit judges are not alone in these views. Former Virginia Supreme Court Chief Justice Harry L. Carrico advises that counsel should "[f]ocus upon a few well-defined issues rather than firing a broadside of vague allegations of error." Former Kansas Supreme Court Justice Richard W. Holmes writes that "[b]rief only the strongest arguments, winnow out weak issues, and those that are likely to be harmless error." The late Andrew D. Christie, former Delaware Supreme Court chief justice, counseled, "[o]mit arguments and assertions which are obviously without merit." Oklahoma Supreme Court Justice Marian P. Opala says, "[e]xcessive contentiousness on immaterial issues distracts attention from what really counts." Former Missouri Supreme Court Chief Justice Charles B. Blackmar adds, "[a]ppellate counsel must exercise careful judgment in selecting the points to be pursued. Too many points tend to distract the court and to divert attention from those which are the most troublesome. They consume pages and argument time."

These views are echoed in academia as Chicago-Kent Law Professor Marcia L. McCormick, formerly of the appellate division of the Illinois Attorney General, advises:

> Framing the issues comes down to asking yourself a few basic questions. The first question should be: What is this case, at its essence, about? The second question should be: Why, given what this case is about, should my client have prevailed at the trial level? The final question should be: What do I think this court should do about it?
>
> These are the three most elemental issues of any appeal. Your answers will provide you with a theory of your case, a solid reason for ruling in your favor, and a road map of how to rule in your favor in a way that properly reflect everybody's interest.
>
> Keep in mind that when you answer these questions, you have to make the answers concrete enough that when they are written down, the court will understand what the salient facts of the case are. Every word counts, and including the information in your issue that you believe will determine the outcome of the appeal tells the court where you are going to take it. It also insures at the drafting stage that you are focused on your goal.[8]

---

8. Marcia L. McCormick, *Selecting and Framing the Issues on Appeal: A Powerful Persuasive Tool*, 90 Ill. B.J. 203 (2002).

§ 9.5 The Appellee's Issues

One golden rule exists for the brief of the appellee: place your issues in the same sequence as the appellant. Artistic license permits you to depart from this only when your responding brief covers more issues than the appellant's brief. It is absolutely critical that you indicate in your statement of issues exactly where the response to specific points raised by the appellant may be found.

This is not to say that the appellee's phrasing of the issue must be an exact copy of the appellant's. Often the wording cannot be duplicated because the appellant's choice of terms is inappropriate for your purposes, or just plain incorrect. Paramount in setting forth the responding issues is giving clear directions to where the response is located. Appellate lawyers must understand what I have previously described as the environment of brief reading. Very seldom do appellate judges read one brief all the way through and then read the other. More often than not, I read the appellant's point, then immediately turn to the appellee's response. Often interspersed in this process is a rereading of relevant portions of the trial court's opinion.

In a consolidated appeal from multiple appellants—often in a criminal case—we generally have a single appellee's brief. Most United States Attorney's offices, but not all, handle this very well by succinctly and accurately cross-indexing the rejoinder to those questions that have been duplicated in the several briefs.

The bottom line. The framework of the appellee's statement of issues should provide a road map for the judge who reads your brief.

§ 9.6 How Many Issues?

The most important decision you make in writing a brief is to limit the issues to about three, no more. Judges react differently to the stimuli of advocacy. I recognize that our initial impressions vary, of course, but I must confess to an idiosyncracy. When faced with a brief that raises no more than three points, I breathe a sigh of satisfaction and conclude that the brief writer may have something to say.

I probably react in the same manner, or perhaps to a slightly lesser degree, when four or five points are presented. Beyond this point, I must confess, a small beast bearing the name of intolerance begins to nibble at my habitually disinterested judgment. Even when we reverse a trial court, rarely does a brief establish more than one or two reversible errors. When I read an appellant's brief that contains more than six points, a presumption arises that there is no merit to *any* of them. I do not say that this is an irrebuttable presumption, but it is neverthe-less a presumption that reduces the effectiveness of the writer's brief.[9]

Justice Robert H. Jackson commented:

> Legal contentions, like the currency, depreciate through overissue. The mind of an appellate judge is habitually receptive to the suggestion that a lower court committed an error. But receptiveness declines as the number of assigned errors increases. Multiplicity hints at a lack of confidence in any one. Of course, I have not forgotten the reluctance with which a lawyer abandons even the weakest point lest it prove alluring to the same kind of judge. But experience on the bench convinces me that multiplying assignments of error will dilute and weaken a good case and will not save a bad one.[10]

Many of my friends at the bar have a sort of Pavlovian reaction when they encounter my distaste for shotgun briefs: "We don't know what may attract the attention of the given court at any time," they say, "so we have to file briefs that touch all bases; we have to use the shotgun approach. We just don't know what the court will consider to be important." I respond with a simple, three-word riposte: "You *should* know!" With the availability of computer-assisted legal research and the wealth of fine law libraries in the states, counties, cities, and law schools, any reasonably competent researcher should be able to deter-mine which aspects of a given subject have or have not commanded the interest of a given court and, therefore, which ones will or will not do so in the present case. But this presupposes that the reasonably competent researcher has actually done the research. Judges expect as much.

How many issues then, should be raised? It depends. Certainly in a criminal case the question of the Sixth Amendment right to competent counsel makes even the most expert appellate advocates lean on the side of too many, rather than too few. I will venture some purely subjec-tive guidelines for civil cases, all of which are subject to the caveat that they do not apply in unusual and extraordinary circumstances.

---

9. Just as James Russell Lowell wrote to Charles Eliot Norton, "In general those who have nothing to say, contrive to spend the longest time in doing it."

10. Robert H. Jackson, *Advocacy Before the United States Supreme Court*, 37 Cornell L.Q. 1, 5 (1951).

Litmus Test: Number of Issues in the Brief

Number of Issues	Judge's Reaction
Three	Presumably arguable points. The lawyer is *primo*.
Four	Probably arguable points. The lawyer is primo minus.
Five	Perhaps arguable points. The lawyer is no longer primo. Probably no arguable points.
Six	The lawyer has not made a favorable initial impression.
Seven	Presumptively, no arguable points. The lawyer is at an extreme disadvantage, with an uphill battle all the way.
Eight or more	Strong presumption that no point is worthwhile.

This litmus test is arbitrary, to be sure, but veteran appellate judges are virtually unanimous in complaining that today's briefs are too long.[11] Former Nebraska Supreme Court Chief Justice William C. Hastings says, "[o]ne of my pet peeves is the shotgun approach in assigning error which too often consists of two or three valid points which are split up and restated until they number twelve or fifteen. My advice to young lawyers has been to remember that the name of the document is a brief and that is what it should be." In 1991, former

---

11. But former Missouri Supreme Court Chief Justice Charles B. Blackmar (nationally known for his co-authorship of Federal Jury Practice and Instructions), adds this caveat:

> It is easy for me to say that counsel should limit the number of issues presented. But there are problems about generalizing. I remember from my practice, many years ago, that a younger lawyer was working with me on a brief. He suggested an additional point and I tried to argue him out of it because we had too many but he persisted and I included it in the brief. We got a favorable opinion which led off with his point, after which it said: "This point is dispositive, and so we do not have to consider the other interesting issues presented and arguments made."

Utah Supreme Court Chief Justice Gordon R. Hall reported, "[i]t has been my experience over the past twenty-two years that the most effective briefs are those that are the most brief, the most direct, and by all means, the most candid."

Judge Fred I. Parker of the second circuit advises that "there may be situations in which asserting a large number of claims on appeal may be the proper thing to do, in the vast majority of cases, no more than three or four issues should be raised. In my view, this is probably the maximum number of claims which an advocate can clearly and completely argue in the limited space of the brief as well as the approximate maximum number of claims I can give full consideration to in one case before I begin to lose both my mind and track of the other claims."[12]

The reality of a judge's workload also plays a role in the need to keep a brief precisely that. Judge Parker's colleague, former Second Circuit Judge Lawrence W. Pierce, notes:

> From a practical standpoint, a more concise, cogent brief presenting the strongest points and arguments usually makes the most sense . . . [C]onsider that if one counts the number of appeals scheduled to be heard by a panel of judges on a particular day, and if one multiplies that by one brief for each party, plus a joint appendix, a reply brief, and an occasional sur-reply brief, in addition to the applicable cases and statutes, one can readily calculate the enormous amount of reading with which a judge and a judge's staff are faced to prepare for each sitting day. One may agree that it is better to have a shorter brief that will be read and studied in preparation for argument than a longer one that is skimmed and put aside for future study.[13]

---

12. Fred I. Parker, *Appellate Advocacy and Practice in the Second Circuit*, 64 Brook. L. Rev. 457, 460-461 (1998). *See also* Abner J. Mikva, *Counsel Lack Selectivity in Appellate Advocacy*, Legal Times, Nov. 15, 1982, at 10. ("Asking attorneys to highlight the meat and potatoes of the case does not mean that the spices included in the entree or the dessert that follows should be taken off the menu. But it does suggest that serving eight different vegetables will detract from the main course.")

13. Lawrence W. Pierce, *Appellate Advocacy: Some Reflections from the Bench,* 61 Fordham L. Rev. 829, 835–836 (1993).

§ 9.7 Perspectives from the Bench

Much of what I say in these pages emanates from personal experience as a state trial judge from 1961 to 1968 and as a circuit judge of the United States Court of Appeals for the Third Circuit since 1968. I have been influenced also by participation as a faculty member and later as associate director of the judicial education programs for state supreme court justices at Professor Robert A. Leflar's Senior Appellate Judges Seminars sponsored by the Institute for Judicial Administration at New York University.

As I prepared the first edition of this book in 1990, many of my seminar colleagues had become chief justices of their states, and I drew upon their experiences for suggestions. For this edition, I have solicited the contributions of current state chief justices and Federal court of appeals chief judges. As I now begin to discuss the heart of the brief—the argument—I share with you a sample of their observations.

§ 9.7.1 State Chief Justices

Chief Justice and State	Comment
Charles E. Jones, *Arizona*	Be concise and direct. Written work should predominately reflect the active voice, not the passive. Omit weak arguments that are largely, if not completely irrelevant, and focus exclusively on the most persuasive, authoritative arguments that will lead to the disposition of issues. State the strongest and best arguments first. Try to anticipate the difficult questions and provide answers. The latter point is also valid in preparing for oral argument.
Mary J. Mullarkey, *Colorado*	Limit the number of issues raised on appeal.
Ronald T. Y. Moon, *Hawaii*	Write in a concise and direct fashion, minimizing the utilization of long, rambling footnotes.

Mary Ann G. McMorrow, *Illinois*	Points made in a brief should be explained and argued and not simply listed without elaboration. The writer must carry the reader through the steps necessary to understand, apply, and dispose of the issue presented. In addition, the argument must be presented in a logical and organized manner, especially in those instances where the case is complex and several issues are presented. The structure of the brief should move from the general to the specific, with appropriate transitions.
Leigh Ingalls Saufley, *Maine*	Always provide a brief, nontechnical summary of issues presented at the beginning of the brief and a clear and explicit indication of the relief requested at the end of the brief.
Stephen N. Limbaugh, Jr., *Missouri*	Do not be repetitive. The persistent recapitulation of arguments—as if that is necessary to beat the arguments into the judges' heads—is often counterproductive because judges will find it irritating rather than enlightening.
Karla M. Gray, *Montana*	Set out only the facts pertinent to the issues raised. Long statements of fact tend to leave the impression that you are making a jury argument because your legal issues are not going to be very strong.
Judith S. Kaye, *New York*	Know your case. Nothing is more appreciated by judges—who have lots of briefs to read—than a clear, concise, cogent writing. That can be accomplished only when you truly understand, and argue, what's important about your case.

Thomas J. Moyer,
Ohio

Be concise. Do not repeat arguments. Do not gratuitously demean the intelligence or skills of opposing counsel. Judges who are reading hundreds of pages to prepare for oral argument simply have no time for redundancies and irrelevant comments. Conciseness in the writing of an appellee's brief includes the realization that the judge does not need to read the statement of facts twice. The appellee should indicate which portions of the statement of facts and statement of the case with which the appellee agrees and devote your efforts to clarifying the appellant's statement and adding facts that are favorable to the appellee's case that may not have been mentioned in the appellant's statement of facts.

David Gilberson,
South Dakota

Lead with your best punch. Go with one or two of your best issues that will really decide the case. A brief with fifteen or twenty assignments of error tells me the attorney is desperate and really is grasping at straws. No trial judge I ever knew was so bad as to make that many errors. As far as oral argument, do the same. Some of the best presentations I have seen discussed only one crucial issue, which usually decides the case. The attorney went directly to that issue, spoke for seven minutes and waived the rest of his time.

Sharon Keller,
*Texas Court of
Criminal Appeals*

And—a little thing—headings and subheadings are good things

Gerry L. Alexander, *Washington*	[I like] brevity. Orderly train of thought set forth only outcome determinative facts summary paragraph, [and] short, clear sentences. I think lawyers should make their written argument as concise as possible. What they submit to us are called "briefs" and not "longs," and it is helpful to the judges who are reviewing this case along with other cases to have the argument presented efficiently. This requires editing.

§ 9.7.2 Circuit Court Chief Judges

Chief Judge and Circuit	*Comment*
Michael Boudin, *First Circuit*	In brief writing, my aim was always to write a brief that was as close as to how a reasonable opinion on the issue might look while still coming out my way.
John M. Walker, Jr., *Second Circuit*	The poorest, least persuasive briefs are all too often those that the lawyer has not taken the time to reduce to its essence. Be highly selective in choosing the few points that have the best chance of prevailing. How often has the fourth or fifth point raised ever resulted in a victory for the appellant?
Edward R. Becker, *Third Circuit*, 1996–2003	Limit the number of points. You will rarely win on more than one or two points. Over-briefing impairs your credibility.
Anthony J. Scirica, *Third Circuit*	You must focus on the dispositive issue or issues only.
Carolyn Dineen King, *Fifth Circuit*	Pick the most important issues, deal with them thoroughly, and omit the others. Be concise.

Deanell Reece Tacha, *Tenth Circuit*	In the typical case there are usually only one or two outcome-determinative issues. Whether one is appellant or appellee, the question to be answered precisely is: "What is it that the court must decide to decide in my favor?" If counsel honestly and analytically answers this question, the brief and the oral argument are very clearly targeted to reaching that answer.
Haldane Robert Mayer, *Federal Circuit*	Be clear and concise—write and rewrite until the issue and answer can be identified in one short sentence. This will also aid the practitioner in culling out the real issues for appeal.
Patricia M. Wald, *D.C. Circuit, 1986–1991*	The more paper you throw at us, the meaner we get, the more irritated and hostile we feel about verbosity, peripheral arguments, and long footnotes. In my [many] years on the court we have by judicial fiat first shortened main briefs from seventy to fifty pages, then put a limit of 12,500 on the number of words that can go in the brief, and in complex, multi-party cases our staff counsel threaten and plead (we get into the act ourselves sometimes) with co-counsel to file joint or at least nonrepetitive briefs. It's my view that we can, should, and will do more to stem the paper tidal wave. Repetition, extraneous facts, over-long arguments (by the twentieth page, we are muttering to ourselves, "I get it, I get it. No more for God's sake.") still occur more often than capable counsel should tolerate. In our court counsel get extra points for briefs they bring in under the fifty-page limit. Many judges look first to see how long a document is before reading a word. If it is long, they

automatically read fast; if short, they read slower. Figure out yourself which is better for your case. Our politicians speak often of judicial restraint; I say let it begin with the lawyers whose grist feeds our opinion mills.

§ 9.7.3 Other United State Circuit Judges

Circuit Judge & Circuit	Comment
Carlos F. Lucero, *Tenth Circuit*	Attorneys should avoid briefs that are too long at all costs. I detest briefs that are sixty-four pages where every word counting rule has been bent. Avoid repetition in briefs. Avoid long string cites. And, for oral argument, I would say this: take a look at the work of typical circuit judges across America. Typically, we'll hear twenty-four cases in one week of oral argument—six cases a day for four days. If the appellant's brief is fifty pages, the response is always fifty pages, and the reply is twenty-five. That's 125 pages of reading on that case. Multiply that by six and that equals 750 pages. Multiply that by four and you are now approaching 3,000 pages of reading
Bobby R. Baldock, *Tenth Circuit*	You really are shooting yourself in the foot by not streamlining your briefs. I don't want to read *War and Peace*.
Diana Gribbon Motz, *Fourth Circuit*	Generally, there should be no more than four questions; do not repeat the same question in different ways. Often a case presents only one or two questions. Very occasionally a case presents many questions. It is, however, almost impossible to treat adequately more than four issues in a thirty-five to fifty-page brief.

§ 9.8 Yet, Lawyers Continue to Write Too Much

If I attempt a ballpark figure of the number of briefs that I have read as a state and federal judge, I would put the figure at about fifty thousand. This means I have read over two million pages. Probably less than half of these pages were necessary. The comments of the judges set forth above dramatically confirm my impressions. They send this very loud message to the appellate bar: *You write too much. Prepare better and write less.* I emphasized this point in my first edition. Over a decade later, most lawyers continue to ignore the uniform advice of the appellate judges who decide their cases.

This a phenomenon not limited to the nation's highest courts. Judges of intermediate appellate courts echo these complaints. In the Fourth District of the Florida District Court of Appeal, for example, the judges strongly favor shorter briefs. The comments of former Judge James C. Downey are typical: "I prefer a concise brief that makes it easy [to review], instead of a law review article that makes it hard." Former Fourth District Judge Gavin Letts concurred:

> Make the briefs short as possible because of the volume we have. I have a limited time for each brief. I don't have longer time to spend on longer briefs. The specialists are usually brief. They know which of our bells to press and their standard of practice is very high.[14]

A heavily overwritten brief makes me suspect that one of two things has occurred: an associate with minimal appellate experience wrote the brief, or as has happened to several of my former law clerks, their drafts were sent back by their seniors with the notation, "Beef this up!" These senior law office functionaries often belong to the more-is-better school. They may be good trial lawyers, perhaps great ones. They may be highly successful and deal everyday with piles of depositions and file cabinets or even rooms full of exhibits. They measure trial time in terms of weeks and months. They are used to paper storms generated by scores of tactical motions with accompanying memoranda and supporting documents with pages numbered in the thousands. They may know a great deal of trial tactics, but they know very little of the appellate decision-making process or the environment in which briefs are examined on appeal.

Listen to the judges who consider the final product. A good beginning would be to read again the comments of the experienced appellate

---

14. *Oral Arguments and Written Briefs—DCA Judges Comment,* 62 Fla. B.J. 23, 24 (1988).

judges in the preceding tables. Listen also to the late attorney John P. Frank of the Phoenix firm Lewis & Roca: "A brief should be brief, and if you have to go over thirty-five pages, you have nothing to say!" And it would not be a bad idea to ask former clerks of appellate judges about the dynamics of the appellate decision-making process.

I see a confounding prolixity from law firms where the people in charge were too timid or too unprepared to wield the red pen. Briefs are not pared down to the essentials but are puffed up with all sorts of extras. Perhaps this practice reflects the attorney's uncertainty as to what issue will draw the court's attention and the belief that the client's best interest is served by including every conceivable argument. The justification for this "Teflon® philosophy"—to throw everything against the wall and see what will stick—is not valid outside the walls of law school and the trial courtroom. Weak issues in a brief are more than surplusage. They have a definite tendency to infect the entire brief because they detract from the efficacy of your good issues. Your brief will be much improved, and your chances of winning greatly increased, if they are discarded.

More than fifty years ago, in his *Treatise on Evidence,* Dean John H. Wigmore made this point very clear in reacting to many thousands of judicial opinions he had studied. Some of the criticisms he set down then, are unfortunately, still appropriate today in an evaluation of briefs:

> Overconsideration . . . shows faithfulness and industry, for which we should be and are grateful. But it tends to remove the decision from the really vital issues in each case and to transform the [brief] into a list of rulings on academic legal assertions. The [brief] is as related to the meat of the case as a library catalogue is to the contents of the books. This is far from exercising the true and high function of an appellate court.[15]

---

15. 1 John H. Wigmore, *Evidence in Trials at Common Law* § 8a, at 617 (1983).

Chapter 10

THE BRIEF: STATING THE ISSUE(S)

§ 10.1 How to State an Issue

You are the judge. Which of the two statements of the same issue immediately informs the judge what point you intend to make?

- The appellant was denied due process.

- The appellant was denied due process when the court denied him the right to counsel in his trial for bank robbery.

Properly stating your issues is the first opportunity to persuade the court. Almost all court rules call for some statement of "issues presented for review," or "points," or "propositions," or "questions presented," or "headnotes." You must frame the issue in terms of your court rules. In general, the issue should be expressed in succinct terms with circumstances of the case and without unnecessary detail.

I will say it now and repeat it later:

If your rules permit, express the issue in the form of a simple declarative sentence phrased so that the court may adopt it as a topic sentence in its opinion in your favor.

Unless the rules require, do not be a "whether-man," phrasing the issue with "Whether . . ." Unless the rules require, do not express the issue in the form of an interrogatory. Write with the power of positive thinking. Give the court a simple categorical statement of the issue in a declarative sentence, fairly stated, yet psychologically inclined in your favor.

Yet, there are times when an interrogative is necessary. Seeing a splendidly crafted statement is a real joy. Consider the workmanship of this example:

Should *Enmund* be applied retroactively, or should the state be permitted one last cruel and unusual punishment before *Enmund* takes effect?[1]

I am impressed by the California practice. In interpreting state appellate Rule 14(a)(1)(B),[2] the court has said that each point should

---

1. *Jones v. Thigpen*, 741 F.2d 805, 811 (5th Cir. 1984).
2. Cal. R. 14(a)(1)(B).

be stated in the form of a proposition which if sustained would lend substantive support for the disposition requested by the preparer.[3]

The rules of the United States Supreme Court contain advice that I think should be followed everywhere: "The questions should be short and concise and should not be argumentative or repetitious . . . The statement of a question presented will be deemed to comprise every subsidiary question fairly included therein."[4]

Many formulations of issues, however, are obviously written without much thought and thus are not very helpful to the court. Here is an example of a type commonly used in appellate briefs:

> Point I: The trial court committed reversible error by denying defendant's motion.

This formulation is useless. It tells the court nothing. But point headings that are devoid of substance are not the only obstacle to understanding. Consider this one:

> Point I: The trial court erred in giving flawed essential elements instructions to the jury and thereby denied the defendant due process and fundamental fairness since it is error to give the jury, within the essential elements instructions, one statement containing more than one essential element of the crime and requiring of the jury simple and singular assent or denial of that compound proposition, fully capable of disjunctive answer, which if found pursuant to the evidence adduced would exculpate the defendant.[5]

This tells the court too much in confusing, at times, incomprehensible, language.

Philadelphia attorney James D. Crawford offers this excellent advice:

> Write the questions presented so that they inspire the answers you want. This is the first place you can be sure of presenting your legal contentions to the court. You will nowhere else present them with such brevity. If the court's attention and sympathy are not caught here, they may well never be caught at all.

3. *Lady v. Worthingham*, 130 P.2d 435 (Cal Ct. App. 1942).

4. S. Ct. R. 14(1)(a) (1999).

5. S. Eric Ottensen, *Effective Brief-Writing for California Appellate Courts*, 21 San Diego L. Rev. 371, 377 (1984)

A remarkable number of briefs contain statements of questions in the form: "Whether the court below properly or improperly granted summary judgment in favor of the defendant, the appellee herein." These questions tells the court almost nothing about the question before it. More important, it does nothing to make the court want to know about the case.

A well-written question explains precisely the issue before the court. A brilliantly written question not only fairly describes the issue before the court but makes the court want to decide that issue in favor of the author's client.

Everyone is familiar with the fact that experts who prepare public opinion polls have substantial control over the responses they get by the questions they frame. A scientific pollster attempts to frame neutral questions in order to get honest answers. An able lawyer, on the other hand, tries to frame questions which, without misleading the court, inspire the answer his or her client desires.

Some true professionals were at work in the briefs in *United States v. Nixon*, in which the president sought to withhold his taped conversations from judicial proceedings. James D. St. Clair was counsel for the president, and Leon Jaworski was the special prosecutor. Compare the excellent, if not textbook, statements of issues presented by the president as petitioner and the United States as respondent:

Petititioner: Point I: This internal dispute within co-equal branches does not present a justiciable case or controversy within the meaning of Article III, Section 2 of the Constitution.

Respondent: Point I: This dispute between the United States, represented by the special prosecutor, and the President—two distinct parties— presents a live, concrete, justiciable controversy.

Petitioner: Point II: A presidential assertion of privilege is
                              not reviewable by the courts.

Respondent: Point II: The courts have both the power and
                              the duty to determine the validity of a claim
                              of executive privilege when it is asserted in a
                              judicial proceeding as a ground for refusing to
                              produce evidence.

Petitioner: Point III: The judicial branch cannot compel
                              production of privileged material from the
                              President.

Respondent: Point III: Courts have the power to order the
                              production of evidence from the executive when
                              justice so requires.[6]

Attorney Jordan B. Cherrick also has offered some excellent practical suggestions:[7]

> Suppose you have a case in which the jury returned a
> $10 million verdict for your client, the husband of the
> late Karen Smith. Dr. Smith, a brilliant young physician,
> was killed when the airplane in which she was traveling
> exploded over the ocean. Your problem is that the trial
> court granted the defendant's motion for a judgment not-
> withstanding the verdict. The court concluded that your
> case was insufficient because your expert witness was
> not competent to testify that the explosion was caused by
> defective engines manufactured by the defendant.
>
> What is your appellate strategy? You decide to concentrate
> on two issues: the ample evidence supporting the jury's
> verdict and the trial court's failure to apply the proper
> standard in setting aside the verdict. Argument on the first
> point will show that an injustice occurred. The second will
> identify the legal error at stake.
>
> With this general approach, you begin to write, starting
> with the question presented. Here are two ways it could be
> done:

6. 418 U.S. 683 (1974), Briefs for Petitioner and Respondent.

7. Jordan B. Cherrick, *Issues, Facts, and Appellate Strategy*, 16 Litig. 15, 16–7 (1990).

> Should the trial court's judgment n.o.v. be reversed because plaintiff's expert witness, an aviation mechanic with more than twenty years of experience, was competent to render an opinion "based on reasonable scientific certainty" that the explosion that killed Dr. Smith was caused by defendant's defective engines?

or

> Should the court of appeals conclude that the trial court erred in granting defendant a judgment notwithstanding the verdict?

The first version is far better. It outlines the equitable heart of the appeal and implies the legal problem involved. The second formulation just sits there, arid and lifeless. It makes the case indistinguishable from all other appeals of J.N.O.V.s–most of which are affirmed. Your statement of issues must do more: It must, from the first page, acquaint the court with why your case is different.

How do you frame the case for the appeals court if you represent the appellee? Again, there are good and bad ways to do it. Compare this statement . . .

> Did the trial court properly enter judgment N.O.V. for the defendant because plaintiff's expert, a mechanic with no engineering training, was not competent to testify that electronically complex jet engines caused the airplane's explosion?

. . . with this one:

> Should the trial court's judgment notwithstanding the verdict be affirmed because the court properly concluded that the plaintiff's expert was not competent to testify about the accident?

Again, the first version is better. It conveys the trial court's primary reason for entering a J.N.O.V. in forceful terms. Reading it, the appeals court knows, at one glance, the essence of the appellee's argument. The second version is much inferior. It merely asks whether the J.N.O.V. should be affirmed. This statement ignores the real problem in the case: Was the plaintiff's expert witness competent to opine on causation, and how did his dubious competence affect the plaintiff's case?

A word of warning on framing the issues. Though it is wise to weave the facts through the legal question, do not go overboard. It is one thing to convey crisply what the case is about. It is another to engage in strident special pleading. In our crash case, this would *not* be good form:

> Did the trial court's reversal of the jury's careful verdict wrongly depend on the conclusion that plaintiff's expert was incompetent to testify that a jet engine's slipshod design caused a shattering explosion that, in a searing flash, snuffed out the life of a brilliant young physician over the chilly waters of the Atlantic?

That is not a statement of the issue on appeal. It is part of a jury summation.

§ 10.2   Issues: A Capsulization

To capsulize, if the rules permit (those of the United States Courts of Appeals and Supreme Court do), my advice is: (1) *do not* phrase the issue in the form of a "whether" statement; (2) *do not* phrase it in the form of an interrogative; and (3) *do* phrase it as a single declarative sentence that will form the topic sentence of your discussion under "Argument," and, with a little bit of luck, will be adopted by the court when its opinion appears in your favor.

§ 10.3   Meeting the Issue Head-On

It is a pleasure to pick up a brief and see that the parties meet the issue head on and do not dance around it. You see the clear outlines of the syllogism. You note complete agreement on the middle and major terms in the major premise and a conflict only as to whether the minor term is a part of the class represented by the major.

Appellant: According to the Supreme Court, "An arrest warrant founded on probable cause implicitly carries with it the limited authority to enter a dwelling in which the suspect lives when there is reason to believe the suspect is within." *Payton v. New York*, 445 U.S. 573 (1980). The evidence indicates that the officers had no reason to believe the suspect was in the residence at the time of the raid. Therefore, the officers' warrantless entry was unjustified. The district court's conclusion to the contrary was clearly erroneous.

Appellee: In *Payton v. New York*, 445 U.S. 573, 603 (1980) the Supreme Court recognized that ". . . for Fourth Amendment purposes, an arrest warrant founded on probable cause implicitly carries with it the limited authority to enter a dwelling in which the suspect lives when there is reason to believe the suspect is within." *United States v. Underwood*, 717 F.2d 482 (9th Cir. 1983), *cert. denied*, 465 U.S. 1036 (1984).

The district court found that the officers had probable cause to believe that the suspect was at the house and were justified in entering the house to arrest her. This finding is amply supported by the record.

Appellant: I. The appellant's conviction must be reversed because there was no substantial evidence that he conspired with anyone else to defraud the United States in collection of revenue.

II. In the alternative, the district court committed reversible error in admitting evidence of the appellant's subsequent acts of uncharged misconduct, in admitting his tax returns, and in refusing his requested instruction regarding the failure of the United States to produce evidence regarding the Bahamian loan.

1. The district court committed reversible error in admitting evidence of the defendant's subsequent acts of uncharged misconduct.

2. The trial court committed reversible error in admitting the defendant's tax returns.

3. The district court committed reversible error in failing to instruct the jury that the government failed to follow established procedures for obtaining information to the Bahamian loan.

4. The errors were not harmless.

III.   The district court abused its discretion in failing to grant defendant's motion for a bill of particulars.

Appellee: A. The evidence was sufficient to sustain the jury's verdict of guilty on count one, conspiracy to defraud the United States.

B. The district court's admission of evidence that the defendant sent cash hidden in a suitbag to Miami and did not declare excess cash carried through United States Customs did not constitute an abuse of discretion.

1. The suitbag evidence.

2. The currency report violation.

C. The district court's admission of the defendant's income tax returns was not an abuse of discretion.

D. The district court's ruling denying defendant's requested instruction on the government's alleged duty to investigate foreign sources of non-taxable income did not constitute an abuse of discretion.

E. The district court's denial of a bill of particulars did not constitute an abuse of discretion.

Author's Comment: The accepted practice is to identify a major point with a Roman numeral, a subpart with capital letters, its subpart with an arabic numeral and its subpart with a lowercase letter. Note here and in other excerpts of briefs the free range of numbering and lettering.

§ 10.4   Single-Issue Briefs

Appellant: The court's charge to the jury on specific intent was inadequate and warrants the granting of a new trial.

Appellee: The district court properly charged the jury that the specific intent required was intent to defraud.

Appellant: The district court erred when it held that it did not have the authority to amend its sentence pursuant to Rule 35(a) to consider the entire sentence if that consideration would result in a reduction in the sentence.

Appellee: The district court properly ruled that it lacked jurisdiction to reduce the defendant's sentence pursuant to Rule 35(a) when the time for presenting a motion for reduction of sentence pursuant to Rule 35(b) had expired.

§ 10.5   How *Not* To State the Issue

Appellant: The following conclusions of law are in error and should be reversed in favor of the Findings of Fact proposed by the plaintiff:

1. Conclusion of Law number 4 is erroneous.

2. Substitute Conclusion of Law 4.

3. Conclusions of Law Numbers 8, 10, 11, and 12 are erroneous.

4. Substitute Conclusions of Law 8, 10, 11, and 12.

Appellee: The district court's determination that the plaintiff was not the victim of discrimination should be affirmed.

A. The disparate treatment theory.

B. The disparate impact theory.

C. The district court's evidentiary rulings were correct.

The Court: In 1986, the Forest Service rejected the plaintiff, a black woman who served as Civil Rights Director for the

Food and Nutrition Services, for appointment as Equal Employment Manager in the United States Department of Agriculture's Southwest region. The position went instead to a white woman who was then the Administrative Officer for the Mt. Hood National Forest and Director of the Forest Service's Equal Employment Office program. Because the plaintiff failed to satisfy her burden of persuasion under either a disparate treatment or disparate impact theory of the case, the trial court found for the Forest Service. We affirm.

§ 10.6   More Examples of Issue Statements: *See* Appendix *B*

§ 10.7   Describe the Issue Fairly

You must fairly describe the issue before the court. This is critical for several reasons. The court must get the impression that the question presented will control the decision. The judges must also be confident that the proposition stated may be affirmed or denied as a legal precept. To be sure, the value judgments required in affirming or denying the proposition of necessity must differ, but the proposition itself must be fashioned so that the court can fairly accept it or reject it.

Justice Frankfurter once wrote: "In law also the right answer usually depends on putting the right question."[8] My late colleague Judge Abraham Freedman used to say, "How you come out here depends on how you come in." Unfortunately, we often encounter skewed statements of issues in briefs. We see issue statements gone awry. An example of a slanted and unfair statement comes to mind (this time from the Court's opinion and not a brief). It emanated from Justice Fortas, writing for the Court in *United States v. Yazell*: "Specifically, the question presented is whether, in the circumstances of this case, the Federal Government, in its zealous pursuit of the balance due on a disaster loan made by the Small Business Administration, may obtain judgment against Esther Mae Yazell of Lampasas, Texas."[9] With the "question" framed in such a subtly biased fashion, could there be any doubt about the "answer?" Although judges may have leeway in making such statements in opinions, lawyers do not have the privilege of inserting hyperbole in the statement of the issue.

---

8. *Estate of Rogers v. Comm'r,* 320 U.S. 410, 413 (1943).

9. 382 U.S. 341, 342–43 (1966).

§ 10.8 Arrangement of Issues

Your most important point should be presented first. Always lead from a position of strength. Picking this point requires you to come up with an intelligent answer to the following question:

> What argument, objectively considered, based on precedent and previously stated policy concerns of the court, is most calculated to persuade the court to your point of view?

You cannot make this decision in a casual manner. It cannot be based on a hunch or a guess, even an educated one. It must be based on careful study of the decisions of the court and must follow a reflective analysis of the decision-making methodology of the judges—an understanding of factors that trigger their decisions.

The most important point is the one that has a reasonable probability to persuade. I define "probability" as being more likely than not and distinguish it from a mere "possibility," or something that may or may not succeed, or something that lies between probable and impossible. You play the odds here. It is the percentages that count. You cannot make this decision until you have checked out the particular appellate court, its caselaw and the decision-making methodology of its judges.

You lead with your strongest suit in this judicial card game because you are in the persuasion business. You cannot save the best argument until last. This is not a drama of the theater, nor the Pulitzer Prize novel. Make a favorable impression on the decision-maker as soon as possible. Listen to Judge Myron H. Bright of the eighth circuit:

> If an appellant can't win on the strength of the strongest claim or claims, he stands little chance of winning a reversal on the basis of weaker claims . . . The court needs to know just where the heart of the matter lies; distracting attention from the most important issues can hardly help an appellant's cause.[10]

If we ranked the metaphysical factors that go into decision-making, the initial impression received by the judge who reads your brief may be more important than any other aspect of the art of persuading. You do

---

10. Myron H. Bright, *Appellate Briefwriting: Some "Golden" Rules*, 17 Creighton L. Rev. 1069, 1071 (1983).

not get a second chance to make a first impression. I remind you of what I said before about the environment under which briefs are read and the crushing caseloads facing appellate judges. Unfortunately, the judge does not possess the luxury of time for leisurely, detached meditation. You had better sell the sizzle as soon as possible. *The steak can wait.*

There is one exception to this rule. Prior to reaching the main issue of the merits you may be required to address a threshold matter, like jurisdiction or some procedural question. In that case, the preliminary housekeeping matters must be addressed.

With respect to jurisdiction, you may have addressed the issue in papers filed with the court prior to filing the brief. Nonaction by the court indicates that the question is still open. My advice for both the appellant and the appellee is to repeat the jurisdiction arguments in the briefs—*do not* rely on the previously filed papers. Making the judge rummage through preliminary briefings when considering the briefs-in-chief does not make your position more acceptable.

Having decided on the lead issue, in what order do you set forth the others? You will often find that several issues rise in logical order, with some issues subordinate to others. You have already determined the major thrust of the brief and decided what points will support the dominant theme. I offer these suggestions for issue arrangement:

- The issues should be listed in order of importance. If you cannot resist including a throwaway issue, save it until last.

- At times, the arguments must be listed in logical order. Often a series of syllogisms is linked, with conclusions of previous ones forming the premises of those which follow. Where one point follows the other in logical order, the statement of issues takes the form of an inverted pyramid. If you lose the top, or fattest issue, you lose the entire argument, for each subsequent point is dependent on the acceptability of the previous one.

- If at all possible, then, construct your brief with points that are independent of each other. In this manner you give the court an alternative basis for decision, so that if the judges reject your major point and those subsequent to and dependent on it, you may be entirely successful on an independent, alternative ground. Here your statement of issues more resembles an egg carton with self-contained supports than a single inverted pyramid.

§ 10.9 Choosing the Theme

Your strongest point should also serve as the unifying theme of your argument. Although I refer to "point" and "theme" in the singular, it may well be that your argument will contain more than one theme, but generally a successful brief contains a single knock-'em-in-the-eyes theme that will persuade the reviewing court to reverse (in the case of an appellant's brief) or to affirm (in the case of an appellee's brief).[11]

The theme is the unifying focus of your brief. It directs the court's attention, as Judge Bright said, to where "the heart of the matter lies," or to what Jordan Cherrick called "the equitable heart of the appeal." It answers the question in the mind of every judge addressing a brief for the first time, the question succinctly phrased by the former Wyoming Chief Justice Walter Urbigkit as: "WHAT IN THE HECK IS THE MESSAGE?" Drawing on his experience as my law clerk for two years, and later as a partner in the Washington, D.C. firm of Covington & Burling, Bobby R. Burchfield writes:

> A brief should have a strong opening, forcefully but concisely stating the argument, or if the brief presents multiple arguments, the theme unifying those arguments. (*E.g.*, "Appellant's arguments miscomprehend this Court's scope of review.") This opening can be in the introductory paragraph or in the summary of argument. A one sentence statement of the grounds for reversal or affirmance is best.

Cherrick also emphasizes the necessity of having a theme in mind when you prepare the issues: "Careful drafting is essential. The way issues are written will govern the court's important first impression of the merits. Whatever the theme, each issue statement should incorporate specific facts and legal principles in a simple, concise, and accurate manner."[12]

§ 10.10 How to Structure an Issue

In every issue formulation be certain to state expressly or implicitly a legal proposition that the court will immediately accept as settled law. This is the stated or implied major premise. For the court to accept a *conclusion* that you proffer, it first has to agree absolutely with your major premise.[13]

---

11. I address this point in detail more properly in chapter 14, The Brief: State Your Theme.
12. *Cherrick*, *supra* note 8, at 16.
13. The logical structure of an argument is discussed in greater detail in chapter 16,: The Brief: The Required Logical Form for Each Issue.

Gary L. Sasso, a Florida appellate specialist at Carlton Fields, makes the important point:

> In constructing your affirmative case, be sure to start at the beginning—not the chronological beginning, but the logical beginning. Every argument has a predicate. You must identify it and establish it before moving on. This is a rule that is usually honored in the breach. Countless briefs just jump into the middle of a legal analysis. They start arguing a point of view before laying the groundwork. Such a brief will do little to persuade someone who does not subscribe to that point of view from the start.
>
> Your objective in constructing an affirmative case should be to start with a proposition that the court—whatever its bent—must accept; then reason, logically, step by step, to your conclusion. If you do this well, you will arrive at your destination with the court right beside you. Your conclusion will make sense, not just because you say so, but because the court will have reasoned along with you. In a way, the technique is one familiar to cross-examiners. You nibble toward your destination with a series of points or questions that can only be answered yes. The main constraint on this approach is the page limit on your brief and the realization that judges do not have all day to read.[14]

Be absolutely certain that your statement of an issue is a proposition that the court must accept—that is, a rock-bound precedent, a statute with a settled interpretation, an unambiguous procedural rule. This is required no matter where the flashpoint of controversy lies between the parties: in the choice of competing precepts, in the interpretation of a controlling precept or in the application of an integral precept to the found facts.[15]

An additional benefit springs from a series of clear, concise, argument headings. Those headings will appear in order in the table of contents of the brief. If they are well written, they will provide an outline for your entire brief on the first page where they will immediately catch the eye of the judges. This outline, together with the statement

---

14. Gary L. Sasso, *Anatomy of the Written Argument*, 15 Litig. 30 (1989).

15. We will treat this subject in some detail later in chapter 15, The Brief: Identify the Flash Point of the Controversy.

of the questions presented, enables you to initially inform the judges of the legal issues they should be thinking about.

§ 10.11 State the Issue as Narrowly as Possible

The objective of appellate advocacy is to win on appeal—to win *this* appeal. Accordingly, state the issue as narrowly as possible to achieve your objective. There is a difference between succeeding as an advocate and mounting a full-scale assault to expound a cause in which you passionately believe. The law develops incrementally; there are few sea changes. Do not expect the court to change the law drastically in a single case.

Be satisfied if the court will rule in your favor as narrowly as possible. Remember that the lawyer's primary obligation is to a *client*, not to a *cause*. To insist that the court give you a full loaf when half a loaf will do may result in nothing but crumbs for your client. Save the broader expansion of the law to another case.

Chapter 11

THE BRIEF: STATEMENT OF THE CASE

§ 11.1 Overview: Statement of the Case

"How did you get here?" Justice Felix Frankfurter once asked a nervous advocate appearing before the Supreme Court. "By the B & O Railroad, sir," came the reply. That was not what the justice wanted to know, of course. He was looking for a statement of the case, which briefly explains the nature of the appeal, the course of the proceedings, and the disposition in the tribunal below.

A succinct statement of the case in your brief tells the appellate court "how you got here." In this portion of the brief you verify the procedural history of the case by answering these questions:

Who: Who won in the trial court? Who is taking the appeal?

What: What is the general area of law implicated in the appeal, and what specifically are the issues?

Where: Where has the case been so far? A trial court, administrative agency, or intermediate court?

When: When was the alleged error committed? During the pretrial, trial, or post-trial stage?

How: How was the case resolved? By summary judgment, a directed verdict, a jury verdict, or a nonjury award?

§ 11.1.1 Examples from the Briefs

Consider the following examples of statements of the case contained in actual briefs:

This case involves a prosecution of twenty-one defendants on charges, *inter alia*, of conspiring to violate the Racketeer Influenced Corrupt Organizations Act, 8 U.S.C. § 1962(d), under a twelve-count indictment returned August 19, 1985.

Appellant Matthew P. Boylan was retained specifically and solely as local counsel in pretrial proceedings for the defendant; Milton M. Ferrell, Jr. was also retained to participate in pretrial proceedings. Milton M. Ferrell, Sr., was the defendant's sole trial counsel. The trial commenced on November 16, 1986, before the Honorable Harold A. Ackerman in the United States District Court for the District of New Jersey.

On February 16, 1988, the trial was recessed when the defendant informed the court that Milton M. Ferrell had been diagnosed as having advanced and incurable cancer and could no longer continue to represent him.

The defendant asked the court to sever his prosecution from that of the other defendants as a result of his counsel's illness. On February 25, 1988, following a February 24 hearing, Judge Ackerman denied the defendant's motion for severance and ordered Mr. Boylan and his firm, Lowenstein, Sandler, Kohl, Fisher & Boylan, to represent the defendant at trial, which Judge Ackerman scheduled to resume on March 21, 1988. Judge Ackerman further ordered Douglas L. Williams, the new law partner of Milton M. Ferrell, Jr., to assist in that representation. Mr. Boylan and the Lowenstein firm refused to comply with that order and on February 29, 1988, were held in civil contempt by Judge Ackerman and subjected to sanctions of $2,500 and $10,000 per day, respectively, for that refusal.

That same day, a Notice of Appeal was filed, and a three-judge panel of this court entered an order staying the order of the district court and scheduling this matter for expedited appeal.

Author's Comment: Does this statement explicitly explain that this is an appeal by the lawyers on contempt sanctions? Does the first sentence suggest this?

This case involves "the ongoing controversy over logging in old growth forests in Oregon and Washington and the impact of that logging on the northern spotted owl." Old-growth forests are favored natural habitat for the northern spotted owl, *Strix occidentalis caurina*. The bird's current range extends from northern California, through the coastal and cascade regions of Oregon and Washington, and into southern British Columbia. Because of logging and land conversion activities, approximately 90 percent of suitable habitat for northern spotted owls now occurs on government land. The Forest Service manages 79 percent of the habitat on federal land, and the Bureau of Land Management manages 14 percent of it; the remaining 7 percent is on National Park Service land. Sixty percent of northern spotted owl habitat on federal land is in areas classified as "timber production land."

In the late 1980's respondents—the Seattle Audubon Society, the Portland Audubon Society, and other environmental groups—filed actions in the Western District of Washington and the District of Oregon challenging the federal government's efforts to continue logging old-growth timber in government-owned forests located in the Pacific Northwest. During the pendency of those federal court proceedings, Congress enacted Section 318 of the Department of the Interior and Related Agencies Appropriations Act, 1990, Pub. L. 101–121, Tit. III, 103 Stat. 745–750 (1989), also known as the Northwest Timber Compromise. Section 318 "sets terms and conditions applicable only for fiscal year 1990 for making timber sales on Federal lands in Oregon and Washington, for managing habitat for northern spotted owls, and for minimizing fragmentation of significant old growth forest stands." H.R. Conf. Rep. No. 264, 101st Cong., 1st Sess. 87 (1989). Its purpose was to "balance the goals of ensuring a predictable flow of public timber for fiscal year 1990 and protecting the northern spotted owl and significant old growth forest stands." *Ibid.*

The district courts in Oregon and Washington concluded that Section 318 operated as a "temporary modification of the environmental laws" invoked by respondents in their lawsuits. Accordingly, the district courts determined that the statute by its terms precluded respondents' claims for relief.

The Ninth Circuit reversed, holding that one part of Section 318—the first sentence in Section 318(b)(6)(A)—violates the constitutional principle of separation of powers set forth in *United States v. Klein*, 80 U.S. (13 Wall.) 128 (1872). The court of appeals determined that Section 318(b)(6)(A) "does not establish new law, but directs the court to reach a specific result and make certain factual findings under existing law in connection with two cases pending in federal court." In the court's view, "[t]his is what *Klein* and subsequent cases agree is constitutionally proscribed." *Ibid.* The court of appeals thus remanded the cases to the district courts for consideration of the merits of respondents' challenges.

Author's Comment: Clear writing explains a complicated problem.

This appeal arises from a final judgment of claims between plaintiffs and one defendant entered under Rule 54(b), Fed. R. Civ. P., in three consolidated class actions filed in the United States District Court for the Eastern District of Pennsylvania. The complaints assert tort and warranty claims on behalf of all public elementary and secondary schools in the country against approximately fifty manufacturers and producers of asbestos-containing materials, some of which were used in the construction of some of the plaintiffs' school buildings. The plaintiffs have alleged that the district court has jurisdiction on the basis of diversity of citizenship. *See* 28 U.S.C. § 1332(a). The class is certified under Rule 23(b)(3), and apparently contains 35,711 members.

On February 29, 1990, the district court entered judgment pursuant to Fed. R. Civ. P. 54(b), and Pretrial Order No. 212 finally approving the 1989 agreement of settlement with defendant Lac D'Amiante Du Quebec, Ltee. By this final judgment, the court dismissed with prejudice the claims of all class members against defendant LAQ. U.S. Gypsum filed a timely notice of appeal on March 21, 1990.

Author's Comment: This statement of the case inadequately describes the general area of law and says nothing about the specific issues.

Plaintiffs Nationwide Mutual Insurance Company, et al., by whom defendant H. Bruce Cornutt had formerly been employed, brought this action to enforce certain provisions of the contract by which Nationwide had employed Cornutt. Before a hearing on a preliminary injunction could be scheduled, Cornutt moved for summary judgment based on the provisions of the Agreement. The district court granted Cornutt's motion for summary judgment as to paragraph 11 the Agreement,* but left for trial Nationwide's entitlement to enforcement of paragraph 12 of the Agreement.

Thereafter, a settlement was reached among the parties to permit review of the trial court's grant of summary judgment. By this settlement, Cornutt agreed to a final injunction with respect to paragraph 12 of the Agreement, and agreed to the preservation of Nationwide's right to appeal from the trial court's summary judgment with respect to paragraph 11. A timely notice of appeal was thereafter filed by Nationwide.

[Text of footnote]

*Paragraph 11 of the Agreement provides:

> 11. Agent agrees that he/she will not, either directly or indirectly by and for himself or as agent for another or through others as agent, engage in or be licensed as an agent, solicitor, representative or broker in any way connected with the sale, advertising or solicitation of fire, casualty, health or life insurance in the area described below for a period of one year from the date of the voluntary or involuntary termination of employment with the Companies or, should the Companies find it necessary by legal action to enjoin Agent from competing with the Companies, one year after the date such injunction is obtained in the following area: within Twenty Five miles of the principal place of business . . . .

Author's Comment: The crux of the appeal is the text of paragraph 11 of the Agreement. It should not have been demoted to a lowly footnote but summarized and included in the body of the statement.

The appeal is from a decision of the U.S. Tax Court entered March 30, 1989. The appeal was timely filed on June 27, 1989.

The Tax Court opinion is reported as 92 T.C. No. 38 (March 1989).

Author's Comment: The minimalist style is not effective, and it is never justified, even in a complicated and technical tax case. Always answer the five questions.

§ 11.2   Summary

The statement of the case is a streamlined account of the proceedings to date. It tells the court "how you got here." The challenge here is expressed in Blaise Pascal's lament, "I am sorry to have wearied you with so long a letter but I did not have time to write a short one."

Chapter 12

THE BRIEF: STATEMENT OF FACTS

§ 12.1 Overview: Statement of Facts

The statement of facts is as important as any portion of the brief. The statement should be written, rewritten, and then rewritten again before being placed in final form. The statement is designed to inform. But a good statement does more; it engages the reader's interest, making the judge look forward to working on the case. The statement of facts tells the story of your case. This does not give you a license to embellish or to throw in irrelevant but juicy facts to liven up the plot. Stick to the essentials. But remember, it is not unconstitutional to be interesting.

In his noteworthy works, *Brief Writing and Oral Argument and Law Students Manual on Legal Writing,* Professor Edward D. refers to the ABCs of legal writing: Accuracy, Brevity, and Clarity.[1] Follow these in preparing your statement of facts. To achieve brevity, however, the brief writer will often sacrifice clarity. Do not do this. Avoid such shortcuts as resorting to initials or acronyms when identifying parties or participants in litigation—this can be both annoying and cumbersome. "USS" may be the United States Steel Company, the Universal Statistics Service, or the Underwriters Society of San Francisco. The desirability of clarity is easier achieved by using a generic term such as "the company," or "the consortium," or "the underwriters," rather than making the reader of the brief fight the battle of trying to remember which initials go with which participant.[2]

You do not begin to write the facts until you have made the decision on the precise issues you intend to discuss. Never put the fact-writing cart before the issue-stating horse. In this manner, you limit the narrative only to those facts that are germane to the issues before the court. The judge will appreciate that you are not cluttering with facts that have no bearing on the decisional process.

---

1. Edward D. Re and Joseph R. Re, *Brief Writing and Oral Argument* 8 (6th ed. 1987).

2. *See, e.g.*, Alex Kozinski, *How You Too Can . . . Lose Your Appeal*, Mont. Law., 5 (Oct. 1997). ("In a recent brief I ran across this little gem: 'LBE's complaint more specifically alleges that NRB failed to make an appropriate determination of RPT and TIP in conformity to SIP.' Even if there was a winning argument buried in the midst of this gobbledegook, it was DOA.")

§ 12.2   What Facts Should be Set Forth?

You must understand that experienced appellate judges may form their first, and probably their most lasting, impression of your side of the case from reading your statement of facts. Do not let facts that are merely decorative obscure those that are important. In a murder case, for example, the installation of a stained glass window on the fiftieth floor of a building may be interesting, but what matters is that the victim was thrown out of the window.

In selecting the facts, the brief writer walks on a very tight rope. The job requires consummate skill, because the writer must constantly seek balance on several levels—the balance between being scrupulously accurate and putting the most favorable emphasis on your version of what happened; the balance between furnishing the relevant facts favoring your client and protecting yourself from a possible charge by your opponent that you have withheld vital facts from the court; and the balance between putting your best evidence before the appellate court and adhering to the actual findings in the trial court. The exceptional advocate balances these conflicting duties and still conveys the impression that his or her client deserves to win.

I approach the selection of facts as an unreconstructed common law lawyer. *Stare decisis* counsels us "to stand by the decisions," and a decision is a mix of the material facts and the legal consequences flowing therefrom. Material facts must stand out because they form the predicate of the legal rule you are urging upon the court. The brief writer must ensure that all material facts necessary to the rule of law urged upon the court are set forth in the narrative. At this point in the brief writing task, it is worth recalling the words of some of the giants of the common law:

- Roscoe Pound: Rules of law are "[p]recepts attaching a definite detailed legal consequence to a definite, detailed state of facts."[3]

- Edward H. Levi: "[T]he scope of a rule of law, and therefore its meaning, depends upon a determination of what facts will be considered similar to those present when the rule was first announced. The finding of similarity or difference is the key step in the legal process."[4]

---

3. Roscoe Pound, *Hierarchy of Sources and Forms in Different Systems of Law*, 7 Tul. L. Rev. 475, 482 (1933).

4. Edward H. Levi, *An Introduction to Legal Reasoning*, 15 U. Chi. L. Rev. 501, 502 (1948).

Philadelphia attorney James D. Crawford says that writing the facts in an appellate brief should not be entrusted to a junior litigator: "Many of the most effective appellate lawyers have told their junior partners and associates: 'You write the law. Let me write the statement of facts because that is where the biggest difference can be made.' " Others suggest that the facts should be written in the first instance by the person most familiar with the case. Familiarity can breed obscurity in the narrative, however. You may know the facts so well that you are unable to put yourself in the position of someone unacquainted with the case. Collaboration with colleagues can overcome this problem, producing a statement that is both comprehensive and comprehensible.

It is essential that the statement of facts command and retain the reader's attention. Do not bore the judge. Do not make the brief difficult to read. Do not clutter the narrative. Come closer to Ernest Hemingway than Beltway bureaucratese. Catherine Drinker Bowen kept a sign posted above her desk to discipline herself as she wrote her books: "Will the reader turn the page?" What Barbara Tuchman described in *Practicing History* as the responsibility of the historian is equally applicable to the lawyer writing the brief:

> The writer of history, I believe, has a number of duties *vis-à-vis* the reader, if he wants to keep him reading. The first is to distill. He must do the preliminary work for the reader, assemble the information, make sense of it, select the essential, discard the irrelevant—above all, discard the irrelevant—and put the rest together so that it forms a developing dramatic narrative. Narrative, it has been said, is the lifeblood of history. To offer a mass of undigested facts, of names not identified and places not located, is of no use to the reader and is simple laziness on the part of the author, or pedantry to show how much he has read.[5]

§ 12.3 Translating the Record into the Statement of Facts

Margaret D. McGaughey, appellate chief of the United States Attorney's office in Maine, is a veteran appellate lawyer who regularly appears in the United States Court of Appeals for the First Circuit. She offers some excellent advice on how to cope with the record and to use it in preparing an effective statement of facts:

---

5. Barbara Tuchman, *Practicing History* 17–18 (1981).

For many lawyers, the most difficult part of appellate practice is not researching the law, writing about it, or even arguing it orally. Instead, it is the significantly less glamorous task of digesting the record and writing the statement of facts. This job is daunting because of its tedious and time-consuming nature. Where an argument of law may be perfected in an afternoon, a good statement of facts may take entire days, even weeks, to complete. Moreover, the statement of facts has tremendous significance to the outcome of the appeal. Cases turn far more frequently on their facts than they do on the law.

In part, writing a statement of facts is intimidating because of the sheer size of the appellate record. Especially in complex or multi-party cases, it is not at all unusual for the record to consist of several thousand pages of transcript and an equal volume of pleadings and memorandum decisions. The prospect of attempting to impose order on such an unruly mass of information can seem overwhelming.

The job is complicated by the substantial differences in considerations that influence the presentation of evidence at trial on one hand and the organization of a statement of facts for appeal on the other. When they can, trial lawyers organize their witnesses and evidence not chronologically, but instead in a way that maximizes the advantages and minimizes the liabilities of the case. The success of a criminal prosecution, for example, may depend on a single cooperating informant whose memory is weak and who may be able to testify only to events that occurred in the middle of the conspiracy period. Yet trial of that case may begin with that same vulnerable witness simply because the trial lawyer cares less about logical progressions than about getting the evidence into the record so that it can be used in summation. As often as not, the order of witnesses at trial is dictated by the simple imperative of who is standing in the corridor at the time a witness is needed.

On appeal, these sorts of tactical considerations disappear and a different priority surfaces. It is to organize the thousands of disjointed bits and pieces of evidence from the trial record into a coherent unit that fosters favorable resolution of the legal issues on appeal. Appellate judges want to know how much attention the disputed ruling occupied at trial so that they can decide whether the legal claim was preserved for review. At the same time, they want to see the larger picture of the trial as a whole in order to determine whether the evidence supporting the ultimate outcome was minimal or overwhelming, and thus the error was reversible or harmless. In writing a statement of facts, the appellate attorney's job is to create a framework that will meet all of these competing expectations.

§ 12.3.1 Digesting the Record

Before a statement of facts can be written, the record must be mastered. McGaughey suggests that in all but the shortest cases, a digest of the record should be prepared, and that one method of digesting the record is to make a page-by-page summary of the transcripts that converts the questions and answers into a few complete sentences that can later be joined together to make paragraphs in the statement of facts. This summary can be tabbed with the names of the witnesses so that the writer can flip back and forth among them to fit the pertinent facts into their proper place in the organization.

Many experienced appellate attorneys believe that, when a digest has been prepared by someone else, the person who ultimately writes the brief and argues the case orally should read the actual record through at least once. This personal reading enables the writer to understand the complete story before becoming mired in collateral issues or excessive detail. It helps to ingrain the facts in the writer's mind for use in writing and in oral argument. It provides the greatest opportunity for the varying nuances in the record to be discovered and used to best advantage.

§ 12.3.2 Writing the Statement of Facts

The basic theory behind writing a statement of facts is to make the case easy for the appellate judges to decide the advocate's way. This means preparing a statement of facts that is simple to follow and to accept as reliable. A statement of facts should read like an interesting story.

Your statement should adhere to a consistent theme, be written with true-to-life language, and have a cohesive organization. Because it is not fiction, however, literary license is unacceptable. A statement of facts should be an accurate reflection of *facts* found by the fact-finder, not simply the favored *evidence* you introduced at trial. Remember, in a jury verdict, the presumption is that the facts found are derived from the evidence presented by the verdict winner. Write them on the basis of evenhanded advocacy. Both the good and bad should appear. The aim is to have the appellate court rely on counsel's statement of facts, not the opponent's statement of facts. It must inspire and be worthy of the appellate court's trust.

Widener University Law Professor Brian J. Foley and Rutgers University clinician Ruth Anne Robbins teach future lawyers that the most powerful tool for persuasion may be the story. They compare the courtroom to the theater and quote David Ball: "Story is the strongest non-violent persuasive method we know. Tell me facts and maybe I will hear a few of them. Tell me an argument and I might consider it. Tell me a story and I am yours. That is why every persuasive enterprise from the Bible to television commercials relies on story."[6]

It is a given that lawyers should "tell a story" in the facts sections of briefs. Foley and Robbins elaborate on what my law clerks call an "Aldisertism": it is not unconstitutional to be interesting. So, how does one tell a story? The first thing to do is to understand what a story is. Surprisingly, few books on writing actually define "story." Perhaps, as with pornography, we know a story when we see (or hear or read) one. That said, here is an example of about as close as any of these books gets to defining "story": "A dramatic novel embodies the following characteristics: it focuses on a central character, the protagonist, who is faced with a dilemma; the dilemma develops into a crisis; the crisis builds through a series of complications to a climax; in the climax, the crisis is solved. The elements most useful and accessible to lawyers are character, conflict, resolution, organization, and point-of-view, and perhaps, setting."[7]

§ 12.3.3 McGaughey's Four Rules of Thumb

I set forth verbatim McGaughey's *Four Rules of Thumb:*

Number 1: Don't use a fact in the argument portion of your brief that was not set forth in the statement of fact.

---

6. David Ball, *Theater Tips and Strategies for Jury Trial* 66 (1994).

7. Brian J. Foley and Ruth Anne Robbins, *Fiction 101: A Primer for Lawyers on How to Use Fiction Writing Techniques to Write Persuasive Fact Sections*, 32 Rutgers L. Rev. 459, 465 (2001).

Unless a fact is included in the statement of facts, it should not be used in the argument. One reason for the requirement of a statement of facts is to provide the appellate court with an objective account of what occurred before the twist of advocacy is added to the cold facts. Thus, ways must be found to weave together both facts that are obviously important and those that merely lend an aura of credibility or provide a human interest factor to keep the judges reading.

The reverse side of this rule is that if opposing counsel has, will, or should rely on a fact for argument, that fact should be covered as well. Including adverse facts fosters a sense of trustworthiness. At the same time it enables the advocate to blunt any negative impact. Do not fear that appellate judges will kill the messenger. They are much more likely to chastise the advocate who withholds the bad news about a case than they are to criticize the lawyer who faces the adverse facts squarely and attempts to place them in perspective.

Do not use opposing counsel's brief as the gauge of what is a significant fact in either the positive or the negative sense. Dangerous as it is to do, opposing counsel may ignore potentially adverse facts in the idle hope that they will be overlooked or disappear. It is equally common that opposing counsel fails to notice factual points that are helpful to that side of the case. In writing a statement of facts, counsel's job is to make an independent judgment about whether each fact is important or not.

There is yet another reason to be objective and fair. Part of a law clerk's unarticulated job description is to find critical facts and case authorities that the lawyers have not addressed. Doing so proves to the judge the law clerk's worth. Thus, when in doubt as to whether a fact is important, include it.

Number Two: Write the statement to reflect the orderly process of litigation. Tell the underlying story from the initial pleading to verdict.

The statement should be written to reflect both the orderly progress of litigation from the initial pleading to verdict and the need to tell the underlying story. What happened before trial, during trial, and on post-trial motions should be handled in that order. Within that framework, the events should be described chronologically. Thus, if there was a hearing on a motion to dismiss followed by a hearing on a motion for summary judgment two weeks later, those events should be handled in the order in which they took place in the district court.

By contrast, the evidence from a testimonial hearing should never be organized witness by witness or exhibit by exhibit. That approach is repetitive when more than one witness observed the same fact, of almost no use to the appellate court, and simply boring. Instead, the event that produced the litigation should be described chronologically from beginning to end, regardless of the order in which the evidence about it was presented at the hearing. Framed another way, the writer should present the historical facts as if a camera had begun to film them at the first operative point and had continued to run until the last event concluded. A statement of facts concerning a contract dispute, for example, should begin with the circumstances that led up to reaching an agreement, followed by a description of the how and when the contact was signed, and then explain how the breach occurred and what damage resulted.

Often this chronological account can be accomplished best by organizing the evidence around one or two witnesses who have the broadest knowledge of the event being litigated. The identity of these principal storytellers often surfaces during the initial broad-brush reading of the transcripts. Corroborating evidence or witnesses can be woven into the principal storytellers' account to keep the chronology moving forward in time. A witness who testified the first day of trial can be linked efficiently to a corroborating document that was admitted at the end of trial this way: "Corroborated by his telephone records and flight coupons, the informant testified that he called the defendant on January 1 just before the informant boarded a Delta Airlines flight to New York."

A word of caution is in order. Care should be taken to avoid resting too heavily on any one witness or exhibit. Too much reliance on an isolated portion of the evidence may set the case up to fail on a harmless error analysis. Whenever possible, make clear that critical points find factual support in more than one source in the trial record.

Within the chronological framework, certain procedural issues, such as objections, sidebar conferences, and rulings must also be covered in a statement of facts. Unless it is obviously awkward to do so, these procedural events should be addressed at the same point in the historical story where the fact that was the subject of the contested ruling appears. An example is: "When the informant began to describe his January 2, 1989 telephone conversation with the undercover agent, a sidebar conference was held on a hearsay objection." In dealing with a ruling that is contested on appeal it is critical to point out whether an objection was made or not and what legal theories were advanced.

This enables the appellate court to anticipate a procedural argument that may preclude considering the issue on appeal. Once the nature of the objections and ruling are covered, the writer can return to the historical story.

> *Number Three:* Support every sentence in a statement of facts by reference to the pages in the record where those facts appear.

This enables the appellate judges to focus directly on the disputed portions of the transcripts. Even the most experienced advocates cannot always anticipate accurately what fact an appellate judge will find to be critical. Rather than take chances, it is best to cover all bases with record citations.

Someone other than the writer should check the final draft of the statement of facts against the record. This means that every record reference at the end of each sentence should be verified against the transcripts and appendix to make certain that the cited pages say what the writer says they do. Numbers can become transposed in typing and render the record citation useless to a judge attempting to find that portion of the record. Moreover, different eyes can read the same passage different ways. This system of double-checking the record gives both inaccuracies and variations in interpretation a chance to be resolved before opposing counsel exposes them to anyone's embarrassment.

A record cite-check also provides a safety net against panic at oral argument. In framing questions, some judges paraphrase, or even quote verbatim, the parties' briefs. The advocate who has verified the statement of facts can be confident that the point that has caught the judge's attention is factually accurate. Rather than be diverted by the fear of being proven wrong, the advocate can concentrate on the legal significance the judge attaches to that point.

> *Number Four:* End the statement of facts with a bang, not a whimper.

In most cases, this means concluding with the verdict or the final order. Thus, the reader knows that the story has ended and the task of analyzing it under legal principles can begin.

§ 12.4 Narrate the Facts Found, Not the Evidence Present

I repeat for emphasis that what counts are the facts found by the factfinder. When a jury determines the facts, the appellate court is required to assume that the jurors accepted the evidence presented by the verdict winner. Too often appellants attempt to argue their evidence unsuccessfully presented to the jury. I do not exaggerate to say that during every court sitting in which I have participated since 1968, there is a least one case where an attorney has done this. Successful appellate lawyers do not.

The biggest offenders in this respect often are extremely effective trial lawyers. They are very successful before a jury, but when they appear before an appellate bench they conduct themselves as if they are still addressing the lay factfinders. Summarizing the facts in an appellate brief is not a summation to a trial jury. In both briefs and oral arguments, these lawyers set forth the evidence they presented at trial and not the facts found by the jury. Think about three baseball umpires arguing about calling balls and strikes. The first umpire says, "I call 'em as I see 'em." The second disagrees, "I call 'em as they are." The third clarifies, "Ball or strike . . . they ain't nothin' till I call 'em." *Your evidence at trial ain't facts until the jury calls 'em.*

The purpose of a brief, as I have emphasized continually, is to persuade the court to your point of view. When you open your brief with a narrative of facts that picks and chooses those items of evidence favorable to your case at trial but ultimately rejected by the factfinder, you immediately lose substantial credibility. Selecting only the bits and pieces of evidence favorable to your client will not go undetected. Appellate judges read trial court opinions and appellees' briefs. They soon get the complete picture. Judges may still respect and admire a lawyer with whom they disagree in interpreting the law, but the same measure of regard does not extend to the lawyer who misrepresents the facts.

Consider again the procedures judges use to study briefs. I first read the appellant's statement of issues. I then look to the opinion of the trial court and carefully examine the statement of facts in that opinion and turn to that court's discussion of those issues presented in the appeal. It is here that I get the "flavor" of the case. Thus, before reading the appellant's statement of facts, I already have examined the trial court's account. I then read the appellant's statement of facts and then the appellee's statement.

You start off on the wrong foot when you steal the facts. It may sound harsh, but "stealing the facts" is exactly what you are doing when you try to pass off carefully selected bits of evidence as the facts found by the factfinder. Judges need to see the picture with all its blemishes and imperfections; they do not want a retouched photograph.

Reading a skewed statement of facts quickly disillusions the brief reader. It is bad enough when this occurs later in the brief-reading process, but when it occurs at the onset, you lose a serious initial impetus, one which you will never regain. You have destroyed the reader's initial neutral attitude, replacing it with a "What's-this-lawyer-trying-to-pull-off-here?" state of mind. As set forth in chapter 1, the appellant always has an uphill battle; mathematically, the odds of succeeding are against you. Do not increase these odds by creating the impression that you have misrepresented the facts.

In many cases, however, the questions at issue require a detailed statement of the actual evidence that was presented. This is particularly true in appeals from the grant of summary judgment, from directed verdicts, from judgments as a matter of law or notwithstanding the verdict (j.n.o.v.) and in challenges to jury instructions. Here, the reviewing court will measure the quantum of evidence against the controlling legal precept in the same manner as did the trial court.

§12.4.1 Summary Judgment

Since the U.S. Supreme Court's important 1986 trilogy of cases,[8] summary judgment has become an important part of modern litigation. Under Fed. R. Civ. P. 56, a party seeking to recover upon a claim, counterclaim, or cross-claim may move for summary judgment in the party's favor upon the entire case or any part thereof. The general practice is for the moving party to augment the motion with factual support contained in affidavits, depositions, or answers to interrogatories. Once the movant's papers are served, the adverse party must respond with specific facts showing that there is a genuine issue as to any material fact.

Success in an appeal from summary judgment depends, of course, on the existence of a genuine issue of material fact—not just any fact, but a material fact, and not just any dispute, but one based on evidence sufficient to pass a minimum threshold. Accordingly, on an appeal from an adverse summary judgment, the statement of facts is crucial. Your appeal stands or falls in these few pages. Two critical requirements must be met:

1. MATERIAL FACTS. The evidence must show a dispute about facts that are material, that is, essential to the adjudication. The evidence, if believed, must be substantial enough to justify a jury in

---

8. *Celotex Corp. v. Catrett*, 477 U.S. 317 (1986); *Anderson v. Liberty Lobby, Inc.*, 477 U.S. 242 (1986); *Matsushita Elec. Indus. Co., Ltd. v. Zenith Radio Corp.*, 475 U.S. 574 (1986).

returning a verdict for the nonmoving party. Peripheral and incidental evidentiary data do not rise to the level of material facts.

2. APPENDIX OR EXCERPT OF RECORD. In addition to indicating in your statement of facts where the evidence appears, be sure to include copies of relevant documents in your appendix or excerpt of record filed in the appellate court. Do not rest on your pleadings.

§ 12.4.2 Sufficiency of the Evidence

Sufficiency of the evidence often serves as a major point on appeal. We see it on the civil side after the plaintiff's suit is dismissed by the granting of a motion for failure to state a claim (at common law, a "demurrer"), by directed verdict, by j.n.o.v. and where a defendant is held not to have proved an affirmative defense. In criminal appeals, the defendant often argues that the government did not present sufficient evidence to prove the elements of the crime beyond a reasonable doubt.

In these cases, you must set forth evidence in your statement of facts. Do not pick and choose the goodies that you present. Save yourself and the court valuable time by describing the evidence in the light of the verdict winner. When I am confronted with a sufficiency issue, I immediately read the appellee's statement of facts before trudging through the appellant's account.

At oral argument of these points, I typically tell appellant's counsel, "Give me the worst-case fact scenario against you. We might as well know it now before your friend gets up to speak." My advice to brief writers on issues questioning the sufficiency of evidence is: *write in terms of the worst-case scenario—remember that the judges will be reading your opponent's statement of facts too.* In so doing you will immediately win points with the court. You will generate an initial positive impression by not filching the facts.

Unfortunately, many lawyers simply gamble. They are willing to take the chance that their factual presentation will sneak past a judge on appeal because of forensic fatigue or some other lapse of standards. But do not bet on it. Appeals are heard by more than one judge. You may get a fastball high and on the inside corner past one judge, but the odds are that you will not get it past the others.

The bottom line. When composing a statement of facts in a sufficiency-of-the-evidence appeal, remember that the facts are always construed in light of the verdict winner. Do not waste your time on a throw-away issue. Lapse of persuasiveness (and credibility) here dilutes the possible effectiveness of other, more convincing, arguments. If your sufficiency of the evidence argument will not survive in light of the worst case scenario, drop it and play your next highest card.

§ 12.4.3 Facts as Predicate for Jury Instructions

Often your major issue on appeal is that the trial court improperly instructed the jury on a point or that it improperly rejected your suggested point for charge. Because this presents a mixed question of law and fact, your statement of facts must set forth the precise evidence of record which, if believed by the jury, would support the requested instruction. Narrate the facts carefully in your statement. Set forth a sufficient factual predicate, but do not clutter.

A jury instruction is a statement in lay terms of a rule of law. According to Roscoe Pound, legal rules are "precepts attaching a definite, detailed legal consequence to a definite, detailed state of facts."[9] Accordingly, the trial judge charges: "Members of the jury, if you find fact A, then you must reach conclusion B." In stating facts in your brief, all that must be shown is that evidence supporting fact A was in the record.

Here, the statement of facts must reflect quality, not quantity. Help the appellate judge reach your way of thinking by making the narrative of facts resemble as closely as possible the material facts set forth in the legal precedent upon which you hinge your assertion that the trial court erred in instructing the jury. You do not help the appellate court, or yourself, if the judge has to struggle through a thicket of extraneous narrative before finally discovering the relevant factual nuggets.

§ 12.5 When the Narrative Should Cite to the Record

Appellate judges appear to be divided as to whether each fact contained in the narrative should be supported with a reference to the transcript, appendix, excerpt of record, or legal file. Former Missouri Chief Justice Charles B. Blackmar states: "You must make reference to the transcript, the legal file, or the record, for every assertion in the statement of facts." My own preference is for selectivity. The best approach is that when you are in doubt, cite.

I prefer a minimum of clutter, which permits smooth reading without a series of literary hiccups. Even in the most fiercely contested trial, a large body of facts is not disputed. Record references should not

---

9. *Pound, supra* note 3, at 482

be necessary to support these, but are always necessary where the facts are controverted. If the appellant misrepresents, then the appellee can make the counterstatement with proper references to the record. If the appellee has been the culprit, the appellant can cite to the references in the reply brief.

The record references in the following excerpt would not be necessary if the facts were not controverted:

> Donald Driver was operating his Dodge Dart in a northerly direction on State Street, App. at 12, and Len Lazy was proceeding southerly, App. at 13, when Peter Pedestrian, the plaintiff below, was walking across the street from east to west, App. at 14.

In discussing this practice with my law clerks over the years, most have disagreed with my preference for selective record citations. They do the cite-checks in my chambers, and, as a result they generally have been less charitable with brief writers than I: "Too many lawyers lie. When I go to the record, it doesn't support what they say. They're always paraphrasing what the witness said or the document revealed." Indeed, this subject has provoked spirited discussions of ethics in my chambers. The clerks say that they have heard that in certain law offices it is proper advocacy to put a special, if not questionable, gloss on what was said in the record.

Philadelphia attorney James Crawford instructs his junior lawyers: "Every fact should have support in the record, and every important fact should be accompanied by a record citation. Moreover, that record citation should fully support the statement for which it is cited." As we have seen, McGaughey agrees completely.

The bottom line. Play it safe. In your first draft of the statement of facts include a record reference. Later, as you build your argument, return to the narrative and decide if it is necessary to keep all references. Furnish *each* appellate judge with an appendix or excerpt of record that contains the referenced record. It is not enough to supply the clerk of the court with a record. A reference to a record on file in the clerk's office in Philadelphia—3,000 miles away—does not help me in Santa Barbara, where I am working on the case.

§ 12.6   The Polestar is Accuracy

The principal directive in narrating the facts is accuracy. Be honest. Do not steal the facts. Judges have been criticized for misstating the facts in an opinion. A report of the American Bar Association warned that "[e]xtreme care must always be taken to assure a fair and impartial statement. This is particularly true with respect to the facts favorable to the side which is going to lose on the appeal. It has been said that a lawyer may forgive a judge for mistaking the law. But, not so if his facts are taken away from him."[10]

San Francisco lawyer Moses Lasky, obviously burned in a case, makes a melancholy observation of judges that also can be directed to lawyers:

> An opinion writer is entitled to the greatest leeway in his law as in his reasoning, for they are his. But honesty allows no leeway in his statement of the facts, for they are not his. There is no substitute whatever for adherence to the exact and precise record in the case. No "result-orientation" can justify omission of a single relevant fact or the inclusion of a single factual statement that is false. This should go without saying. Unfortunately it needs saying.[11]

Judges who encounter such conduct in lawyers react with the same disdain. They may well forgive a lawyer for reading a putative precedent differently than they do, but they find it difficult to forgive a misstatement of fact. Indeed, a lawyer may gain sympathy in misconstruing a point of law but be written off as untrustworthy in misstating the facts.

§ 12.7 Examples of Statements of Facts: *See* Appendix C

§ 12.8 Materiality

To determine what facts are or are not material, the brief writer has two initial chores:

1. To acquire a complete understanding of the case you are presenting as putative precedent, e.g., one whose facts are identical or similar, and of the case from which you seek to draw an analogy—one whose facts demonstrate a high degree of resemblances.

---

10. American Bar Association, Section of Judicial Administration, *Committee Report: Internal Operating Procedures of Appellate Courts* 31, reprinted in B. Witkin, Manual on Appellate Court Opinions 102 (1977).

11. Moses Lasky, *A Return to the Observatory Below the Bench*, 19 Sw. L.J. 679, 689 (1965).

2. To learn something about the jurisprudential idiosyncracies of the judges before whom you are appearing. What
   types of facts have they deemed material in the past?

The brief writer must then recall the analytical process of determining what facts are material from § 8.3: (1) establish the holding
of your chosen case to understand the legal consequences attached
to the specific set of facts; (2) exclude any dictum from the decision;
and (3) determine whether the holding is a binding precedent for a
succeeding case containing prima facie similar facts. Remember that
this last step involves a double analysis of stating the material facts
in the putative precedent and then attempting to find those which are
material in the compared case.

When it comes to material facts, what is one person's meat is another
person's poison. To assist in selecting them for your brief, you should
consider the interrelationship between two terms that sound alike, but
whose meanings diverge in the decisional process: "reasonable" and
"reasoning."

A judge's decision on the choice, interpretation, and application of
a legal precept may involve a value judgment justifiable in his or her
mind because the decision is "reasonable," in the sense that it is fair,
just, sound, and sensible. One judge may believe that it is "reasonable"
to maintain the law in harmony with existing circumstances and precedents and may accede to the magnetic appeal of consistency; another
may assert that the issue should be considered pragmatically and
respond only to its practical consequences.

What is "reasonable" in given circumstances gives rise to endless
differences of opinion. This is as it should be. The inevitably varying
views found in multijudge courts is one of the most vital traditions in
the growth of the common law. So is the balance between respect for
and ongoing reexamination of precedents. We are all influenced by the
traditional Holmes-Pound-Cardozo philosophy, which tells us that the
great aim of the law is to improve the welfare of society. We seek to
achieve this aim by reaching decisions that are "reasonable."

Determining what is "reasonable," however, is closely related to the
overarching process we call "reasoning," with which we solve a problem
by pondering a given set of facts to discover their relationship and so
reach a logical conclusion. The application of "reasonableness" to "reasoning" is an ever-recurring scenario: if A has been found to be liable in
set of circumstances B, judges have to decide—often without an exact
precedent to guide them—whether A is liable also if B occurs, plus or

minus circumstance C. To do this, judges must determine which facts are material. Given the situation that A is liable if set of circumstances B applies, the judge must decide whether the addition or deletion of circumstance C is material or immaterial.

Two famous cases dramatically illustrate this. In *Rylands v. Fletcher*,[12] the defendant employed an independent contractor to make a reservoir on his land. Because of the contractor's negligence in failing to fill up some unused mine shafts, water escaped and flooded the plaintiff's mine. The case could have been decided solely on the basis of the contractor's negligence, but the court chose to decide it on the basis of strict liability; it determined that the negligence of the contractor was immaterial, and held for the landowner. Compare the actual facts of the case with the facts deemed material by the court:

Actual Facts

- D had a reservoir built on his land.

- The contractor was negligent. (This constitutes additional circumstance C.)

- Water escaped.

- P was injured.

CONCLUSION: D is liable to P.

———

Material Facts as Seen by the Court

- D had a reservoir built on his land.

- Water escaped.

- P was injured.

CONCLUSION: D is liable to P.

---

12. Moses Lasky, *A Return to the Observatory Below the Bench*, 19 Sw. L.J. 679, 689 (1965).

Thus, by the determination that circumstance *C* was immaterial, the doctrine of absolute liability was established in 1868. It is still alive and kicking today.

In *Brown v. Board of Education*,[13] the Court addressed circumstance *A*—African-American children in segregated schools. It decided, under the doctrine of "separate but equal," that no African-American school could be considered "equal." In *Mayor of Baltimore v. Dawson*,[14] the Court again confronted a segregation issue—this time, minus circumstance *A* (that is, minus the context of segregated schools). The Court affirmed the Fourth Circuit's ruling that the *Brown* decision would nevertheless apply to end segregation in public beaches and bathhouses. Segregation minus circumstance A led to the same result in *Holmes v. Atlanta*[15] (municipal golf course) and *Gayle v. Browder*[16] (buses). When *Browder* came down, it was recognized that, as a matter of law, the entire doctrine of separate but equal was overruled without being limited to the reasons stated in *Brown*: the special and particular problems of segregated education. Rapidly changing social and judicial perspectives had rendered that circumstance immaterial.

The bottom line. To determine what facts are or are not material depends on many factors. At one end of a scale of difficulty are the slam dunk cases where the controlling case is a precedent *fortissimo* —the facts and the law are equally clear. At the other end are cases where no strong case stands out; what you have at best is a precedent *pianissimo*—a case that is going to require a real selling job on your part to convince the court what facts are or are not material. In still another situation, where there is no case, weak or strong, to guide you, you must depend on the rule of analogy, where you rely only on examining the factual resemblances and differences in the compared cases.[17]

§ 12.9 Summary

Take the time and do it well. Writing the statement of facts is always a challenge, because the narrative must be scrupulously accurate and free from argumentativeness, and yet—and this is a big "yet"—convey a clear impression that the brief writer's client deserves to win on appeal.

---

13. 347 U.S. 483 (1954).

14. 350 U.S. 877 (1955).

15. 350 U.S. 879 (1955).

16. 352 U.S. 903 (1956).

17. For a more detailed discussion of material facts and analogies, *see* Ruggero J. Aldisert, *Logic for Lawyers: A Guide to Clear Legal Thinking* 229–35 (3d ed. 1997).

The narrative often forms, in large part, the appellate court's first impression of your client's cause. It is usually a lasting one. If you handle this job well, you give your entire case the high gloss that marks a professional. Conversely, stealing the facts and obscuring the issues, intentionally or through simple neglect, diminishes both the court's confidence in counsel and sympathy for his or her client.

Chapter 13

THE BRIEF: SUMMARY OF THE ARGUMENT

§ 13.1 Overview

In 1994, the Federal Rules of Appellate Procedure were amended to make mandatory what theretofore had been only a suggestion. The new amendment at Rule 28(a)(8) now provides that briefs of the appellant and appellee must contain:

> a summary of the argument, which must contain a succinct, clear, and accurate statement of the arguments made in the body of the brief, and which must not merely repeat the argument headings.

In earlier editions I referred to old Rule 28(a)(5) and commented: "Although this language is permissive, the good brief writer will consider it mandatory." I cannot overemphasize that every appellate brief should contain a summary of the argument even if your specific state rules may not require it. In many ways, the summary of the argument is the most important part of the brief.

To understand my strident recommendation, you must recall the manner in which appellate judges study briefs. They generally read the appellants' statement of issues first. If the trial court has written an opinion, they then read the court's treatment of those issues. The next step, which is crucial, is to turn to the appellant's summary of the argument—if there is one—and then to the appellee's summary. This provides the "flavor" of the case.

The summary is critical because it gives the reader a concise preview of the argument. The summary should be crafted so as to allow the judge to construct a practical outline of a memorandum. Alas, this often does not occur, because the brief writer either has not prepared a summary or has slapped one together without the thought necessary to create a statement that is both comprehensive and concise.

Preparing an effective summary may be the brief writer's most challenging and most important task. Former Mississippi Supreme Court Justice James L. Robertson remarks:

> I think the most important part of the brief is the Summary of the Argument. I invariably read it first. It is almost like the opening statement in a trial. From clear and plausible argument summary, I often get an inclination to affirm or

reverse that rises almost to the dignity of a (psychologically) rebuttable presumption.

I do not mean to denigrate the importance of a fully developed and technically sound argument. But I read the subsequent argument in a "show me" frame of mind, testing whether it confirms my impression from the summary of the argument.[1]

Loyola Law School Dean David W. Burcham, one of my former clerks who went on to clerk for Justice Byron White, and to practice law with a large Los Angeles firm before donning academic robes, offers these comments: "A brief writer should understand that the summary of argument will likely create the first, and perhaps last, impression of the Court toward the legal merits of the client's case. It should be the structural centerpiece of the entire brief."

§ 13.2   The Critical Opening Paragraph

Readers of appellate briefs tend to be very busy. As a result, they have highly selective reading habits. They need and expect to know what a given case is about, and the opening of the summary of argument should tell them immediately. Detective mysteries and narratives with O. Henry-style surprise endings have their place—in fiction. But apply these techniques to brief writing and you risk losing your audience. In reading a summary, judges are impatient. They want to know up front what the case is about. They do not want to wait until the end. With the number of appeals constantly increasing, it is important that the brief writer give an early signal to the reader. That signal is the opening or orientation paragraph of the summary of the argument.

The introduction of your summary—the *exordium* in the schema of the rhetoricians—must let the reader know, in a few sentences, the scope, theme, content, and outcome of the brief. It sets the stage for the discussion to follow. It dispatches your argument to the reader at once in succinct, concise, and minimal terms. It describes the equitable heart of the appeal.

The critical portion of your summary is the orientation sentence or sentences that announce the theme of your argument. To craft the theme or focus of your argument takes skill and concentration. It is the *first* thing you write and the *last* thing you rewrite. It is the dominant argument of maximum potency that must be compatible with ruling

---

1. James L. Robertson, *From the Bench: Reality on Appeal*, 17 LITIG. 3, 5 (1990).

case law or consistent with known policy considerations of the judicial tribunal before which you appear. The theme should be all-inclusive and subsume the various points to be discussed in the brief. It should be aphoristic, in the sense of being a short, pithy, pointed sentence containing some important legal precept, one that Cardozo, in a related context, described as "a brief and almost sententious statement at the outset of the problem to be attacked."[2] If you are proceeding on alternative theories, you necessarily will have multiple themes.

Justice William A. Bablitch of the Wisconsin Supreme Court reminded us that, as a basic principle of good writing, "a reader should not be forced to confront details before the writer has provided a framework for understanding."[3] Thus, the introductory paragraph must alert the reader to the upcoming issues, their importance and any conclusions to be drawn.[4] You may have the opportunity to write an effective introductory paragraph in other parts of your brief, depending on the court's rules, but it is essential that you prepare one as the introduction to your argument summary and repeat it in your first point of the argument. Justice Bablitch aptly observes:

> It is not easy to write a good introductory paragraph. It takes great effort, but it is time well spent. A properly written introduction makes the rest of the brief-writing task comparatively easy. If you are unable to write a cogent, succinct, encompassing introduction, you probably do not have a solid grasp of the subject matter.
>
> The fundamental question is, "What does the reader need to know to decide the final resolution?" If the introduction offers context before detail, then the reader is able to discern the important from the unimportant.[5]

Appellate lawyers are professional writers. Whether they write well or poorly, they write for a very discriminating audience, an audience of professional readers of legal text. By force of circumstance, everything the brief writer does must be expressed in words, preferably with a high degree of clarity and precision. Other writers may have the assistance of elegant typography and graphic illustration. The appellate lawyer is armed only with the pen.

---

2. Benjamin N. Cardozo, *Law and Literature*, 14 Yale L.J. 705 (1925), reprinted in Selected Writings of Benjamin Nathan Cardozo 339, 352–53 (M. Hall ed. 1967).

3. William A Bablitch, *Writing to Win*, Compleat Law, Winter 1988, at 11.

4. *Id.*

5. *Id.*

Judges crave an immediate sense of overview. At the beginning of a brief, they are not interested in hearing all the details of the case. They want to know what kind of case this is and what issues the brief addresses. Only then are they prepared to digest, in Cardozo's words, "a fuller statement of the facts, rigidly pared down, however, in almost every case, to those that are truly essential as opposed to those that are decorative and adventitious. If these are presented with due proportion and selection, our conclusion ought to follow so naturally and inevitably as almost to prove itself."[6]

If you have trouble expressing the theme of the brief in the introductory pages of your summary of argument, look to West Publishing Company's headnote writers for guidance. These people are highly professional; they are trained to describe an issue as comprehensively as possible, with minimal wordage. If you still have trouble, look to the *exordium* or introductory paragraph of judicial opinions written by those judges who spend much care in fashioning the opening.[7] A sampling of some excellent opening sentences from United States Supreme Court justices in volume 484 of United States Reports in 1987 discloses how one can combine tight writing with excellent orientation.

---

6. Benjamin N. Cardozo, *supra* note 2, at 352–53; *see also*, Frank Coffin, *The Ways of a Judge* 159 (1980) (explaining how the first words of an opinion slowly emerge on the blank sheet of paper).

7. For examples of good openings in judicial opinions *see* Ruggero J. Aldisert, *Opinion Writing* 77–79 (1990).

Justice Marshall

In this case, we must decide whether § 505(a) of the Clean Water Act, also known as the Federal Water Pollution Control Act, 33 U.S.C. § 1365, confers federal jurisdiction over citizen suits for wholly past violations.

Justice Brennan

The question to be decided in this case is whether a federal court has authority to review a decision of the National Labor Relations Board's General Counsel dismissing an unfair labor practice complaint pursuant to an informal settlement in which the charging party refused to join.

Justice O'Connor

This case requires us to decide whether a state-court judge has absolute immunity from a suit for damages under 42 U.S.C. § 1983 for his decision to dismiss a subordinate court employee.

Justice Stevens

As a sanction for failing to identify a defense witness in response to a pretrial discovery request, an Illinois trial judge refused to allow the undisclosed witness to testify. The question presented is whether that refusal violated the petitioner's constitutional right to obtain the testimony of favorable witnesses.

Justice Blackmun

Respondent Thomas M. Egan lost his laborer's job at the Trident Naval Refit Facility in Bremerton, Wash., when he was denied a required security clearance. The narrow question presented by this case is whether the Merit Systems Protection Board (Board) has authority by statute to review the substance of the underlying decision to deny or revoke a security clearance in the course of reviewing an adverse action.

Justice Scalia   This case requires us to determine whether either the Confrontation Clause of the Sixth Amendment or Rule 802 of the Federal Rules of Evidence bars testimony concerning a prior, out-of-court identification when the identifying witness is unable, because of memory loss, to explain the basis for the identification.

I freely concede that because Supreme Court justices take only limited questions on certiorari (or petitions for review in the state systems), it is easier for them to fashion an opening in one or two sentences than it is for a lawyer writing a brief that raises more than one question. But remember that the theme or jugular issue in a brief may center on a single question of law. In expressing that point, you would do well to emulate the crisp, focused technique employed by judges and justices.

§ 13.3   Examples of Good Openings

The following are good examples of the opening sentence or paragraph to the summary of argument:

Single issues

The question for decision in this appeal is clear cut and straightforward: Does the president have the power to remove a United States Marshal from office? We say that he has that power.

———————

The district court erred when it used its contempt power to compel Attorney Matthew P. Boylan and his firm to assume representation of the defendant fifteen months into an ongoing, massive, twenty-one-defendant criminal case.

Multiple Issues

For the reasons that follow, Appellant is requesting this court to reverse his conviction under the federal extortion statute, 18 U.S.C. § 876. He contends that the statute is unconstitutional because it is overbroad and vague. Should the court reject this challenge, Appellant asks that the court vacate the judgment and order a new trial because the government, during its cross-examination of him, referred to statements made by appellant in a magistrate's pretrial inquiry regarding his eligibility for appointed counsel, and that this reference violated appellant's rights protected under the Fifth and Sixth amendments.

This appeal requests this court to hold that the district court erred in injecting a notice requirement into the doctrine of constructive discharge under Title VII of the Civil Rights Act of 1964, 42 U.S.C. §§ 2000a-2000h. Subsumed in this problem are two somewhat related but distinct subordinate inquiries: whether the existence of notice *vel non* is a question of fact, and if so, was the court clearly erroneous in finding no notice (a) on the basis of imputed notice to the employer based on actions of and notice to supervisory employees or agents of the employer, or (b) on the basis of inferred notice to the employer given the small size of the business enterprise and repeated unsuccessful attempts by the employee to reach the employer to complain about acts of gender discrimination.

§ 13.4 The Summary of Summaries

The summary of argument should be a terse synopsis of the argument rather than a verbatim repetition of the statement of issues. United States Supreme Court Rule 24(f) likewise provides that all briefs on the merits must contain "[a] summary of the argument, suitably paragraphed, which should be a succinct, but accurate and clear, condensation of the argument actually made in the body of the brief." This rule cautions that "a mere repetition of the headings under which the argument is arranged is not sufficient." Fed. R. App. P. 28(a)(8) now tracks this language.

Philadelphia attorney James Crawford similarly advises: "In your summary of argument, do not merely restate your questions presented or headings. The summary should be a neat balance between the absolute condensation of the questions and headings and the extensive discussion contained in the argument itself."

If a judge has not read the entire brief prior to oral argument or has read it well in advance of argument, the summary of argument can serve as a valuable substitute or refresher which the judge can glance at prior to the hearing. Many advocates firmly believe, therefore, that the summary of argument is one of the most important sections of the brief, recapitulating the central issues in the case. But beware: most of these summaries are too long. Judge Leonard I. Garth of the Third Circuit recommends to his students that no summary should exceed one-and-a-half pages.

§ 13.5 More Examples of Summaries of Arguments: *See* Appendix *D*

Chapter 14

THE BRIEF: STATE YOUR THEME

§ 14.1   Overview

It is now time to start writing your argument. What is the first thing you do? That is easy: *carve out adequate time in your schedule*. Ideas need time to percolate. Crucial cases get overruled or reversed during the briefing process. Colleagues offer vital help and then get pulled away on another matter. Illness or emergency invades your schedule. Modern technical miracles fail as deadlines approach. If you arrange to have your brief ready for filing a week, or at least two to three days early, none of these events need concern you.

§ 14.2   Finding Your Theme

When a lawyer discusses a case informally with another lawyer, like standing at a bar having a drink with a friend, he or she usually can encapsulate the issue in a few sentences: "This case I had this week . . . The jury came in against me, but I think a have a good issue on appeal. The trial judge allowed this garage mechanic to testify as an expert witness and he challenged the design of a new gear box on a $100,000 BMW. I got socked to the tune of a million bucks!"

In those few sentences, the lawyer described the theme of the appeal: the trial court abused its discretion in allowing the testimony of an unqualified expert. That is it. Everything to be said in the appellate brief should relate to this theme and should not be hidden in fifty pages or fourteen thousand words analyzing six different and cluttered issues.

"Most cases can be woven into a simple and consistent theme," writes Loyola Law School Professor Henry Deeb Gabriel, a long-time appellate litigator for the United States Department of Justice.[1] I completely agree. He says that the theme usually derives from a simple point: "You should take the opportunity to go beyond the technical, legal points of your case and give the court a common sense, simple reason why all the technical stuff in your brief makes sense. Also remember that the only major concept or theme from your oral argument will likely be retained by the writing judge when she sits down and starts to draft the opinion. This theme, if possible, should be grounded in broad equitable reasons."[2]

---

1. Henry D. Gabriel, *Preparation and Delivery or Oral Argument in Appellate Courts,* 22 Am. J. Trial Advoc. 571, 583 (1999).

2. *Id.* at 584.

§ 14.3   Crafting Your Theme for an Appellate Forum

You already know how to write your first sentence. You wrote it as the orientation paragraph (the *exordium*) in your argument summary. Repeat it here. It is your strongest point. *Your strongest point is that argument, objectively considered, based on precedent and previously stated policy concerns of the court, most calculated to persuade the court to your point of view.* You want to hit the judges between the eyes with it. You aim for the best possible initial impression. You do not get a second chance.

The orientation paragraph of your summary of argument should be repeated as the opening of your argument in chief, the topic sentence(s) of the text under your first heading. Recall how your first-year college English composition instructor explained that the topic sentence sets forth a theme. Do the same thing here. The skeletal structure of a good brief may contain three or possibly four points, perhaps some independent of one another; to the extent possible, endeavor to declare and support a unifying theme that will run throughout the brief.

The theme not only sets the flavor of your argument but also sets the mood. It is both the focus and the thesis. It directs the judges' attention immediately to where the trial court's error took place and explains straightaway why the trial court was wrong or, when used by the appellee, why it was right. It tells the appellate court what relief you want.

The best briefs contain a unifying theme or possibly coequal themes that immediately focus the argument: the trial court's findings of fact were clearly erroneous, and this is why; the plaintiff did not meet the burden of proof and here is the controlling law, and this is the critical element not proved; under the circumstances, the trial court's range of discretion was severely restricted as indicated by ruling case law, and here is how there was an improper exercise of that discretion; this is a case where the trial court erred as a matter of law by choosing, from competing legal precepts, the wrong one; the trial court erred in construing the relevant statute; or the trial court erred in applying settled legal precepts to the facts found by the fact-finder.

§ 14.4   Examples of Stated Themes

This case of original impression requires this court to consider the effect of a 1977 proclamation by President Jimmy Carter granting a pardon for violations of the Military Service Act between August 4, 1964 and March 28, 1975. Specifically, the court must decide whether one convicted of violating provisions of the Act is entitled to an expunction of all court records relating to his conviction by virtue of receiving the Presidential pardon. The district court granted the motion to expunge.

The United States appeals and requests the court to reverse the judgment. For the reasons that follow, the government argues that the district court lacked the power to expunge the criminal record on the basis of the pardon. Alternatively, it contends that this particular case is not one warranting expunction.

The appellants are five Philadelphia residents and taxpayers. They are not now, nor will they in the future, be involved in the construction business. They appeal from the district court judgment dismissing, for lack of standing, their claims against the city and its officials. The complaint asserted an equal protection violation resulting from the application of minority business enterprise participation requirements to a city construction project. The question for decision is whether appellants have standing to assert this equal protection claim based on their status as residents and taxpayers. Appellants request that this court reverse the judgment of the district court that denied them standing.

In this appeal from the dismissal by the district court of a civil rights suit brought by a prisoner, the major question for decision by this court is whether a witness who testifies at a preliminary hearing is entitled to absolute immunity from a subsequent civil rights suit for damages based on alleged perjured testimony given at those proceedings. The court must also decide whether the district court properly abstained from adjudicating certain civil rights claims which, in essence, seek to attack the validity of a state court conviction, while an appeal of that conviction remains pending in state court. The appellees respectfully request this court to affirm the judgment of the district court in all respects.

§ 14.5 Criteria of Structure

You can jump quickly into the little boxes in the judges' minds by framing your briefs along certain criteria of structure:

(1) After stating the overarching theme or focus of your brief, proceed into the argument in a highly compartmentalized, issue-by-issue format. This is not the time for cross-pollenization. The statement of your issue is the argument heading as well as the topic sentence of the text. Only matters relevant to that statement and which support that statement should be set forth in the discussion under that heading.

As any formal essay is divided in discrete parts, often you will require subheadings. These subheads are designed to support the point and they, too, should be compartmentalized. Your headings and subheadings must be full enough and clear enough so the court can understand them. If the judges cannot understand your argument, they cannot be persuaded by it. Your headings and subheadings must be convincing enough to make the court want to accept them.

Do not wander, ramble, or digress. Do not get unglued and meander. Think logically and write logically. Make your point and then move to another.

(2) Incorporate the proper standard of review in the topic sentence(s) introducing each point. You have already stated the various standards of review as set forth in chapter 5, Issue Preservation and Standards of Review, with the necessary citations, preferably from the appellate court before whom you now appear. At this point, it is not necessary to repeat the legal authority for the standard. You simply state the standard in a clear declaratory sentence: "The trial court's findings of fact are clearly erroneous in that . . . "; "The trial court erred as a matter of law in awarding summary judgment because . . . "; or "The trial court abused its discretion in . . . "

(3) Identify the precise jurisprudential flashpoint of conflict between the parties—choice of law, or interpretation or application of the precept to facts found by the factfinder. Confine your discussion to this conflict. Do not wander or overwrite.

(4) Decide whether the several issues chosen by you are independent of each other or are interrelated. You must decide whether the major premise of a subsequent issue is dependent upon the conclusion reached in the prior issue. Understand this, so you will not be surprised when a judge recognizes it at oral argument.

(5) If a number of issues are raised in the appeal but only one issue is dispositive, always brief the dispositive issue first. Explain why it is dispositive and why the appellate court need decide only this issue.

(6) Consider the consequences of the rule you are urging upon the court. Be prepared to predict how far the rule will carry in future cases.

(7) Determine whether the rule is consistent with or contradictory to some binding legal precept of your jurisdiction.

(8) Determine whether the conclusion is coherent in the sense of being a sound, sensible, just, and desirable norm for the guidance of affairs.[3]

In implementing these criteria, you must observe the basic canons of inductive and deductive logic in forming the premises of your argument. To conform faithfully to the rules of logic, it is imperative that your analysis be free from formal and material fallacies. I make a passing reference to logical order at this time, and will treat it in summary fashion in chapter 15, The Required Logical Form for Each Issue.

§ 14.6 Standards of Review

Standards of review have already been covered in detail in chapter 5, Issue Preservation and Standards of Review. Keep in mind the different standards of review that apply to appeals where it is alleged that a judge or hearing tribunal (a) made findings of fact which are clearly erroneous, (b) improperly exercised discretion, or (c) committed legal error.

---

3. These final three were promulgated by University of Edinburgh Professor Neil Mac-Cormick. Neil MacCormick, *Legal Reasoning and Legal Theory* 119 (1978).

§ 14.7   The Experts Speak

Judge or Lawyer	*Comment*
Howard J. Bashman, Esq., *Buchanan Ingersoll, Philadelphia, PA*	Appellate judges are incredibly over-worked. They are forced to read approximately one thousand pages of text to prepare for a single day of oral argument. If your brief is unnecessarily long and complicated, it may not get read completely, it may not get read carefully, or worse, it may not be understood. Moreover, most appellate judges are generalists, not specialists. They do not have an expert's understanding of every substantive area of the law. Nor, of course, do appellate law clerks, who usually arrive at that job fresh from law school.

Even the most complex factual and legal concepts can be made easy to understand if presented properly to the reader. My advice is not to avoid complexity; instead, make complicated concepts understandable to someone who may be confronting the matter for the first time.

Before I file an appellate brief that I have drafted, I ask another lawyer in my office who has had no prior involvement in the case to read it over and let me know whether he finds it understandable and persuasive. Unless someone who knows nothing about your case can understand and be persuaded by your appellate brief, the document is worthless.

Judge or Lawyer	*Comment*
Sarah B. Duncan, *Justice, Texas Court of Appeals at San Antonio*	The secret ingredient of a good legal argument is the flow—that is, an argument which proceeds like the current of a stream naturally, uninterrupted, and logically from beginning to end. It is important that the appellate court be swept along by the current; that it understand every logical step along the way and arrive with the litigant at the ultimate point of concluding in the same frame of mind.
Patricia M. Wald, *Chief Judge Emeritus United States Court of Appeals, D.C. Circuit*	Visualize the whole before you begin. What overriding message is the document going to convey? What facts are essential to the argument? How does the argument take off from the facts? How do different arguments blend together? Better still, if it's a brief, visualize the way the judge's opinion should read if it goes your way. (Too many briefs read as if the paralegal summed up all conceivably relevant facts, and then the lawyer took over with the legal arguments, and never the twain doth meet.)

Chapter 15

THE BRIEF: IDENTIFY THE FLASHPOINT OF CONTROVERSY

§ 15.1 Identify the Precise Jurisprudential Conflict

For each point in your argument, identify the precise flashpoint of controversy between the parties. There are three potential conflicts:

1. Where the law and its application alike are plain or, to put it another way, where the rule of law is clear and its application to the facts as found by the factfinder is equally clear.

2. Where the rule of law is clear and the sole question is its application to the facts. In Cardozo's formulation, "[T]he rule of law is certain, and the application alone doubtful."[1]

3. Where neither the rule nor, a fortiori, its application, is clear.

The brief writer should not waste effort or unduly lengthen the brief if the point falls within category 1. One or two sentences with relevant citations should suffice. If the point fits into category 2, do not waste effort on justifying the controlling rule. Concentrate only on the conflict, the application of the rule to the facts. If the point comes within category 3, it is necessary first to identify the flashpoint of the conflict. Here, too, I suggest there are three subcategories:

a. *Finding the law*. Here, you must choose among competing legal precepts to determine which should control. This requires the deepest development in the brief, because after you choose among the competing precepts, you must also interpret that precept.

b. *Interpreting the law*. Here, there is no dispute about which competing precept controls, but only the question of interpreting what has been chosen. This arises most frequently in statutory construction. If the conflict falls within this category, do not discuss choice of other precepts; discuss only interpretation of the law. You then apply the facts to your intrepretation.

c. *Application of the law to the facts*. Here, you need only discuss the application of the precept—as chosen and interpreted—to the facts as found by the factfinder.

---

1. Benjamin N. Cardozo, *The Nature of the Judicial Process* 164 (1921).

§ 15.2 Examples from the Briefs

The Choice: Finding the Law

This appeal requires Pennsylvania to decide the question of whether injury to an allegedly defective product itself is compensable in tort. The majority rule, set forth in *Seeley v. White Motor Co.*, 63 Cal.2d 9, 403 P.2d 145, 45 Cal. Rptr. 17 (1965), seeks to preserve a proper role for the law of warranty by precluding tort liability if a defective product injures only itself, causing economic loss. The decision in *Santor v. A & M Kargheusian, Inc.*, 44 N.J. 52, 207 A.2d 305 (1965), embodies the minority approach. That case held that a manufacturer's duty to make nondefective products encompasses injury to the product itself, whether the defect creates an unreasonable risk of harm. For the reasons that follow we ask this court to adopt the majority rule.

This court must decide whether the captain of a merchant ship violated applicable maritime law when he buried at sea a seaman who died of a heart attack on the return trip of the vessel eight days from its next port-of-call. After seaman James Floyd died, the captain conducted a burial-at-sea ritual. Maria Floyd, the seaman's daughter, for herself, as executrix of her father's estate, and for the next-of-kin, sued the vessel's owner for improperly disposing of her father's body. The district court granted summary judgment in favor of Lykes Bros. Steamship Company. Maria Floyd has appealed. This court should affirm.

Appellant contends that state tort law has established that the spouse or next-of-kin is entitled to possession of a body for the purpose of arranging for final disposition of the remains, *see, e.g., Blanchard v. Brawley*, 75 So. 2d 891, 893 (La. Ct. App.1954), and that violation of the right of possession and burial is an actionable tort. *See, e.g., Papieves v. Lawrence*, 437 Pa. 373, 263 A.2d 118, 120 (1970). She argues that this state law tort precept should be incorporated into general maritime law. She says that currently recognized maritime authority deems burial at sea anachronistic and improper when the next-of-kin are not notified in advance.

We respond that this case is not governed by state tort concepts, but by federal maritime law. Relying on *Brambir v. Cunard White Star, Ltd.*, 37 F. Supp. 906 (S.D.N.Y. 1940), *aff'd mem.*, 119 F.2d 419 (2d Cir. 1941), we ask this court to hold that maritime law does not provide a cause of action for burial at sea.

Interpreting the Law

Appellants are two coal producing companies requesting this court to reverse the grant of summary judgment in favor of the government. This is a case of statutory construction that requires an interpretation of the expression "coal produced by surface mining" under the Surface Mining Control and Reclamation Act, 30 U.S.C. § 1201-1328.

This is not a mere semantic exercise, because upon your decision depends the extent of tonnage upon which a reclamation fee of 35 cents per ton may be levied by the Secretary of the Interior. The government argued, and the district court found, that tonnage of "coal produced" includes the weight of rock, clay, dirt and other debris mined with the "coal" that was delivered by the companies to a coal washing and sizing plant. We borrow from Gertrude Stein's "a rose is a rose is a rose" and argue that coal is coal and it means a mineral that is combustible. Accordingly, we ask this court to conclude that the district court erred in determining that all the material mined by appellants was subject to the reclamation fee, and that under a proper interpretation of the statute, "coal produced" means only the mineral coal and does not include rock, clay, dirt, and other debris that was excavated with the coal.

The major question for decision is one of first impression in the United States Courts of Appeals. This court must decide whether a claim deemed filed in a chapter 11 (reorganization) proceeding remains effective when the debtor converts the chapter 11 case into one under chapter 7 (liquidation). The issue requires that the court construe relevant statutes and the rules of practice and procedure in bankruptcy. The bankruptcy judge, 43 B.R. 937, and, after appeal, the district court, 52 B.R. 960, held that listing the claim on the debtor's schedule, which was filed under chapter 11, did not preserve the claim under chapter 7. We ask this court to reverse.

―――――――

The principal issue presented for decision is whether a private cause of action for damages against corporate directors is to be implied in favor of a corporate stockholder under 18 U.S.C. § 610, a criminal statute prohibiting corporations from making "a contribution or expenditure in connection with any election at which Presidential and Vice Presidential electors . . . are to be voted for." We ask this court to conclude that implication of such a federal cause of action is not suggested by the legislative context of Section 610 or required to accomplish Congress's purposes in enacting the statute. This court should hold, therefore, that it has no occasion to address the questions whether Section 610, properly construed, proscribes the expenditures alleged in this case, or whether the statute is unconstitutional as violative of the First Amendment or of the equal protection component of the Due Process Clause of the Fifth Amendment.

Applying the Law to the Facts

The major question for decision raised by these two appeals from a judgment in favor of plaintiff in a diversity action brought under Pennsylvania law is the extent to which delay damages may be awarded under Rule 238, Pa. R. Civ. P. Here, defendant obtained a directed verdict at the close of the first trial, but, after a retrial was ordered by this court, ultimately lost on the merits. Because defendant lost and because he never made a settlement offer, plaintiff was awarded Rule 238 delay damages totaling $247,500. This award included damages for the time the case was on appeal from the directed verdict, but, because of plaintiff's mathematical miscalculation, did not include damages for the 17 days immediately preceding the final verdict.

The defendant, at No. 82-5711, argues that the delay damages award was excessive. As appellant, the plaintiff below, appeals at No. 82-5836, contends that the delay damages were insufficient and we ask this court to so hold.

This appeal requires the court to decide whether Blue Shield's prepaid dental service program in Pennsylvania violates the antitrust laws. Several Pennsylvania dental associations and individual dentists appeal from a summary judgment dismissing their antitrust and state law claims brought against the Medical Service Association of Pennsylvania, doing business as Pennsylvania Blue Shield. Appellants argue that Blue Shield engaged in a price-fixing conspiracy and a group boycott in violation of § 1 of the Sherman Act, 15 U.S.C. § 1, attempted to monopolize and monopolized in violation of §2 of the Act, 15 U.S.C. § 2, and that the district court abused its discretion in refusing to certify a subclass of cooperating dentists for treble damages purposes. This court should conclude that appellants' contentions are without merit, and affirm the judgment of the district court.

§ 15.3   Determining the Interdependence of Issues

The ideal brief is where two or more of the issues are completely independent of each other. It is ideal because the court may completely reject one issue, but nevertheless rule in your favor on the basis of another. It is ideal because you have alternative, independent reasons supporting your submission.

In other cases, you do not have the luxury of alternative choices. Instead, you have arguments that are dependent upon resolution of preceding ones. Separate and interrelated arguments (issues or points) fit into the category of what logicians describe as a "prosyllogism," whose conclusion is used as the major premise of the following syllogism, or an "episyllogism," which derives its major premise from the conclusion of the preceding syllogism.

I asked a lawyer who was in the process of completing his year of clerkship with another federal circuit judge to give me his "pet peeve" after reading a year of briefs. His response:

> The major flaw I've seen in the briefs submitted to this court is that the writers don't tie the issues together. Frequently, the viability of one discrete issue turns on the merits of another issue. This may require nothing more than an "if the court finds in our favor on this issue, then the remaining two issues are moot; otherwise these remaining issues must be addressed." Often, the relationship among issues

is a positive point that should be explained to the appellate court: if a positive result on Issue A logically necessitates a similar result on Issue B, the advocate should point out this relationship to the appellate court. Any logical paradigm that can make the court's job easier should be highlighted by the advocate.

When the advocate does not point out issue relationships to the court, it may appear that the advocate does not really understand either issue, and has simply flicked an "issue paint brush" against the paper canvas hoping that something sticks. On the other hand, the advocate who can point out the relationship between the issues shows that she truly understands the case and instills confidence in the reader.

The bottom line. If at all possible, have points that independently and alternatively support your position. Where points are interdependent, explain that if the court accepts a preceding one, the subsequent ones must logically follow. Where one point is controlling, explain that the court need not meet the ones that follow.

§ 15.4   Consider the Consequences of Your Analysis

The analysis of the law set forth in your brief does not operate in a vacuum. The immediate objective of an appellate advocate is limited—to persuade the court to accept the conclusion supported by the argument. The means you employ, however, must far transcend your immediate objective. The court has an obligation that goes far beyond *jus personam*, or considering the specific demands of the parties before the court. There must also be *jus rem*, fidelity to what has been decided in the past as a guide to setting the course for the future. The brief writer must realize at the outset that the submission always will be tested by judges in terms of the institutional or precedential consequences of that urged upon the court.

You must remember what your law school professor did to you after you recited the case in your first-year contracts course. The professor worked you over—exposed you in front of all your classmates. The ogre did this by offering a hypothetical in which the facts were changed somewhat (a little or a lot) and inquired whether the added or subtracted facts would make a difference in the result. Many of you breathed the proverbial sigh of relief when you received your J.D. degree and left the Socratic tyranny of the classroom. But I have news for you. The agony continues. Appellate judges pick up where the professors left off. Only this time, if you are not prepared, it is not a question of classroom embarrassment. If you are not prepared, your client loses the case. And if your client loses a substantial number of times, you end up losing the client. Appellate judges follow the Socratic method in evaluating every brief you write and every oral argument you present.

Throughout every consideration of your argument, the judicial analysis takes place in a kind of forensic Einsteinian relativity. The precedential or institutional consequences are always considered. They are considered in all dimensions of your presentation—whether you choose among rival precepts, interpret a precept, or decide to apply a chosen and interpreted precept to the facts.

Judges require lawyers to evaluate resemblances and differences in the fact patterns of the compared cases, and these are constantly tossed about in a sea of analogies. They do this to decide whether the particular rationale supporting your submission can legitimately support the same result in other fact patterns, and if so, why. They do this because judges always must consider the consequences of every decision. Judges constantly inquire whether the lawyer has seriously considered the policy concerns that are necessarily involved in extending or contracting the law in a given field. At work always is the jurisprudential equivalent of Immanuel Kant's categorical imperative: "Act as if the maxim of your action were to become through your will a universal law of nature."[2]

Modern adjudication, however, demands more than strict adherence to the common law tradition. Because of the precise nature of today's litigation, judges must now cautiously and carefully consider —especially in the dynamic fields of criminal law, tort law, and constitutional law—exactly what social, economic, or political consequences will follow from their decision. Consider, for example, the emphasis on drinking and driving, treble damages under RICO and antitrust, employer discrimination, products liability, professional malpractice, or new concepts by which pecuniary loss or punitive damages are allocated. In the allocation of pecuniary loss, the pendulum now swings in favor of the injured and away from traditional property rights. These views, light years away from "lawyer's law" of another era, require judges to consider consequential concerns in varying degrees when evaluating an issue.

---

2. Immanuel Kant, *Groundwork of the Metaphysics of Morals* 89 (Paton trans. 1964).

University of Edinburgh Professor Neil MacCormick has pinpointed the problem:

> We face the question: What, if any, limits can govern the judicial choice of rulings to test, and how, in any event, can judges begin to frame any ruling appropriate to fit the concrete case when so vast a range of possibilities is open?[3]

Lawyers must always recognize that for a judge, in a given case, to choose among possible competing rulings means, among other things, to choose which will best serve to create a model for human conduct in our society. For example, on the one hand, manufacturers should take reasonable care in preparing and packaging consumer goods and should be made liable for damages to anyone injured by their failure in that respect; alternatively, the law does not require them to take such care and does not make them liable for failure to do so. To take that disjunction seriously as posing a real choice in a real society, the judge must then ask what the difference is.

The answer must be that the difference is determined, borrowing from MacCormick, by the three Cs: the different *consequences* that would follow from actually adopting and applying one or the other of these rival suggestions; the requirement that the choice be *consistent* with some valid and binding rule of the system; and the notion that it be *coherent* in the sense that it is a sound and sensible, just or desirable norm for the guidance of appeals.

§ 15.5   Psych Out the Court

No bright-line rules are available to predict how a multijudge court will consider the consequences of your analysis. The process is intrinsically evaluative. You must inquire about the acceptability or unacceptability of consequences, and this requires at a minimum that you have thoroughly researched the jurisprudential idiosyncrasies of the members of the court before whom you are appearing. *Know the court. Know this court. Know the court that will be reading your briefs.* It is not enough that you have a case written by a distinguished judge from another jurisdiction or from another circuit. It is not enough that you have a case written by a long-gone judge of the court.

Find out how the judges react to the controlling general principles involved in your case. Do your homework. Study the court and see what makes it tick. With the availability of Westlaw and Lexis, you can

---

3. Neil MacCormick, *Legal Reasoning and Legal Theory* 119 (1978).

ascertain how individual judges react to definite and particular concepts. Read their opinions with the view of learning something about their societal concerns, political preferences, economic hypotheses, behavioral interests, sociological bias or prejudice and jurisprudential idiosyncracies. (For example, are they slaves to precedent or do they perceive the court as an instrument of social change?)

Study "your" judges from the standpoint of what MacCormick has said about the theory of consequentialist arguments: the reasons given by judges in deciding cases are articulated in terms of arguments "based on the consequences of rival possible rulings about validity or bindingness in certain generic contexts."[4] Ascertain how they evaluate relevant consequences. If you can, learn the extent to which this evaluation depends on stated or implied criteria of "justice" and "common sense" (defined for this purpose as a rough contemporary consensus on social values to which judges conceive themselves as giving effect). If you can, learn also if this process draws upon fundamental assumptions about political philosophy, and of course, in the dynamics of constitutional law, how the process draws upon assumptions about the proper distribution of authority among the various organs of government. Learn what their "underpinning" reasons are.

To comprehend and assimilate ingredients that make up the jural philosophies of appellate judges today does not require that you research generations of judges. For example, the active judges on the U.S. Courts of Appeals have not been in office for many years. The chief judges are usually the most senior in active status, and a whirl around the circuits reveals they became judges in the following years: D.C. circuit in 1986, first circuit in 1992, second circuit in 1989, third circuit in 1987, fourth circuit in 1984, fifth circuit in 1979, sixth circuit in 1979, seventh circuit in 1983, eighth circuit in 1991, ninth circuit in 1979, tenth circuit in 1985, eleventh circuit in 1986, and federal circuit in 1987. From this, you can assume that, with limited exceptions, the active judges have been on a court for a shorter time. To examine the philosophical idiosyncracies of the majority of the judges who will decide your case does not require you to research past generations of judges on that court.

No trial lawyer worth his salt will appear before a trial judge cold. The legal profession in a given community has a "book" on every trial judge. The "book" is not written, although some large litigating firms may have reduced comments to writing. Rather, it is the sum total of impressions by lawyers who have appeared before the judges. How

---

4. *Id.* at 139.

does the judge rule on evidence questions or react to opening and closing statements? How far afield can I go in cross-examination? In personal injuries cases is the particular judge plaintiff-oriented or defendant-oriented? What about sidebar conferences? Suggested jury instructions? Trial memoranda (or must we sell the law clerk)? Are we chained to the counsel table or the lectern or may we wander around the room when we ask questions?

Make your book on the appellate judges for whom you are writing the brief. Have they written any law review articles? Have they made any speeches before bar groups or at law schools? In their opinions on this subject do they quote any commentators? How do they treat precedents? Measured by Karl Llewellyn's "strict" or "loose" scale, do they put only the narrowest interpretations of past cases, deciding that the putative precedent "holds only of redheaded Walpoles in pale magenta Buick automobiles?"[5] Do you detect any particular approach to statutory construction? Do they like references to legislative history? Are they quick to find an abuse of discretion? Are they likely to upset the factual findings of trial judges as clearly erroneous? How do they regard the court—as a strict tribunal for deciding narrowly only the issue before it, or as an instrument for social change?

The brief writer must always must focus his vision on the court before which he or she is appearing. As Wisconsin Supreme Court Justice William A. Bablitch advises brief writers, "Your vision is to your client, ours must be to how our decision will affect others in the future." For this reason, he cautions:

> Be aware of our institutional function. Our decisions must provide predictable remedies for the rational resolution of problems that arise in future social and economic life. We paint on a large canvas. We are concerned, first and foremost, with the effect of our decision on the state of the law, not on your client.[6]

There is no reason, however, to assume that the process of determining how the court reacts to consequences involves evaluation in terms of a single scale, e.g., as the Benthamite scale of supposedly measurable aggregates of pleasure and pain. Sometimes, when lawyers present the case for and against given rulings, they characteristically

---

5. Karl Llewellyn, *The Bramble Bush* 56–69 (7th prtg. 1981).

6. William A. Bablitch, *Writing to Win, Compleat Law.*, Winter 1988, at 12.

refer to certain criteria as "justice," "common sense," "public policy," "convenience," or "expediency." To the extent that these criteria are defined and explained in their application to the argument, they serve a useful purpose. To the extent that they are used only as buzzwords, they may not be very effective.

For a decision to be influenced by consequential factors, the brief must first respond to the rules of inductive or deductive logic, but not all decisions are governed by relentless rules of logic. Critical decision points in judicial decision-making are based on "value judgments." To choose between rival legal principles is a value judgment. To place a certain interpretation on a statute is a value judgment. To decide whether the material or adjudicative facts in one case resemble those of another is a value judgment. Max Weber, the European social theorist, suggested that "value judgment" refers "to practical evaluation of a phenomena which is . . . worthy of either condemnation or approval." He distinguished between "logically determinable or empirically observable facts" and the "value judgments which are derived from practical standards, ethical standards or views."[7] Decisions do necessitate the use of value judgments, but it is desirable always to explain why a particular value is chosen over another.

Set forth the rationale in your brief and explain your value-based choice, but do not dwell for long in the murky waters of subjectively defined buzzwords. Remember Humpty-Dumpty, who proclaimed that any word he used "means just what I choose it to mean—neither more nor less." We all know what happened to that hubristic egghead.

Judges who evaluate consequences of rulings of other courts give different weight to different criteria. Not surprisingly, we do not agree as to what degree of either perceived injustice or predicted inconvenience will arise from the adoption or rejection of a given ruling. Sometimes we differ sharply and even passionately as to the acceptability of a ruling under scrutiny. At this level there can simply be irresoluble differences of opinion—hence, the necessity of a multijudge court as a reviewing tribunal, one that applies thorough ratiocination in its elaboration of reasons.

---

7. Max Weber, *Value Judgments in Social Science*, in Weber Selections 69 (W. Runciman ed. 1987).

§ 15.6   The Requirement of Consistency

What institutional device do we have to keep the brakes on free-wheeling concepts of what are and are not desirable consequences? Fortunately, the system does provide such a device. Just as fortunately, this goes to the heart of the common law tradition. Appellate decisions at all times should be congruent with and not antagonistic to some valid and binding rule of the system. Judges should respect at all times the notion of consistency.

We are no longer in the year 1215, when the barons forced King John to issue the Magna Carta at Runnymede, marking the start of the common law tradition in England. Our own country has a tradition that goes back more than two centuries, originating in an era when we had already absorbed further centuries of the English common law experience with cases, recorded at least since the days of Sir Edward Coke and, later, Sir William Blackstone. Our nation's oldest appellate tribunal, the Pennsylvania Supreme Court, has been handing down recorded decisions since 1686. We have a long history of judicial experience to ensure consistency.

Justice William O. Douglas noted the reservoir of authority to aid decisions in hard cases: "There are usually plenty of precedents to go around; and with the accumulation of decisions, it is no great problem for the lawyer to find legal authority for most propositions."[8] The tradition of *stare decisis* places the judge under an obligation to follow prior judicial decisions unless exceptional circumstances are present.[9] Here, of course, I may be begging the question because any judicial decision that departs from precedent already implies that the circumstances are exceptional.

Adherence to the tenet of consistency keeps the march of the law at a measured cadence. The point riders can go just so far; the outriders must keep close to the flanks; and the drags must not fall too far behind.

In his discourse on *The Seven Sins of Appellate Brief Writing and Other Transgressions*, United States Circuit Judge Harry Pregerson says that the first sin is "Long, Boring Briefs" but a close second is "Incoherent, Unfocused, and Disorganized Briefs."

---

8. William O. Douglas, *Stare Decisis*, 49 Colum. L. Rev. 735, 736 (1949).

9. In a small percentage of cases, no legal principles exist for guidance. These cases require the court to examine some justificatory principle of morality, justice, and social policy. *See* Ruggero J. Aldisert, *The Judicial Process: Readings, Materials and Cases* (2d ed. 1996).

Inconsistency is an aggravated form of incoherence. In one recent case, counsel insisted that the crucial term in the statute before us had a plain and unambiguous meaning and then attempted to support that claim by citing a half-dozen cases, each of which defined the term differently.

To avoid incoherence, you should ask someone unfamiliar with the matter to read your brief carefully for consistency, clarity, and logic. Such an independent reader can point out areas that are confusing and may make the difference between an intelligible brief and an incoherent one.[10]

§ 15.7   The Tenet of Coherence

We must also consider coherence, a concept closely related to, but in several senses somewhat different from consistency. As Judge Pregerson formulates it, inconsistency may be considered as an aggravated form of incoherence. Yet an action may be consistent without being coherent. It may be consistent in the sense of establishing a set of norms that do not contradict one another, but at the same time, the action may pursue no just or desirable value or policy.

Thus, it can be said that "coherent" means connected naturally or logically as by a common principle. The child who constantly lies to his parents is certainly consistent, but there is a question whether the conduct follows any tenet of coherence.

Two sets of statutes come to mind, which are internally consistent, but rather incoherent. Some years back, when the Social Security system began to hurt for funds, some bright-eyed "bean counters" in the Social Security Administration came up with an idea that they unblushingly pronounced a work of genius. They had found a way to save, they alleged, some money for the funds they had sworn to protect. They decided that those of us born between 1917 and 1921 (and I am one) should receive a lower replacement rate to calculate our preretirement income than those born before or after this limited period, and that accordingly, those of us born between these years should receive lower benefits. We became known as "notch babies." (The same notch babies, as it happened that made up the bulk of those who served in World War II). Consistent? *Yes.* Coherent? *Of course, not.*

---

10. Harry Pregerson, *The Seven Sins of Appellate Brief Writing and Other Transgressions*, 34 UCLA L. Rev. 431, 434–35 (1986).

The other statute was enacted by the Italian parliament. A majority could not agree on a uniform speed limit for the *autostrade*, the nation's superhighways or toll roads. The objective of the legislation was automotive safety. Before that time, the *autostrade* resembled the Indianapolis 500, with speed limited only by the vehicle's power and the driver's inclination. At some curves, drivers had to slow down sharply—to 130 kilometers (almost 80 miles) an hour. The legislative solution was to set one limit for small Fiats, another for mid-sized cars, and still another for luxury sedans and sports cars. Moreover, each automobile owner had to purchase and post on the rear a decal to identify the vehicle's proper speed limit. Consistent? *Yes.* Coherent? *Well, you guess.* Has it worked? *Absolutely.* No one puts decals on cars. And the Italian road police make no effort to enforce it. So goes it in *il bel paese.*

§ 15.8   The Brief's Conclusion

Having set forth your argument, point by point, you are not quite finished. You must now write a separate section titled "Conclusion," in which you advise the court precisely the relief you seek. Tell them what you want.

Some lawyers recapitulate the argument in the conclusion. Often this is very effective, especially if the written argument has been lengthy, but the conclusion should be extremely concise; it should not be a reprint of your summary of argument and should not exceed a few sentences. In most cases, however, a recap is not necessary. Also, in most cases, the relief requested may be clear from the status of the case, but in a good number of cases this is not so. If you are seeking a remand with a direction to enter j.n.o.v., say so. Otherwise, the court may conclude that your are requesting a new trial. If you are requesting a remand with a direction to dismiss the complaint or to enter judgment in favor of your client, say so. Be very specific.

§ 15.8.1   Examples of Conclusions

For the foregoing reasons, appellant requests the court to reverse the judgment against him, and remand the case to the district court for entry of a judgment of acquittal. Barring that relief, he prays that the judgment be reversed and the case remanded for a new trial.

For these reasons, and for the reasons stated in the briefs filed by the other appellees, the judgment of the district court should be affirmed.

For the above reasons, appellant requests the Court to reverse the judgment of the district court.

For the foregoing reasons, appellant requests the Court to vacate the judgment of the court below and remand these proceedings with a direction to enter judgment in its favor.

Wherefore Brophy Corporation, as appellee and cross-appellant, requests that the judgment of the district court be affirmed except insofar as that court declined to permit Brophy Corporation to supplement its application for attorney's fees, costs, and expenses to include those attorney's fees, costs and expenses devoted to the litigation of the fee application itself. In that latter regard, the judgment of the district court should be vacated and the case remanded for further proceedings.

Should this Honorable Court agree with appellants that fees are not properly awardable under 28 U.S.C. § 2412(d), we request a remand to the district court with instructions that it consider Brophy Corporation's alternative basis for an award of fees under 28 U.S.C. § 2412(b).

Complete the conclusion with a signature line signed by at least one lawyer or, if applicable, the name of the law firm, followed by an address, the name of the party represented, and its role in the case, whether appellant, appellee, intervenor, or amicus. In some states, the lawyer's bar number must be added to all court papers.

§ 15.9   The Perfect Brief and Pet Peeves

At the 1990 Tenth Circuit Judicial Conference, two United States circuit judges were asked this question: "How do you define what a perfect brief is, and what would be your pet peeves in the briefs you do see?"[11]

§ 15.9.1   Perfection

Judge Bobby R. Baldock

"[A] terrific brief that I enjoy is one that is very precise and gets to the point of the issues that have been raised, so that I know exactly what it is that you claim as an appellant. The brief needs to identify what the alleged reversible error is, taking into consideration the standards of review that we have to apply, because that standard in many instances determines the outcome. We can't substitute our judgment for the trial judge's, even if something that happened at the trial was very important to the outcome.

For an appellee, a good brief is one that goes directly to the heart of the matter. It is not one of those briefs that just says, 'Well, we won in the trial court; therefore, we should win in the appellate court.' Those briefs are absolutely no help. These issues sometimes are very close.

---

11. These responses are reprinted from *What Appellate Advocates Seek from Appellate Judges and What Appellate Judge Seek from Appellate Advocates*, 31 N.M.L. Rev. 265, 265–267 (2000).

A terrific brief is one that is straight to the point. It tells us what happened, why there was error, and what law supports the claim that the judgment below is reversible. The appellee, of course, does just the opposite, explaining why the judgment below should be upheld. So that is a terrific brief, and it doesn't take 150 pages to do that. You can do it easily with less than fifty pages."

Judge Carlos F. Lucero

"To me a terrific brief is one that concisely, precisely, and meticulously states the issues for our consideration, and why they compel reversal of what the trial court did below."

§ 15.9.2 Peeves

Judge Carlos F. Lucero

Number one is briefs that do not have a compelling reason *as a matter of law* for reversal. That is to say, the brief just says, 'I lost below, and please reverse.' Well, losing below presents no basis for appealing a case, let alone for persuading an appellate court to reverse.

My second pet peeve is an unfocused statement of the issues that presents no compelling error that we should address or no novel and creative issue that is being advanced for the creation of law that should grab our attention.

Another pet peeve is a brief that does not contain a summary of the argument or that contains a summary of the argument that is of little, if any, help. A summary of the argument should be able to tell an appellate court precisely and concisely what error the trial court made below that requires us to take the extraordinary step and consume and utilize the judicial resources necessary to retry that case. I think litigants who don't put in a summary of the argument have done themselves a grave disservice, and those who don't use the summary properly are close behind.

The last of my pet peeves is briefs that use too much of their valuable space stating unnecessary facts and thereby consume too much of the judge's time, to the point that he or she loses interest. These briefs fail to isolate the really relevant facts on appeal—the facts that are truly critical to addressing the contended error. Some attorneys really blow it by failing to include citations to the record on those critical facts. That is the worst brief."

Judge Baldock

Why don't we see more concise briefs? That's the problem we have. I think those people who are frequently working at the appellate level understand these things and we don't usually see the type of briefs with the pet peeves we're talking about. Where we see these mistakes are from trial lawyers who only do an appellate brief once in a great while.

The Tenth Circuit has provided a guideline book on how to approach briefs. But it's amazing; time after time after time we get briefs that totally ignore those guidelines. We see briefs that appear to totally ignore the Tenth Circuit rules on how to prepare the brief. I think a lot of this is due to the fact that attorneys who don't have a very large appellate practice get a little bit negligent in really trying to conform to the rules. The time constraint is important too. But you've got one shot at the appellate court, and you really need to put your best foot forward. We see your brief first. That's why it's so important that you follow the court guidelines. We're aware of your time constraints. But you still have to follow the rules.

Chapter 16

THE BRIEF: THE REQUIRED LOGICAL FORM
FOR EACH ISSUE

§ 16.1 Overview

Oliver Wendell Holmes is often quoted for his famous statement:

> The life of the law has not been logic; it has been experi-
> ence. The felt necessities of the time, the prevalent moral
> and political theories, intuitions of public policy, avowed or
> unconscious, even the prejudices which judges share with
> their fellow-men, have had good deal more to do than the
> syllogism in determining the rules by which men should be
> governed.[1]

But Holmes was speaking in 1881 of only of a type of *deductive* logic
that has fixed premises. Over a century later, we now know that it is
clear that by *inductive* logic we witness the drama of developing law to
meet felt necessities of the times, current moral and political theories,
intuitions of public policy, and the hopes, dreams, and aspirations of
an informed society. What you write today as a brief is measured by
its persuasive power, and do not kid yourself, persuasion depends upon
the force of its formal logic.

What Holmes was saying must always be considered in the context
of his message: an appeal that the law adjust to changing social conditions, that we should not be bound by rigid legal precepts that were
once justified by good reasons but are no longer viable in a changing society. His appeal did not go unnoticed. Aided by the writings of Roscoe
Pound and Benjamin Cardozo, our jurisprudence moved from a rigid
German *Begriffsjurisprudenz*, which Rudolf von Jhering styled as a
jurisprudence of concepts.[2] The current spirit was eloquently stated by
Professor Harry W. Jones of Columbia: "A legal rule or a legal institution is a good rule or institution when—that is, to the extent that—it
contributes to the establishment and preservation of a social environment in which the quality of human life can be spirited, improving and
unimpaired."[3]

---

1. Oliver Wendell Holmes, *The Common Law* 1 (1881).

2. Rudolf von Jhering, *Der Geist Des Rominischen Rechts* (1887).

3. Harry W. Jones, *An Invitation to Jurisprudence*, 74 Colum. L. Rev. 1023, 1025 (1974).

Although it can be said that formal logic is not an end-in-view of law, it is one of the important means to the ends of law, perhaps the most important. Logical form and logical reasoning have never been subordinated in the judicial process. We all know the "why" of logic in the law. Justice Felix Frankfurter said it best on his retirement after twenty-three years on the Supreme Court: "Fragile as reason is and limited as law is as the expression of the institutionalized medium of reason, that's all we have standing between us and the tyranny of mere will and the cruelty of unbridled, unprincipled, undisciplined feeling."[4]

The common law tradition demands respect for logical form in our reasoning. Without it we are denied justification for our arguments before a court. Logical form is only a means to the ends of justice. But the canons of logic are nonetheless critical tools of argument; they are the implements of persuasion. When it comes to brief writing, they form the imprimatur that gives legitimacy and respect. They are the acid that washes away obscurity in your own argument and obfuscation in your opponent's argument.

Logical argument is a means of determining the soundness of a purported conclusion. We do this by following well established canons of logical order in a deliberate and intentional fashion. In the law, we must follow a thinking process that emancipates us from impulsively jumping to conclusions, or from argument supported only by strongly felt emotions or superstitions. That which John Dewey said for teachers in generations past is still vital and important today: reflective thought "converts action that is merely appetitive, blind, and impulsive into intelligent action."[5]

The purpose of an appellate brief is to persuade. It is to persuade a group of highly trained legal professionals. Whatever form an argument may take before a lay audience, when presented to appellate judges, it must employ inductive or deductive reasoning and be free from both formal and material fallacies. I now turn to a quick summary of concepts to be employed by brief writers.[6]

---

4. *Time*, Sept. 7, 1962 at 16.

5. John Dewey, *How We Think* 17 (2d ed. 1933).

6. I set forth this thesis in detail in my book, *Logic for Lawyers: A Guide to Clear Legal Thinking* (3d ed. 1997), by analyzing logical components as used in the law and illustrating concepts with excerpts from cases. It is not my intention to repeat that effort here, but only to synthesize certain concepts that should be followed in appellate advocacy. The reader is directed to *Logic for Lawyers* for a more comprehensive study.

§ 16.2 The Required Logical Structure of each Issue

What we have set forth so far in previous chapters is but prologue. We now come to the make-or-break part of your brief: how to effectively discuss each issue in your brief.

It is the discussion of issues that formally constitutes your argument. An argument is a group of propositions in which one is claimed to follow from the others—the others being treated as furnishing support for the truth of the original. An argument is not a random collection of propositions, but rather a formally structured grouping.

The purpose of a brief is to persuade the court to accept the conclusion you present. You must not do this "in the nude," using the felicitous expression of Loyola Law School Dean David W. Burcham. A naked exhortation for the court to accept a proffered conclusion will not suffice because the conclusion you urge will take the form of a rule of law. Roscoe Pound taught that rules of law "are precepts attaching a definite detailed legal consequence to a definite, detailed state of facts."[7] And a rule of law promulgated by a court is valid only to the extent that sound reasoning supports it.

Because reason must always support the conclusion presented for acceptance, we turn to some basic concepts of legal reasoning to assist the brief writer.

§ 16.3 Concepts of Reasonable, Reasoning, Reasons, Reason

It is necessary to repeat and expand on some elementary, yet indispensable, concepts of logic for lawyers that we have previously mentioned. Involved in the judicial process is an interrelationship among four terms that sound alike, but whose meanings diverge in the decisional process: "reasonable," "reasoning," "reasons," and "reason."

Reasonable

A judge's decision on the choice, interpretation, and application of a legal precept involves a value judgment justifiable because he or she is convinced that the decision is fair, just, sound, and sensible, and, therefore, "reasonable." One judge may believe that it is "reasonable" to maintain the law in harmony with existing circumstances and precedents, and accede to the magnetic appeal of consistency in the law; another may assert that the issue should be considered pragmatically, and will respond only to its practical consequences. What is "reasonable" in a

---

7. Roscoe Pound, *Hierarchy of Sources and Forms in Different Systems of Law*, 7 Tul. L. Rev. 475, 482–487 (1933).

given set of circumstances may permit endless differences of opinion. This difference inevitable among multijudge reviewing courts ensures the vitalizing growth of common law.

Reasoning

Determining what is "reasonable" is closely related to the over-arching process we call "reasoning," which is defined as a progression of thought based upon the logical relation between truths. Logical thought is reflective thinking, which may be understood as an "operation in which present facts suggest other facts (or truths) in such a way as to induce belief in what is suggested on the ground of real relation in the things themselves, a relation between what suggests and what is suggested."[8] Reasoning involves recognizing a "link in actual things, that makes one thing the ground, warrant, evidence, for believing in something else."[9] The ability to adjudicate cases depends upon the power to see logical connections in the cases and to recognize similarities and dissimilarities. This means solving a problem by pondering a given set of facts to perceive the relationship among those facts and thus reaching a logical conclusion.

Reasons

To solve problems in the proceeding manner we resort to "reasons." These are the various premises utilized in the reasoning process. In the judicial review process, deductive reasoning is the centerpiece, and "reasons" constitute the major and minor premises of the categorical syllogism.

Reason

Finally, "reason" is often used as a shorthand expression that inquires into the validity or cogency of "reasoning" and the truth of the factual component of "reasons." The application of "reasonableness" to "reason" is an ever-recurring scenario.

Judges of a trial tribunal or reviewing judges always appraise a specific argument from two separate, but related, analyses. First, from the sole vantage of examining its reasoning to determine whether, in the language of the logician, it is valid or cogent, without at the same time troubling over the truth and falsity of its premises. Second, from the sole vantage of the truth and falsity of its premises, without troubling over the validity or cogency of its reasoning. Arguments that have both valid or cogent reasoning and true premises are sound arguments. An

---

8. *Dewey,* supra note 5 at 12.

9. *Id.*

argument fails to be sound if either (a) the reasoning it employs from premises to conclusion is not acceptable, or (b) one or more of its premises is false.[10]

§ 16.4   Introduction to Deductive Reasoning

Deductive reasoning is a mental operation that a student, lawyer, or judge must employ every working day of his or her life. Formal deductive logic is an act of the mind in which, from the relation of two propositions to each other, we infer, that is, we understand and affirm, a third proposition. In deductive reasoning, the first two propositions which imply the third proposition, the conclusion, are called *premises*. The broad proposition that forms the starting point of deduction is called the *major premise*; the second proposition is called the *minor premise*. They have these titles because the major premise represents the *class*; the minor premise, something or someone included in the class.

The major premise of the issue usually takes the form of a rule of law, enunciated in a previous case, that usually appears as the topic sentence of the discussion of each issue and is represented as a legal precept on which all members of the court will agree is a rule of law.

- Your major premise is a detailed legal consequence attached to a detailed set of facts. Example, ALL MEN ARE MORTAL.

- If the major premise is not true, your entire argument fails. All is lost. All the facts you set forth, all the citations that follow, will not help you.

- Your minor premise consists of the facts found by the fact-finder. Your purpose is to show that these facts (the subject of your Minor Premise, usually called the Minor Term) come within the detailed set of facts set forth in the major premise. Example, SOCRATES IS A MAN.

- Your conclusion then will logically follow. SOCRATES IS MORTAL.

- The bottom line: be absolutely certain that you accurately state the rule of law—the detailed legal consequence attached to a detailed set of facts—that anchors your entire deductive argument as the major premise in your discussion of the issue.

---

10. *Aylett v. Sec'y of Hous. & Urban Dev.*, 54 F. 3d 1660,1667–1668 (10th Cir. 1995).

§ 16.4.1 Deductive Reasoning in the Discussion of Your Issue

I now turn to the major logical framework of the issue(s) you discuss. In most cases you will utilize what logicians describe as the categorical deductive *syllogism*. You all know it by the familiar form:

Major Premise:	All men are mortal.
Minor Premise:	Socrates is a man.
Conclusion:	Therefore, Socrates is a mortal.

Apply this inference from two other propositions to the opinion of Judge Cardozo in *MacPherson v. Buick Motor Car Co.*:[11]

Major Premise:	Any manufacturer who negligently constructs an article that may be inherently dangerous to life and limb when so constructed is liable in damages for the injuries resulting.
Minor Premise:	A manufacturer who constructs an automobile in which the spokes on a wheel are defective creates an article that is inherently dangerous to life an limb.
Conclusion:	Therefore, a manufacturer who constructs an automobile in which the spokes on a wheel are defective is liable in damages for the injuries resulting.

The classic means of deductive reasoning is the syllogism. Aristotle first formulated this theory and offered this definition: "A syllogism is discourse in which, certain things being stated, something other than what is stated follows of necessity from their being so. I mean by the last phrase that they produce the consequence, and by this, that no further term is required from without to make the consequence necessary."[12]

From this definition we can say that a syllogism is a form of implication in which two propositions rub together to create a third.[13] This syllogism must appear—in one form or another—in almost every issue you discuss in your brief. If you only argue the superficial merits of your conclusion, be prepared to have the strength of your logical foundation tested at oral argument. An argument that is correctly reasoned

---

11. 227 N.Y. 382, 11 N.E. 1050 (1960).

12. L.S. Stebbing, *A Modern Introduction to Logic* 81 (6th ed. 1948) (quoting Aristotle, Analytica Prior.a 24b).

13. *Id.*

may be wrong, but an argument that is incorrectly reasoned cannot ever be right.

§ 16.5 Introduction to Inductive Reasoning

Deductive reasoning and adherence to the Socrates-is-a-man type of syllogism is only one of the major components of the common law logic tradition. Inductive reasoning is equally important. In law logic, it is very often used to alter either the major or the minor premise of the deductive syllogism.

In legal analysis, a statute or specific constitutional provision qualifies as the controlling major premise. It is the law of the case, with which the facts (appearing in the minor premise) will be compared, so as to reach a decision (conclusion). Where no clear rule of law is present, however, it is necessary, using Lord Diplock's phrase, to draw upon "the cumulative experience of the judiciary" and then fashion a proper major premise from existing legal rules—the specific holdings of other cases. This is done by inductive reasoning.

Deductive reasoning moves by inference from the more general to the less general to the particular. Inductive reasoning moves in the direction: from the particular to the general, or from the particular to the particular.

§ 16.5.1 Inductive Generalization

Let us start with the all-men-are-mortal major premise. The premise, in general form, resulted from the process of *enumeration*: it was created by the counting of millions of particulars to create a general statement. The world is inhabited by millions of men, we know all these men to be mortal, thus we are armed with an example of *inductive generalization* that concludes: Socrates is mortal.

It should be clear that the truth of the conclusion drawn from this inductive process is not guaranteed by the form of the argument, not even when all the premises are true, and no matter how numerous they are. We always run the risk of the informal fallacy of hasty generalization. We can say, however, that the creation of a major premise in law by the technique of inductive enumeration, although not guaranteed to produce an absolute truth, does produce a proposition more likely true than not. This permits the premise to be modified as new cases are decided. Formulating a generalization, that is, enumerating a series of tight holdings of cases to create a generalized legal precept, is at best a logic of probabilities. We accept the result, not because it is an absolute truth, like a proposition in mathematics, but because it gives our results a certain hue of credibility. The process is designed to yield workable and tested premises, rather than truths.

§ 16.5.2 Analogy

A proper analogy should identify the number of respects in which the compared cases, or fact scenarios, resemble one another (let us call these similarities positive analogies) and the number of respects in which they differ (negative analogies). Unlike the method of enumeration, numbers do not count in the method of analogy. Instead, what is important is *relevancy*—whether the compared facts resemble, or differ from, one another in relevant respects. John Stuart Mill asked the question: "Why is a single instance, in some cases, sufficient for a complete induction, while in others myriads of concurring instances, without a single exception known or presumed, go such a very little way towards establishing an universal proposition? Whoever can answer this question knows more of the philosophy of logic than the wisest of the ancients, and has solved the problem of induction."[14]

Judge Cardozo estimated that at least nine-tenths of appellate cases "could not, with semblance of reason, be decided in any way but one," because "the law and its application alike are plain," or "the rule of law is certain, and the application alone doubtful."[15]

I totally agree that this is a conservative estimate and this is not guesswork: recall again the reversal statistics set forth back in chapter 1. The case most often presenting an arguable question for decision is Cardozo's second category when the law is certain but the application doubtful. Where there is an absolute right of appeal to an appellate court, this is the type of case that forms the largest number of counseled appeals. And to determine whether the application of facts found by the fact-finder apply to the rule of law, we must perforce compare those facts to those contained in the governing rule of law. In doing this, we resort to tenets of inductive analogy.

Let us assume as the controlling rule of law: where all facts A, B, and C are present, legal consequence X follows. Assume now that in the case at bar, the facts D, E, and F were found by the factfinder at trial. To say that the material facts are or are not analogous by merely repeating them and saying so is not enough. To persuade the court

---

14. John Stuart Mill, *A System of Logic Ratiocination and Inductive* (8th ed. 1916).

15. Benjamin N. Cardozo, *The Nature of the Judicial Process* 819 (1921).

that they are or not, you must discuss the components of the analogy doctrine.

In an opinion I wrote for the third circuit, I discussed these in an important class action antitrust case where the principal argument on appeal was whether the holding in a case called *Newton* applied to the case at bar:

> The precise holding in *Newton* was that the facts common to the members of the class did not predominate. No new legal precept was created; no new nuance of interpretation was forthcoming. It was merely the application of ruling case law in this court to the facts of that case.
>
> The process of justifying a court's decision always requires application of a legal precept to a particular factual situation. The application may be purely mechanical, as it is in most cases. If the facts are similar to those in an earlier case announcing a rule of law, the doctrine of precedent becomes operative. Where there is no quarrel over the choice and interpretation of the legal precept, here Rule 23(b)(3), the root controversy usually is traced to a value judgment of whether there is sufficient similarity between the fact situations under comparison. Edward R. Levi amply described this kind of assessment when he stated: "the scope of a rule of law, and therefore its meaning, depends upon a determination of what facts will be considered similar. . . . The finding of similarity or difference is the key step in the legal process." To predict a court's actions in a precept-application controversy, therefore, requires a prediction of what facts in the compared cases a given court, at a given time, will deem either material or insignificant. The facts considered material are adjudicative facts, described by Hart and Sacks as "facts relevant in deciding whether a given general proposition is or is not applicable to a particular situation."
>
> For Appellants' argument to prevail, therefore, they must demonstrate that the facts in *Newton* are substantially similar to the facts in the case at bar, what logicians call inductive reasoning by analogy, or reasoning from one particular case to another. To draw an analogy between two entities is to indicate one or more respects in which they are similar and thus argue that the legal consequence attached

to one set of particular facts may apply to a different set of particular facts because of the similarities in the two sets. Because a successful analogy is drawn by demonstrating the resemblances or similarities in the facts, the degree of similarity is always the crucial element. You may not conclude that only a partial resemblance between two entities is equal to a substantial or exact correspondence.

Logicians teach that one must always appraise an analogical argument very carefully. Several criteria may be used: (1) the acceptability of the analogy will vary proportionally with the number of circumstances that have been analyzed; (2) the acceptability will depend upon the number of positive resemblances (similarities) and negative resemblances (dissimilarities); or (3) the acceptability will be influenced by the relevance of the purported analogies.[16]

For Appellants to draw a proper analogy, they had the burden in the district court, as they do here of showing that the similarities in the facts of the two cases outweigh the differences. They cannot do so, for two significant reasons. First, in *Newton* it was clear that not all members of the putative class sustained injuries; here, all members sustained injuries because of the artificially increased prices. Secondly, in *Newton* there were hundreds of millions of stock transactions involved, thus making the putative class extremely unmanageable; here, an astronomical number of transactions is not present. The classes are manageable.[17]

---

16. Irving M. Copi & Keith Burgess-Jackson, Informal Logic 166 (3d ed. 1996); Arthur L. Goodhart, *Determining the Ratio Decidendi of a Case*, 40 Yale L.J. 161, 179 (1930); John H. Wigmore, *Wigmore's Code of the Rules of Evidence in Trials at Law* 118 (3d ed. 1942); John Stuart Mill, *A System of Logic Ratiocinative and Inductive* 98–142 (8th ed. 1916). ("Two things resemble each other in one or more respects; a certain proposition is true of one; therefore it is true of the other.")

17. *In re Linerboard Antitrust Litig.*, 305 F.3d 145, 156–57 (3d Cir. 2002).

How my panel discussed this issue here could offer some guidance to brief writers in presenting an argument based on analogy.

§ 16.6 Testing the Conclusion of Each Issue

Your conclusion can be true only when (1) the other propositions (premises) are true, and (2) these propositions imply the conclusion. The conclusion is always inferred from the other propositions.

Not all means of persuasion are based on reflective thinking or formal logic. For example, rhetoric is a means of persuasion. Seekers of public office, columnists, television commentators, editorial writers, advertising experts—and trial lawyers—are all masters of persuasion. They often appeal to emotions rather than to reason. Their aim is to induce belief, not to demonstrate a conclusion by pure logical means. These presentations may be works of art, but they do not always demonstrate the logic that distinguishes legal argument from impassioned summations to a jury.

This is not to say that all good reasoning must be stated in the order of formal correctness. Often, the conclusion is stated first: "Socrates is a mortal because all men are mortal and Socrates is a man"; or in a Supreme Court case, "It could hardly be denied that a tax laid specifically on the exercise of those freedoms would be unconstitutional. Yet the license tax imposed by this ordinance is, in substance, just that."[18]

At times, the argument can skillfully be compressed to a single sentence. Thus, in *Roe v. Wade*, Justice Blackmun wrote:

> This right of privacy, whether it be founded in the Fourteenth Amendment's concept of personal liberty and restrictions upon state action, as we feel it is, or, as the District Court determined, in the Ninth Amendment's reservation of rights to the people, is broad enough to encompass a woman's decision whether or not to terminate her pregnancy.[19]

18. *Murdock v. Penn.*, 319 U.S. 105, 108 (1943).

19. 410 U.S. 116, 163 (1973).

Implicit in this statement was the following syllogism:

Major Premise: The right of privacy is guaranteed by the Fourteenth (or Ninth) Amendment.

Minor Premise: A woman's decision to terminate her pregnancy is protected by a right of privacy.

Conclusion: Therefore, a woman's decision whether to terminate her pregnancy is protected by the Fourteenth (or Ninth) Amendment.

Chapter 17

THE BRIEF: SHORTENING THE ARGUMENT

§ 17.1   How To Cut the Flab

All the judges quoted in this book have one bit of advice in common: emphasize the muscle of your brief and cut out the flab.

When you start to write the argument, you know by then that you have jurisdiction. You know that the issues have been properly noticed in the trial tribunal. You know what issues you want to discuss. You are ready to take them on, one by one. It is here, in the argument portion of the brief, where the judges direct their closest attention. And it is here where you must buckle down and demonstrate superior writing skills.

In their briefs, many lawyers seem—like the poor little lambs in Yale's "Whiffenpoof Song"—to have lost their way. Many briefs are no longer instruments of persuasion or explanation. Rather, they emerge from the word processors as instruments of commentary, looking more like wide-blade axes than precision decision-making tools.

A promiscuous uttering of citations has replaced the crisply stated, clean lines of legal reasoning. We often see a mishmash of citation in text and footnotes. String cites are rarely useful or impressive. Generally, the latest case from the court should be sufficient. Judges do not need a show-and-tell exercise to reveal how smart you are. It is not too unkind to suggest that often what poses as a work of scholarship is actually a work of journalism. In Charles Rodell's words, "A pennyworth of content is most frequently concealed beneath a pound of so-called style."[1]

Historian Barbara W. Tuchman sounded a call for "clear, easy-reading prose" from the writing community. She asked all writers to avoid "the Latinized language of academics with their endless succession of polysyllables, their deaf ear for sentence structure, and unconcern for clarity."[2]

A stuffy style and fluffy padding shows that the legal profession suffers from a crippling case of acute and possibly terminal pedantry. We seem to forget that all lawyers and judges are naturally called upon to be professional writers. The tools of the trade consist entirely of words. Professional writers know and accept the hard truth that

---

1. Charles Rodell, *Goodbye to Law Reviews*, 23 Va. L. Rev. 38 (1936).
2. Barbara W. Tuchman, *An Author's Mail*, 54 Am. Scholar 313, 322 (1985).

prose, like any other art, calls for frequent compromise among desirable aims—sound and sense, force and fluidity, clearness and precision, emphasis and nuance, wit and truth. The very need for balance rules out consistency in writing. Each word, each sentence, each paragraph is a special case.[3] Yet judges and lawyers alike stand guilty of bombastic propositions and legal dialectics in "[l]ong sentences, awkward constructions, and fuzzy-wuzzy words that seem to apologize for daring to venture an opinion."[4]

What miracles we achieve, effortlessly managing to be both turgid and turbid, sometimes committing both sins in the same sentence. Many of us, *mirabile dictu*, manage the feat without even being sure what these words mean! Multisyllabic jargon and verbal distortions are the rule, not the exception, and exemplify neatly what was once as "Haig-ese," in honor of a former secretary of state who holds a patent on the practice.[5] Professor Charles Alan Wright once said, "The great goal in writing and speaking is clarity."[6] Oklahoma Supreme Court Justice Yvonne Kauger echoes this good advice: "Avoid 'legalese.' Use simple sentences. I try to write my opinions so that my mother, a non-lawyer, can understand them."

Many brief writers suffer chronic cases of literary hiccups. They insert citations as often as possible, three or four in a simple declaratory sentence, irrespective of how these interfere with the flow of the prose, the rhythm of the presentations, or the order of argument. Such static impedes easy comprehension.

Habits like this stem perhaps from a skewed view of legal writing—that it must be technical in subject, multisyllabic in form, and highly complex in sentence structure. To be sure, the writing must be technical in the sense of being supported by appropriate legal authorities. But writing works best when it is clear and to the point.

---

3. Jacques Barzun, *Behind the Blue Pencil*, 54 Am. Scholar 385, 387–88 (1985).

4. *Rodell, supra* note 1, at 39.

5. According to a story popular inside the Beltway, an aide to the Secretary of State, General Alexander Haig had the audacity to ask for a raise in pay. Although you or I might have used a single word to respond in the negative, General Haig—more generous with the language than we are—replied: "Because of the fluctuational predisposition of your position's productive capacity as juxtaposed to government standards, it would be momentarily injudicious to advocate an increment." Lord Alfred Denning, *The Closing Chapter* 62 (1983).

6. Charles Alan Wright, *Foreword* to Bryan Garner, *The Elements of Legal Style* viii (1991).

Brief writers would be well served if they posted a little sign on their desks: "Why and for whom am I writing?" Remember that you are writing for appellate judges for the sole purpose of persuading them. Your briefs will be shorter and more to the point if this is remembered. Wisconsin Supreme Court Justice William A. Bablitch observed:

> When the desire to impress becomes more important than the desire to persuade, it can lead to awful results. In an attempt to be eloquent, intellectual, and erudite, the unfortunate result all too frequently is legalese and legal jargon put in the form called a legal brief. Hundreds of footnotes and string citations are unimpressive. We know you haven't read them anyway. There is a place for law review articles, but that place is not in the briefs filed in the court.[7]

Nor are these observations the product of forensic fatigue from a judge who has spent many years on the bench. John W. Davis had this to say about brief writing way back in 1940:

> I assume also that briefs are not overlarded with long quotations from the reported opinions, no matter how pat they seem; nor over-crowded with citations designed it would seem to certify to the industry of the brief-maker rather than to fortify the argument. . . .

> I assume further that they are not defaced by supras or infras or by a multiplicity of footnotes which, save in the rare case where they are needed to elucidate the text, do nothing but distract the attention of the reader and interrupt the flow of reasoning. . . .[8]

All this has not been emphasized to suggest that effective legal writing should be graded purely for literary style. Rather, I stress these observations because the purpose of all legal writing is persuasion. Without clear writing, communication is lessened. To the extent that we complicate communication, we dilute our powers of persuasion.

---

7. William A. Bablitch, *Writing to Win*, Compleat Law., Winter 1988, at 11.

8. John W. Davis, *The Argument of an Appeal*, 26 A.B.A.J. 895, 895–96 (1940).

§ 17.2 Listen to Leading Appellate Judges

Chief Justice and State	Comment
Charles E. Jones, *Arizona*	Be concise and direct.
Ronald T.Y. Moon, *Hawaii*	Write in a concise and direct fashion, minimizing the utilization of long, rambling footnotes.
Stephen N. Limbaugh, Jr., *Missouri*	Do not be repetitive.
Karla M. Gray, *Montana*	Be focused and concise: say it once, say it well, and move on. Set out only the facts pertinent to the issues raised.
Judith S. Kaye, *New York*	Know your case. Nothing is more appreciated by judges—who have lots of briefs to read—than clear, concise, cogent writing
Thomas J. Moyer, *Ohio*	Be concise. Do not repeat arguments.
Frank F. Drowota II, *Tennessee*	State the issues clearly and concisely.
Sharon Keller, *Texas Court of Criminal Appeals*	Briefs should always be concise.
Gerry L. Alexander, *Washington*	Dislikes: Irrelevant Facts. Long briefs. I think lawyers should make their written argument as concise as possible.

Chief Judge and Circuit	Comments
John M. Walker, Jr., *Second Circuit*	Be concise, do not repeat arguments or facts. The poorest, least persuasive briefs are all too often those that the lawyer has not taken the time to reduce to its essence.

Edward R. Becker, *Third Circuit, 1996–2003*	Limit the number of points. You will rarely win on more than one or two points. Overbriefing impairs your credibility
Anthony J. Scirica, *Third Circuit*	Focus only on the dispositive issue or issues.
Carolyn Dineen King, *Fifth Circuit*	Pick the most important issues, deal with them thoroughly, and omit the others. Be concise.
Douglas H. Ginsburg, *D.C. Circuit*	Be as brief as possible.
Haldane Robert Mayer, *Federal Circuit*	Be clear and concise.
Patricia M. Wald, *Chief Judge Emeritus,* *D.C. Circuit*	The more paper you throw at us, the meaner we get, the more irritated and hostile we feel about verbosity, peripheral arguments and long footnotes. Repetition, extraneous facts, over-long arguments (by the twentieth page, we are muttering to ourselves, "I get it, I get it. No more for God's sake.") still occur more often than capable counsel should tolerate.

§ 17.3   Footnotes

If it is important enough to say, say it in the text of your brief, not in a footnote. The only hard and fast rule is: "When in doubt, do not use them." But there is a caveat here.

I recommend the use of footnotes to supplement or authenticate certain statements in the briefs where, if the authority were placed in the text, the additional material would detract from the argument and diminish the persuasive power of the text.

I strongly discourage the use of footnotes for the making of remarks and asides, in the manner of a character in a play sharing a private joke with the audience. These marginal comments, often with piddling objections to minor points in the opponent's brief or the lower court's opinion, add little to and subtract much from the impact of your brief.

David O. Boehm, retired associate justice of the New York Supreme Court, offers another reason to avoid footnotes: "Their usage has been called, with good reason, the Ping-Pong Ocular Syndrome. A footnote jerks the smooth flow of argument to an abrupt stop by the command that you immediately transfer your attention from the text to the footnote. The interruption is hardly worth it. What ordinarily appears in a footnote is a reference that, without injury, could have been incorporated into the main text or, in most cases, omitted entirely."[9]

An additional word of caution: judges know the brief writer's trick of resorting to single-spaced footnotes when the draft runs over the page limits set forth in the court rules. They also deplore the conduct of bold and foolish persons whose briefs were bounced back by the clerk's office for over-pagination, but who returned the same text in smaller type to get the same words on fewer pages. Many courts now have rules establishing a minimum type size—pay attention to them. In any event, briefs that promote eyestrain will not promote the judges' attention and inspire enthusiasm.

§ 17.4 Tight Writing is Effective Writing

Writing successfully is to sell effectively. Being successful means selling your argument to your reader. Excessive citation, compulsive footnoting, and pedantry are three mighty horsemen running against your purpose. The result is a text that emphasizes trifling points of learning, shows a questionable sense of proportion, and makes no distinction between what is important and what is merely interesting to the writer. To put it less delicately, this approach confuses what is necessary to the argument and what is pseudo-academic show-and-tell. The common law tradition demands no more than a clear statement of reasons. Judges expect no more.

The ability to write clearly and memorably may or may not sometimes be a gift granted at birth. Without question, it can be perfected by studious attention and constant application, much like a muscle that is strengthened by proper and continuing exercise. To do the writing, editing, and rewriting required for polished text, takes time.

---

9. David O. Boehm, *Clarity and Candor Are Vital in Appellate Advocacy*, N.Y. St. B.J., Sept./Oct. 1999, at 52, 55.

Time, unfortunately, even with computers, e-mail, and laser printing, is severely rationed these days.

Francis Bacon's Seventeenth century criticism of legal writers still applies four centuries later: "They make imaginary laws for imaginary commonwealths; and their discourses are as the stars, which give little light because they are so high."[10]

§ 17.5 The Multiplication of Cases and Statutes

The argument must be clear. Develop your analysis in depth, but use precedent selectively. Lawyers and judges both have an obligation to evaluate the effect of previous cases. Add to this the responsibility of deciding which cases to rely upon explicitly and which to exclude as duplicative. Precedents should not be used to validate the obvious.

I expect that the response to this criticism will probably follow two lines of attack. First, one might say that the common law tradition demands authority to support propositions asserted in the brief and in the opinion. With the passage of time, obviously, more authority and more precedent are available for citation, and this proliferation explains why many more cases are cited today than in the era of Oliver Wendell Holmes, Benjamin Cardozo, and Learned Hand. Indeed, as we have said before, West Group now reports 54,059 published appellate cases each year.

The second argument is that we are in the midst of an explosion of congressional legislation along with a race to see which agency can generate the most regulations. For example, bills to expand federal jurisdiction are proposed at a rate of no less than one hundred per year. This legislative and administrative feast fattens the body of law. Briefs should reflect that expansion with thorough citation to all pertinent authorities.

I concede the validity of these arguments but offer a rebuttal. The proliferation of legislation and administrative regulations not only fattens the body of the law, but clogs its arteries, quickens its heart rate, and generally weakens the body. Many of these new regulatory statutes do little more than add a gloss to a relatively small number of long-recognized disciplines of the law. To regulate business practices, these statutes simply provide that idiosyncratic definitions, such as fraud,

---

10. Francis Bacon, *The Advancement of Learning, Book II* (1705), quoted in 3 *The Works of Francis Bacon* 475 (J. Spedding ed. 1876).

may be used in conjunction with time-tested tort principles.[11] They may set standards for interpreting contracts[12] or proclaim restrictions on the use of real or personal property[13] or restrict liberties[14] or declare certain conduct to be an offense against society.[15] Most congressional activity in the criminal field works to deem a federal crime conduct that was fairly well recognized as a state crime or, arbitrarily, to make a violation of a certain federal regulation a penal offense. In each of these cases and in the many others like them, citation to and analysis of the statute usually can be quite brief.

To the precedent "explosion" argument, my answer is that very few cases really bring about fundamental changes in the law. Most of the federal appellate cases reported each year come within the two categories suggested by Cardozo in 1921, those in which "[t]he law and its application alike are plain" and those in which "the rule of law is certain, and the application alone doubtful."[16] In my view, 90 percent of the cases appealed to the courts of appeals fall within these two categories.[17] This leaves only 10 percent of our swollen caseload about which it can be said that a decision one way or the other will count for the future, will advance or retrench the development of the law. Citations

---

11. *See, e.g.*, Securities Act of 1933, 15 U.S.C. §§ 78a–77bbbb (1981 & Supp. 1991); Securities Exchange Act of 1934, 15 U.S.C. §§ 78a-78kk (1981 & Supp. 1991).

12. *See, e.g.*, Investment Companies and Advisers Act, 15 U.S.C. § 80a(46) (1981 & Supp. 1991) (validity of contracts); 29 U.S.C. § 103 (1973 & Supp. 1991) ("yellow dog" contracts); 41 U.S.C. § 10b (1987 & Supp. 1991) (contracts for public works).

13. *See, e.g.*, Mineral Lands Leasing Act, 30 U.S.C. § 187 (1986 & Supp. 1991) (restrictions on assignment or subletting of leases); 21 U.S.C. § 123 (1972 & Supp. 1991) (Secretary of Agriculture authorized to quarantine livestock); 21 U.S.C. § 331(f) (1972 & Supp. 1991) (refusal to permit entry or inspection of premises prohibited); Surface Mining Control and Reclamation Act, 30 U.S.C. § 1256 (1986 & Supp. 1991) (permit required to engage in strip mining).

14. *See, e.g.*, Fair Labor Standards Act, 29 U.S.C. § 212 (1965 & Supp. 1991) (prohibition on child labor); 26 U.S.C. § 6702 (1989 & Supp. 1991) (statute used to prosecute tax protestors for filing frivolous tax returns).

15. Organized Crime Control Act of 1970, Racketeer-Influenced and Corrupt Organizations Act (RICO), 18 U.S.C. §§ 1961–1968 (1984 & Supp. 1991) (federal treble damage remedy for conspiracy to commit fraud).

16. Benjamin H. Cardozo, *The Nature of the Judicial Process* 164–165 (1921).

17. Cardozo estimated that at least nine-tenths of appellate cases in 1924 "could not, with semblance of reason, be decided in any way but one." Benjamin H. Cardozo, *Growth of the Law* 60 (1924). In 1961, Judge Henry Friendly wrote: "Indeed, Cardozo's nine-tenths estimate probably should be read as referring to the first category alone. Thus reading it, Professor Harry W. Jones finds it 'surprising' on the high side . . . ; so would I. If it includes both categories, I would not." Henry Friendly, *Reactions of a Lawyer— Newly Become Judge*, 71 Yale L.J. 218, 222-23 (1961) (quoting: Jones, *Law and Morality in the Perspective of Legal Realism*, 61 Colum. L. Rev. 799, 803 n.17 (1961)).

to all relevant authority does not clarify the law; it muddies the waters. The number of cases has exploded. Developments in the law have not.

Our British cousin Lord Patrick Devlin would agree. He has suggested that "at least nine-tenths of the judiciary spends its life submerged in the interested application of known law. Indeed, to say that one-tenth rises above the waterline that is marked by notice in the legal journals would probably be an exaggeration."[18]

§ 17.6   The Epidemic of "Citationitis"

The infatuation with citing precedent is older than any of us. No less venerable a critic than James Boswell had this to say in *The Life of Samuel Johnson*: "Dr. Johnson observed that 'authority from personal respect has much weight with most people, and often more than reasoning.'"[19] Johnson himself commented, "The more precedents there are, the less occasion is there for law; that is to say, the less occasion is there for investigating principles."[20] These words can be used to describe current legal writing. Although the citable cases are available by the thousands, few add very much to legal fundamentals. Additionally, over-citation creates the contrary impression that American law has undergone massive changes. This simply is not true. Over-citation is both a self-fulfilling prophecy and a self-inflicted wound.

The brute fact is that not all precedent represents currency of equal value. An authoritative gradation of legal precepts does exist. Some precedents are much more important than others. Recognition that a hierarchy of value exists is essential if judges are to find the proper grounds of decision; if lawyers are to find the basis for predicting the course of decision; and if citizens are to obtain reasonable guidance in conducting themselves according to the demands of legal order. Even more important—much more important—is the need to bring greater order to the design of law by identifying clearly, and at the earliest opportunity, the family of law implicated in the case.

The time has come for lawyers to simplify, rather than complicate, current legal issues. The time has come to identify clearly the controversy in each case and to isolate the branch of the law governing that controversy. The first step must be to concentrate on the tree's trunk and its main branches, rather than to fuss over the buds and blossoms that continually sprout and grow, but with the fall will be gone.

---

18. Patrick Devlin, *The Judge* 4 (1979).

19. James Boswell, *Life of Samuel Johnson* 615 (1906).

20. *Id.* at 417.

This arboreal metaphor brings to mind Dean Wigmore's criticism of overemphasis on the technique of legal rules in detail, with corresponding underemphasis in policies, reasons, and principles. This is a difficult thing to describe to those who do not sense it without description, but it is very marked. It is the kind of thing that is like the dead bark on the outside of a tree, in contrast to the living, growing inner core. Too much of our law is dead bark—at least in judicial opinions.[21]

We must emphasize basic legal precepts because the starting point of every judicial decision must be a recognition of controlling dogma, doctrine and fundamental principles. Only this recognition will make our decisions consistent and coherent. To accomplish this, all judges need help from all lawyers. Simplicity and order in briefs promotes progress in the law, not regress. It creates better communication between lawyer and judge and between judge and community. It removes from judicial decisions everything that is idiosyncratic, and in its place establishes predictability and reckonability.

§ 17.7   An Outline for Editing

A. Edit the work.

    1. Check spelling. Run a spell check. Ensure correct spelling of all proper names. Then double-check.

    2. Edit like a reader. Identify problems you encounter as a reader.

        a. Determine whether the sequence of ideas flows smoothly and logically.

        b. Determine whether the ideas are adequately supported.

        c   Recall the judges' major criticisms of briefs: they are too long. Is every point in this brief necessary? Does a weak point detract from a strong one? Have I fallen in love with my writing, or am I looking at it from the standpoint of a reader judge who will see all its warts and blemishes? If I stay with the points, should I cut some of the supporting text. Have I over-discussed some of the cases? Are all the citations absolutely necessary?

        d. Look for conspicuous omissions.

        e. Look for needless repetition.

---

21. John H. Wigmore, *Evidence in Trials at Common Law* § 8a, at 617.

3. Edit like a writer. Assess your writing techniques and mark up the first draft as an editor would.

    a. Read certain passages aloud, if necessary, and train your ears to detect errors reliably.

    b. Assess the "beat" of your writing. There is a difference between writing for reading and writing for speaking, even though each form has both mood and rhythm. Is the mood exaggerated? Do the words come through as a stentorian roar or as a "soft sell," soothing but nonetheless persuasive?

4. Edit to conform to page limitations. How long is the brief? Do I really need fifty pages to make my argument? Would the judge be impressed if I cut down the number of pages instead of presenting a forty-seven to fifty-page effort? What will sell here? A lean, mean machine or a fat, flabby one?

5. Edit to see that pages are correctly numbered and properly assembled. Check to see that your appendix is paginated and contains a table of contents.

B. An appellate lawyer is a professional writer.

1. Follow the practice of all professional writers and editors. Never rely entirely upon your memory. Keep a select library of the best reference materials at your elbow: a reputable dictionary, a comprehensive thesaurus, a good book of quotations, and of course, *The Elements of Style* by Strunk and White.

C. Read constantly.

1. Make outside reading a lifetime professional commitment. The best writing trains your ear, helping you to listen. The worst writing helps you to learn what to avoid.

2. Concentrate on masters of "the plain style," such as Mark Twain, George Orwell, James Thurber, E.B. White, Ernest Hemingway, Henry James, and Jonathan Swift, who provided models and weapons against the convoluted, lumbering style of legal prose.

D.   Never become complacent with your writing.

1.   Remember, effective writing is a lifetime goal, never a final accomplishment.

   a.   Become your own best critic.

   b.   Try to write so that when you finish you can look at the result and honestly say, "I have just done the very best I am capable of at this stage of my literary development."

   c.   Regularly review your past writing.

      i.   Ask yourself how it appeals to you.

      ii.   Assess improvement or deterioration in your writing style. Ask yourself whether your words remain as persuasive as they first seemed and whether they do a good job of expressing the thoughts you intended when you began.

   d.   To improve, work consciously to ensure that everything you write will be better than anything you wrote before.

   e.   Keep always in mind that writing is like exercising a muscle: the more you write, the easier it becomes.

Chapter 18

THE BRIEF: WRITE TO PERSUADE

§ 18.1   Overview

The purpose of a brief is to animize the art of persuasion. The lawyer must convince the judicial reader of the rightness of his or her cause. A writer friend once sent me a letter in which he said: "The first job for any piece of writing is to entice the reader into reading it, start to finish. That accomplished, the words must convey clearly what the writer wants them to convey. Finally, the text must perform the missionary act of persuasion, reinforcing the support of those who agree with the author and changing the minds of those who do not."

To write effectively is to sell effectively. That is why I can comfortably think of judges and lawyers as salespeople, a function they do not always recognize and one that many would probably deny. In this sense, objections notwithstanding, being a successful lawyer or judge means selling your argument to the legal community.

§ 18.2   The Mechanics of Persuasion

Other than the suggestions I have set forth in these chapters, are there really any specific yet undiscovered "mechanics of persuasion" a lawyer may use to craft his or her appellate brief and argument? To compile these "tools of the trade," I posed this very question to judges of the U.S. Courts of Appeals for the Third and Tenth Circuit, as well a few experienced appellate lawyers.

§ 18.2.1   Judges' Recommended "Tools"

Joseph F. Weis, Jr., Senior Circuit Judge, *United States Court of Appeals, Third Circuit*	After getting a firm grasp on the facts and doing the required research on the law, counsel should figuratively step back and, before picking up the pen (or turning on the word processor), ask himself or herself, "What is really the heart of this case? What should the law say about it?" Serious, objective and, not necessarily brief, consideration of these questions can give the sharp focus that a good brief and argument require.

Stephen H. Anderson,
Circuit Judge,
*United States Court of
Appeals,
Tenth Circuit*

Every conceivable device should be used to promote the quick understanding, and lasting impression of that understanding, of the most important points and issues raised. Thus, in addition to law, an appeal to reasonable policy grounds supporting points and issues will go a long way toward promoting the position one wants the judge to adopt. For example, legislative history is in fact a good tool when properly used (despite Justice Scalia). Also, drawing on a parade of horribles or ultimate absurdity, unworkability, or untenability to show the fallacy of an opposing argument when carried to its logical extreme, is effective. In the same vein, comparisons to settled law with similar objectives such as comparing a line of authority under one civil rights law to an issue under another civil rights law helps.

The art of persuasion under the subheading of helping the court to "understand" should take into account that examples of this art that are all around us. We are literally drenched in Madison Avenue propaganda and enticements, in political spin doctoring, in sound bites, and so on. They are all effective in their own way, and lawyers should pay attention to the quick, colorful, slanted illustration of points in ways and embedded in compelling contexts used every day by professional persuaders. The ancient arts of parable, allegory, analogy, and so on are eminently helpful tools for helping the listener understand and for driving a point home—if short and "catchy"—anchored in the judges' common experience, and attached to a generally accepted bias of some sort.

Wade Brorby, Senior Circuit Judge, *United States Court of Appeals, Tenth Circuit*	Counsel should be honest and candid with the court. In addition to honesty, counsel should tell the court why it should adopt the proffered reasoning.
David M. Ebel, Circuit Judge, *United States Court of Appeals, Tenth Circuit*	I see three essential ingredients in a persuasive argument: (1) gaining credibility by the advocate; (2) focusing the court's attention on the dispositive matters; and (3) combining both a *reason* to rule a particular way with a roadmap as to *how* such a ruling can be fashioned. A fourth element—style—could also be added. An informal, give-and-take style, is always more persuasive than prepared remarks that are too heavily scripted and adhered to. Lawyers should trust their instinct and allow the "force" to be with them during their argument.
William J. Holloway, Jr., Senior Circuit Judge, *United States Court of Appeals, Tenth Circuit*	*First,* from the opening of the briefs of both sides, in their all-important summary of the argument, and likewise in the beginning of their oral arguments, the lawyers should convincingly show *why* his or her client deserves to win the case, identifying the paramount equities in the client's favor and the distressing injustice that would follow if the client loses. After making that important pitch, the lawyer must flesh out specific means to make this showing so that the court *wants* to rule for the client. *Second,* in the majority of cases, but not all, the lawyers should try to choose one powerful horse to ride with confidence all the way to victory at the finish line. This technique by counsel will tend to keep the judges' focus on the strong points counsel wishes to press. Along the way, meritorious objections and rough spots should be acknowledged and dealt with by counsel, but his or her main theme should not be forgotten. That theme should be confidently reasserted in the peroration of counsel's argument and in the conclusion of his or her brief.

Paul J. Kelly, Jr.,
Circuit Judge,
*United States.Court
of Appeals,
Tenth Circuit*

I have always thought that in addition to a good brief an advocate needs to figure out a theme for her oral argument that is perhaps different from the brief and which is designed to highlight one or two of the best points. An imaginative theme can capture a panel's interest and perhaps change initial impressions.

John C. Porfilio,
Senior Circuit Judge,
*United States Court
of Appeals,
Tenth Circuit*

It seems to me there is one common failing among advocates that inhibits their credibility and, therefore, their persuasiveness. In the attempt to present their cases in the light most favorable to their position, lawyers seem to sublimate the fact there is no perfect case. Indeed, the other side has issues of some weight or the case would not be before the court. Thus, in their enthusiasm to prevail, they naturally tend to ignore facts or issues which are more helpful to the other side than to them. When questioned about those points, as they will undoubtedly be, they become evasive or dismissive. To me, that sort of response immediately calls counsel's credibility into question, and even counsel's good arguments tend to lose their punch.

My advice to an appellate counsel, therefore, is to become as well prepared on the strong points of an adversary's case as you are on your own. More importantly, be prepared to demonstrate why those seemingly strong points bear no weight against the strength of your case. If you cannot make such a demonstration, ask yourself why you are in court because you must expect to prevail on the strength of your issues, not the weakness of your adversary's.

Finally, do not avoid a direct response to a question from the bench. In most cases, the judges will not let you get away with such a tactic anyway; so you must have a ready answer. By doing so, you demonstrate your issues have strength, your presentation is credible, and that you should prevail is evident.

Deanell Reece Tacha,
Chief Judge,
*United States Court
of Appeals,
Tenth Circui*

Whether one is appellant or appellee, the question to be answered precisely is: "What is it that the court must decide to decide in my favor?" If counsel honestly and analytically answers this question, the brief and the oral argument are very clearly targeted to reaching that answer. The appellant must answer in a focused manner: What issue or issues will require the appellate court to reverse the judgment of the court below, and what cases and/or facts precisely address that issue? For appellee, the question is perhaps even more straightforward: What issue requires that the appellate court affirm the district court, and what facts or cases support that result?

As I have worked with advocacy classes, I have been struck by the difficulty that advocates have in answering those questions precisely. Either because of a lack of focus or the difficulty of honing a case to that particularity. Lawyers seem to have an exceedingly difficult time answering directly these pivotal questions.

Leonard I. Garth,
Senior Circuit Judge,
*United States Court
of Appeals,
Third Circuit*

To persuade a panel of the Court to adopt counsel's view of the case, counsel should, in the short time permitted, zero in and focus his oral argument on the strongest issue presented on his appeal. This means that the plethora of subsidiary issues peppering his brief should not receive the attention accorded to the significant focal issue. Moreover, in preparation for argument before the Court, it is strongly advised that a mock argument be held with other members or associates of counsel's firm so that the weaknesses and strengths of his argument can be assessed in advance of appearing in court. If this practice which is employed regularly by the Solicitor General's Office and by the United states Attorneys' Office is good enough for them, it should, and will have merit, for other appellate counsel.

Richard L. Nygaard,
Circuit Judge,
United States Court of Appeals,
Third Circuit

The most effective tool the lawyer has for winning on appeal is his or her brief. Long after the echoes of a brilliant argument die down in the courtroom, the Judge will still have the brief in hand. There is absolutely *no substitute* for a commanding knowledge of the record and all cases critical to the appeal. Misstating either the record or a case that either supports you or which you must distinguish, *severely* weakens the lawyer's credibility in the eyes of the court.

Just as a lawyer must have a command of the record and the law, the lawyer should assume that the Judges do as well. I find it annoying when an attorney arguing on appeal states an argument or a response to a question as, "If you read the record . . . ," or "If you read the district court's opinion . . . ," or "If you read the case of such and such. . ." I will usually interject, "I *have* read the record (or that case), now *you* tell *me* where it supports your argument."

The best way to prepare for oral argument is to prepare your own brief. Farming it out to associates or, worse still, a research or brief writing organization is a poor substitute. When you write your *own* brief, you will have performed the first test of your theories, the facts, and the law.

Marjorie O. Rendell,
Circuit Judge,
United States Court of Appeals,
Third Circuit

There is great merit to the concept of leading from strength. Perhaps in the context of brief writing and appellate argument it should be rephrased as leading with strength. Always put your best argument first, both in the brief and in your oral remarks. In fact, the most impressive oral arguments I have heard have begun with an opening sentence that captures the essence of why the case should be affirmed or reversed. Very often, this is based on either the standard of review or the fact that the case was decided by a jury trial. A cogent, forceful opening can clinch the case at the outset.

Attorneys do not like to be questioned, since it detracts from what they would like to say. But what they fail to realize is that one or more of the judges on the panel probably *have* questions; that is very often the reason the panel schedules the case for argument. The job of the attorney, therefore, is not to make the panel listen to what counsel wants to say, but, rather, it is to try to determine as early as possible which judges have questions and what those questions are. *A welcoming attitude toward questioning is important.*

I have observed that it can impress the court if appellant's counsel, during rebuttal, references the court's astute questioning of appellee's counsel. This somehow reinforces in the court the feeling that it is aligned with appellant's thinking. If employed subtly, this can be persuasive.

One technique that is seldom used, but which I have found convincing, is for the lawyers to point out the pitfalls attendant to the court's deciding the case the other way. That is, very often a court is being called upon to rule in a way that is simply too broad, impractical, or not capable of application. We often find ourselves asking counsel, "What rule would you have us espouse, and how should our opinion flow in terms of anlysis?" We ask this because very often, in fact, it will not "write" in the way that counsel is advocating. For opposing counsel to point this out can be very helpful.

Max Rosenn,
Senior Circuit Judge,
United States Court of Appeals,
Third Circuit

I have some familiarity with appellate advocacy as a lawyer who made his first appellate argument before the Supreme Court of Pennsylvania in 1933, and as an appellate judge who has heard arguments since 1970. I believe that an effective and persuasive appellate advocate must win the confidence of the judges. To do this, counsel must know the facts of the case, be fully familiar with the pertinent principles of law, and argue fairly and logically. A lawyer should impress the court with candor in response to its questions and the argument of the opponents, with the soundness of his or her argument, intellectual honesty, the thoroughness of preparation and visible confidence in his or her case. Counsel should speak clearly, not too rapidly, and address the court directly and with ease. Counsel's credibility and effectiveness are severely damaged when overzealousness leads a lawyer to exaggerate the strength of a legal position or the holding of a court. All of this presupposes that counsel has submitted a well-prepared, reliable, and tidy brief.

Dolores K. Sloviter,
Circuit Judge,
United States Court of Appeals,
Third Circuit

I really believe that a lawyer cannot persuade a good appellate court to adopt his or her view on the case unless the case itself is a winning case. Because we read the briefs as carefully as we do, I will go out of my way to find some basis to decide for a party if I think he, she, or it is right, unless the issue has been waived. Therefore, even the most beautifully written and argued brief cannot persuade me if I believe the facts or the law are contrary to that party's position. Furthermore, because we do not sit alone, if I miss a basis to hold for a party that has written a poor brief, usually one of my colleagues will see through the brief and find the missing piece. Therefore, the mechanics of persuasion are, in my view, limited to finding a good case with winning facts or law.

§ 18.2.2 Lawyers' Recommended Tools

Nancy J. Arnold,
Judge,
Cook County,
Illinois Circuit Court,
(Former president of
the Appellate Lawyers
Assocation)

Starting at the deeper end, I believe that my most important technique as an appellate lawyer consisted of obtaining my own confidence in the logic of my reasoning and the research of authority establishing its principles. I rigorously composed an outline which required me to set out each step in the reasoning process and all the authority and facts to support them. I insisted on never making a leap—no unexpressed assumption or conclusion—no hole in authority—no twists of legal reality. I sought self-assurance that the premises leading to my conclusions were solid in authority and fact and that the premises did lead logically to the conclusion reached. To be persuasive, an argument must instill confidence in the listener. The essential thing is to assure that the advocate himself has that confidence, appropriately.

In the middle of the spectrum is technique relating to the statement of facts. I always considered that to be a very important part of the argument because it tells the story of the case. The case will be defined by the argument, and the argument has already been drawn in detailed outline form. The facts chosen to include in the statement of facts must tell the story so that the argument will grow from it. The facts set out must be accurate and deliberately chosen, complete but without any thing that is unnecessary. The statement of facts should give the court reason to have confidence in it.

Paul J. Brysh,
Assistant United States
Attorney,
Western District of Pennsylvania,
Pittsburgh, Pennsylvania

In those cases in which the application of a legal rule to the case is questionable, counsel on both sides should address the reason or purpose for the rule. Needless to say, the proponent of the application of the rule should attempt to demonstrate that the reason or purpose would be served by applying the rule in that case. Conversely, the opponent should endeavor to show that the reason or purpose is not present in the case or is outweighed by countervailing considerations.

One of the most advantageous things the appellate lawyer can do is to convey effectively to the court a general view of the case that is favorable to his or her position. The lawyer should be conscious of that fact throughout the brief-writing process, in particular. When drafting the statement of facts, the summary of argument, and the argument, the lawyer should have as one of his or her objectives to paint a picture that is as favorable to her or her client or position as accuracy and faithfulness to the record allow.

James D. Crawford,
Senior Counsel,
Schnader, Harrison,
Segal & Lewis,
Philadelphia, Pennsylvania

The techniques we use—or should use—are simple:

Speak directly to the court; maintain eye contact at all times; never read anything but a piece of language—statutory, contractual, etc.—whose exact wording is crucial; answer a question fully, frankly and when it is asked; never try to talk past the red light; avoid personalities; speak clearly and plainly;

know the names of the judges and use them—and be aware when they have written or participated in controlling or crucial cases; know your record cold and have it indexed so that you can find important testimony or exhibits; and, most of all, do not try to deliver a prepared speech in lieu of engaging in a dialog with the court. These are the tricks of our trade, but they are not magic bullets that will arm your readers with the tools of victory.

Edward F. Mannino,
Akin Gump Strauss Hauer & Feld, Philadelphia, Pennsylvania

Remember that judges are people too. Treat this presentation as a *closing argument* to a jury of experts. Demonstrate in your briefs and at oral argument why the issue presented is important.

Demonstrate why fairness requires that the case be decided in favor of your client. Identify the consequences of an adverse ruling to the judicial system and to society as a whole. Remember to place the issues presented in a broader social context, and demonstrate how that context requires the result you are seeking.

Demonstrate how the result is *consistent with precedent*, including the Court's prior decisions. Utilize *logic*, not histrionics or bombast. Respect the Court's *intelligence*. Be *respectful*, not condescending or lecturing. *Answer* the questions posed; each question represents a life line thrown to you if you choose to rasp it firmly.

Howard J. Bashman,
Buchanan Ingersoll,
Philadelphia, Pennsylvania

Your brief must make sense and be persuasive to someone who knows nothing about your case and next to nothing about the areas of law involved. Pursue your strongest and most significant issues and leave the rest behind. Size matters, and quality matters too. Keep your brief as short as possible, and make sure that every cite to the record and to the law is impeccably accurate.

Michael R. Reagan,
Herbolsheimer, Lannon,
Henson, Duncan & Reagan,
Ottawa, Illinois

I believe in the study of the craft of persuasion. But the craft of persuasion is secondary to presenting a well-conceived optimal solution to the problem before the court. Arriving at what that proposed solution should be is the starting point of persuasion, and not a byproduct. The greatest persuasive technique is to be in possession of that well-conceived solution. Determining what that solution should be requires early and sustained effort. Ideally, planning for, or against, the prospect of an appeal should commence at the time of the preparationof the complaint or answer in the case, with knowledge as to where the issues are, or can be, embedded within the various stages of the litigation. However, because many appellate lawyers have their first encounter with a case near the end of the trial court process, those planning opportunities are limited. But they still exist, in different form. Before the brief writing begins, it is crucial to identify which issues have the prospect of success. It may be, particularly in the representation of an appellee, that a fresh issue can indeed be generated, and that it is necessary to do so because the research reveals that there are difficulties with the existing issues. Doing that type of work early in the process immeasurably adds to the prospects of success. In contrast, evaluating the strength of the issues in the case for the first time in preparation for oral argument is usually futile.

Chapter 19

THE BRIEF: PERFECTING THE ARGUMENT

§ 19.1 Trial Afterthoughts, or Brief Writing on Back Burners

Any football coach worth his salt will not dare go into a contest without a game plan. No competent trial lawyer will participate in a trial or hearing without a definite theory or strategy supporting the contention or defense. The coach prepares for the entire game, for all four quarters. Most lawyers do not. They prepare only for the first half, the trial itself. If an appeal is necessary, they will wing it. They are like the coach who goes into the second half without a previously determined strategy.

I do not think that I am being unduly cynical when I suggest that most trial lawyers hope to win on the facts, that the bulk of trial work is fact-specific, both in discovery and at trial. In the event that the factfinder finds against them, in many cases, too many lawyers immediately file a notice of appeal without having much in mind on which to base it. Once the notice is filed, if the trial lawyer belongs to a large firm, some juniors are called in and given their marching orders: "Get a transcript and help me find some trial error. I am very busy with this next case. You will note that I made some objections in evidence rulings, and I submitted some points for charge that were rejected. Look over the transcript and then get back to me." Then they start to write the brief. This is the first time they consider the issues in the case from the perspective of an appeal—although the horse may have escaped from the barn long ago. To be sure, this is one extreme. But from my long experience as an appellate judge, I am convinced that this happens frequently enough to cause concern.

At the other extreme is the ideal scenario: preparation for an appeal starts with the filing of a complaint or indictment, with counsel constantly keeping one eye cocked on the appellate process, knowing that without careful planning and monitoring a possible trial error may not be preserved and trial strategy not directed toward ultimate protection on appeal.

Certainly before the last pretrial conference, when you decide upon your *trial* strategy, you should also lay plans for the *appeal* in the event that the factfinder goes against you. This will take some doing, but here you will be acting as a real lawyer and not some paralegal collecting facts. The full-game strategy requires you to develop alternative tactics. Your plan should require the trial court to make rulings of law or to exercise discretion at designated, predetermined points at pretrial and trial, and in post-trial motions. If at all possible, you devise alternative legal theories of prosecution of claim or defense, with one theory being predicated on the basis that facts *A* will be found and another on the possibility that facts *B* will be found.

At trial, court rulings generally will deal with questions of evidence, directed verdict and jury instructions. Keep in mind our discussion in § 5.4.2, Ultimate Facts: Mixed Questions of Law and Fact. If you win the verdict, you want to be certain that the facts found are "basic" or pure facts; if you are a loser, you want to argue that a legal component exists in the found "facts" in order to have some chance on appeal.

Objections to evidence at trial are often casually made—perhaps, too casually. This results in too many problems. First, you deprive yourself of a strategic advantage at trial by not having the evidence admitted or rejected. Second, you have not laid the proper groundwork for success on appeal. Often, upon reflection and study, appellate judges may conclude that the trial court was wrong on an evidentiary ruling, but we will not disturb it because the reasons asserted on appeal were not given to the trial court in the heat of battle. It is one thing to say, "Objection, the evidence is inadmissible." It is something else to say, "I am objecting under Rule 403 and I am requesting to be heard with the appropriate cases."

In the early 1950s, I was co-counsel with Edward Bennett Williams in a high-profile case in Washington, D.C. I learned many things from this true master at the bar. I still remember that Williams had a separate file of every witness that we and our opponent intended to call. On one side of the open-faced file was a summary of what the witness would probably say; on the other side was a digest of the appropriate law of evidence, including case citations, covering the expected testimony. The true name of the game is preparation.

To summarize, the broad contours of your appellate theory should be sketched out, replete with alternatives, at the same time your trial tactics and strategy are developed. There is time to do it. Cut down on useless, cost-ineffective discovery. It is time to put the horse before the cart. Instead of spending thousands, if not hundreds of thousands, of dollars in discovery in search of a theory of claim or defense, decide first upon a long-range theory for the trial and appellate courts. In 1976, I commented that litigants are "over-discovered, over-interrogatoried, and over-deposed; as a result [they are] over-charged, over-expensed, and overwrought."[1] The inordinate amount of time expended in useless discovery could be well spent in "thinking like a lawyer," in planning the legal theory you will be presenting at both the trial and appellate levels.

The bottom line. You must prepare your game plan for all four quarters—not just the trial, which is only the first half of the game. At the outset, you must anticipate adverse rulings on evidence and jury instructions and lay the proper groundwork. On a more cosmic level, your trial strategy must present alternative theories of law and fact so that all your eggs will not be placed in a single "fact basket."

§ 19.2   The Use of Precedent

"The conclusion we urge in this appeal is mandated by the controlling case of *Alpha v. Bravo*. The facts here are on all fours with those in this controlling precedent. The trial court erred in not applying the rule of *Alpha*."

We see statements like this so often in the briefs. But the problem is that there are precedents *fortissimo* and precedents *pianissimo*, cases that are "just a little bit precedent" and cases that cannot be considered as precedents at all, because they emerge from other jurisdictions and qualify only as persuasive argument.[2]

It is also important to understand how judges determine the longevity of a precedent. Justice Robert H. Jackson addressed this very point:

> The first essential of a lasting precedent is that the court or the majority that promulgates it be fully committed to its principle. That means such individual study of its background and antecedents, its draftsmanship and effects that at least when it is announced it represents not a mere acquiescence but a conviction of those who support it. When that thoroughness and conviction are lacking, a new case

---

1. Ruggero J. Aldisert, *An American View of the Judicial Function,* in Legal Institutions Today: English and American Approaches Compared 72 (American Bar Association 1976), *reprinted in The Role of the Courts In Contemporary Society*, 38 U. Pitt. L. Rev. 437, 467 (1977).

2. This is not the place to analyze the elements of precedent, but I have treated this subject in detail in Ruggero J. Aldisert, *Precedent: What It Is and What It Isn't; When Do We Kiss It and When Do We Kill It?*, 17 Pepp. L. Rev. 605 (1990).

presenting a different aspect or throwing new light, results in overruling or in some other escape from it that is equally unsettling to the law.[3]

Former Justice Walter V. Schaefer of the Illinois Supreme Court also observed that:

an opinion which does not within its own confines exhibit an awareness of relevant considerations, whose premises are concealed, or whose logic is faulty is not likely to enjoy either a long life or the capacity to generate offspring.[4]

Judges do not apply precedents blindly. The putative precedent must be analyzed carefully to determine whether material facts and issues in the compared cases are similar. It must be studied to determine whether the precept deduced therefrom is the holding of the case or merely dictum. More than sixty years ago, Benjamin Cardozo noted that:

precedents are the basic juridical concepts that are the postulants of judicial reasoning, and farther back are the habits of life, the institutions of society, in which those conceptions had their origin, and which, by process of interaction, they have modified in turn.[5]

Cardozo also condemned legal research consisting of search, comparison and little more, which he called the color-matching process, stating:

Some judges seldom get beyond that process in any case. Their notion of their duty is to match the colors of the case at hand against the colors of many sample cases spread out upon their desk. The sample nearest in shade supplies the applicable rule. But, of course, no system of living law can be evolved by such a process, and no judge of a high court, worthy of his office, views the function of his place so narrowly. If that were all there was to our calling, there would be little of intellectual interest about it. The man who had the best card index of the cases would also be the wisest judge.[6]

---

3. Robert H. Jackson, *Decisional Law and Stare Decisis*, 30 A.B.A. J. 334, 335 (1944), reprinted in Walter v. Schaefer, *Precedent and Policy,* 34 U. Chi. L. Rev. 3, 10 (1965).

4. Walter V. Schaefer, *Precedents and Policy*, 34 U. Chi. L. Rev. 3, 10 (1965).

5. Benjamin Cardozo, *The Nature of the Judicial Process* 19 (1921).

6. *Id.* at 20–21

Appellate judges ask themselves questions. Has the precept emerging from the prior case originated in a thorough, well-reasoned opinion that was itself based upon clear and binding precedents? Is the precept seriously weakened by a trenchant dissent, or by a concurring opinion that casts doubt upon the wisdom of the majority opinion? Is the precept found in a single case, or has it been restated and applied in several cases that have reaffirmed its value and social desirability? The answers to these questions tell us that the value of precedents varies widely. They are not all currency of equal value.

§ 19.3 How to Cite and Discuss Cases and Yet be Concise

If one message has come clear from these pages, with virtually uniform support from the state chief justices, it is that lawyers should shorten their briefs. The tightening process must cover all components of the brief. Condense your procedural history to a minimum, reduce the number of issues, limit the statement of facts to those that are material and adjudicative and give the judges a short summary of your argument.

I now turn to what may be the most difficult aspect of tightening up the brief: how to explain the holdings of relevant case authority, replete with facts and reasoning, and still keep the brief concise. This is not easy to do, but remember, no one ever represented that appellate advocacy was a walk in the park. At times it is not enough merely to give a citation, because you feel that this puts an additional burden on the judge to look up the case. At other times, especially in appellee and reply briefs, you want to expose why certain cases relied upon by your adversary are irrelevant. There is a solution to the problem, but some preliminary considerations must be reviewed in order to understand the resolution that I will suggest. Let us review some basic theory of the common law tradition:

- *Case holding.* The holding of a case is expressed in terms of what Roscoe Pound described as a legal rule in the narrow sense.

- *Legal Rules.* "These are precepts attaching a definite detailed legal consequence to a definite, detailed state of facts. If one likes, they are definite threats of definite, detailed official action in the case of definite, detailed state of facts."[7]

---

7. Roscoe Pound, *Hierarchy of Sources and Forms in Different Systems of Law*, 7 Tul. L. Rev. 475, 482 (1933).

- *Precedent.* "A judicial precedent attaches a specific legal consequence to a detailed set of facts in an adjudged case or judicial
  decision, which is then considered as furnishing the rule for the
  determination of a subsequent case involving identical or similar material facts and arising in the same court or a lower court
  in the judicial hierarchy."[8]

- *Material facts and analogies.* Material facts are the lifeblood
  of legal analogies. Analogy does not seek proof of an identity of
  one thing with another, but only a comparison of resemblances.
  It does not depend upon the *quantity* of instances but upon the
  quality of resemblances between things. Reaching a conclusion
  by analogy has the benefit of the high degree of similarity of the
  compared data. The degree of similarity is always the crucial
  inquiry in analogies. Here the skill of the advocate will often
  be the determining factor. Plaintiff's lawyer may argue that the
  historical events of entity *A*—in law, a precedent—bears many
  resemblances to the case at bar *B*. The opponent will argue that
  although the facts in *A* and *B* are similar in some respects, this
  does not mean that those similarities are material and therefore
  relevant, or that the cases are similar in other respects; he or she
  will argue that a false analogy is present. What is one person's
  meat is another person's poison. What is one attorney's material
  and relevant fact in analogical comparisons is the other attorney's immaterial and irrelevant fact. Often the art of advocacy
  resolves itself into convincing the court which facts in previous
  cases are indeed positive analogies, and which are not.[9]

- *Reasoning, reasons, and reasonableness distinguished.* The objective of adjudication is "reasonableness"—judgments that are sound,
  sensible, fair, and just. "Reasoning" is a logical process. "Reasons"
  are the premises used in the reasoning process to achieve reasonableness. Lawyers give "reasons" to prove that their conclusion is
  reasonable.

How then do we apply these concepts to the problem at hand? Understand that appellate judges are interested only in the material facts
and the legal consequences attached to them.

It often becomes necessary to condense the material facts in discussing a particular case. Limit the fact recitation in the cited cases

---

8. *Allegheny Gen. Hosp. v. NLRB*, 608 F.2d 965, 969–70 (3d Cir. 1979).
9. *See* Ruggero J. Aldisert, *Logic for Lawyers: A Guide to Clear Legal Thinking* 87–12 (3d ed. 1996).

to critical facts. These are the adjudicative facts. Decide which facts were important to the ruling and which were not. What you say in your brief depends on why you are citing the case. First, you may be citing the case for the purpose of analogy, for the purpose of comparing the material facts here with those of the compared case. Second, you may be citing the case only for the reasons stated in the compared case; you cite the case because you like the reasons; you like the reasons because they support your theory. But if the compared case is fact-specific, then the reasons may not be too critical. Third, you may be interested only in the conclusion of the case and are citing it only to support the public policy argument asserted to support your brief's conclusion.

The dimensions of your discussion of the case you cite, therefore, are determined by why you have cited it—for the facts, for the reasons, or for the conclusion, or for any combination of the three. You must balance the desire to present something that is tightly written with the necessity of furnishing the court with sufficient tools to accept your argument. The question is always: why have I cited the case? The answer to this depends upon the overarching question: where does this case fit into the theme or focus of the brief?

When you answer this question, you recognize that a case should not be cited, in Loyola Law Dean David W. Burcham's words, "in the nude"—that is, without any explanation for it. The historical purpose and function of citing cases is to record the holding. It is to validate the statement of a legal rule, as we have described in the Poundian sense, a detailed legal consequence to a definite, detailed state of facts. To take an example: "Driving a motor vehicle at sixty miles an hour through a twenty-mile-an hour school zone on the wrong side of the road while intoxicated is a breach of the standard of due care and will impose liability in damages if the conduct is the proximate cause of the injuries sustained."

§ 19.3.1 Use the Parenthetical

In recent years, the parenthetical has become very popular, and I strongly recommend its use. If a case is cited to show resemblances or differences in the facts, a parenthetical disclosing the material facts of the cited case will be very effective: *Fisher & Sons v. Gilardi*, 345 F.4th 666, 678 (9th Cir. 2012) (holding that the reuse of burial caskets differs from the reuse of funereal urns under the statute).

The parenthetical can also be used to state the reasons that supported the conclusion of the cited case: *Gandolfini v. HBO, Inc.*, 543 F.4th 123, 126 (2d Cir. 2004). ("Where a party has not performed to a substantial extent of the contract, the other party is entitled to damages for the missing degree of performance.") The parenthetical also may be used to state the legal rule that constitutes the holding: *Upton Sinclair Muckraking Indus. v. Jimmy Dean Co.* ("Where the parties agreed to sell and purchase a specific number of dressed hogs and live hogs and the seller failed to deliver the live hogs as promised, there was not substantial performance of the contract, and the purchaser is entitled to damages for the missing degree of performance.")

Accompanying a citation with a parenthetical serves three important purposes—(1) it tells the brief reader why you are citing the case, (2) it shows where the case fits into the theme or focus of your brief, and (3) it achieves the objective of concise brief writing.

An example of an excellent use of parentheticals by the United States Supreme Court appears in Justice Stephen Breyer's opinion in *Meyer v. Holley.*[10]

> The Fair Housing Act itself focuses on prohibited acts. In relevant part the Act forbids "any person or other entity whose business includes engaging in residential real estate-related transactions to discriminate," for example, because of "race." 42 U.S.C. § 3605(a). It adds that "person" includes, for example, individuals, corporations, partnerships, associations, labor unions, and other organizations. § 3602(d). It says nothing about vicarious liability.
>
> Nonetheless, it is well established that the Act provides for vicarious liability. This Court has noted that an action brought for compensation by a victim of housing discrimination is, in effect, a tort action. *See Curtis v. Loether*, 415 U.S. 189, 195–196 (1974). And the Court has assumed that, when Congress creates a tort action, it legislates against a legal background of ordinary tort-related vicarious liability rules and consequently intends its legislation to incorporate those rules. *Monterey v. Del Monte Dunes at Monterey, Ltd.*, 526 U.S. 687, 709 (1999) (listing this Court's precedents that interpret Rev. Stat. § 1979, 42 U.S.C. § 1983, in which Congress created "a species of tort liability," "in light of the background of tort liability" (internal quotation marks omitted)). *Cf. Astoria Fed. Sav. & Loan Assn. v. Solimino,*

---

10. *Meyer v. Holley*, 123 S. Ct. 824, 828–829 (2003).

501 U.S. 104, 108 (1991) ("Congress is understood to legislate against a background of common-law . . . principles."); *United States v. Texas,* 507 U.S. 529, 534 (1993). ("In order to abrogate a common-law principle, the statute must 'speak directly' to the question addressed by the common law.")

§ 19.4 String Citations and Other "Dont's"

Don't use string citations. They are generally irritating and useless. Former California Supreme Court Chief Justice Malcolm Lucas emphasized, "Do not use string cites: explain the application of each case or other authority to your argument. Back up your arguments with direct, analogous, or otherwise persuasive authority."

If a single case in the jurisdiction is on point, citation to that case will suffice, particularly if it is relatively recent. Especially irksome are string cites following a well-established legal precept, such as, "A party must have minimum contacts with the forum state before personal jurisdiction can be constitutionally exercised." The brief writer who follows this assertion with a string cite runs the risk of engendering brief-reader wrath.

This is not to say that multiple citations should never be used. I suggest that there is a difference between string citations, in the sense condemned, and what I call multiple citations—a display of numerous authorities of various courts to show support for a given proposition. They are clearly proper and necessary where an issue is open in the jurisdiction and the brief writer wants the reader to know what courts are lined up for and against the proposition. The bottom line: multiple citations are not disfavored; unnecessary citations from the same court repeating the same holding deserve the opprobrious title "string" and are citations *non grata*.

Don't misuse case authority. Whether as a result of sloppiness or overzealous advocacy, a brief writer who stretches the holding of a case beyond a reasonable interpretation will most assuredly antagonize the brief reader. We see this much too often. Recall what I said about my colleague, William H. Hastie, and how he described citing a case for a proposition far beyond its actual holding as "trampling on graves." It is one thing to draw an analogy from a citation and identify it as such; it is quite another to attribute nonexistent characteristics to it. The misdeed begets ill effects that fulminate far beyond one bad citation. The judge may apply *falsus in unus, falsus in omnibus*, and your credibility will suffer severely.[11]

Don't use long quotations. It is a strong judge who can resist the temptation to skip all or a part of a long, unindented quotation.

Don't quote phrases or sentences out of context. This is the fallacy of vicious abstraction. Your credibility suffers. Judges do not like it, and opponents can discover it and pounce on you.

§ 19.5 The Appellee's Brief

The appellee's brief should follow the same suggestions we have made for the appellant: proper statement of issues, a summary of the argument, the enunciation of a theme or focus, and a point-by-point discussion in the argument as presented in this chapter. Some differences in appellate advocacy, however, present themselves. First, you have the advantage of defending a judgment, order, or decision in your favor and often are armed with the statement of reasons offered by the trial court or agency. It is your adversary and not you who has the burden proving that the judgment should be disturbed. Second, in the style of the Greco-Roman rhetoricians, your argument must be a combination of *confutatio* (refuting your opponent's argument) and *confirmatio* (confirming what the court did below).

§ 19.5.1 The Appellee's Statement of Facts

Where you agree with the appellant's statement of facts, even if the literary style or length is not what you would have offered, it may be well to say that you accept it. If you disagree, you probably have two choices: (1) accept with some modifications of your own, or (2) present your own statement.

If you keep in mind the environment in which briefs are read, you will seek to reduce the judges' reading time to a minimum. Keep in mind also the distinction between material or adjudicative facts on the

---

11. This is not to say that judges, and some of our most outstanding ones, do not indulge in the grave-trampling process. They do. And, if they are on the highest courts, they can get away with it. One case that comes to mind was the United States Supreme Court's decision in *Craig v. Boren*, 429 U.S. 190, 197 (1976), the seminal decision that created a new, intermediate scrutiny of statutes in Equal Protection cases: the state action "must serve important governmental objectives, and must be substantially related to the achievement of these objectives." When Justice Brennan first stated this he cited *Reed v. Reed*, 404 U.S. 71, 76 (1971), as authority. *Reed*, however, simply followed the rational basis test: whether the challenged statute "bears a rational relationship to a state objective that is sought to be advanced by the operation of" the statute. *Boren* purported to rest on precedential authority when in fact it did not. A brand new tenet of constitutional law was conceived by artificial insemination.

one hand and surplus narrative on the other. If your quarrel is with the Mickey Mouse trivia in the appellant's statement of facts, let it alone and save your big guns until later. If there has been an omission or misrepresentation as to material facts, however, you may say, "We accept appellee's statement of facts, except that it omits the following [then insert the material with an appendix or record reference] and mistakenly says [so and so] when the record actually says [such and such with a page reference]."

If these factual omissions or errors are important, and you expose them, then your adversary's blood spills on the floor early in the judge's reading of the brief. If you have chosen to restate the facts because there are too many errors or omissions, at the conclusion of your statement it will be helpful to summarize the omissions and inaccuracies.

Ohio Supreme Court Chief Justice Thomas J. Moyer makes the same point: "Conciseness in the writing of an appellee's brief includes the realization that the judge does not need to read the statement of facts twice. The appellee should indicate which portions of the statement of facts and statement of the case with which the appellee agrees and devote your efforts to clarifying the appellant's statement and adding facts that are favorable to the appellee's case that may not have been mentioned in the appellant's statement."

§ 19.5.2 Comment on the Appellant's Authorities

The best case scenario for the appellee unfolds when the appellant has neglected to cite a controlling case of the highest court of the jurisdiction or of the court in which you now appear. When this occurs, you hit your adversary between the eyes as soon as possible. But do it skillfully with a powerful *ad rem* approach. Avoid the *ad hominem* accusation that the appellant is deceiving the court. The judges will probably take it over from there at oral argument.

Does the appellee comment on all the authorities cited by the appellant? The conventional wisdom is that you should, but there are certain caveats. You are not in a law school class reciting the entire case cited by the appellant; you are before a busy appellate court. It is sufficient to note that the holding of the case is not as represented; if you can get a one-sentence direct quote laying out the law, put it in. It is sufficient also to note that the material facts in that case differ from the instant one and quickly show the distinction. It is sufficient also to show any difference in the procedural postures of the two cases. This may become very important when the appeal is from summary judgment or from a jury or bench trial and the cited case emanated from a Rule 12(b)(6) motion (judgment on the pleadings); point out the distinction and succinctly explain why it makes a difference.

The rule of thumb is that the appellee should have an answer to every authority cited by the appellant, but the response need not be unduly prolix. Often totally irrelevant citations are thrown in as make-weights in the appellant's brief. These do not deserve the dignity of measured response, and here perhaps is where a footnote may tidily dispose of them.

But where the flashpoint of dispute is choosing among competing legal precepts or interpreting the legal material selected or applying the resulting legal precept to the cause, it is not enough merely to say that your choice is the better (or majority) view, or that your interpretation or application is superior; you must explain why yours is the preferable view. Always give the court a supply of reasons, not only to persuade them to make the decision in your favor, but also to furnish material that the judges may properly use in their justification of the decision—the opinion they will write.

A word about logic. It is not enough for the appellee to charge that the appellant's "reasoning was flawed." Be very specific and identify precisely why and how the logical progression fails. The judges will be impressed. Besides, it will straighten out your thinking. Often, when one says that the "reasoning is flawed," what is meant is that one disagrees with the judgment call used to choose the major premise; such is not a quarrel with canons of logical reasoning, but a disagreement with the value judgment employed by the court. Do not fall into this trap.

Finally, when you (and ostensibly the trial court) insist that a certain case is controlling, be sure to explain why.

§ 19.6   The Reply Brief

The reply brief can be both the best of times and the worst of times. It is at its best when it addresses a point not raised in the appellant's opening brief, such as an argument or error in the appellee's brief, or a new decision handed down since the filing of the opening brief. It is at its worst when an appellant simply rewrites the opening brief and restates what was said before.

Someone who did not know a thing about how appellate judges decide cases has preached a gospel to many appellants' lawyers to file a reply brief in every case: "Always have the last word."

Since 1968, I have been reading reply briefs by the thousands in appellate courts all over the country, and maybe 500 genuinely qualified as reply briefs. Most simply repeat arguments contained in the opening brief.

The bottom line. Prepare a reply brief only in the following situations:

- if the appellee cites a case not covered in the opening brief and you are able to show that it is either not controlling or does not stand for the proposition asserted;

- if the appellee advances an important argument not covered by your opening brief and you have a convincing rebuttal to it;

- if the appellee has raised a question of jurisdiction not covered in your opening brief;

- if relevant cases have been handed down since filing your opening brief;

- if the appellee has made a misstatement of fact or an irrelevant argument;

- if the appellee has failed to respond to a principal argument you made in your opening brief. Here, you succinctly say that the appellee has apparently conceded this point.

Before you write a reply brief, think of analogous situations at trial. Redirect examination is limited to new matters brought out in cross-examination. The reply brief serves the same function on appeal, so it should be subject to the same limitation. Your case in rebuttal is likewise limited to new matters that were brought up in your adversary's case. Again, the same considerations apply in an appeal. An attempt to use redirect or rebuttal simply to rehash points already made would call down the wrath of the trial court. Recycling your opening brief as a reply brief has the same effect on the appellate court.

My advice:

- Put your best foot forward in your opening brief. Reply briefs are not the favorite children of appellate judges.

- An appellant should never deliberately save for the reply its response to an argument it knows that the appellee will advance. The opening brief should be drafted as persuasively and completely as possible. This means that you include all relevant argument. Those who wait may be too late. Moreover, in courts that are absolutely current, often the judges will receive the briefs in chief before the reply brief, and they read these briefs and form tentative impressions before the reply briefs arrive. This is especially the case in accelerated briefing schedules.

- Do not file a reply brief unless you can explicitly justify it in terms of the purposes I have presented here. If none of these situations obtains, do not file a reply brief.

University of South Carolina Law Professor Thomas R. Haggard offers some additional impressive advice on reply briefs.[12]

- Do not nitpick. Appellant should focus on the major, substantive errors that respondent has made in its brief. Appellant should not quibble over whether respondent has correctly stated the "holding" of some obscure precedent, whether respondent has slightly mischaracterized a minor factual point, whether some quotation has arguably been taken out of context, or whether all the cases the respondent cites truly support the proposition for which they are cited—except in extreme cases of abuse, of course. Judge Friedman in the Federal Circuit expressed it this way: "Do not file a reply brief, as some lawyers do, that is primarily concerned with correcting minor errors the other side has made. Such a brief is a sign of weakness: it suggests that you have no good answers on the merits, and therefore are nitpicking at the periphery."

- Do not indulge in invective. Appellants generally feel that their original briefs were as sharp as the Excalibur sword and that respondent's brief has now blunted the point and severely nicked the edges of the blade. At this point, things begin to get a little personal, and the temptation is strong to refer to respondent's brief as a viper pit of deception and engage in other harangues. This is counterproductive. The reply brief can be the *pièce de résistance* of the appeal; or it can be its Waterloo. Appellants should not be casual in how they approach the project. Realizing that appellate courts are always reluctant to reverse lower court decisions, that the burden is on the appellant, and that the chances of winning on appeal are not good, appellant's opening brief should have been a solid, legally compelling and well written effort. Respondent has had the opportunity to take its best shot, and the message of appellant's reply brief is that the shot missed.

---

12. Thomas J. Haggard, *Writing the Reply Brief*, Scrivener, Mar./Apr. 2001, at 42.

§ 19.7 Advice from an Appellate Specialist

Herb Fox, an attorney from Santa Barbara, California, specializes in appellate advocacy and authors a monthly column on appellate court practice. He offers three suggestions to follow in drafting appellate briefs:

1. Leave ample time to revise and edit the brief. If your analysis of the record, legal research and first draft takes fifty hours, plan to spend another twenty-five hours rewriting and editing.

2. Understand the reasons for revising and rewriting: The first draft is to demonstrate to yourself that you have command of the procedural history, facts, and law. The second draft is to demonstrate to opposing counsel why they are wrong. The third draft is to demonstrate to trial counsel and the client that you have a handle on the case and to invite their comments which, once received, should largely be discarded. The fourth through twenty-fifth draft is for the appellate court: by the fourth draft you have a rough idea of what the case is really about, and now it is time to make the brief sparkle, sing, and persuade.

3. Send a draft to trial counsel and clients for comments, they may catch grammatical errors. As a general rule, all other comments should be ignored. Trial counsel is usually making the case for the client, and both probably know little about the appellate standard of review, writing, or the art of obtaining reversal.

§ 19.8 Brief Writing: A Summary

Above all else, the argument should be convincing. The brief should do its job even when the case poses difficult questions and your opponent's brief raises serious arguments that your brief may not answer completely. Your brief should state the strongest possible position for your client and should do so in a manner that convinces the court that your position is worthy of acceptance or at least serious consideration.

If you cannot do this, you should not be filing the brief at all. Except in the case of a criminal defendant who has a constitutional right to pursue even a weak argument that has a remote chance for success, there is no excuse for filing a brief that cannot convince its own author. Even in the criminal case, the brief should persuade the court that at least its author is convinced.

Chapter 20

THE BRIEF: FORMAL AND INFORMAL FALLACIES

§ 20.1 Overview

Several types of fallacies rear their ugly and unwelcome heads in the law. One type of fallacy occurs when we neglect the rules of logic and fall into erroneous reasoning. Other fallacies, generally called informal or material fallacies, meticulously follow logical form but suffer from improper content or emphasis. A fallacy then is not merely an error, but a way of falling into an error.

The name comes from the Latin, fallax, which suggests a deliberate deception, but most fallacies are not intentional. Fallacies are dangerous because they are false conclusions or interpretations resulting from processes of thinking that claim or appear to be valid but fail to conform to the requirements of logic.[1] A fallacy can be defined as "any argument that seems conclusive to the normal mind but that proves, upon examination, not to establish the alleged conclusion,"[2] or more succinctly, a form of argument that has intuitive appeal but does not withstand rational scrutiny. They have been identified as such ever since Aristotle described these arguments: "That some [lines of] reasoning are genuine, while others seem to be so but are not, is evident. This happens with arguments, as also elsewhere, through a certain likeness between the genuine and the sham."[3] Common fallacies abound in all writings—speeches, commentaries, legislative debates, political oratory, TV editorials, columns, articles, household and family discussions, and personal conversations.

§ 20.2 A Listing of Formal Fallacies

Formal fallacies arise when there is an error in the logical or formal structure of the argument quite apart from the content of the premises. They can be discovered without any knowledge of the subject matter with which the argument is concerned. Our inquiry into formal fallacies begins with the categorical syllogism. The rules of the categorical syllogism form guidelines upon which a deductive or inductive argument in proper logical form may be based. Conversely

---

1. Rosental J. Creighton, *An Introductory Logic* 208 (1898).

2. Ralph Monroe Eaton, *General Logic* 332 (1931).

3. De Sophistics Elechis, in *The Works of Aristotle* (W.D. Ross trans. 1928).

stated, to depart from any of these rules is to commit a logical fallacy of form; it is to commit what is known as a formal fallacy.

I furnish now only a catalog or listing or tally of formal fallacies without describing or defining them. Here again for further study I refer you to *Logic for Lawyers*.[4]

§ 20.2.1   Fallacies in Categorical Syllogisms

Categorical syllogisms contain three terms, two premises, and one conclusion. The premises and conclusion we have discussed above. The three terms are defined as follows:

- The *major term* occurs once in the major premise and once in the conclusion. It expresses the general class or attribute with which we are concerned.

- The *minor term* occurs once in the minor premise and once in the conclusion. It identifies the particular instance that we want to include in the general class.

- The *middle term* occurs once in each premise. It is the connector we use to establish a relationship between the major term and the minor term.

These then are the rules that you must follow to avoid formal fallacies:

> *Rule 1*: A valid categorical syllogism must contain exactly three terms, each of which is used in the same sense throughout the argument.

> *Rule 2*: In a valid categorical syllogism, the middle term must occur in at least one premise.

> *Rule 3*: In a valid categorical syllogism, no term can occur in the conclusion which does not occur in a premise.

> *Rule 4*: No categorical syllogism is valid if it has two negative premises.

> *Rule 5*: If either premise of a valid categorical syllogism is negative, the conclusion must be negative.

> *Rule 6*: No valid categorical syllogism with a particular conclusion can have two universal premises.

Violation of any of these rules is a formal fallacy and renders the argument invalid.

---

4. Ruggero J. Aldisert, *Logic for Lawyers: A Guide to Clear Legal Thinking* (3d ed. 1997).

§ 20.2.2   Fallacies in Hypothetical Syllogisms

In law we often encounter a compound proposition called a hypothetical or conditional proposition. Hypothetical or conditional propositions are the darlings of law professors and of appellate judges asking questions at oral argument: "If we follow that rule, what will be the result in a case where . . . " This type of compound proposition is not categorical, for it does not directly assert the existence of a fact. Instead it contains a condition—"if," "unless," "granted," "supposing"—and it is divided into two parts: the *antecedent* and the *cosequent.*

- If the offer is accepted before the offeror revokes, the revocation is invalid.

- *Antecedent*: the offer is accepted before the offeror revokes

- *Consequent*: the revocation is invalid

The conditional proposition can be combined with other propositions to form a hypothetical argument.

- If the defendant was denied due process, the conviction is invalid.

- The defendant was denied due process.

- Therefore, the conviction is invalid.

Valid hypothetical arguments cannot be constructed by making either of the following moves, which constitute the two fallacies in this area:

1. Denying the antecedent

2. Affirming the consequent

§ 20.2.3   Fallacies in Disjunctive Syllogisms

Disjunctive propositions present their conditions as alternatives. A disjunctive proposition expresses an "either-or," or an "if, then-not" relation between at least two component propositions. A disjunctive syllogism may consist, for example, of a disjunctive proposition as the major premise, a minor premise categorically affirming or denying one of the alternative propositions, and a conclusion that categorically affirms or denies the other alternative. Such arguments are subject to the fallacy of the imperfect disjunctive.

§ 20.3   A Listing of Material or Factual Fallacies

Material, or factual, fallacies do not result from violations of formal logic rules. They are called "material" because they exist not in the form of an argument, but in its factual content or matter. For this reason, they cannot be set right without some knowledge of the subject. It is difficult to condense into a single definition everything encompassed by material fallacies, yet two basic tenets of logic provide keys to their understanding:

- Logical reasoning presupposes that the terms shall be unambiguously defined and used in a uniform manner throughout.

- The discipline of logic demands that the conclusion be derived from the premises rather than assumed.

Material fallacies can sneak up on us as readily as do fallacies of form. Logicians, scientists, and other careful scholars are especially adept at detecting and avoiding them. Professors William and Mabel Sahakian describe them as "numerous, deceptive and elusive—so elusive that a person untrained in detecting them can easily be misled into accepting them as valid."[5] Logicians differ as to the precise categorization of material fallacies, because some resemble or relate to a type of argument rather than a type of logic, but for my purposes, I will follow in major part the classification set forth by the Sahakians.

§ 20.3.1   Fallacies of Irrelevant Evidence

Fallacies of irrelevant evidence are arguments that miss the central point at issue and rely instead upon emotions, ignorance and other irrelevant matters.

1. *Fallacy of irrelevance* (or irrelevant conclusions, *ignoratio elenchi*)

2. *Fallacies of distraction*

   a. *Argumentum ad misericordiam*, or the appeal to pity

   b. *Argumentum ad verecundiam*, or the appeal to prestige

   c. *Argumentum ad hominem*, or the appeal to personal ridicule

   d. *Argumentum ad populum*, or the appeal to popular opinion

---

5. William and Mabel Sahakian, *Ideas of the Great Philosophers* 11 (1966).

e. *Argumentum ad antiquitam*, or the appeal to tradition

f. *Argumentum ad terrorem*, or the appeal to fearsome consequences

§ 20.3.2 Miscellaneous Material Fallacies

1. *Fallacy of accident* (or *dicto simpliciter*): applying the general rule to exceptional circumstances.

2. *Converse fallacy of accident* (or the fallacy of selective instances or hasty generalizations): deriving a general rule from an inadequate sample of instances.

3. *False cause* (or *post hoc ergo propter hoc*): concluding from the conjunction of two events that one caused the other.

4. *Conclusion that does not follow* (or *non sequitur*): employing premises that do not support the conclusion reached.

5. *Compound question* (or poisoning the well): phrasing the question so as to prefigure the answer.

6. *Begging the question* (or *petitio principii*, arguing in a circular): assuming as true what is to be proved.

7. *You yourself do it* (or *tu quoque*): meeting criticism with the argument that the other person engages in the very conduct hoe or she is criticizing.

§ 20.3.3 Linguistic Fallacies

1. *Fallacy of equivocation*: using terms that are vague or signify a variety of ideas.

2. *Fallacy of amphibology*: using statements whose meaning is unclear because of the syntax.

3. *Fallacy of composition*: concluding that a property possessed by one member of a group is also possessed by all members of the group.

4. *Fallacy of division*: concluding that a property possessed by the whole is also possessed by each of the parts individually.

5. *Fallacy of vicious abstraction*: taking a statement out of context.

6. *Argumentum ad nauseam*: sustaining one's position by repetition or other needlessly lengthy argument

§ 20.4 Fallacies: A Final Word

Our understanding of fallacies can be sharpened in the course of daily life. Read editorials and opinion pieces, and put the reasoning to the tests. Are the authors guilty of erecting strawpersons and knocking them down, thus committing the fallacy of irrelevant conclusions? Do they beat their breasts over an answer expressed in a news conference by the president or governor or mayor when the question was loaded with three or four compound parts? Does the content of the piece truly follow logical form? Does it appear as a categorical, hypothetical, or disjunctive syllogism? Do you see *ad hominems* or other fallacies?

Pay attention to TV correspondents in their sixty-second sound bites following news accounts. Are they guilty of the fallacy of hasty generalization by prophesizing broad consequences from one single event in a fast-breaking story? Do you detect any fallacies of distraction? Appeals to pity or to the masses? Are they guilty of *dicto simpliciter*, attempting to project a general rule from that which obviously is an exception to the rule? For the apogee of political science fiction, analyze carefully the comments of senators and congresspersons who blithely offer comments on sudden events without a whit of understanding of the underlying factual premises.

Or at the friendly corner tavern, listen to the loud defense of conclusions on church, school, family, religion, and politics. Without entering the discussion yourself (do not ever try to use reflective reasoning in a bar), attempt to identify the premises employed by the discussants. Are there any premises? Listen to conclusions that they draw from current facts. Are these permissible inferences, that is, inferences that would reasonably follow in logical sequence based on past human experience, or are they sheer speculation? How about: "I know the game was fixed! How could a team lose three in a row to the Mets when they beat them six times straight."

In the tavern or the cocktail lounge, take an end seat and drink deeply of *non sequiturs* and *post hocs*.

But do not get smug. All of us commit fallacies every day in reaching judgments—all of us, and that includes judges, lawyers, professors, preachers, and authors of books. We do this because our thinking is not always reflective. We are "thinking" every waking moment of the day. At any time, there is always a penny for our thoughts. We have daydreams and reveries. We build castles in the air. We conjure up mental pictures and random recollections. We sometimes "think" and "conclude" because we want a certain conclusion. We think that wishing will make it so.

Sometimes, we unwittingly insert a note of invention and add it to a faithful record of observation. We simply want to believe something. We are certain our kids do not do the bad things that others do. We are totally convinced that our best friends did not say what others reported that they said. We are constantly influenced by emotions, beliefs, and social wants and demands. We are human; we are not computers.

So sometimes we do draw conclusions by a process that lies somewhere between a flight of fancy and a dispassionate weighing of the relevant considerations that should be employed to reach a reasoned conclusion. We must all confess to this. But by now you have learned that what is derived is reflective thinking and that this involves more than a sequence of ideas. To do our jobs as members of the legal profession, and of community and family units, and to earn the respect of those who know us, and the accolade that we are clear thinkers, we have an obligation. That obligation is to employ reflective thinking when called upon to solve a problem, any problem whether at home, school, church, office, business, or in our social relations. We must respect the canons of reflective thinking, what John Dewey called "a *con*-sequence—a consecutive ordering in such a way that each determines the next as its proper outcome, while each outcome in turn leans back on or refers to, its predecessors."[6]

What John Dewey said over three-quarters of a century ago is important and should be our watchword:

> The successive portions of a reflective thought grow out of one another and support one another; they do not come and go in a medley. Each phase is a step from something to something. . . . The stream or flow becomes a train or chain. There are in any reflective thought definite units that are linked together to a common end.[7]

If we follow these watchwords, we will go a long way in avoiding the pitfalls of fallacy.

---

6. John Dewey, *How We Think* 4 (2d ed. 1933).

7. *Id.* at 4–5.

Chapter 21

THE BRIEF: A COMPENDIUM OF ADVICE

§ 21.1   Writing the Argument: A Recap

Brief writing for appellate advocates is not easy. As my Marine Corps boot camp drill instructor used to say in 1942: "We didn't promise you a rose garden!"

Your finished product must demonstrate substance, acceptability, and continuity. Your product must display an awareness of broad relevant considerations and be faithful to the canons of logic. Such an effort does not come about automatically. It results from the brief writer's participation in the scholarly life, succinctly described by Gilbert Highet:[1]

> It is a curious life we lead, the life of scholarship . . . Consider first the life of learning. It is based on certain principles which people outside the academic field seldom fully understand or appreciate.
>
> The first of these is devotion: devotion and diligence. The Germans pithily call it Sitzfleisch, "flesh to sit on" because they admire the will power that keeps a man at his desk or laboratory table hour after hour, while he penetrates inch by inch to the heart of a problem. But many of us now find that Sitzfleisch is not so important as what newspaper men call "leg work."
>
> The second principle of scholarship . . . is humility . . .
>
> The third principle of scholarship is far easier to apply now than it has ever been throughout history. This is organization. Closely allied to this intellectual ideal is a fourth principle of scholarship . . . collaboration.

Never dictate a brief. Prepare your first draft with whatever tool helps you to work and think most effectively: pen, pencil, typewriter, word processor, whatever. You will not be able to complete it in one sitting so devise a strategy that will enable you to get back to it with a minimum of wheel spin. Ernest Hemingway is said to have stopped

---

1. Gilbert Highet, *The Scholarly Life*, 41 Am. Scholar 522 (1972).

the day's work at a point when he had clearly in his head what he was going to write on the following day. I know a professional who, when he starts a day with writer's block, gets back on track by retyping the last page he wrote the day before.

So, you have now battled through the "block" and written the argument. Now, rewrite it. Put it aside again and come back to it later. Let it cool off for awhile. The length of time depends upon your schedule. Maybe put it aside for a few hours. Preferably a couple of days, or even a week. Then revise it again. Rewrite. Rewrite. Rewrite. Do not feel incompetent. Remember when it comes to professional writing, appellate brief writers *are* professional writers.

There is no such thing as good writing; there is only good rewriting. Approach revision as a stranger, as an outside reader and editor who is seeing the copy fresh for the first time.

Edit your own work. *Edit like a reader*: identify the problems you encounter as a reader; determine whether the sequence of ideas flows smoothly and logically; determine whether the ideas are adequately supported; look for conspicuous omissions; look for needless repetition. Then edit like a writer: assess your writing techniques and mark up your draft like an editor would; read certain passages aloud, if necessary, and train your ear to detect errors reliably; avoid the trap of falling in love with your writing—love often blinds.

I like Wisconsin Supreme Court Justice William A. Bablitch's phrase, "Develop the skill of distance." He describes this as "the ability to distance yourself from your written work so as to see it through the eyes of a first time reader." He suggests that you "[r]oleplay yourself into being a first time reader."

> Next concentrate on the sentence and paragraph you are reading. Don't let your mind to wander ahead of your text. When you wrote it, you knew where you were going, but the first time reader does not. Then ask yourself, does this sentence make sense? Does this sentence and paragraph flow logically from the preceding?
>
> The more you force yourself to do this, the more you will see gaps, ambiguities, and lack of clarity in your writing. You will begin to understand the trap so many writers fall into when they know their subject either too well or not well enough. You will see where the connecting bridges are missing between sentences or between paragraphs, where

sentences that seemed to make sense when you write them will make little sense to the first time reader.[2]

Assess the "beat" of your writing. There is a difference between writing for reading and writing for speaking, even though each form has both mood and rhythm. Is the mood exaggerated? Do the words come through as a stentorian roar or as a "soft sell," soothing but nonetheless persuasive?

Never become complacent with your writing. Remember, effective writing is a lifetime goal, never a final accomplishment. Become your own best critic. Try to write so that when you finish you can look at the result and honestly say, "I have just done the very best I am capable of at this stage in my literary development." Regularly review your past writing. Ask how it appeals to you now. Assess improvement or deterioration in your writing style. Ask yourself whether your words remain as persuasive as they first seemed and whether they do a good job of expressing the thoughts you intended when you began. Keep always in mind that writing is like exercising a muscle: The more you write, the easier it becomes.

Check and double-check your spelling. Run the entire brief through the spell check on the word processor. But do not stop here. Read the draft again because some words may be properly spelled but contextually erroneous. Obey the rules of grammar.[3]

Make certain that you include a year date for every citation. Some supreme court justices fail to do this, but you can excuse them, for rank hath its privileges. And never include a Federal Reporter citation without identifying the circuit.

§ 21.2 State Chief Justices Speak

Charles E. Jones,
Arizona

Be concise and direct. Written work should predominately reflect the active voice, not the passive. Omit weak arguments that are largely, if not completely irrelevant, and focus exclusively on the most persuasive, authoritative arguments that will lead to the disposition of issues. State the strongest and best arguments first.

---

2. William A. Bablitch, *Writing to Win*, Compleat Law., Winter 1988, at 12.

3. *See Appellate Judicial Opinions* 195–96 (Robert A. Leflar, ed. 1974) (offering a delightful spoof on writing style).

Mary J. Mullarkey, *Colorado*	Develop a coherent theory of the case. Give analytical framework to reach the result you want. Be as accurate and precise as possible. You build credibility by fairly characterizing the law and the facts. Limit the number of issues raised on appeal.
Ronald T.Y. Moon, *Hawaii*	Follow the appellate rules on briefing scrupulously. Write in a concise and direct fashion, minimizing the utilization of long, rambling footnotes. Maintain credibility by presenting argument in a civil, reasonable, and professional manner.
Stephen N. Limbaugh, Jr., *Missouri*	Concede points that need to be conceded, To do so is no sign of weakness, and judges will appreciate the candidness. Double-space and use large type size, if not otherwise required by local rules of appellate practice. This makes the briefs more user-friendly for judges, like me, whose eyes glaze over from so much brief reading.
Karla M. Gray, *Montana*	Be focused and concise: Say it once, say it well, and move on. Set out only the facts pertinent to the issues raised. Long statements of fact tend to leave the impression that you are making a jury argument because your legal issues are not going to be very strong. Meet adverse authorities head on and, where you cannot do so with a reasonable legal analysis, concede the issue and save your credibility for other issues.
John V. Hendry, *Nebraska*	Failure to recognize and structure the brief around the standard of review. The standard of review is the engine that drives the opinion. Failure to recognize this, and to incorporate one's argument around it, is tantamount to driving the engine off the track. Failure to accurately set forth the record. One that fails in this regard raises questions on the accuracy

of other aspects of the brief and diminishes the credibility of the brief. Failure to provide a scholarly analysis of the pertinent cases. Failure to provide such analysis leaves the appellate court with the impression that one has simply chosen to throw everything at the court, hoping the court will find "something on its own that will stick."

Patricio M. Serna,
New Mexico

Be conscientious in complying with appellate rules of procedure, such as informing the court of the manner in which an error was preserved in the lower court and including citations to the record for assertions of fact. Alert the appellate court to the proper standard of review and present the argument in the context of the standard of review. Be honest and forthright about the facts and the law, even if they appear to hinder an argument, because any perceived concealment will be far more damaging.

Judith S. Kaye,
New York

Know Your Audience. This means knowing, and abiding by, all rules of the court—both as to form and as to substance of the brief. Know Your Case. Nothing is more appreciated by judges—who have lots of briefs to read—than a clear, concise, cogent writing. That can be accomplished only when you truly understand, and argue, what's important about your case. Win Your Reader. Briefs are private oral argument time with the reader. Inform your reader, clearly and simply, right at the outset as to what your argument will be; build it carefully with an accurate, persuasive statement of the facts and authorities; and then gently remind the reader of what you have established. The brief you want to write is the one the judge turns to when deciding how to vote and composing the opinion.

Thomas J. Moyer,
Ohio

The most effective briefs present the facts in a narrative, accurate, and persuasive style and present the legal issues in a manner that draws the interest of the reader. You want the judge to believe that he or she is required in your case, to decide a very important legal issue. Be concise. Do not repeat arguments. Do not gratuitously demean the intelligence or skills of opposing counsel. Judges who are reading hundreds of pages to prepare for oral argument simply have no time for redundancies and irrelevant comments. Conciseness in the writing of an appellee's brief includes the realization that the judge does not need to read the statement of facts twice. The appellee should indicate which portions of the statement of facts and statement of the case with which the appellee agrees and devote his or her efforts to clarifying the appellant's statement and adding facts that are favorable to the appellee's case that may not have been mentioned in the appellant's statement of facts. Be faithful to the record. If you misstate facts or unreasonably stretch the holdings in cases, you will lose credibility with the reader that will diminish the ability to be persuasive regarding points upon which you should prevail.

Ralph J. Cappy,
Pennsylvania

Appellate advocates owe a duty of professional responsibility, not only to their clients, but to the court. Far too frequently, members of the bar push the boundaries of proper advocacy in their fervor for success. Thus, while it should go without saying, as a foundational requirement, counsel must provide, with candor, a complete recitation of the facts at issue and an accurate characterization of the relevant law. Appellate advocates will be more successful if they are cognizant of the role that appellate courts play in interpreting the meaning of the constitution and legislative enactments, and in advancing the common law. Appreciation of this role should lead the advocate to go beyond merely seeking relief for his or her client; rather counsel must understand, and explain to the court with clarity, what precise legal holding it is that he or she desires. While an appellate court grapples with the law in the context of an appeal involving particular parties, the review process is incomplete without some consideration of the practical ramifications of a particular interpretation or holding on the greater body of law involved and on society as a whole. Thus, appellate counsel is well advised to provide to the court, via explanation and even concrete example, an understanding of the broader statewide, and perhaps even national, implications of its decision.

Frank J. Williams, *Rhode Island*

List relevant standard of review before each rgument and confine argument to the applicable standard; use summary of the case section to give more detailed background of the case so that reader may be educated before he or she proceeds to the argument sections; be vigilant about maintaining perfect organization, spelling, grammar, and citation.

David Gilberson, *South Dakota*

Lead with your best punch. Go with one or two of your best issues that will really decide the case. A brief with fifteen or twenty assignments of error tells me the attorney is desperate and really is grasping at straws. No trial judge I ever knew was so bad as to make that many errors.

Frank F. Drowota II, *Tennessee*

Summarize the relevant facts in a non-argumentative, chronological narrative rather than a witness-by-witness account. State the issues clearly and concisely. Make your strongest arguments first. Do not ignore opposing authority.

Sharon Keller, *Texas Court of Criminal Appeals*	It is helpful if a brief summarizes the argument at the beginning. Briefs should always be concise. And, a little thing, headings and subheadings are good things.
Gerry L. Alexander, *Washington*	An argument presented efficiently requires editing. It is important for the attorneys to tell us up front and in conclusion what relief they seek from our court. It is helpful if the brief is divided into sections with good headings and clear transitions between issues.
Shirley S. Abrahamson, *Wisconsin*	When writing a brief, keep in mind that the result you want is an opinion in your favor. Make it easy for the judges to write that opinion by including all the necessary facts, legal precedent, and policy analysis in your brief. If the court will have to announce standards and criteria to be applied in future cases, try to suggest them in your brief. Adapt the style and mechanical details of your brief to human realities. Judges do not always have the law library and case record available to them. They read briefs in bed, in cars, and on planes. Quote the relevant statutes and make sure the appendix is sufficient to give the flavor of the record. Do not ignore unfavorable precedent. Ethically, you are obligated to inform the court of binding precedent in the controlling jurisdiction. Strategically, an unfavorable case will do far more damage when it is emphasized by your opponent, or worse, when the court discovers it after oral argument and you no longer have the opportunity to explain or distinguish it or ask that it be overruled.

§ 21.3 United States Circuit Chiefs Speak

Michael Boudin,
First Circuit

Be clear and concise—write and rewrite until the issue and answer can be identified in one short sentence. This will also aid the practitioner in culling out the real issues for appeal. Do not use footnotes—they distract and disrupt the reader. If the information is important enough to include, it is important enough to weave into the text. Remember your audience—the judge reading the brief has not spent the last few years living the case. Before filing the brief, let someone who has not been working on the case review it. If the argument is not clear to him, the brief is not finished.

John M. Walker, Jr.,
Second Circuit

Be concise, do not repeat arguments or facts. The poorest, least persuasive briefs are all too often those that the lawyer has not taken the time to reduce to its essence. Be highly selective in choosing the few points that have the best chance of prevailing. How often has the fourth or fifth point raised ever resulted in a victory for the appellant? Be careful with the mechanics of spelling, citation, and avoiding typographical errors (such as a line repeated or dropped on the word processor). Such mistakes subconsciously convey the lawyer's lack of concern for his client's cause.

Edward R. Becker,
Third Circuit,
1996–2003

Limit the number of points. You will rarely win on more than one or two points. Overbriefing impairs your credibility. Acknowledge the vulnerable points in your position and then tell the Court how to deal with them. Make sure your argument is logically arranged. Clarity of writing is key.

Carolyn Dineen King,
Fifth Circuit

Pick the most important issues, deal with them thoroughly, and omit the others. Deal directly with cases, statutes, and policy arguments that are adverse to your position. Be concise.

Douglas H. Ginsburg, *D.C. Circuit*	Be as brief as possible. Clearly outline the arguments. Conclude with a specific request for relief.
Haldane Robert Mayer, *Federal Circuit*	Be clear and concise—write and rewrite until the issue and answer can be identified in one short sentence. This will also aid the practitioner in culling out the real issues for appeal. Do not use footnotes—they distract and disrupt the reader. If the information is important enough to include, it is important enough to weave into the text. Remember your audience—the judge reading the brief has not spent the last few years living the case. Before filing the brief, let someone who has not been working on the case review it. If the argument is not clear to him, the brief is not finished.
Patricia M. Wald, Chief Judge Emeritus, *D.C. Circuit*	Visualize the whole before you begin. What overriding message is the document going to convey? What facts are essential to the argument? How does the argument take off from the facts? How do different arguments blend together? Better still, if it's a brief, visualize the way the judge's opinion should read if it goes your way. (Too many briefs read as if the paralegal summed up all conceivably relevant facts, and then the lawyer took over with the legal arguments, and never the twain doth meet.) Make the facts tell a story. The facts give the fix; spend time amassing them in a compelling way for your side but do not omit the ones that go the other way. Tackle these uncooperative facts and put them in perspective (Too many times the judge reading both briefs will not recognize they are about the same case.). If you're appealing, make it seem like a close case, so any legal error will be

pivotal. Above all, be accurate on the record; a mistaken citation or an overbroad reading can destroy your credibility vis-a'-vis the entire brief. Describe what happened low-key ("Just the facts, ma'am") with no rhetorical or judgmental flourishes—well done, the facts should make your case by themselves. Think hard before writing what the "Issue" is. This provides the lens through which the judge-reader filters the rest of the brief. Avoid abstractions; make it a concrete, easily understood question to which the answer is inevitable after you read the upcoming "Fact" section (If your facts are terribly unsympathetic, you may be driven to describing the issue in abstract, formalistic terms, but do so only as a last resort.). Use neutral words; don't mix it up with argument or rhetoric; be especially fair in stating the real issue. Be sure and tell why it is important to come out your way, in part by explaining the consequences if we don't. The logic and common sense of your position should be stressed; its appropriateness in terms of precedent or statutory parsing comes later, i.e., the state of the law allows this result, rather than requires it. In complex cases, you need to fully understand the real-world dispute to write accurately or convincingly about consequences; more cases are decided wrongly by judges because they don't understand the underlying problem than because they read cases badly. Perceived confusion or ignorance on the part of counsel about "what really happened" can be fatal. In the same vein, don't over-rely on precedent; few cases are completely controlled by it. If yours isn't, don't pretend it is.

§ 21.4 Other Circuit Judges Speak

Roger J. Miner,
Second Circuit

Ethical considerations first come into play for the appellate lawyer in the decision on whether to undertake representation on appeal. This is often a difficult question for the attorney. The Code prohibits unwarranted appeals, and frivolous appeals are sanctionable under the Federal Rules of Appellate Procedure. On the other hand, the Code requires diligent and zealous prosecution of arguably meritorious appeals. My own view on this issue is that far too many frivolous appeals and far too many non-meritorious issues are presented to appellate tribunals. An examination of the volume of *Anders* briefs filings supports my view. . . . If appointed counsel for indigent appellants presenting *Anders* briefs and the appellate courts that examine these briefs can undertake searching examinations of the record and find no basis for appeal in a substantial number of cases, how many meritless appeals must there be in civil and criminal cases in which appellants are represented by retained counsel? From where I sit, the answer is 'plenty,' and this is to say nothing of the criminal appeals presented by court appointed attorneys who should have filed *Anders* briefs but did not. Pressing appeals that have no merit in these times of limited appellate court resources and burgeoning caseloads is especially irresponsible, for it delays the disposition of meritorious cases and issues.

Fred I. Parker,
Second Circuit

The appellant's brief bears a particularly heavy burden. It must get the judge to start thinking "reverse." The great advantage an appellant has, however, is that in the natural order of things, the appellant's brief is read first. Advocates should be very careful not to destroy that advantage. If I read an appellant's brief which, clearly and accurately, sets out the facts, tells me what the district court did, explains why the district court found in appellee's favor and then goes on to explain why that decision was in error, I get engaged in a case and stay with that brief. Such a brief is a joy to read because it allows me to understand the entire case without wasting any time. If the brief has also made me think that the equities or the law suggest reversal, then it has been truly successful. On the other hand, if it leaves me wondering what happened other than that the district court ruled in a way that upset the appellant, it has accomplished nothing. The presentation of the legal argument in the case should also be guided by the principles of clarity and accuracy. These principles apply to the drafting of the legal argument in the following ways: first and foremost, cite cases accurately. Misleadingly cropped quotations and other misstatements of holdings will be caught, either by your adversary or by the court. While I certainly do not know the vast expanse of the law off of the top of my head, I do possess a good sense of what the law is not, and I am, therefore, able to quickly spot distortions of precedent. Even if neither I nor one of my colleagues spots a misstatement in our review of the brief or during argument, any misstatements will be caught when a member of the bench sits down to write the opinion, leaving a judge who is somewhat upset with you to write the disposition of your case. Needless to say, having this happen is not in the best interests of your client. I would also like to recommend that all advocates distinguish contrary authority, even in their opening brief. If there is bad precedent out there for your case, you can assume your adversary will cite it to us, or we will independently find it. If the first time I see an adverse case is in the answering brief, then my initial reaction is that the appellant does not have a good explanation as to why that case is inapposite. While a response in the reply brief may dispel this initial impression, it may not. Therefore, by failing to mention contrary precedent in the opening brief, the advocate makes that precedent more weighty than it perhaps should be. In sum, the guiding principles in brief writing should be clarity, conciseness, and honesty. I realize that I am not breaking new ground here, but I will state that I do not believe that I have ever found that an advocate has lost a case because his or her brief was too short or because his or her sentence structure was too simple. A simple argument stated simply is far more effective than a convoluted argument stated loquaciously.

Joel F. Dubrina,
Eleventh Circuit

First, organize your thoughts and think about what you want to say to the court. Define the issues in your mind, and as you think about what the issues are, reduce your ideas to writing. A definition of the issues is important because the formulation of issues determines which facts are material and what legal principles govern. If you represent the appellant, you must review the record for possible grounds of error. If there is a transcript of an evidentiary hearing or trial, you need to read it in its entirety. No one right way of writing a brief exists. Anyone undertaking to announce authoritative rules of good writing invites debate and comparison. In a leading text on good writing, the authors acknowledged that "[s]tyle rules . . . are, of course, somewhat a matter of individual preference, and even the established rules of grammar are open to challenge." An exclusive style of writing does not exist. However, good writing can be distinguished from poor writing and I can assure you that appellate judges appreciate the former. A few characteristics of bad writing are worth discussing. Most lawyers write too much. More often than not, they try to convey too much information and cover too many issues. Lawyers fail to separate the material from the immaterial. When writing a brief, a lawyer should say no more and no less than he or she needs to say. A brief should express ideas accurately, briefly, and as clearly as possible, leaving little room for inappropriate interpretation. Precision is the main concern of good writing. Many legal writers lack the ability to write simple, straightforward prose. In order to write with clarity and precision, the writer must know precisely what he or she wants to say and must say that and nothing else. Frequently, lawyers have a tendency to overgeneralize. When lawyers are not sure of a legal principle or how to state it precisely, they decide to cover up by using vague expressions. Of course, painstaking and thoughtful editing is essential for precise writing. This means going over the brief, sentence by sentence, and eliminating the surplusage. A sound brief is the reflection of a logical process of reasoning from premises through principles to conclusions. Good organization will be like a road map to the judges, enabling them to follow from the beginning to the end without getting lost.

§ 21.5 Rehearing en banc

What do you do when the court decides against you and you are convinced that it is wrong? Under Fed. R. App. P. 35 and 40, you may file for rehearing of a panel decision by the full court or by the three-judge panel that issued it. Be warned: the odds against obtaining rehearing are considerable. No procedural step should be taken without a searching inquiry into whether doing so would waste the client's time and money. Rehearing requests are confined to written presentations; no oral argument is available.

The essential difference between the two forms of review is that the Rule 40 rehearing seeks to persuade the original panel to correct errors of fact or law in its own opinion. A Rule 35 petition seeks to persuade a majority of all the active judges in the circuit that the issues are important enough to invoke the extraordinary step of consideration by the full court. State practice regarding in banc rehearings generally tracks the federal experience: Granting the petition is the exception and not the rule.

Rule 35, a suggestion for rehearing in banc by all the active judges of the circuit, provides:

> (a) When Hearing or Rehearing in Banc Will be Ordered. A majority of the circuit judges who are in regular active service may order that an appeal or other proceeding be heard or reheard by the court of appeals in banc. Such a hearing or rehearing is not favored and ordinarily will not be ordered except
>
> (1) when consideration by the full court is necessary to secure or maintain uniformity of its decisions, or
> (2) when the proceeding involves a question of exceptional importance.

Rule 35 states that the petition for rehearing must follow the form provided for briefs in Rule 32. Some courts of appeals also provide additional requirements; many require that you file a separate petition for rehearing and petition for rehearing in banc, because the reasons for seeking panel rehearing are different from those governing rehearing in banc. Check your local rules. The third circuit, for example, treats all petitions as requests for both panel and in banc rehearing unless otherwise specified in the petition.

In a panel rehearing petition, be concise with the discussion of the proceedings and of the facts. Remember that you are speaking to the judges who decided the case earlier and to the law clerks who spent hours poring over your arguments and the record. They do not want you to rehash the same argument. Refresh their memory. Then get to the point.

In most courts of appeals, the authoring judge will pay the most attention to the petition, although copies of it will be circulated to the chambers of each panel member. Realistically, however, the authoring judge is the one you should target.

The petition for rehearing is also an opportunity to point out errors in the panel's treatment of the law. The lawyer may use the petition to ask the panel to tone down or excise aspects of its decision. A litigant may also have an interest in the development of law and may wish to shape the legal rules in ways that will not necessarily benefit him or her in the present case, but will be helpful later.

This too must be said. Judges have egos—and while sometimes willing to admit mistakes freely or grudgingly—they do not appreciate having their noses rubbed in an alleged mistake. Make it as easy as possible for judges to retract their earlier decision. Offer alternatives. Above all, do not accuse either the authoring judge or the panel of stupidity, bias, or prejudice. You may frankly believe that, but *ad hominem* attacks on those before whom you plead your case will not help.

Circuit rules generally warn against the filing of unnecessary suggestions for rehearing in banc. Because many circuits have penalties for frivolous petitions,[4] the in banc suggestion should be reserved for extraordinary situations. Rule 35 states that the suggestion will not be granted unless full court consideration is necessary to secure or maintain uniformity of its decisions" or the case "involves a question of exceptional importance."

In federal appeals, the boy-who-cried-wolf syndrome runs rampant. Far too many petitions and suggestions are filed. The rehearing rules are flagrantly abused; as a result, judges are universally aggravated. Too many lawyers file these requests routinely every time they get an adverse result. They make no effort to demonstrate that the panel decision conflicts with circuit or Supreme Court precedent. They simply want to get a second bite of the apple. Too many lawyers describe every holding as a question of exceptional importance. Because active circuit judges are inundated by so many frivolous requests, the sheer volume infects the rehearing process. The inundation minimizes the

---

4. *See, e.g.*, 8th Cir. R. 35A(2); 5th Cir. R. 35.1.

efficacy of those rare requests that are worthy of reconsideration by the panel or the full court.

The third circuit attempted to stem this tide by setting forth guidelines in its circuit rules:

- Rehearing in banc is not favored.[5]

- "[The] court does not ordinarily grant rehearing in banc where the panel's statement of the law is correct and the controverted issue is solely the application of the law to the circumstances of the case."[6]

- Where the petitioner for rehearing in banc is represented by counsel, the petition shall contain, so far as is pertinent, the following statement of counsel:

  I express a belief, based on a reasoned and studied professional judgment, that the panel decision is contrary to the decisions of the United States Court of Appeals for the Third Circuit or the Supreme Court of the United States, and that consideration by the full court is necessary to secure and maintain uniformity of decisions in this court, to-wit, the panel's decision is contrary to the decision of the court or the Supreme Court in [citation to the case or cases] or, that this appeal involves a question of exceptional importance, to-wit [set forth in one sentence].[7]

Perhaps the third circuit rule has had a minimal effect on the tide. From where I sit, I can conclude that many lawyers are willing to certify a "reasoned and studied professional judgment" that a case qualifies for consideration under the rules when in fact it is little more than an exercise in both frivolity and futility.

A recent improvement in my home court procedures has brought some semblance of order to the barrage of questions from fourteen judges during oral argument. A ceasefire is in effect for the first five minutes of argument. Counsel is free to make an uninterrupted presentation during this time without being bombarded with questions from the bench.

---

5. 3d Cir. R. 34.5.

6. 3d Cir I.O.P. 9.3.2.

7. 3d Cir. R. 34.5.

§ 21.5.1 Judge Patricia M. Wald's Comments

Patricia M. Wald, Chief Judge Emeritus of the United States Court of Appeals for the D.C. Circuit, discusses en banc in her delightful essay, *Nineteen Tips from 21 Years on the Appellate Bench.*[8] Although her comments describe the experience on her court, her observations are generally descriptive of most en bancs. While serving as an active judge, I often have said, "This case is too important to be en banced." With minor editing, her commentary follows:

> Let me talk a bit about en bancs. They spell cruel and unusual punishment for all concerned. Think before you ask for one. We get hundreds of petitions but grant on average less than six a year. Fed. R. App. P. 35 says that en bancs are disfavored and ordinarily will not be ordered except when necessary to secure uniformity or for a question of exceptional importance.
>
> Those have not been the de facto criteria in my experience. En bancs most often occur when a majority feels strongly that the panel is wrong about something they care a lot about or which may be precedential outside the confines of the immediate case. Every judge writes panel opinions (or dissents) in the shadow of an en banc and when there is the threat of one, panel majorities will often try to conciliate opponents or temper rhetoric in a supplemental opinion on rehearing; they may pull back from excessive rhetoric, too-broad holdings, or clarify the scope of the original opinion.
>
> En bancs usually follow a strong dissent, but can also be provoked by a unanimous panel composed of a philosophical minority on the court. I once sat on a now-notorious panel that had three unanimous decisions en banc-ed and one reheard by the panel to forestall an en banc.
>
> At any rate, remember four things about en bancs before you jump to ask for one when you lose before a panel:
>
> (1) They take a long time, often up to two years before the court can assemble itself and get all the opinions written. If your case is really hot, you could be up on certiorari long before, and chances are either you or your opponent will

---

8. 1 J. App. Prac. & Process 7 (Winter 1999).

go for certiorari anyway afterwards. As court of appeals dockets go up, the Supreme Court's steadily declines—only eighty-six cases argued last year.

(2) There are apt to be many en banc opinions written—likely a plurality and several other unclassifiable opinions rather than just a majority and dissent—so that the law is not necessarily the clearer or cleaner for the exercise.

(3) An en banc is like a constitutional convention. Everything—in circuit law—is up for grabs. The decision may emerge on grounds argued by neither party and desired by neither party. Advocates lose control since judge power is at its zenith; except for Supreme Court precedent, the decision can go anywhere. You, the counsel, no longer hold the road map.

(4) Since en bancs so often occur in fundamental value-conflicted cases, astute counsel can pretty well predict the outcomes on the basis of past positions taken by the judges. If you don't have a shot at winning an en banc, all you do is risk an even stronger set of nails in your coffin.

Oral argument in an en banc is an especially perilous undertaking. The mere fact that an en banc has been commenced usually means that the court is divided and panel members in the majority are already unhappy. Many more of the judges' questions in en banc arguments seem to be motivated by the desire to establish rather than explore positions or to defuse the positions of other judges. The counsel is often the woman in the middle of an intramural contest. She may not be aware of the real reason why the en banc was voted or what the court thinks is really at stake. The judges may have their own agendas as to what precedential underbrush the en banc will clear out or even what brand new doctrinal formula it will encapsule into law—with or without aid of counsel. It's also harder to control the flow of questioning from eleven judges than from three. More judges means more interruptions, cross-conversations between judges, and attempts to bind counsel to or divorce him from another judge's articulation of the issue or the acceptable resolution of it.

In sum, more is not always better, so think before en bancing. A really important case will likely go up anyway; a really wrong decision is worth a preliminary try at the en benc, but most of the rest brings much hassle and little success.

PART FOUR
NUTS AND BOLTS OF PREPARING
AND DELIVERING ORAL ARGUMENT

Chapter 22

PREPARING FOR ORAL ARGUMENT

§ 22.1 How Judges Prepare

Judges follow different chambers practices. Our work habits differ. Our experiences differ. I came to the federal appellate bench after an active career as a trial lawyer and state trial judge. I served as an adjunct law professor for twenty-three years. I like to study, do research, and write. My chambers practice is a mix of the pragmatic and the scholastic. Let me describe what takes place in my chambers prior to oral argument.

1. We receive the briefs and appendices a minimum of four weeks (usually six or seven weeks) in advance of the calendar week.

2. I am the first in chambers to read the briefs and the appendices. Depending on the circuit, there are at least six to eight cases each day on the week's calendar. This is how I read the briefs:

   (a) Read the statement of issues in the appellant's brief.

   (b) Read the district court's opinion with special emphasis on the facts and that portion of the opinion dealing with the issues raised on appeal.

   (c) Read appellant's summary of argument

   (d) Read appellee's summary of argument.

   (e) Read appellant's brief cover to cover.

   (f) Read appellee's brief cover to cover.

   (g) Skim, not read, reply brief to see if any point is legitimate.

   (h) If appellant raises a point with which I am not familiar, I do not proceed to next point. Instead, I immediately read the appellee's brief on this point.

   (i) I reach a tentative decision.

3. I dictate a bench memorandum in each case analyzing the issues. If I am not familiar with controlling cases, I go to the Reporters and often have the full text of cases photocopied and attached to my memo together with excerpts from the record. I then make three decisions: (1) whether I desire oral argument; (2) whether my clerks should do further work on the case; and (3) reach a very tentative decision as to disposition.

4. After dictating the memo, I then prepare a document entitled "Synopsis." I synthesize the *major* contentions in the brief. By typing it myself rather than dictating, I am able to summarize the contentions, and ascertain, wherever possible, the single theme on which the appeal will stand or fall.

5. If the case is important enough for oral argument, I require my law clerks to prepare a detailed, formal bench memorandum, separate and apart from the one I already prepared. I instruct that their analysis and recommended disposition be their own product and they not be influenced by my original analysis. The clerks examine the relevant cases cited, do original research, and prepare a quality memorandum. Their memos are written in a formal style so that if the presiding judge assigns the case to me for an opinion, I can use excerpts from their memo for use in the first draft of the opinion. While preparing their bench memos, the clerks often confer with me.

6. Where another judge on the panel requests argument in additional cases, those too are assigned to the clerks for the "full court press."

7. I carefully study the bench memoranda prepared by the law clerks, either approving them or ordering more research and analysis.

8. In the week prior to argument, my clerks and I devote at least a day to what I call "Case Conference." The day before Case Conference I reread all bench memos and will list on a "pink sheet" any questions I might have. My clerks (and sometimes interns) and I then sit around a conference table and discuss every case on the calendar—emphasizing those that will be argued but also those in which the clerks have not written a memo. My "position papers" at the conference are at least two bench memoranda: mine and the law clerks. During the course of discussion, I may order additional materials to be affixed to the memoranda, such as excerpts from the briefs, parts of the record and photocopies of cases. Often, I will have a clerk prepare a concise account of our conference summarizing our discussions and indicating what questions I may ask counsel. This is listed on a document entitled "Case Conference Notes." The law clerk who had worked on the cases leads this discussion, and I lead the discussion on the cases to be submitted without argument.

9. The law clerks then prepare a thick, spiral-bound "Bench Memorandum" that includes a table of contents, my bench memo, the

clerk's memo, my "pink sheet" and Case Conference Notes, all opinions of the trial court or administrative agency, and full text copies of *all* relevant cases. This is the document that I have before me on the bench during oral argument. I also require that all briefs and appendices be on the bench as well.

We then travel to the city where the court will be sitting. On the morning of the argument, before I ascend the bench, my clerks and I meet again for about forty-five minutes to discuss the day's calendar.

Even with all this preparation, I recognize that a sort of chambers inbreeding takes place. I require oral argument in all cases except the "slam dunks" to discover whether my clerks and I have missed something in reading the briefs. I await the emphasis counsel will put on the case in their presentations, and I always listen closely to my colleagues' questions. These furnish clues as to their interests or concerns. Unlike other judges, I do not take notes during argument. My clerks do this. Instead, I concentrate completely on what every counsel says.

But each judge has his or her method of preparation. We boil at different degrees. For example, at the Tenth Circuit Judicial Conference in 2003, Judges Robby R. Baldock and Carlos F. Lucero were members of a panel and asked by the panel's moderator about chambers preparation. Their responses follow.[1]

§ 22.1.1 Chambers Preparation by Circuit Judge Bobby R. Baldock

Moderator: What part of the brief do you think is most important and which brief do you read first? Do you read the reply brief first because that's where the issues are joined?

Judge Baldock: I know each judge does things differently. I start with what the trial court did below. It doesn't matter whether it's a criminal or civil case. I want to know what the trial judge was looking at, and what he or she did. Normally, if it's a jury trial, I read the appellant's brief first, since the burden is on the appellant to convince me to overturn the conviction. Then, after making my notes and looking at that, I go to the appellee's brief, and then I go to the reply, if there is one. Doing it in this order helps formulate

---

1. These responses are reprinted from *What Appellate Advocates Seek from Appellate Judges and What Appellate Judges Seek from Appellate Advocates*, 31 N.M.L. Rev. 265, 265–279 (2001).

the issues in my mind. At the end, hopefully I have a clear understanding of what the issue is. And I do my homework. My law clerks don't do a synopsis for me and come tell me what the case is about. The lawyers are trying to convince me—I'm the judge—why I should do something or the other. So I do my own bench memos. The law clerks and I fight a lot about some of these things. Now, I may rely later on a clerk's judgment if the clerk sees the issue differently. But it's your argument to me, and my understanding of your argument, that's important.

Moderator: Let's say there are three issues. When you read the briefs do you read the first issue through all three briefs and the second through all three briefs?

Judge Baldock: I read each whole brief, because so many times the arguments are integrated. You can't separate them because some of the facts will pour over into the other issues. That way I get a clear picture. Then in my analysis I will separate and outline each issue. As I'm trying to formulate my bench memo I do an outline of each issue. But first I have to know how all the facts come into play. . . .

When the briefs are really far apart, or I see citations to cases that are going off in different directions, then I may call the law clerk in and say, "Look, there's something strange here." The lawyers should pretty much be looking at the same line of cases and arguing different analysis. So when lawyers are arguing entirely different cases, then I know that something is wrong with one side or the other. Then I may call the law clerk to do some more extensive research.

§ 22.1.2 Chambers Preparation by Circuit Judge Carlos F. Lucero

Judge Lucero: I'm a creature of habit in reading briefs, and I pretty well follow the same model each time. I pick up the appellant's brief, and I read the statement of the issues and the summary of the argument. I do this because I want to know what the case is about and what the dispute is. The statement and the summary tell me that very quickly. If somebody doesn't include a statement of the issues, they've blown it in a big way because now they're putting a judge in a bad frame of mind by making him try to figure out what the appeal is about.

Having read those two parts of the appellant's brief, I then turn to the appendix and read the trial court's order and judgment. Now, knowing what the issues are, I can focus on what the trial court did, to see whether the judgment of the trial court was right or wrong. This is sort of a preview of coming attractions. Then I turn back to the arguments in the appellant's brief, and, to the extent that I've been persuaded, I carefully consider every aspect of the appellant's brief. If I have not been persuaded by the appellant's argument, I still read the appellee's brief, but with less concern. Finally, I turn to the reply brief, and I come to my preliminary opinion.

Now, where Judge Baldock and I differ is I do use bench memos from my clerks. I will not read the bench memo before reading the briefs, but having read the briefs and come to my preliminary conclusions on the case, I then turn to the bench memos. It is remarkable, quite remarkable, how often you agree pretty well with the bench memo. At that point I come to closure in my mind. Now, if the clerk's recommendation and mine don't square, that is a red flag, and you've got a hot issue here. Then I'll direct more research, and I'll pull cases. The law clerk always attaches key cases to the bench memo, and I'll read those as well. Now the case is ready for oral argument.

§ 22.2 The Tradition Continues

After over forty years as a judge, I still feel a profound excitement as I leave the robing room and ascend the bench. The old heart still beats a little faster in anticipation of oral argument, yet I felt the same way many years ago when I took the bench every morning as a member of a state trial court still bearing the name it had in colonial days—the Court of Common Pleas. The judicial robe always carries a sense of history.

The tradition and the majestic history of any courtroom always electrifies, but you feel the atmosphere in the court of appeals to be especially charged; it is the court of last resort for more than 99 percent of the cases.[2] The history, tradition, and heavy responsibility all contribute to the massive discharge of psychic energy by the judges, because the argument demands high concentration and unflagging attention. Judges recognize the importance of oral argument because, insofar as the case is concerned, it is the last half of the ninth inning.

All the weeks of preparation in chambers—reading the briefs, researching the authorities, contemplating the outer perimeters to which a decision one way or another will take the law, ruminating the broad policy questions involved in the issues—all of this, comes down to an oral presentation of fifteen minutes, at the most thirty minutes, a side. And for all of this, the lawyers must be prepared. Prepared for the most intensive courtroom participation in the life of a litigator. Most lawyers are not ready.

You must prepare. When you look at the black-robed figures sitting on the dais, your first thought should be, "Lemme at 'em." You should be straining at the leash to get to the judges. An attorney once told me, "If you feel comfortable sitting, waiting for your turn to argue, your mental attitude is all wrong. You should feel that you are in the starting blocks, totally trained and ready, longing for the starting gun to go off, longing to let the judges know what you know about the important parts of the case, and thus believe what you believe about the Rightness, not just correctness, but the Rightness or Righteousness of your position."

You must prepare. The most important step in getting to the lemme-at-'em frame of mind is total preparation on the facts and the law.

You must prepare. You must know and—what is important—you must *believe* that you know more about the case than anyone else in the courtroom, including the judges. You want the judges to think that you are the "Master of the Universe" insofar as this case is concerned. If the judges get this feeling, then they will be more likely to trust what you say and believe what you believe. And if you have this feeling, then you will have no apprehension about having hypotheticals thrown to you at oral argument. You will have the attitude that you are ready for anything. Advice on how to acquire this attitude is contained in the pages that follow.

---

2. In the twelve months ending September 30, 2002, the court of appeals terminated 56,586 cases. During the same period, the Supreme court received 6,343 petitions for certiorari in federal cases; of these, 118 were granted. Director of the Administrative Office of the United States Courts, 2002 Annual Report of the Director, Tables B, B-2, at http://www.uscourts.gov/judbus2002/contents.html.

§ 22.3   Advice from State Chief Justices

Charles E. Jones *Arizona,*	State the strongest and best arguments first. Try to anticipate the difficult questions and provide answers. The latter point is also valid in preparing for oral argument.
Mary J. Mullarkey, *Colorado*	Practice your argument before you appear. Review the record. Nothing is more disheartening to the judge than asking questions about the record and being told that the attorney has not looked at the record since writing the brief. Respond to questions as they are raised. Don't try to postpone or evade answering the judge. The point of oral argument is to address the court's concerns, not to give a flawless speech.
Ronald T.Y. Moon, *Hawaii*	Oral argument is not a speech but a discussion with the appellate judges. Prepare thoroughly by knowing the facts, the record, and the applicable case law. Anticipate questions touching upon the weaknesses in your case and the reasonable arguments of your opponent; practice your answers.
Mary Ann McMorrow, *Illinois*	Speak clearly and with conviction that your position is correct. An otherwise good argument, presented in an overly meek or apologetic manner, loses its effectiveness and conveys the impression that the speaker lacks conviction in the validity of the argument. Be respectful and courteous. Do not appear confrontational, and do not belittle the justices or their questions.
Leigh Ingalls Saufley, *Maine*	Do not waste time reciting the facts or procedural history as an introduction to argument. The court has always read the briefs and bench memo before oral argument begins and repetition only detracts from the amount of time you will have to address the important issues of the case. Begin your argument by going right to the heart of your strongest point, and never read from your brief. Oral argument should be a dynamic flow of questions and answers getting

to the heart of the concept. You will not persuade the court by rereading matters that have already been read. Never respond to a question from a justice with "I'll get back to that." Be sufficiently familiar with all issues in your case so that you can flexibly respond to questions on different issues in a short period of time.

Maura D. Corrigan, *Michigan*

To succeed at oral argument, you should: Prepare. Advocates should participate in as many moot court arguments as possible. You must know every aspect of your case, from the record to the standard of review, in order to successfully address the questions asked. Answer truthfully. Don't be afraid to concede that you haven't thought about a particular line of questioning. Answering truthfully and asking to file a supplemental brief on the issue is far better than talking yourself into a corner and compromising your argument. Know your audience. Take the time to research the particular concerns of the court and tailor your argument accordingly. You do your client a great disservice if you fail to focus on issues and arguments the court considers important.

Stephen N. Limbaugh, Jr., *Missouri*

Concede points that should be conceded. Understand the purpose of oral argument, which is not so much to allow the lawyers to rehash the argument in their briefs, but, instead, to allow the judges to ask questions in order to better understand those arguments. Supplement charts, graphs, blown-up photographs, or other visual aids, for use in oral argument with small, individual copies for each judge that the Marshal can distribute beforehand. This makes the argument more user friendly.

Karla M. Gray,
Montana

Think long and hard before attempting to "split" your oral argument time with another lawyer. It almost never works out well. Answer questions from the bench when they are asked; do not say you will get to it later. Sometimes you run out of time and, in any event, the question may remain in the judge or justice's mind until answered and distract attention from your other points. During preparation, check for—and be familiar with—related cases decided after the briefs were filed in your case.

John V. Hendry,
Nebraska

Evading questions: Appellate courts ask questions to alert the advocate of issues which are troubling. To evade the question, or to refuse to answer the question, simply reinforces the feeling of the appellate court that the issue in all likelihood ought to be decided against that advocate's position. Failure to familiarize oneself with the record: Unfamiliarity with the record diminishes the confidence the appellate court has in the positions being advocated. Failure to concede issues which are, for all practical purposes, uncontested: Such failure could, in some instances, diminish the credibility of the advocate's overall position.

Patricio M. Serna,
New Mexico

Clarify and explain rather than reiterate material in the briefs. Focus on the strongest arguments from the briefs and account for time to answer questions in allocating time between arguments. Be familiar with the facts so the argument is not distracted by counsel rifling through the record.

Judith S. Kaye,
New York

Know Your Audience. Oral argument should be tailored to the bench you are addressing. Will it be a "hot bench," or do you need to begin with the facts? Are time allotments serious? Does the court prefer a "jury summation" type argument? I am often surprised to see even very seasoned lawyers observing our courtroom the day before their argument, doing their homework. *Know Your Case.* Knowing your case really well is a first principle, whether in brief writing or oral argument. That instills confidence, facilitates an orderly presentation and helps you field questions, especially the unexpected ones. I cannot overstate the importance of listening to and answering the court's questions when asked, even if they seem irrelevant, inartful or downright silly. Decorum matters. Judges do notice how you behave in the courtroom. Make your arguments with conviction, because weakness and discomfort show—if you don't believe in the correctness of your position, why should I? Be respectful and attentive when your adversary is arguing—no grimacing, gesticulating or body contortions. Be sure to finish with a "thank you"—before your time expires.

Thomas J. Moyer, *Ohio*

Know the court. Know whether the judges typically ask questions of counsel. Be prepared to move in and out of your prepared oral argument in the midst of questions from the court. Do not assume that a judge's question is hostile to your position; the judge may be simply removing barriers to a vote for your client. If you did not try the case, be familiar enough with the transcript hat you never respond to a question from the court with, "I am sorry Your Honor, but I did not try the case." Attempt to anticipate questions in order to cite to the brief and even more impressively, to the record.

Ralph J. Cappy, *Pennsylvania*

The most effective oral advocate is one whose "argument" is not only persuasive, but more importantly, educational. Thus, appellate counsel must, when a judge or justice asks a question or is troubled by a particular aspect of the appeal, immediately (or at the earliest opportunity) answer the question or address the concern that the judge or justice may have. Appellate advocates have a duty to be selective in choosing the issues to speak on at oral argument. By limiting the issues to be discussed at oral argument to only those one or two aspects of the appeal that are most important (or perhaps most complex) counsel will make best use of the limited time available for oral argument and be of greatest benefit to the court and to his or her client. Although difficult for an advocate, appellate counsel should know when it is appropriate to concede a point. While you may be sacrificing one aspect of your appeal, you will have increased your stature with the court that will transcend the immediate matter and benefit you as a professional far into the future.

Frank J. Williams, *Rhode Island*	State the standard of review during argument and confine argument to the applicable standard. If you don't know the answer to a question, say so directly and move on to the next point. Do not give detailed background of the case. Assume the justices are familiar with the facts and begin and limit your discussion to the most important issues.
David Gilberson, *South Dakota*	During oral argument, answer questions from the bench directly and do not try to mislead the court. If you have a weak point in your case admit it because it is probably already apparent to the court and your opponent will really work you over on rebuttal if you try to slide by without informing the court. Oral argument before an appellate court is not a jury argument. Leave the theatrics at home.
Frank F. Drowota II, *Tennessee*	Be familiar with the court, the judges, and the court rules. Preparation for oral argument will vary depending upon whether the court is "hot" or "cold." Do not treat questions from the bench as interruptions. Be flexible. Be candid. Be honest. Shading the facts or law will undermine your

credibility as an advocate. Be attentive when opposing counsel is presenting argument so that you will be able to respond to questions the judges asked opposing counsel. These questions sometimes emphasize areas in your adversary's case that the judges consider weak.

Sharon Keller, *Texas Court of Criminal Appeals*

During oral argument, lawyers should tell the court where they are going by briefly summarizing the points to be made. Argument should focus on the points that are critical to their case and avoid side issues. Lawyers should refrain from making jury arguments and stick to the legal issue.

Gerry L. Alexander, *Washington*

On oral argument, any statement of the facts should be brief. Counsel should assume that the judges are familiar with the facts by virtue of reading the briefs. Counsel should also let us know early in his or her argument what relief they seek for their client. A strong ending is important. Counsel should not end like many do with "if there are no further questions I will stop now."

Shirley S. Abrahamson, *Wisconsin*

Have clearly in mind the key points you want to make. Make them in the first few minutes and keep coming back to them. Do not plan on restating every argument set out in your brief. Focus on your best points. Start with your strongest argument, because if the court has many questions you may not get beyond your first point. Read articles on oral argument and brief writing. They tend to be very repetitive, because the advice given is good. If you cannot answer a question, say so. If you want to take a shot at it, say, "My immediate reaction is . . . " If the question raises an important point that neither party considered, ask permission to address the issue in a letter to the court and opposing counsel within three days of the oral argument.

§ 22.4 Advice from United States Circuit Chiefs

Michael Boudin, *First Circuit*	In oral argument, I have only one critical piece of advice: take up a yellow pad with a one-page outline, if you must, and nothing more, and if possible, take nothing at all (the idea is to have an organized conversation with the judges rather than to make a speech).
John M. Walker, Jr., *Second Circuit*	Be completely prepared for all foreseeable questions. Master the record and the relevant statutes and case law. Practice with a moot court. Have a strategy that, amidst all of the questioning, results in bringing home the two or three points that you want the court to absorb, if nothing else. Open your argument with a carefully planned statement that plays to your strength: the law, the facts or, hopefully, both.
Edward R. Becker, *Third Circuit, 1996–2003*	Limit the number of points. You will rarely win on more than one or two points. Overbriefing impairs your credibility. Acknowledge the vulnerable points in your position and then tell the Court how to deal with them. Make sure your argument is logically arranged. Clarity of argument is key.
Anthony J. Scirica, *Third Circuit*	You must prepare. You know the record and the law. Although you are necessarily focused on winning your case, be aware of the appellate court's role in enunciating the law in similar cases. If you are asked what legal standard the court should adopt, you should have an answer.
Carolyn Dineen King, *Fifth Circuit*	Address the most important issue first; you may never get to the others. Be absolutely candid and honest with the court. Focus only on those facts or procedural history, if any, that are critical to the outcome; don't get into a long recital on these items; the court is familiar with them.

Deanell Reece Tacha,
Tenth Circuit

The most common failing I see in both oral argument and brief writing is the failure to be analytically precise about the issues addressed on appeal. It seems to me that before ever writing a brief, and certainly before oral argument, counsel should have a very candid discussion with himself or herself about what precisely the issues are that will result in a favorable decision on appeal. The most common complaints I hear from appellate judges relate to . . . lack of focus, covering too many issues, and scattering case authority and facts throughout the brief and argument so that they lose their impact on the issues to which they are most germane. I therefore urge discipline in both brief writing and preparation for oral argument with respect to answering with clarity these central questions.

Douglas H. Ginsburg,
D.C. Circuit

Do not argue with a judge in response to a judge's question. Do not simply repeat in oral argument what is in the briefs. Get your important points across as succinctly and quickly as possible.

Haldane
Robert Mayer,
Federal Circuit

Argue the law—the appellate court's primary function is to insure that the lower court has not committed reversible legal error. Given the standard of review, if the lawyer is arguing facts, he is fighting an uphill battle. Do not use exhibits—exhibits waste time, are distracting, and draw attention away from the advocate. However, if a lawyer insists on using exhibits, he should take care not to argue the facts. Advance the ball—the judges have read your briefs, do not stand at the podium and rehash them. Use the time to answer the court's questions and address your opponent's arguments.

Patricia Wald,
Chief Judge
Emeritus,
D.C. Circuit

Apart from an acceptance of the "life is not fair" motif to oral argument, probably the most important thing for an appellate lawyer is to "know the record." It is not good enough that the paralegal or the associate who drafted the brief knows the record inside and out; the lawyer who argues the case must. I concur with Chief Justice Rehnquist's lament about oral advocates who depend too heavily on their subordinates in writing the brief, and who cannot answer questions about the basic case or the record. The more arcane the subject matter, the more intimate with the record the advocate needs to be. All the questions of fact and expert opinion that the brief may have raised in the judges' minds will surface at argument, and nothing frustrates a bench more than a lawyer who does not know the answers. Your credibility as a legal maven spurts as soon as you show familiarity with the facts of the underlying dispute. When a lawyer cannot smoothly answer a question securely rooted in his knowledge of the record, the specter of a remand for inadequate explanation by the agency comes quickly to the fore. If you watch, we don't ask you so many questions about the meaning of precedent as we do about the underlying dispute in the case: What is it really all about? Why does one party care so much about a few words in an agency rule? Of course counsel can always offer to submit record cites after argument, but inability to locate them onsite definitely detracts from the image of her being in complete control of the case.

§ 22.5 Advice from Other United States Circuit Judges

Other United States Circuit Judges give similar advice.

Karen J.
Williams,
Fourth Circuit

During oral argument, it is impossible to focus the court's attention on the most relevant facts and legal analyses with the required precision if you have not invested the time in thorough preparation. To accomplish this end, you must become completely familiar with your case. As you prepare for argument, learn or reacquaint yourself with the parties, the facts, the record, and the proceedings below. Review all of the briefs. Know the arguments on all sides of your issues, including those of any amici. Know the significant cases cited in each of those briefs, including the facts, the holdings, and how your case is distinguishable. You must master both the relevant facts and the relevant law. There is simply no excuse for ignorance of what occurred below or of what an important precedent holds. As you prepare an outline of argument, you may want to include citations to significant decisions and statutes so that it becomes second nature for you to identify which citations relate to which arguments. As you prepare for argument, it is important to take off your advocate's hat and take stock of your case with the objective eyes of the judges who will hear your appeal. In the process of reviewing the already-prepared materials, it is important to consider what your briefing has, and has not, accomplished. Switch places with the court and consider what the judges hearing your case will need and want to know. Do not waste your opportunity to persuade the court to your view of the case by treating oral argument as a summary of what you said in your briefs: the judges have read the briefs. To be thoroughly prepared for oral argument, you need to try to begin thinking about your appeal from the point where you ended in the briefs. Identify those points of law upon which the outcome of the case is likely to turn and which, when viewed objectively, could be resolved in favor of either party. Those isues should be the focus of your oral argument. Make notes on what points are clear and unclear as discussed in your briefs. You should concentrate on clarifying the most important points for argument. If we review only for abuse of discretion, the advocate must clearly demonstrate an obvious error, or no relief will be forthcoming. Under the de novo standard of review, however, we are free to reverse a judgment call in a grey area. Also, many areas of substantive law have complex, multi-part tests that need to be mastered.

Jacques L. Weiner, Jr., *Fifth Circuit*

The best way to prepare is to familiarize yourself thoroughly with the record and with your brief, and with your opponent's brief. Know each important case thoroughly and know its significance and its holding. Likewise, be familiar with and understand each pertinent statute as well as its legislative history and purpose. Plan to begin your presentation with a short, attention-getting "simple and direct" introduction of the points you plan to make, leaving plenty of time to address each of them even if a substantial portion of your allotted time gets siphoned off by questions from the court and by your answers to those questions. Don't waste your limited time replicating your written statement of facts or your written arguments verbatim: we are ahead of you in that respect. You will serve your clients and the court best by going directly to the most significant points of your case. If you have deposed yourself well, you should have a pretty fair idea of why your case is before our court for oral argument and, distilled to their simplest forms, which are the truly important issues in need of discussion. Clarify misconceptions resulting from your opponent's brief; disarm the opposition by conceding those facts and legal issues that are clear "losers" for you. If you represent the appellant, describe the worst error committed by the trial court and how your case was harmed by it. Clarify possible misconceptions we might harbor as the result of the district court's rulings and reasons. And, to repeat it for emphasis, save lots of time for questions from the court. If you represent the appellee, make certain that the appellant has stated the facts accurately and completely. Focus on wrongly stated facts and issues; and, as in your brief, hit the appellant's arguments head-on, issue by issue. Tell the court the legal and moral reasons why your victory below should be preserved. Do all that you can to support the district court. If alleged errors are not errors, tell us why; if they truly were errors, don't deny it— just show how they are harmless or give us one or more alternative reasons on which we can sustain the district court's result, even if its reasoning was skewed. Remember, rebuttal is for rebuttal only. When you represent the appellant, you will likely have reserved some time for rebuttal. Before appearing at argument, do all that you can to anticipate the appellee's strategy. Be well prepared to rebut points that the appellee is sure to advance. Often, you will have saved five minutes of your alloted twenty minutes for rebuttal, so use it wisely.

Joel F. Dubina,
Eleventh Circuit

The following are sixteen simple suggestions that should help a lawyer achieve success in orally arguing a case:

1. Be courteous and polite.
2. Get right to the issues.
3. Don't dwell on the facts.
4. Answer the judges' questions directly and precisely.
5. Learn to overcome fear.
6. Cite to Supreme Court authority and [circuit or state] authority.
7. Check slip opinions the day before oral argument to see whether recent law impacts your case.

8. Keep in mind that the brief is critical.

9. Know the standards of review.

10. If you represent the appellee, track the argument of the appellant.

11. Know the record.

12. Don't make a jury argument.

13. If you represent the appellee and the district judge committed error, you will do better to admit it and argue that it was harmless.

14. When concluding your argument, tell the court what you want.

15. Educate and teach the court.

16. PREPARE!

Roger J. Miner, *Second Circuit*	Most oral arguments are made by attorneys who "wing it." The lack of preparation is apparent in these arguments. Counsel often seem to be taken by surprise at a question from the court. A frequent response is "I'll get to that" by attorneys who never do. An attorney once responded to my question this way: "Why do you ask the question, judge?" A frequent answer to the question is, "That is not this case." The questioner generally knows that the questions assume facts not in the case, but may be testing the basis of counsel's theory and its applicability to future cases. A properly prepared attorney is ready to distinguish the facts and the law from those in his or her case. [Recently retired Deputy Solicitor General] Lawrence Wallace, who has argued more cases before the Supreme Court than any other lawyer in recent times, has said, "If you can't answer the question, 'What are the strongest points to be made for the other side?' you're not really prepared to argue the case."
Fred I. Parker, *Second Circuit*	The following specific guidelines may be of use when responding to questioning from the bench: First, and most obviously, always be respectful. It is somewhat surprising how excited some advocates can become during the course of the argument, but remember that cutting off the questions of a judge is never a good way to win points with the panel.

However, being respectful does not mean that you should not be forceful. Simply because a member of the panel is trying to make a specific point from the bench does not necessarily imply that the questioner is correct. If you disagree, simply state for instance: "I understand your point, your Honor, however, as I read *Jones v. Smith* . . . " Second, just like in brief writing, confront the negative precedent. Recently, there was an advocate who was asked, "Doesn't *Jones v. Smith* bar your client's claim?" The advocate responded, "Your Honor, as I've noted in my brief, not as I read it. However, to the extent you may think it does, I think *Jones v. Smith* is wrongly decided and this panel should overrule it." Honesty and clarity always win points with the panel. Third, always answer the question that was asked. The best practice is to always begin your answer with a "yes" or "no," and then continue on with an explanation, a qualifier or whatever else you may want to add.

§ 22.6 Is It a Hot or Cold Court?

Should you proceed to oral argument on the assumption that the court has read the briefs? It depends. You must learn in advance as much as possible about any appellate bench before whom you appear. Find out if the judges traditionally receive the briefs before oral argument and if so, how much in advance. If the judges receive briefs at the last minute, as is the case in some state appellate courts and in at least one of the United States courts of appeals, you may assume that it is a cold court and that there has not been much advance study of the briefs.

Investigate to see if the court has published internal operating procedures, or communicate with a former law clerk who has served with the court to learn their practices. For example, from the Third Circuit's Internal Operating Procedures you can learn that "Briefs and appendices are distributed sufficiently in advance to afford four full weeks' study in chambers prior to the panel sitting."[3]

---

3. 3d Cir. I.O.P. 1.1.

§ 22.7 Preparing for the Questions: A Checklist

The judges will question you. Prepare for it.

Every brief submitted by counsel and every point to be covered at oral argument must be meticulously examined and reviewed from the point of view of a judge who is either skeptical or downright hostile. That judge will toss hypotheticals at you in an attempt to show that your position will damage controlling case law or clash with traditional legal precepts. Prepare for this inquisition.

The very process of preparing for the worst onslaught will strengthen your hand. It will help build a strong intellectual framework for your presentation. Step aside from your written brief and argument outline and go through a checklist of questions:

- What do you want? What are you asking the court to hold?

- What rule do you want the court to adopt to justify the holding you request? Is there any other rule that would satisfy you?

- How will the rule work? What are the practical consequences? How far will the rule carry? How far will the law go? Will it expand or contract existing case law? If we extend claims, demands, or defenses, at what point can we draw the line before it conflicts with a competing legal precept? If we contract claims, demands, or defenses, will we now or in the immediate future be overruling settled case law? Would we be modifying it? If so, are there strong policy reasons for a potential change in the law? Will it change current practice? Will it generate additional litigation?

- Is there a legally respectable argument for the rule? Is it supported by relevant authorities? Is it consistent with what the court has done before? Is it coherent in the sense that it hangs together in fact and law?

- Why should the court accept your argument and your proposed rule? What values and interests would be advanced? Would opposing values and interests be accommodated? How thoughtfully and disinterestedly have the social interests been weighed? How fair and durable does the adjustment of any interest-conflicts promise to be?

- Why is your rule superior to an alternative? To the one advanced by the trial court? By your opponent?

- Is the court in a position to announce your rule? Do the record facts and procedural posture furnish the adequate background? If it is a Rule 12(b)(6) matter (judgment on the pleadings), would it be better cast as a grant of summary judgment? If a summary judgment, should the court have the benefit of a full trial record?

- Where is the flashpoint of conflict between you and your adversary? Is it in the choice of competing legal precepts? Are you quarreling simply over construction of a controlling precept? Or only over application of a chosen and interpreted precept to the facts found by the factfinder?

- Are the points constituting your argument mutually independent? Does the whole argument depend upon the court accepting your first point? If the court rejects one point can it still rule in your favor? Or is the opposite true: that each subsequent point depends upon its predecessor, that is, the first point is but a prosyllogism to the succeeding episyllogism so that the conclusion of the first argument becomes the major premise of the next?

- How substantial is the major premise of your argument? Is it the text of a case holding or statute or constitution's clause? Or are you depending upon inductive reasoning to generalize a proposition from a series of holdings? If so, is there a sufficient enumeration of instances? If you have analogized to one or two cases or statutes, are the resemblances sufficient to draw the analogy?

- Are there any formal fallacies in the argument? Any material fallacies?

- In reviewing your brief at this eleventh hour, do you spot any weakness? To avoid a grilling from hostile judges, are you willing to concede any points? If so, does this strengthen or weaken your remaining arguments?

- Do you know the essential part of the record like the back of your hand? Will you be able to turn to it in a moment, or will you leaf through pages, or look with dismay at your junior colleague at the counsel table?

Go through an inventory of questions like these—or prepare your own—in order to frame answers to possible questions in the calm and friendly environment of your office, where you will have the advantage of time and research and consultation with colleagues. If you do not do this, consider the alternative: standing alone at the lectern with the minutes and seconds of rationed time ticking away and being forced to think of an immediate answer to a question that never before had entered your mind.

§ 22.8 The Mandatory Rehearsal

I strongly recommend that you rehearse your presentation before several office colleagues, not intimately familiar and emotionally influenced by the case, but who have taken the time to read the briefs and are willing to assume the role of judges and that of your adversary. This is as important as any other phase of preparation. To do this is not to demean your abilities; rather, it is to demonstrate high professionalism. It is not a waste of time and is a legitimate part of your billable hours.

Here, you do not want to engender tunnel vision or participate in an sycophantic romance with your associates telling you what a fantastic lawyer you are. It is important that the "judges" study both sets of briefs in advance and thus acquire more than a superficial understanding of what the case is all about. They should be prepared to interrupt you with the type of questions that you might expect at the official performance. In particular, they should throw at you hypotheticals: "Counsel, before us are facts A, B, and C, and you are asking us to accept a legal proposition, X, to govern them. Suppose the next case we have includes an additional fact, D. Would we apply your rule? Or suppose we have only facts A and B?" Anticipate such questions and be prepared to answer them. Do not simply say, "Of course, your honors, but that is not the case before the court." The judges know this.

Your office "judges" should test both your inductive and deductive reasoning. Be prepared to defend your analogies. Know the resemblances and differences in the compared cases, vindicate your major premise, and demonstrate that your conclusion logically flows from it.

Prepare for oral argument the way the president might prepare for a press conference. His aides pitch him the hard balls and curves that the press will be throwing. And if such a rehearsal is mandatory for the president, it should be mandatory for you.

Then have your "adversary" make his speech and let the "judges" work him over. You will gain valuable insights from this. You will hear how the strong arguments against you will sound in court. This may influence you to alter your presentation. If you are the appellant, it may give you some intuition in preparing some "spontaneous" rebuttal.

Such a rehearsal is not playacting. It is serious preparation for a fifteen-minute oral presentation that may make or break your case. In recommending this practice, Pittsburgh attorney John H. Bingler Jr. comments: "A rehearsal in front of your colleagues who have read the briefs and prepared to hit you on your weakest points and the strong points of your adversary is very helpful. It is a great confidence builder; best done in front of a TV camera or camcorder. Do it until you feel very good about your performance, or it will be a great confidence killer."

Former Missouri Supreme Court Chief Justice Charles B. Blackmar recounts:

> In preparing the only argument I made before the United States Supreme Court I rehearsed before a bench composed of some of my colleagues at St. Louis University and a retired appellate judge. The questions were more penetrating and detailed than the Supreme Court's. The rehearsal was very helpful to me. I made several revisions in my plan of argument, based on the comments of the panel.

But the question comes: if you are the appellee, how do you rehearse? I think that the best answer is to have one of your colleagues argue your opponent's case as a preliminary so that you may then proceed into a response. Here, it is important that the panel of your "judges" fire away with questions directed to both your opponent and you.

I cannot emphasize too strongly the need to rehearse. Oral arguments before an appellate court do not come every day. Philadelphia attorney Irving R. "Buddy" Seigal explained that this rehearsal should include:

> sessions with experienced as well as inexperienced lawyers in counsel's firm. This kind of preparation is essential. If the case is not "important enough" to justify the legal time necessary for such thorough preparation insofar as fees are

concerned, then, having accepted the appellate assignment, counsel must do what is necessary in the fee area, but still prepare just as if he was being adequately compensated. That is the duty of the lawyer, and particularly the lawyer appearing in the appellate courts.

The rehearsal requires law office teamwork. If properly conducted, you will indeed develop the necessary lemme-at-'em frame of mind. You will be thoroughly prepared. You will be ready for the questions. You will be alert to the potential hypotheticals.

Notwithstanding these views, other distinguished lawyers have different ideas.

As noted in the Foreword, Charles Alan Wright, the late scholar, author, professor, and appellate lawyer, made this comment:

> I would not dream of rehearsing an argument. Indeed I refuse even to discuss a case in the period leading up to when I am going to argue it. At least for my style of argument, freshness and spontaneity are vitally important. I think long and hard about what may be said at oral argument, but I do not put words on paper nor do I discuss the case with others.

Similarly, veteran Philadelphia appellate lawyer James D. Crawford shared Professor Wright's view insofar as he, himself, is concerned, but he seems to think that it is helpful for others in his firm:

> In more than forty years of making appellate arguments, I have never practiced before a moot court—although I have participated in many as a "judge." Even when clients have told me that they require moot courts of their lawyers, I have persuaded them that it doesn't work for me. (Of course, I am always willing to discuss my tentative approach to the argument and to explain how I would answer particular questions; what I won't do is try to get "psyched up" for an argument that doesn't count.)
>
> I recognize that most appellate lawyers don't agree with me. But I have always believed that I would read too much into the moot court and would tend to search for the answers that worked there even if the question or the questioner at oral argument is very different from those in the moot court. That doesn't mean that I don't regularly seek

the help of colleagues in preparing an argument; I will discuss problems in the case, approaches to the argument or even proposed answers to expected questions; I just think it is at best useless, and sometimes harmful, to do this in a formal moot court setting.

§ 22.9   Casing the Joint

For important arguments in unfamiliar locations, especially in the United States Courts of Appeals or the United States Supreme Court, arrive at least a day and a half early. If you can possibly do so, watch the arguments of others the day before you argue. Learn something about the acoustics of the room and the idiosyncracies of the judges. This should be an absolute necessity if you are before the United States Supreme Court. If that Court is not in session, you may wish to listen to tape recordings of arguments which are available through the National Archives and Notherwestern University's Oyez Project, or at least examine transcripts of Supreme Court arguments available online.[4] Never go into that court cold.

Bingler offers this advice:

> On the day before your argument, go through the routine you expect to follow on the day your argue, even the walk/ drive to the courthouse. If at all possible stay at a hotel within walking distance of the courthouse. Get up at the same time, eat the same breakfast, drink the same number of cups of coffee, so you'll know how you will feel the day you argue and so you won't need to think about much else on argument day besides your argument.

At a bare minimum, if you have never been to the court, find out first where the lawyers must report in. Learn whether there is more than one courtroom; how cases are called; whether there is a daily calendar for distribution; where you can find your case on the list; the arrangement of counsel tables (who sits where); how the court controls the length of argument (by lights or cards or whatever); whether a clock can be seen from the lectern; where counsel may place notes or other materials; whether a sound system is used. Learn something about the acoustics; judges do not want to be shouted at, but they should not have to strain to hear what is being said.

---

4. Alderson Reporting Co., *Argument Transcripts*, at http://www.supremecourtus.gov/oral_arguments/argument_transcripts.html.

§ 22.10 Supplemental Citations

If you have cases that you have discovered or which have come up subsequent to the filing of your brief, forward them to the court under the procedures set by the court. Do not wait until the day of the argument. United States circuit judges are rather liberal in permitting "late citations" in the form of a letter to the clerk with copies to the panel, but I am not enamored with the practice in those courts that permit citations to be handed up to the bench at the beginning of the argument.

If you wait until the day of the argument, you are losing much of the zip. If the case is important enough to be cited, the judges should have the opportunity of studying it before hearing your oral argument. At a minimum, the judges should be permitted to examine it before participating in the decision conference, which usually takes place immediately after the oral argument.

Technically, late citations should be limited to cases which have surfaced subsequent to the filing of the brief. Often however, it is simply tardy research that is responsible for these late citations. Submitting cases at the last minute that should have been in the brief is a sign of sloppy lawyering.

I also believe that it is extremely important to give a reason for the citation. The judges should be told what point the late citation is supporting with a one- or two-sentence summary of the holding of the case or a parenthetical quotation. I admit that Fed. R. App. P. 28(j) concerning Supplemental Authorities is ambiguous: "the letter shall without argument state the reasons for the supplemental citations" (what is argument but a statement of reasons?), but I suggest that you err on the side of furnishing an explanation rather than submitting a citation "in the nude." When I receive a citation at the last minute while on the bench, I immediately send for the reporter and examine the case during oral argument. This is most unsatisfactory because I have to do the reading while I am listening to the argument. Recently in a case on the ninth circuit, our attention was drawn to a last-minute citation represented by counsel to be controlling on a point. I sent for the case, glanced at it on the bench and discovered immediately that the holding was the exact opposite from the characterization given by counsel. I noted also that the presiding judge had written the opinion. I turned to him, handed him the book and pointed out the relevant part. Whereupon the presiding judge, who previously had been silent, took over the questioning and destroyed the oral presentation.

This late citation turned out to be a disaster. Not really understanding the case, the attorney who offered it committed forensic suicide in open court.

Chapter 23

HOW TOP-FLIGHT APPELLATE LAWYERS PREPARE

§ 23.1 Overview

Advice on how to prepare for oral argument comes largely from expert lawyers, rather than from the judges. Judges may offer suggestions on how to make the presentation. They can also sketch out in broad strokes the nature of the preparation necessary to satisfy them. But the nuts and bolts on how to prepare must come from experienced appellate advocates, and it is to them that I now turn.

§ 23.2 Philadelphia Lawyers

§ 23.2.1 Edward F. Mannino (Akin Gump)

Edward F. Mannino, of Akin, Gump, Strauss, Hauer & Feld, is a seasoned appellate lawyer and he offers this advice:

1. Reread your brief and make notes regarding:

    a. The themes;

    b. The key facts in the case; and

    c. The key authorities, which should have been read.

2. Read the entire Appendix (or Excerpts of Record) cover to cover and make notes. Use flags to mark key pages; tabs bend easily and fall off. For easy reference during argument, mark on the front cover of each appendix volume in felt-tip pen, which is easy to read, the page numbers of, and a brief phrase describing, all key record citations. Do this even though a typed digest of key Appendix references is available.

3. Reread the adversary brief and note the key points. Look for the weaknesses in your own case that this brief identifies and be prepared to respond to questions from the court about them.

4. Appellant's counsel especially should reread and make notes on the opinion below. What errors of logic can be identified? Are cases miscited, or have cases been decided recently that should change the result? What are the policy implications if the approach of the court below is upheld? Is the judge below

well-respected and rarely reversed, or is his reputation poor with the appellate court?

5.   Read the key opinions upon which both sides rely.

6.   Select those points upon which you must prevail to win on appeal. Attempt to limit your argument to no more than three points, even in full thirty minutes of argument, although you will understand that fifteen minutes is usually the time allotted. Nevertheless, know the record and briefs on all the remaining points if questions are raised on those points by the court or the adversary.

7.   Prepare an outline based on the notes. Plain white paper, 8½-by-11-inch, can be used, with each point for argument beginning on a new page. The outline should be concise, (preferably limited to one page for each point), and should note key themes, the single best authority (by a panel member where possible), and record citations to the briefs and Appendix. For ease of reference, capitalize all letters and use a very short, nongrammatical key word approach with bullet points.

   a.   The purpose of this outline is to distill the essence of the case for purposes of preparation. It should be completed at least one week before argument, studied very day, and revised constantly. Wide margins should be left for revisions and notes.

8.   Put the outline in a looseleaf or similar notebook. . . . By contrast, index cards always pose the hazard of falling on the way to the lectern or getting out of order.

9.   The notebook should also contain separate pages for reference which summarize key opinions from your court, recording the name of every judge who will hear the argument, with the name of the opinion writer underlined. Should you cite a leading case, you can indicate that Judge *X* sat on that case as well.

10 .   On the day before the oral argument reduce the outline as much as possible, preferably to one page. The notebook and full outline will be available at oral argument should your mind go blank—which it never does. Do not look at anything other than this brief outline during argument, and then only as a roadmap of points to be made when sidetracked by questions.

a. By the day of argument, you must know your case well enough to *talk* about it, not just read notes.

b. One week before, and again the day before, oral argument check current slip opinions, looseleaf trade services, Westlaw and Lexis, or other computer law services.

11. Learn the names of the judges who will hear your case, if it is not a court in banc. Most circuits now identify the panel a week before the argument. If a trial judge or a judge from another circuit or court is sitting, consult Westlaw and Lexis to see if that judge has written any opinion on a point involved in your appeal.

12. Always be thinking of the questions the court will pose. Your adversary's brief will suggest most, but not all, of them.

13. The appellee's counsel must also prepare an outline of key points. While appellee will, to a large extent, be responding to the points raised by the court or made by appellant's counsel, the adversary should not determine the scope or content of the appellee's presentation. Make whatever points are necessary, even if the adversary chooses not to mention them. If the points are *crucial*, do not rely on the brief alone.

14. Know the court's own rules, which may require specific application for oral argument by a particular time in advance of argument.

15. When there are multiple counsel for several appellants or appellees, decide in advance who will argue. One lawyer should represent everyone with a common interest. Dividing time even in a thirty-minute argument, unless there is a conflict in interests or positions, will annoy the court and weaken the presentation.

16. Amici, especially governmental agencies such as the Securities and Exchange Commission, should be contacted for possible help in the early stages of an appeal. They must apply to the court for permission *to* argue, and, *if* permitted to do so, will present their own oral argument. The party with whom they are aligned must coordinate carefully with them, inform them of key points of evidence, and assist them in appearing knowledgeable.

17. Finally, if you are the appellee, be prepared to discard your prepared argument where the court clearly understands the issues, and questions your opponent on your key points. In

such a case, you may choose only to answer questions the court has posed to your opponent, and then ask the court if it has any other questions for you. After you answer them, sit down.

§ 23.2.2 James D. Crawford (Schnader)

James D. Crawford, now senior counsel at Schnader, Harrison, Segal & Lewis, has written extensively on appellate advocacy.

1. *Make Sure Your Legal Argument Is Sound, Convincing, and Concise.* This is the section of the brief in which inexperienced counsel most often tend to write too much. Days, or perhaps weeks, of research have gone into gathering material. Something must be done, they feel, with all the case citations collected on file cards and all the cases themselves xeroxed and neatly filed. In fact, most of the research in a really fine brief is done to determine whether there are flaws in the arguments which flow from the most important cases or statutes on which you rely. There is no reason to inform the court that forty-seven cases in a variety of jurisdictions do not call into question the important rule announced by the very court before which you are arguing in a decision handed down just last year.

2. *Clarity and Inevitability Are the Two Watch Words of a Good Argument.* The court must be able to understand exactly where you are going. More important, the court should be convinced that, on the basis of precedent and reason, there is no where else it would want to go.

3. *Most of All, It Must Be Correct.* Most important of all, however, is that your argument, where the appellate court is an able one, must be not merely clear and convincing, but also correct. It is easy to build an argument from helpful language in cases not on point or to construct arguments from statutory language superficially read. But you can expect the appellate court not merely to read your brief, but to think about it. The only way to prepare for this trap is for you to think about it first.

4. *Never Use Weaker Arguments.* In this respect, it is almost as crucial to avoid weak arguments as it is to make the most of strong ones. Even the strongest of legal arguments may lose its effect if it is surrounded by weaker ones. Judges who have

been convinced by your first argument may begin to doubt their judgment if they read four or five frivolous reasons to do that which they were already prepared to do on the basis of one thoroughly sound argument.

§ 23.2.3 Howard J. Bashman (Buchanan Ingersoll)

Howard J. Bashman, a partner at Buchanan Ingersoll, is also the presence behind *How Appealing*—a delightful and informative Web "blog" devoted to appellate matters.[1]

> The first one or two sentences of your presentation should deliver a roadmap to the main points you plan to address during your time at the podium. "The trial court's judgment should be reversed for three reasons. First, second, and third."

> Respond immediately to the substance of questions from the bench, in a manner that is forthright, not evasive. If you are asked about issue two while you are addressing issue one, answer the question. You can then return to your intended presentation or stay with the issue raised by the question should the judges appear especially interested in it.

> If, before your allotted time has expired, you have answered all of the judges' questions and have addressed the matters you intended to cover, thank the court for its attention and sit down.

§ 23.3 Florida Lawyer Gary L. Sasso (Carlton Fields)

Gary L. Sasso of the St. Petersburg firm of Carlton Fields, has written extensively on brief writing and oral argument.

1. *Keep it simple.* This maxim has been stated so often that it may seem numbingly obvious. But the same might be said of "Thou shalt not kill." Each is repeated a lot because each means a lot. Violating either rule can lead to disaster. Chances are, whatever you *expect* to argue, the court will make you keep it simple by using up your time-asking questions.

---

1. Howard Bashman, *How Appealing*, at http://appellateblog.blogspot.com.

If you represent the appellant, you should have made hard judgments, long before argument, when selecting the grounds for the appeal. Frustrated by an adverse outcome and peeved by many unhappy rulings, large and small, trial counsel often want to appeal on six or eight grounds. Bad idea. Appellate courts are skeptical of scattershot appeals. Appellate courts loathe appeals that (1) take issue with a trial judge's exercise of discretion in gray areas, or that (2) attack rulings that probably had no impact on the outcome. Appellate courts cannot and will not second-guess trial judges on such points. Almost always, appeals that raise too many issues spend too much effort on points that fall into one of these two categories.

2.   *Do not reargue your brief.* Resist the temptation to base the text and structure of oral argument on the contents of your brief. It usually is unwise to organize your oral argument exactly the way you organized your brief. This is so because briefs and oral argument have different functions and conventions. Writing and talking are different activities. What works in one does not in the other. Briefs begin with a detailed statement of the case. Oral argument should not. Begin your oral argument with a concise (one or two sentence) statement of the issues. Then tell the court how you believe the issues must be resolved. Next, state the key facts—not all the facts—that should dictate the outcome. This should take no more than a minute—the oral equivalent of a paragraph.

3.   *Answer questions promptly and responsively.* I have heard even experienced counsel complain about "interruptions" during oral argument by the court. The court's questions should *never* be regarded as interruptions. You are thinking the wrong way if you fail to see questions as the principal reason for oral argument. Questions by the court must be taken as important opportunities to learn what may be troubling the judges. Many judges prepare questions before argument starts. Each question is asked for a reason.

Address the court's questions directly and immediately. In *all* cases, begin your response with "yes," "no," "it depends" or "I don't know." *Then* provide any necessary explanation. *Never* say, "I will get to that shortly" or "I need to provide some background before I answer the question."

4. *Be flexible*. Partly because the court's questions are so important, you must be flexible going into argument. Generally you will be better served by thinking through the implications of your position enough to be able to address hypothetical questions directly and succinctly. This may include making concessions when necessary, while making clear that your client must still prevail in the different, non-hypothetical circumstances of your case.

5. *Maintain a tone of "respectful equality."* You must show the appellate panel deference in presenting your case and in responding to questions. Still, you should not confuse respect with timidity or obsequiousness. Maintain a tone of "respectful equality." In your demeanor and in the force and conviction of your argument, show the court that you are an intellectual peer, but at the same time treat judges courteously. Do not raise your voice, make faces, or show impatience at questions from the bench—and *never* interrupt a judge before he or she completes a question or finishes making an observation. But do not be intimidated into conceding an argument that you believe you should win.

6. *Prepare with the end in mind.* Finally, you should prepare for oral argument with a view to what will actually happen at argument. Many attorneys prepare by planning what they will say uninterrupted by the court. By now, it should be clear that oral argument involves much more than that. You are not the only player. You must anticipate what the other players—the court and opposing counsel—may do.

   Begin by reviewing all the briefs. Make notes of problems that you must resolve by the time of argument, and then resolve them. Become completely familiar with all your weaknesses. Next review the full text of the principal cases cited by the parties. With the benefit of the briefs and the passage of time, you will likely gain new insight into the issues. Having taken this step, update your research to catch developments in the law and in the later histories of the cases you cited.

7. *Do not write out your argument.* Many lawyers do. If you are wedded to this practice, so be it. But if you have not developed the habit (or superstition), do not start; and, if you have, break it if you can. Scripting your argument will reduce your flexibility.

A compromise security blanket is to memorize your opening line (usually a statement of the issues). This will have a calming effect as you first stand at the podium; it will help get you off to a good start. But from that point on, look the judges in the eye and *talk—not* declaim or recite—to them.

8.   *Broaden your preparation.* Having developed a basic idea of what your argument will be, broaden your preparation by reviewing all cases of any significance cited by the parties. You may want to annotate your brief with a one-phrase description of the holding or key facts of each such case. Be prepared to distinguish bad cases that the court may ask you about.

9.   *List all difficult questions that the court may ask.* Put yourself in the court's shoes for this exercise. Keep in mind that the court will be concerned about jurisdictional issues and the procedural posture of the case. It may want to determine the narrowest possible ground on which to dispose of the case. Do not ignore these matters simply because the *parties* have not devoted much attention to them or because you do not intend to raise them in argument. You may not have a choice. Ultimately, you must satisfy the court; you must be prepared to address *its* concerns.

10. *Utilize a moot court.* For important cases, or for your first few appeals, ask colleagues to put you through a moot court. This can be tremendously helpful. Moot court members will see problems— even gestures or fidgeting—you may not know you have. Allow at least one day between moot court and the actual argument to give yourself enough time to research or think through issues that come up for the first time in the practice session—and perhaps to recover your self-confidence.

11. *Condense.* Having prepared your argument, condense your outline to one or two pages if possible. Set forth only the key points, key facts, and key citations that you may need at argument. Use words or phrases rather than full sentences. This will be far more helpful when you are on your feet than a full-text script attractively bound and tabbed in a three-ring notebook.[2]

---

2. Gary L. Sasso, *Appellate Oral Argument*, 20 Litig. 27 (1994).

§ 23.4   Illinois Lawyer-Turned-Judge Nancy J. Arnold

Judge Nancy J. Arnold of the Circuit Court in Cook County, Chicago, had been an experienced appellate lawyer prior to ascending the bench and served as president of the Illinois Appellate Lawyers Association.

> The "techniques" of an attorney engaged in the process of *winning an appeal* span a spectrum running from perhaps mere gadgetry to fundamental substance.
>
> Starting at the deeper end, I believe that my most important "technique" as an appellate lawyer consisted of obtaining my own confidence in:
>
> 1. the logic of my reasoning, and
>
> 2. the research of authority establishing its principles.
>
> I rigorously composed an outline which required me to set out each step in the reasoning process and all the authority and facts to support them. I insisted on never making a leap—no unexpressed assumption or conclusion, no hole in authority, no twists of legal reality.
>
> I sought self-assurance that the total premises leading to my conclusions were solid in authority and fact, and that the premises did lead logically to the conclusion reached. . . .
>
> To be persuasive, an argument must instill confidence in the listener. The essential thing is to assure that the advocate himself has that confidence.
>
> Somewhere here also is the matter of style. We are lawyers. Ours is a proud and noble profession. Our writing and speaking style should reflect our respect for the law and for our profession It should reflect the seriousness of our purpose and our place in society. It should inspire the court to discourse on an elevated plane.

§ 23.5   California Appellate Specialist Curt Cutting

Not only is Curt Cutting of the Los Angeles appellate law firm of Horvitz & Levy one of my former clerks, but he is a founding member of the American Bar Association's Council of Appellate Lawyers—the first national bench-bar organization for appellate lawyers. He has filed appellate briefs and presented oral arguments in state and federal courts, including the United States Supreme Court.

Communicate with the client. Oral argument preparation often begins with a call to the client. I do this well before the scheduled hearing date, to discuss the nature and purpose of oral argument and how I intend to prepare for it. This call may not be necessary when the client has a sophisticated understanding of the appellate process, but when the client is new to the appellate process, the call can be critically important for two reasons:

1. First, it provides an opportunity to explain that the oral argument is most productive when it involves a question-and-answer dialogue with the court, not when it involves the delivery of a preprepared script. There is a common client misconception that appellate oral argument will resemble a trial lawyer's closing argument, in which the lawyer delivers an impassioned speech and the court listens passively. I prefer to dispel this misconception as early in the process as possible.

2. Second, the call provides an opportunity to explain the need for intensive oral argument preparation. Some clients may think that you do not need to spend much time preparing for argument because you have already researched the issues and written the briefs. It is particularly important to explain to these clients in advance what you will be doing to prepare for oral argument and why. Once they understand the necessary steps in the process, most clients are more than happy to have you do whatever is necessary to increase the likelihood of success on appeal.

Reread the briefs and the record. In many courts, there is a significant lag time between the completion of briefing and the scheduling of oral argument. In some courts, this lag time can be a year or longer. During that time, I will have turned my attention to other cases, and my familiarity with the case to be argued will have faded. Therefore, when the court finally schedules a date for oral argument I must first reacquaint myself with the appeal by reviewing the briefs and the major legal authorities relied on by both sides.

In addition to refreshing my knowledge of the briefs, I go back over the appellate record. Some appellate lawyers recommend rereading the *entire* record, but I think this is usually a waste of time, because large portions of the record may have no bearing on the appeal. Instead, I reread the notes I made during my initial reading of the record and I use those notes to identify the portions of the record that pertain to the issues on appeal. I then review these portions carefully and repeatedly, until I am satisfied that I can answer any factual questions the court might ask about them. I must have a complete mastery of the record, because I will not have time at oral argument to fumble through the record or the briefs, and I never want to respond to a question by saying "It's in the record, but I can't tell you where."

Update the research. Next I update the relevant law, looking for any recent developments that could affect the case, i.e., newly decided cases, newly enacted or amended statutes, and orders that have superseded any recent cases I cited in the brief, such as grants of review, rehearing, or depublication. I update the research well in advance of the hearing date, so I have time to call the court's attention to new authorities if necessary.

If I encounter an adverse change in the law, I do not ignore it. The court's law clerks will find it even if my opponent does not. If I think the new authority must be discussed at argument, I will call it to the court's attention by letter, rather than "springing" it on the court at the hearing. The day before the hearing, I update the research again to check for last-minute developments.

Capsulize the arguments and polish the theme. Once I have committed the relevant facts and law to memory, I begin to think about the points I want to make at argument. It is not effective to repeat the arguments in the brief, but at the same time it is inappropriate to raise arguments not covered by the briefs. Instead, I must try to capsulize the arguments in the brief, breaking each one down to its essence in a way that can be easily communicated in a conversation with the court. I also take this opportunity to hone a theme that may gave gotten lost in the more detailed written presentation. I try to think of examples to demonstrate the practical benefits of the position I am advocating, and to illustrate the problems that would be created by the opposing position. Developing these examples gives me a chance to be more colloquial in my presentation, emphasizing the "big picture" at issue in the case.

As I prepare my presentation on each issue, I consider whether my client has an interest in seeking a publication of the court's opinion on that issue, and how my remarks might direct the court to the desired result. Also, I make sure that I am prepared to communicate the precise disposition I am seeking, such as a new trial, a partial new trial, or a reversal with directions.

Finally, I determine in advance whether there are any legal or factual points I will concede at argument. Sometimes I will decide to concede a point that we raised in the briefs, rather than stubbornly pushing an argument that has been undermined by an opponent's persuasive counter arguments or by post-briefing legal developments. Before I concede anything at oral argument, however, I always obtain prior authorization from the client.

Prepare an outline. Once I have capsulized the arguments in the brief and honed the theme, I prepare an outline of the points I would like to raise at oral argument. Obviously, this list cannot include *all* the arguments in the brief. I focus on my strongest arguments, and my answers to my opponent's strongest arguments. Although I arrange these points in an outline format, I do not wed myself to the order of the arguments in the outline. I make sure that each point is a stand-alone modular argument that I can jump to any point, as the flow of the conversation with the court dictates.

Some attorneys take their outlines with them to the lectern during argument, I do not follow this practice because I fear I would have a tendency to use the outline as a crutch, and I would end up looking down and reading from my notes. To avoid this temptation, I reduce my outline to a single piece of paper with only a few key words or phrases, which I can use to get back on track if I lose my train of thought.

In addition to an outline, some attorneys also bring large volumes of materials to oral argument, such as copies of the cases cited in the briefs, volumes of the appellate record (sometimes the entire record), visual aids, etc. This is a matter of personal preference, but I prefer to bring only the bare minimum, knowing that I will not have time during argument to fumble through a stack of materials. I bring only one small binder, usually containing a few key cases and a few relevant pages from the record. Even so, I generally do not bring this binder to the lectern during argument. If I have prepared properly for argument, I will not need to refer even to these few items.

Participate in a moot court. My firm conducts a moot court before each argument as a matter of course, with other lawyers from the firm participating as judges. Ideally, the judges include at least one lawyer who is very familiar with the case and knows the strengths and weaknesses of my position, and one lawyer who is new to the case and will bring a fresh perspective. In some high-stakes cases, my firm has retained one or more retired appellate judges to serve as moot court judges. Whoever the judges are, they must spend time before the moot court reading the briefs and preparing questions. Only a fully prepared judge will be able to ask the tough questions that make moot court worthwhile.

The primary purpose of the moot court is to practice answering tough questions. At the real argument, answering the court's questions is far more important than giving prepared remarks. There is a well known anecdote about a lawyer who forgot this principle during an argument before the California Supreme Court. The court asked the lawyer a question and he responded by saying "I'll get there, your honor." Justice Gibson quickly responded, "You're there now, counsel."

Learn about the court. If I am arguing before an unfamiliar court, I visit the courthouse in advance to observe argument in other cases. This gives me a comfort level with the atmosphere of the courtroom, and it sometimes provides insight into the judicial philosophies or temperaments of the members of the panel.

If I am able to learn the identity of the panel members in advance of the argument, I try to collect and review as much information as possible about them—reputation, published biographies, previous opinions, etc. This information only goes so far, however. Each judge has law clerks providing input on the case, and there is no means of obtaining any advance information about them. And in most cases, parties have no way of knowing which judge will be writing the opinion. For these reasons, I find it is best to let the merits of my case, rather than my knowledge of the court, be the primary force in shaping the argument.

Ideally, when I have completed all of these steps, I have mastered the case so well that I can relax before the court and come across as personable and conversational, but at the same time forceful and authoritative.

§ 23.6 Assistant United States Attorney Paul J. Brysh

Assistant United States Attorney Paul J. Brysh of the Western District of Pennsylvania is a veteran appellate lawyer for the government with extensive experience in the United States court of appeals.

Persuading an appellate judge is a far more subtle endeavor than persuading a jury or even a trial judge. Appellate judges are constrained, not only by the evidence and the substantive law, but also by the often severe limitations on the scope of their review. They tend to be highly conscious of this. They are conditioned not to be receptive to arguments based upon sympathy or other emotions.

Therefore, the most persuasive appellate arguments are sound arguments that are demonstrably faithful to the record and firmly grounded in the law. There is no more persuasive appellate argument than this issue is controlled by X case or Y statute, followed by a cogent explanation.

Many cases are not quite that clear, however, and judges do not enjoy applying the law mechanically if the result is unfair. It is therefore usually worthwhile for the appellate advocate to devote some time and effort to marshaling all of the facts and circumstances suggesting that the result indicated by the law is also equitable and reasonable.

Because the amount of time is usually very limited in oral argument and, the most effective form of persuasion is providing accurate and complete answers to the court's questions, counsel should welcome the questions. The questions enable counsel to use his or her time to address matters that are of concern to the judges, instead of wasting that time on matters that are of little or no concern to the judges.

Counsel should listen carefully to the questions, and then answer them directly, candidly, and fully.

§ 23.7   Washington, D.C. Lawyer Bobby R. Burchfield (Covington & Burling)

Bobby R. Burchfield—another of my former clerks and the co-chair of the litigation group at Covington & Burling in Washington, D.C.— has argued appellate cases before five different United States courts of appeals. He has practiced in the area of complex corporate litigation since joining the firm in 1981 and has had principal responsibility in a variety of high-profile cases. In 1992, he took a leave of absence to serve as General Counsel of President George H. W. Bush's re-election campaign.

Work hard to find the winning argument. To be in this business, we almost have to believe that every case is winnable if only we can find the right argument and make it effectively. Sometimes the winning argument will be unconventional, but if a candid evaluation of the available arguments leads to the conclusion that the conventional arguments cannot succeed, a more creative approach may be necessary.

Believe in your position. Critique your own argument mercilessly, and take account of its weaknesses. By the time of oral argument, you should be confident that your argument is logical, consistent with the record, supported (or at least not foreclosed) by pertinent precedent, and responsive to any argument advanced by your adversary. Until you reach the point of believing in your own argument, it is difficult to expect an appellate court to do so.

State clearly and early why you should win. At the outset of the argument, express concisely and precisely why your client should win. The opening sentence of the argument should simply but powerfully tell the court why you win the case. The rest of the argument should elaborate upon that statement. This principle discourages, and is intended to discourage, [buffet-style] arguments.

Be authoritative. Both in the briefs and at argument your goal should be for the Court to look to you as the most authoritative person in the courtroom with regard to your case. This requires extensive preparation on both the law and the record, as well as painstaking candor. If relying upon critical evidence, direct the court to the location of the document or testimony in the record, give the court time to find it, and read the pertinent language to the court. By doing so, you will assure that the court sees the evidence and appreciates its importance to your case.

Whenever possible, follow the judges. Understand and associate yourself with the views of the judges on your panel to the maximum extent possible. If you know the panel in advance, determine what each judge has written about the issues in your case, and attempt to reconcile your position to that of each judge. Even when the panel in not known in advance, your typed summaries of the important decisions should indicate the author and participating judges so that quick reference is possible immediately before argument. During argument, seize upon questioning by the Court to align your position with the questioning judge. If you are the appellee, you might even pick up on a question asked of the appellant's counsel to demonstrate how the inquiry helps your case.

Simplify complex issues. It is important to understand complex issues, but just as important to simplify them. The goal is to communicate even the most complex factual and legal issues in an accurate but simple and understandable way. Excellent advocates especially excel at this.

Finally, do not neglect the equities. It is as important to explain why a ruling for your client is fair as it is to explain why a ruling for your client is required by existing precedent. Judges strive to reach fair results within the confines of existing precedent. You should strive to make the judges want to rule for you, rather than persuading them that they must rule for you. A judge will often find the way to a fair result, even if apparently applicable precedent seems at first blush to stand in the way. The best "one-two" punch is to explain why a ruling for your client would be fair, and then how precedent compels (or at least allows) your client to win.

§ 23.8 Former United States Solicitor General Seth P. Waxman (Wilmer, Cutler & Pickering)

Seth P. Waxman—Solicitor General of the United States from 1997 to 2001—has argued thirty-three cases in the United States Supreme Court and is now a partner at Wilmer, Cutler & Pickering in Washington, D.C. He is considered to be among the country's premier oral advocates. With Mr. Waxman's permission, I reproduce excerpts of his recommended principals of oral argument from his essay, *In the Shadow of Daniel Webster: Arguing Appeals in the Twenty-First Century*:

I mention Daniel Webster not because of his mastery of American politics, but rather because he is widely regarded as the greatest advocate ever to argue in an American court. *McCulloch v. Maryland, Gibbons v. Ogden, Luther v. Borden,* the *Charles River Bridge Case.* Webster argued them all. Webster's qualities and accomplishments as an advocate have been extolled so often that the highest praise to which any modem lawyer can aspire is to be deemed "almost as good as Daniel Webster." In the realm of advocacy, Webster doesn't merely sit in the Pantheon: He is Zeus himself.

Passion. This first principle is the most fundamental. If you want to be a great oral advocate, you must care passionately about your work. Justice Story recalled Webster's "earnestness of manner, and a depth of research, and a potency of phrase, which at once convinced you that his whole soul was in the cause. . . ." You need only read Webster's published letters to understand that he saw complete dedication as the key to his work—dedication to his client, to his craft, and to the principles to which he believed his profession should aspire. As Chief Justice Fuller once observed, "It is impossible to overestimate the support the Court derives from the bar, and in Mr. Webster's arguments fidelity to the Court is as conspicuous as fidelity to his client. It is not the client first and the conscience afterwards, but duty to both together, one and inseparable."

That passionate devotion to duty has continued to resonate with judges and lawyers from generation to generation. The attitude and preparation of some show that they have no conception of their effort higher than to make a living. Others are dutiful but uninspired in trying to shape their little cases to a winning pattern. But it lifts up the heart of a judge when an advocate stands at the bar who knows that he is building a cathedral.

Preparation. The second principle that Webster's work exemplifies builds on the first. Webster acknowledged, as we all know we should, the absolute importance of comprehensive preparation. Things may not—indeed, they will not—always turn out precisely as we hope, but for lawyers like Webster, it will not be for lack of effort. For lawyers building a cathedral, every argument demands what others might deride as over-preparation. "Accuracy and diligence," Webster said, "are much more necessary to a lawyer than great comprehension of mind, or brilliancy of talent." To be a great lawyer, he recognized, one "must first consent to be only a great drudge." The night before his grand performance in *Gibbons v. Ogden,* Webster worked for eleven straight hours, pausing only to shave, eat, and read the morning paper before appearing at the Court. As Webster understood, the goal of preparation is simply this: *When you walk into the courtroom to make your oral argument, you should know every aspect of the case better than anyone else does.*

Certainly you should know it far better than any judge. You must know the entire factual record. You must comfortably understand all of the relevant law, whatever its source. And finally you must do something else that is far more difficult—you must understand the implications of every principle upon which your case depends.

Every advocate follows his own path, but I generally try to do this in two ways. First, I think about questions. I attempt to identify every question a judge could reasonably ask. I think as hard as I can about what the best possible answer is. And finally I consider what further questions might follow from that answer, and what the answers to those questions should be. This is, for me at least, hard, hard work. It is generally easy to think of a few difficult questions; it is impossible to think of them all. How far down the list of conceivable questions you get, though, is a pretty good indicator of how well prepared you are.

The other thing I often do is to try to explain the case to a non-lawyer. This may seem peculiar, since judges, after all, are lawyers. But I find that explaining the case to someone who is not a lawyer helps me to discern whether there is a basic flaw in my reasoning, and whether I am really able to distinguish what is fundamental about my case from what is not. Preparing to answer all sorts of doctrinally tricky questions is essential, but it may also obscure the forest for the trees. You must be able to see both very clearly when you stand up to argue.

Planting the Kernel. My third and final point relates to the argument itself. Because oral argument is now so very different from what it was in Webster's day, it is difficult to translate the principles for appellate advocacy that might have been used in his time into precepts that will apply today. In all but the rarest of modern appellate courtrooms, for example, we litigate in an environment of interruption, not oration. But even in this very different world. there is a fundamental principle from Webster's day that still prevails, and it is this: When you stand up to present your oral argument facts and law at your command and head crammed with answers to every conceivable question, something else must be at the forefront of your mind. Daniel Webster certainly had it clearly in focus when he stood up to argue.

It is the kernel of the case—the one or two, or at the very most, three points that you must impress upon the court before you sit down.

These points may or may not be those you emphasized in your briefs. Sometimes, in fact, the thorough preparation you make for oral argument leads you to see the fundamentals of your case in a different way. I once came to reconceptualize a case on the very night before oral argument, because, although I had conducted two moot courts in the case, each using a different theme, neither had worked to my satisfaction. My last-minute change worked beautifully in that case, but I would never counsel brinksmanship like this for its own sake, for it is fraught with risk. But my own experience in this unusual case does demonstrate, I think, that however difficult the kernel may be to discern, and however late it reveals itself, you must have it in mind when you appear before the court.

Once you have found the kernel, polish and refine it into its purest, simplest form. And consider carefully how best to present it to the court. Webster understood this precept well, demanding of himself "the greatest effort of power in the tersest and fewest words." In Webster's day the kernel was often planted only after hours spent carefully tilling the judicial mind. Nowadays, the best strategy before a fully prepared court may be to make your point, pellucidly, as soon as you begin. But however you plan to do it, you must be absolutely clear in your mind about what the essentials are, and you must also be confident that when you sit down, the judges will understand both what they are and why they are important.

Questions will come. In the Supreme Court they come in a torrent. You should welcome and embrace questions, not be annoyed by them. An oral argument punctuated by questions may not be as transiently satisfying as a perfectly declaimed speech. Almost certainly, it will not be studied with admiration through the generations. But if those are your objectives, stick to giving speeches or lectures. The oral advocate's job is to convince judges, and questions provide the clearest window of insight into what will accomplish that. Treat each question as a sincere effort to understand your point—even if that might not be the judge's true reason for asking. And answer every question frankly, respectfully, and directly. If you are sufficiently well prepared, you will often see how a judge's question can lead you to a point you need to make in order to help the court understand the kernel of your case. Fish are more assertive today than they were in Webster's time; they will not simply jump into your pocket at the sight of your fishing rod. But once judges start to nibble with questions, with direct and thoughtful answers you can still hope to reel them in.

Before I drown you in metaphor. I will close with one further thought: In modern oral argument, the very best strategy, whether answering questions or making your essential affirmative point, may be to heed the advice with which the great Admiral Nelson admonished his captains: "Never mind maneuvers," he used to say, "always go at 'em." In his own way, in his own time, that is just what Daniel Webster did.[3]

---

3. Seth P. Waxman, *In the Shadow of Daniel Webster: Arguing Appeals in the Twenty-First Century*, 3 J. App. Prac. & Process 521 (2001).

Chapter 24

DELIVERING THE ARGUMENT

§ 24.1 Appearance and Demeanor

When your case is called, you approach the lectern and identify yourself: "I am attorney So and So representing the appellant Such and Such." This is not only necessary for the moment of the argument but if the case is being recorded, in reviewing the tape or a transcript of it, the judges will know exactly who is speaking.

My advice is to dress conservatively. Men should wear a dark business suit and a conservative tie. For women, the basic black dress is always appropriate, as is a traditionally tailored, dark-colored suit. Judges are more tolerant today—much more tolerant than they were when I came to the bar in 1947—but it would not hurt to remember the words of King Lear: "Through tattered clothes small vices do appear."[1] No court will stop a lawyer from arguing if he or she shows up in technicolor splendor; yet keep in mind that the judges appear in black robes in the appellate courtroom—the most formal of settings. How you dress may be of little moment to most judges, but if your appearance offends one judge who is a stickler for proper appearance, then you are starting off on the wrong foot in your responsibility to persuade.

Keep your voice well modulated. Your appearance before an appellate court is not an appearance before a jury. If the lectern is fairly close to the bench, it is well to keep your voice on the same level and in the same tone that you would use in a conversation at a dinner table with one sitting across from you. I recognize that acoustics in many courtrooms will not permit this and you may have to project your voice. In many courtrooms, the bench is somewhat elevated and is set at some distance from the lectern. In this situation, you should pitch your voice accordingly. Some microphones are placed on the podium for amplification purposes. Others are there for recording purposes only. Find out in advance what the situation is.

You should attempt to make your presentation as if you and the judges are sitting around a conference table. When the present courtrooms in the third circuit were designed, we deliberately arranged the design so that the attorney and the judges were almost on eye level. This was to encourage the private conversational give-and-take between counsel and the court.

---

1. William Shakespeare, *King Lear* act 4, sc. 6.

Should the client be present at oral argument? I do not think so. Clients have a tendency to make the sort of suggestions that are least admired by judges. Many times I have had the experiences described by Justice Robert H. Jackson:

> When I hear counsel launch into personal attacks on the opposition or praise of a client, I instinctively look about to see if I can identify the client in the room—and often succeed. Some counsel have become conspicuous for the gallery that listens to their argument and, when it is finished, ostentatiously departs. The case that is argued to please a client, impress a following in the audience, or attract notice from the press, will not often make a favorable impression on the bench. An argument is not a spectacle.[2]

Although I have emphasized the conversational nature of your oral presentation, it is extremely important that you speak loud enough for the judges to hear you. Many lawyers are understandably quite nervous and have difficulty projecting. This is unfortunate. All is lost in oral argument unless the judges understand you; and we cannot understand you unless we hear you. Justice Jackson also adds:

> If your voice is low, it burdens the hearing, and parts of what you say may be missed. On the other hand, no judge likes to be shouted at as if he were an ox. I know of nothing you can do except to bear the difficulty in mind, watch the bench, and adapt your delivery to avoid causing apparent strain.[3]

§ 24.2 Nervous? Yes, We Know

Judges know that appearing before a panel of the court is a formidable experience. There is an accompanying nervousness, and this is to be expected. The stress level is always high as the lawyer stands, ready to sell the case. Alan L. Dworsky put it very well:

> Experienced lawyers feel that way too. In fact, polls show that most people are more afraid of public speaking than dying. To me this only proves that most people who are polled don't think much about the questions. My point is: you're human. Don't interpret your nervousness as personal

---

2. Robert H. Jackson, *Advocacy Before the United States Supreme Court*, 37 Cornell L.Q. 1, 10 (1951).
3. *Id.*

flaw. Be gentle with yourself. Nervousness is a normal human experience in an exciting and scary challenge. It shows that you care about your performance and your case. When you stop being nervous, start worrying. You've either stopped caring or stopped breathing.[4]

There is, however, one antidote to this; and I guarantee that it will work every time. If you walk into that courtroom better prepared on the subject than anyone else in the room, you have nothing to be nervous about. It is *your* case. You have lived with it. You have written the brief after researching and becoming familiar with every case touching the subject matter. You now know more about the subject matter than any judge on the bench. Judges are generalists, not specialists in any idiosyncratic part of the law. It is you who is the specialist. You are there to help the judges by sharing your knowledge.

Notice that I used the phrase "know more about the *subject matter*." I did not say "know more about *your case*." You must have a broad comprehension of the entire branch of the law of which your case is but a part. You will have a ready answer for any hypothetical thrown at you, and *you*, not the judges, are now the master in this little domain. In the words of Franklin D. Roosevelt, "You have nothing to fear but fear itself."

Assume that you are still nervous. Not to worry. Ultimately, judges are interested in what you say; not how you say it. We are not out there judging a debate or a law school moot court competition. We have asked for oral argument because we need a little more substantive help from the lawyers, not an Oscar-worthy performance.

Do not mumble. Always speak clearly so that you may be understood. Oklahoma Supreme Court Justice Yvonne Kauger adds:

> Don't whine. . . . Nervous tension seems to raise voices by octaves. Take a deep breath and lower your register. It should go without saying—but don't chew gum! As incredible as this sounds, it has happened.

---

4. Alan L. Dworsky, *The Little Book on Oral Argument* 3–4 (2000).

§ 24.3 Ten Golden Rules for Oral Argument

John W. Davis, Esq.[5]	*Judge Myron H. Bright*[6]
1. Change places (in your imagination of course) with the court.	1. Know your customer, the court.
2. State first the nature of the case and briefly its prior history.	2. A.B.P.—always be prepared.
3. State the facts. (Follow the three *C*s: chronology, candor and clarity.)	3. Go for the jugular.
4. State next the applicable rules of law on which you rely.	4. Questions, questions, good and bad. Answer directly, then return to your main theme.
5. Always go for the jugular vein.	5. Be flexible and innovative.
6. Rejoice when the court asks questions.	6. One lawyer is better than two.
7. Read sparingly and only from necessity.	7. Look up, speak up.
8. Avoid personalities.	8. Don't snatch defeat from the jaws of victory.
9. Know your record from cover to cover.	9. Believe in your case and be natural.
10. Sit down.	10. Above all, don't kid yourself. Oral argument is important; indeed, it may be crucial.

§ 24.4 Payoff Time: The Actual Delivery

§ 24.4.1 Overview

We all have our own personality, our own way of speaking, our own way of convincing. We say things in a certain manner, communicate in individual styles of tone, modulation, and gesture. We are comfortable as we do this, and we are usually effective.

In oral argument be as natural and comfortable as possible. Be yourself. Do not try to cast yourself in the image of another, because you run the risk of appearing artificial and insincere; you fail to project the appearance of confidence and credibility. When this happens, you lack persuasion. If you have prepared enough, you can afford to be yourself.

To launch your argument you might wish to commit to memory a few opening sentences, but do not start out by reading. To read your argument is to antagonize the court. Never, never do it. Do not even think about it. Have an outline or notes, but your notes must be a

---

5. John W. Davis, *The Argument of an Appeal*, 26 A.B.A.J. 895 (1940).

6. Myron H. Bright, *The Ten Commandments of Oral Argument*, 67 A.B.A.J. 1136 (1981).

safety net, not a crutch. Look at your notes when you are making a short quote from the record or a case. Referring to your notes at this time adds the appearance of reliability to your quoting. If you have prepared sufficiently, or have rehearsed adequately, you should know exactly what to say.

Your oral argument should never exceed three points. You do not have the time to develop more. After identifying yourself, it is imperative to inform the court what issues you intend to discuss. You will then explain that you are relying on the brief for the others. At this point, you may be interrupted by one of the judges who wishes to hear argument on another issue. You should be sufficiently prepared to accommodate the court.

Former Wisconsin Supreme Court Chief Justice Nathan S. Heffernan advises counsel: "At the outset, tell the judges what you are going to tell them, tell them, and if it appears necessary, tell them what you told them."

§ 24.4.2 When to Say What

You always lead off with your best point—your strongest one. Your strongest point is *the argument that objectively considered, and based on precedent, and stated policy concerns of the court, is most likely to persuade the court to your point of view.*

It is what John W. Davis characterized as the "cardinal point around which lesser points revolve like planets around the sun."[7] This determination must be made dispassionately. No matter how great the cause you hope to advance, no matter how deep the passions run, your presentation must be at all stages cool, calculating, and logical. I have had some of the nationally famous civil rights lawyers appear before me over the years, great advocates whose out-of-court interviews and televised sound bites resounded in flamboyant, purple prose. But in courtroom the role-playing and posturing were gone. They were very professional and, in general, extremely effective advocates in the finest tradition.

After setting out your first point, you then move to your second strongest argument, and if there is more, then to the final one. The presentation should be in the form of an inverted pyramid, with the best material presented first and the lesser following after in order of

---

7. Davis, *supra* note 5, at 897.

diminishing importance. This is how reporters are taught to write a newspaper article—to permit the editor to cut it off at the end and still leave a complete and important story.

Ideally, your second or third points should be self-sufficient and independent of the court's acceptance of the first argument. If the first point is rejected by the court, be prepared to shift ground immediately. I have heard too many arguments in which the advocate elected to slug it out with the judges on the first point. The advocate persisted, even though the effort was a manifest failure, and even though counsel was losing valuable time by not moving on to a point that might have gotten a more sympathetic hearing.

§ 24.4.2   Do Not Hide Facts and Cases That Hurt

You are the appellant. There are facts in the record and a case or two that may hurt you. Your opponent is sitting at the counsel table waiting to slam you with them as soon as you sit down. Or even worse, the judges are about to trump your opponent and launch an attack of their own. It is time to take the wind out of your adversary's sails. Mention these facts up front and tell us why they do not hurt you. Explain why the adverse case really is not a death knell. This will defuse any potential attack.

If you do this well, some of the fire and brimstone is taken out of the appellee's main argument. What is more, you have earned the respect of the court because this has heightened your credibility. This does not mean that you should pitch your entire argument as a rebuttal to the appellee's case. Rather, you, not your opponent, must control the direction of your argument.

If this is not done, you will surely get a question from one of the judges: "Help us out. In a few minutes, your friend is going to talk about these facts or this case, may we have your views on this now." Address these points before the court has an opportunity to ask. Where the case is fact-driven, as in a sufficiency of the evidence case, too often the appellant gives us a reprise of a jury speech, arguing evidence that has been rejected by the jury. Avoid this temptation and provide the court, up front, a worse-case scenario of facts against you. This will engender respect every time.

§ 24.4.3 How to Say It

Spicing your argument with a quote from one of the literary masters can be effective if used properly. A familiar quotation can eloquently sum up your position or vividly illustrate the equities that favor your client. Do not repeat it if it appears already in your brief. Do use it if the quote fits perfectly, is memorable, and you are confident that it is well known to the judges. Make certain that it does not provide fodder to your adversary and thus boomerang on you.

Keep your main points simple and hard-hitting. Limit discussion of citations and precedents. It is better to leave detailed discussion of cases to the briefs. Concentrate instead on the logic and force of your position. Keep always in mind the focus of your argument and do not get sidetracked, even by a single judge. Stay with the theme that represents your best hope of winning. Do not waste your severely rationed time on unnecessary elaboration.

Tell the court what you want and why. Explain how the rule you want the court to adopt will work, and show how it is consistent with what these judges have said before. Explain that there is impressive, respectable authority for it and that it fairly accommodates relevant values and interests.

This is but a modern version of the *confirmatio*; your argument confirms the acceptability of the proposition you are urging before the court. It proves the case. At the same time you must set forth what the ancients called the *confutatio*, a refutation of the proposition urged by your adversary.[8] Quickly, forcefully, and effectively show why that position should not be accepted, why it is not supported by good reason or authority and why it will not work.

Know your record cold. Be prepared to answer questions about *all* its relevant parts. Remember, different judges may focus on different aspects of the prior proceeding. One judge may question you about an event or finding, because that judge has already studied the record and is seeking only to question the factual predicate of your position. This is simply a quiz. Another judge may ask about a portion of the record to substantiate that judge's support of your proposition. As we will develop later in this chapter, not all questions asked by judges are zingers. Many are designed to help you. Many are designed as part of an open internal advocacy of positions on the bench.

The corollary of knowing the record is sticking to it. Unless asked by a judge, never go outside the record in oral argument.

As soon as you perceive that the judges understand your point, move to the other issues. When you perceive that they understand

---

8. For an analysis of argument by the Greco-Roman rhetoricians, *see* Ruggero J. Aldisert, *Opinion Writing* 72 (1990).

these arguments, *sit down*. I cannot emphasize too much the necessity to quit while you are ahead.

A certain atmosphere or mood characterizes an argument in every case. Experienced lawyer-observers can sense this as they watch other lawyers' performances. Even law clerks, fresh out of law school but thoroughly acquainted with the case, can sense this. There comes a time when the man or woman at the lectern reaches the maximum possible advantage of the oral presentation. That is the moment to quit talking and sit down. Do not think that talking for a few more minutes cannot hurt. It *will* hurt. It can dispel the positive, confident atmosphere created by your presentation. A somewhat cynical old adage teaches: "Tis better to remain silent and be thought a fool, than to open your mouth and remove all doubts."

There is a level of theater in appellate courtroom rhetoric, with recognized highs and lows. To abandon a high point that has been successfully reached and then proceed to fill the air with meaningless padding and verbal filler is to transform your sizzle into drizzle. But even more dangerous, the anticlimactic speech used to fill the air between the close of your real argument and the expiration of your allotted time may call attention to a weaker point in your position. One of the judges may pick up on this, start probing and wind up destroying the court's prior willingness to accept your argument. I have seen this happen many, many times. Judges carry impressions—weak or strong, good or bad—from the close of oral argument to the decision conference that immediately follows the day's calendar.

§ 24.4.4 A Special Delivery

The Opening. Walk to the lectern. Wait to be recognized by the presiding judge. Then open by saying:

> If it please the court. My name is John J. Jones and I represent the appellant, Santa Barbara Olive Company. We ask to reserve X minutes for rebuttal. We request this court to reverse the judgment of the trial court for the reasons set forth in our brief. Today, I will address two points in support of our position. We will rely on our brief for the other arguments. I request two minutes for rebuttal time. [Pause

for reaction from the presiding judge.] We believe that the judgment should be reversed for the following reasons.

Your outline. Have an outline of your argument, together with supporting papers, at the lectern. Remember: your outline is a safety net, not a crutch.

Maintain eye contact. You look directly at the judges at all times. It is eyeball-to-eyeball time.

Be courteous and respectful. But do not be timorous or overawed. Maintain a position of respectful equality. Do not be disturbed or pushed around simply because a judge disagrees with your position. Stand your ground firmly but with courtesy and dignity.

Be prepared to modify your planned presentation. You may have to modify your argument for several reasons. The judges may agree immediately with one point. If you sense this, move quickly to another point. A series of questions may have taken much time from your planned presentation on one point; when you move to the next point, deliver it in truncated fashion, otherwise time may run out. If you are the appellee, and the questions put to the appellant demonstrate that the judges understand your position on one point, alter your planned argument.

Your closing. Do not let the presentation peter out simply because time has been called. Save time for a concise, punchy summary.

Sit Down. Exactly that.

§ 24.4.5 Watch Your Time

Place your watch on the lectern and keep track of your time. In some courts, a series of lights are placed on the podium. The green light signals the start of your argument; the amber comes on when you have two minutes remaining and the red light signifies that you should stop. When the red light comes on, immediately close your argument in thirty seconds or so; do not antagonize the judges by prolonging the discussion when your time has expired.

Save at least one minute for a summary of your argument. Watch your rebuttal time. If you are the appellant, arrange in advance how much time you are reserving for rebuttal. In some courts you may ask the presiding judge at the beginning of the argument. In other courts, you make arrangements with the clerk in which case you advise the court what you have done.

Do not intrude on your rebuttal time by prolonging your argument in chief. The time will be subtracted from you. Do not expect to use rebuttal simply as a chance to include arguments that should have been made in the case in chief. There are presiding judges, and I was one of them, who were very strict about what could be said in rebuttal. It is not spillover time from your case in chief. The appellee always has the right to respond, so you may not save for rebuttal material what should have been stated earlier.

When the red light goes on or you are told that your time is up, and you are in the middle of a sentence or a thought or a response to a question, it is good practice to ask the presiding judge for a brief moment to conclude. Then wrap it up in fifteen to twenty seconds.

§ 24.4.6 Be Flexible

In the modern appellate argument, you must be able to think on your feet. Watch how the wind is blowing from the bench. When the judges ask persistent questions that seem to indicate that they do not agree with your position, and their questions are really not designed to elicit further information, it is time to shift gears. You may wish to provide a transition by saying, "If the court please, we have stated our position and I believe that your honors understand our argument. Permit me now to address the second point."

Be careful about making concessions. If in the preparation of your argument you believe that it may be appropriate to make concessions, then do it. Do not make careless concessions at oral argument on the spur of the moment. They may come back to haunt you.

When two of the judges engage in private conversation during your presentation, do not stop. Address your argument to other judge or judges. In any event, never stop talking. The judge or judges who are paying attention to you will resent that you have interrupted your delivery to them.

It is a normal reaction to more vigorously try to persuade in the face of a bench that is not buying your argument. If the point in controversy is the major premise on which your second and third arguments depend, you must hang tough. If, however, the point under attack is independent of other points in your argument, as soon as you get the storm signals from the bench, it is time to move on to another argument.

§ 24.4.7 Visual Aids

My experience with visual aids has been mixed. When used properly, they can be very effective; when the props are technically insufficient, you run a serious risk. Because some judges come to the bench equipped with reading glasses only and do not have the eyesight to read at a distance, be certain that your visual aids are large enough to be examined.

I have had some excellent experiences. I recall one with the tenth circuit in Denver. Involved was the interpretation of certain regulations of a federal agency. These regulations were set forth in the briefs and we were fairly familiar with them. Nevertheless, counsel had magnificent blown-up reproductions of the key sections of these regulations. Using a pointer, counsel very effectively led us through the important sections of the regulations suitably highlighted. I believe that the presentation won the case for him.

My colleague, Senior Circuit Judge Joseph Weis, Jr. reports:

> I think that one of the most interesting arguments] that I heard was one involving a copyright where the lawyers used large blowups of prints by Winslow Homer, Monet, and other artists to illustrate a point about artistic expression. I also had a fine experience with a blowup of two pertinent sections of the Internal Revenue Code in a tax case. The blowup made it much easier to follow the argument than referring to the appendix or the brief. Also, I think in some cases blown-up photos could be very effective when an understanding of the facts would help the argument flow smoothly.

Yet there *is* a down side. Setting up visual aids invades your allotted time. Moreover, there are times when a page or two from the Appendix or Excerpts of the Record are more effective. Because you should not assume that every judge has a copy on the bench, have copies available for them to follow along with your argument. Do not proceed on the basis that the judges may look at the Appendix when they return to chambers. The tentative decision-making conference takes place at the end of the day's argument list so make certain they have their copies while on the bench so they have them at conference. Your visual aids propped up in the courtroom do not follow the judges into the conference room.

§ 24.5   Arguing Before a Cold Court

Where judges of an appellate court do not have the opportunity of examining briefs before oral argument, the court is known as a "cold" court. You must tailor your arguments accordingly.

Generally speaking, the court is cold because the sheer volume of appeals prevents pre-argument study of the briefs. Under these circumstances you will be exposed to less questioning and given a shorter time to argue than in a hot court. For the most part, you should follow the same suggestions for preparation previously outlined in chapter 22. Your delivery must be tailored to a different audience.

Primarily, the appellant must open the argument with a one or two-minute orientation statement that should parallel the statement of the case discussed in chapter 11:

- *What*: What is the general area of law implicated in the appeal? What are the issues, and what is the theme or gut issue? Expose the jugular, the focus of your attack.

- *Who*: Who won in the tribunal below? Who is talking the appeal?

- *When*: When was the alleged error committed? Is the appeal from an adverse verdict because of insufficiency of evidence? Is it alleged that error was committed in the pleadings, at pre-trial, trial, or post-trial?

- *How*: How was the case resolved? Was the judgment entered as the result of summary judgment, a directed verdict, a jury verdict, or a nonjury award?

- *Where*: Where does the appeal come from: a trial court, administrative agency, or intermediate appellate court?

Immediately thereafter, you state the material facts as succinctly and interestingly as possible. Do not waste time on any facts except those necessary to support the argument you will be making. Be prepared to answer questions at this time. Some of the judges immediately will want to pigeonhole your case into past decisions. Know the facts completely and do not let questioning lead you astray. Your factual recitation should be guided by what John W. Davis called the three *C*s: chronology, candor, and clarity.

You then identify the points you will argue in support of your main contention, making certain to advise the court that you are relying on your brief for other points. Having identified the issues you will argue, proceed immediately to explain the standard of review for each point.

Then proceed into your argument. Presume that you are before a hot court that has studied the precedents cited in the briefs. However, when you mention a case as precedent or you wish to distinguish a case upon which you know your adversary will rely, give a one-sentence description of its holding. State both the factual component and the legal consequence attached thereto. In a nutshell, you must paint a broader picture before a cold court.

§ 24.6 How to Answer Questions

§ 24.6.1 In General

Oral argument is no longer the formal, uninterrupted presentation characteristic of appellate proceedings of yesteryear. Wisconsin Supreme Court Chief Justice Shirley Abrahamson reports: "At one time oral argument in the Wisconsin Supreme Court was so quiet that you could hear the justices' arteries clogging."

In most appellate courts today, however, oral presentations consist primarily of a dialogue between the judges and the advocate. Answering questions from the judges is a vital part of modern advocacy. Answering them properly is critical to the modern art of persuasion. Certain general suggestions are in order.

To answer a question intelligently, you must first *listen* to the question. Judges recognize that some lawyers may be a little nervous, and understandably so. But judges also recognize that lawyers, just like you and I in private conversation, sometimes have a tendency to "hear" only a part of the question asked. In appellate advocacy, it is important to listen to the entire question and to answer the entire question, not only a discrete part of it.

In listening to the question, be certain that you *understand* it before attempting an answer. This is especially true in federal appellate courts, where the judges deal with specialized subject matter and have a tendency to speak in shorthand expressions. Less experienced lawyers may not be familiar with the jargon used. For example, the court may inquire, "Counsel, do the authorities you rely on come up in the context of a *Teague* matter?" What the court is really asking goes to the distinction between a direct appeal in a criminal case and an appeal on collateral review. If you do not understand the question, say so. You will not necessarily lose any points.

Answer the question directly. Do not evade. If the question calls for a "yes or no" answer, respond with a yes or a no. Then elaborate. You do not have time to beat around the bush, and you do not want to give the impression that you are stonewalling. Do not postpone the answer by saying, "I have not got to that point in my argument yet." The judge will respond, "Yes, you have."

This problem often arises where more than one lawyer is representing a single party. The practice of divided representation is appropriate to avoid conflicts of interest, but it is otherwise disfavored. To be sure, we understand that clients want their own lawyers to argue. We also understand the converse: Lawyers who have lived through the trial and have prepared a brief want a chance to get in at least five minutes of argument (and have their names in the Reporter showing that they argued the case). But, in cases of severely rationed time, judges want to get to the heart of what interests them and do not like to hear, "If the court please, my colleague is handling that part of the argument."

Your responses should be clear and concise. Judges know the time limitations you are under, and ordinarily the questions put are not designed for a lengthy response. One or two sentences usually will suffice.

Yet there are questions that demand a longer response and will take up substantial amounts of your limited time. In this situation, be cheerful, or at least pretend that you are. Do not create the impression that the mere putting of the question annoys you. In my many years on the bench I have received enough responses of this type; they come under the category, "How to Wean Friends on the Bench."

A number of years ago, a constitutional law professor appeared before us, and he had brought along his entire class to witness his dazzling performance as the appellant's lawyer. Early in his presentation, I interrupted and asked him to address the question of our court's jurisdiction in the appeal. He sloughed me off with a scowl, saying that there was no such issue in the case. A little while later I tried again, and he responded with some annoyance, "I've already answered that question." When I was rebuffed the third time, the presiding judge, William H. Hastie, unloaded on him, "Counsellor, answer the question and answer it right now. For your information, the question of jurisdiction has been in this case ever since the moment Judge Aldisert raised it ten minutes ago." The professor glared, and then stumbled, and stumbled some more. The opinion was assigned to me, and we dismissed the appeal for lack of jurisdiction.

When the questions put by the court are relevant—and most of the time they are, especially when more than one judge pursues a particular line of inquiry—it is a clear signal that this is the direction in which the judges are moving. Throw away your planned argument and proceed in the direction of the questions. This probably is the issue the judges will talk about in conference.

It may be that one of the judges goes off on a tangent that is completely irrelevant. We will discuss later how to handle questions from the judge who, by persistent irrelevant questions, appears to have gone off on an intellectual frolic of his or her own. If you are fully prepared on the subject matter of the case, you will know what questions are totally off base.

What do you do when you are asked a point-blank question about a case that you do not know, notwithstanding thorough preparation? My answer: Do not bluff. Be frank with the court, "If Your Honor will refresh my recollection of the holding, I would appreciate it." If the explanation does not ring any bells, my suggestion is that you say, "Your Honor, I'm sorry that I must have overlooked that case. May I please have the opportunity of filing a supplemental brief discussing it within forty-eight hours?" It would be the most hard-hearted judge who would refuse such a request. Counsel should not overlook the opportunity of seeking to file a post-argument supplemental brief where a judge's question plowed novel ground. But to be effective, promise to have the supplement filed in a matter of days, not weeks.

Be careful about making concessions in response to questions. When you go through the questions checklist contained in § 21.7 in preparation for oral argument, you may decide that you are willing to concede some points. This decision can serve two important goals. First, you may wish to clear away the underbrush of questionable points that may possibly detract from the jugular point. It is better to prune than to be subjected to time-consuming interrogation on minor points. Second, it is one thing to plan a concession after calm and careful reflection in the environment of your office; it is quite another thing to concede hastily in open court while under pressure from the bench.

To concede or not to concede a point at oral argument depends upon the extent of your advance preparation. You should know what will hurt or help you. Without sufficient preparation, you may be faced with a dilemma. On this one hand you do not want to concede something that may come back to haunt you, but on the other hand you do not want the judges to conclude that you are stonewalling.

But there is a difference between factual and legal concessions. If the record facts are against you, concede their existence, but hasten to argue that this concession does not destroy your case. Be very careful, however, of legal concessions. If on the way home from the courthouse, you realize that you have made an improvident concession on a point of some significance, all is not lost. It is appropriate to immediately file a supplemental brief by letter that refers to the question and your response and clarifies it. Be certain to serve your adversary with a copy. There is no guarantee that all judges would accept it. I would.

Often the unfortunate situation develops where a very argumentative judge will try to force you to capitulate. Handle this with great diplomacy, but with firmness. Be attentive, but do not be intimidated:

> Your Honor, I regret that I cannot improve on the answer I previously gave the court on that point. With great deference and respect, Your Honor, we see that issue in a very different light. In my view, I believe . . .

§ 24.6.2 Questions: User-Friendly and Otherwise

Many lawyers are instinctively suspicious of questions from the bench, and they answer so cautiously that they sound evasive. When this happens, I am inclined to say, "Look here, all the questions put to you are not designed to trap you. Please listen to the question before attempting an answer." Too many lawyers operate under the impression that bench questions are all cross-examination. Actually, there are several discrete categories.

The most important question is where a judge sweeps away all the clutter and zeroes in on the basic issue in the case. It is the question that sums up the case in a single sentence. If you have prepared thoroughly, you should expect this, notwithstanding the structure of your brief or your game plan at argument. When this question comes thundering down, you can run but you cannot hide. It will reappear in the opening sentence or paragraph of the opinion: "The major question for decision in this appeal is whether . . . " Be ready for it.

Many questions are designed to clarify something in the record. I vote for oral argument often because I need help from counsel in getting to this information. Often the problem is caused in federal courts by an incomplete appendix accompanying the brief. This is especially true in the courts where the judges require only an Excerpt of Record instead of the full appendix. Thus the question will proceed, "Counsel, on page so-and-so of the brief you refer to such-and-such evidence in the record. Will you please tell us where we can locate it?" Often when this factual predicate is established, it will serve as the springboard to other questions.

Many questions relate to the standard of review. Often, counsel will argue the evidence presented at trial instead of the facts as found by the fact-finder. This provokes the questions: "What did the fact-finder find? If the jury found it, can we touch it in view of the Seventh Amendment? If found by the judge, is it clearly erroneous? If found by the agency, was there substantial evidence in the record as a whole to support it?"

Often we get ambiguous standards of review in the briefs. Oral argument provides the opportunity to focus on the correct standard. In many cases, the standard of review determines the outcome of the appeal.

Then there are what I call the quiz questions, which are utilized by individual judges for at least three objectives: Socratic or debating purposes, for internal judicial advocacy, and to communicate outright hostility to the lawyer's position. Judges use the Socratic method to test the validity of the logic employed and to determine by means of hypotheticals where a proposed rule will take the court. Lawyers must expect that the logic of the argument will be put to the test. They must be prepared to defend their reasoning, both in form and content.

Be prepared for the hypothetical. Do not antagonize the court by saying, "Well, those facts are not before the court here. That is a different case." The judges know that. Counsel must understand that there is a limit to every principle, as immutable in the law as the principle may be; that there comes a point when the extension of a legitimate principle brings it into conflict with another, equally legitimate, and the court must decide where along the line the axe must fall. Accordingly, counsel should not try to move the application of a principle too far or too fast.

In a multijudge appellate court, judges do not usually discuss cases in advance. In the United States courts of appeals and state appellate courts, judges often do not live in the same city. They meet for the first time at oral argument, and often questions are put to counsel by a judge solely to test the jural waters. When this occurs, the lawyer is merely a conduit. He or she is simply the medium by which the questioning judge may disclose to the other judges some inclination on the case.

The most difficult question-and-answer colloquy for the lawyer occurs when a judge is blatantly hostile to counsel's stated position. Often the hostile judge becomes the proverbial dog on a bone, who will not let go or let up. Perhaps this type of judge has seen too many episodes of *Law and Order* and expects the lawyer to break down and confess like a witness subjected to Jack McCoy's cross-examination. This is no time for the lawyer to become distraught. The hostility is often a sign that the judge is in the minority, and thus the unrelenting attack is motivated by the frustration that impotency brings. When the lawyer realizes that the judge is trying to achieve a capitulation, the lawyer should respond with courteous, but confident arguments explaining why capitulation would not be appropriate. When the judge says, "Counsel, that argument is simply ridiculous," the response could be, "Your Honor, I respectfully disagree, and I have offered legitimate reasons why it is not. My hope is only that Your Honor, on reflection, will change your mind."

§ 24.6.3   How to Disengage from Persistent Questioning by a Single Judge

§ 24.6.3.1   In General

There is a forensic dilemma in oral argument: when faced with a continuous barrage of questions from a single judge, how can you please the court by answering and yet diplomatically return to the argument you are there to make? This calls for the highest advocacy and impromptu skills.

One method is to announce that you have multiple responses to the question, one of which returns you to your planned format: "If the court please, I have two responses to make to that question." Then proceed to make a direct response to the question and immediately state, "For my second response to the court's question I would add . . ." and then slip in your "indirect, by way of analogy response," which tracks your planned presentation. This sometimes helps prevent interruption until you briefly give your two answers. At worst, it will give you a transition back to your planned presentation.

Keep in mind that the entire purpose of argument is *to persuade*. You do not want to antagonize a judge by calling a question irrelevant. The question may indeed be irrelevant, but do not throw it back in the questioner's face. Instead give a neutral answer: "If the court please, in my view of the case we have not stressed that particular point, and this is why we have not . . ."

A very serious situation arises where a single judge takes over the questioning on matters that you feel are irrelevant, and the questioning is so persistent and continuous that you may be totally precluded from making your argument. That may be the most difficult scenario facing the oral advocate. I have asked the chief judges of the federal judicial circuits for their advice.

§ 24.6.3.2   Advice from United States Circuit Chiefs

How does the lawyer who is being bombarded by a series of questions from a judge who is off on an intellectual frolic—respectfully answer, yet return to the issues that the lawyers and ostensibly the other two judges, deem relevant?

Michael Boudin, *First Circuit*	I used several different techniques when I was in practice but the one that seemed to me to work best was to give a succinct answer to the judge and say firmly something like: "That is about all I can say in response to your question, and in the few minutes I have left, I had better address the remaining two issues in this case." Most of the other alternatives, I found, were too mild to produce results or too strong to be stomached save by a very good-humored judge.
John M. Walker, Jr., *Second Circuit*	Say, "I want to answer your question but then turn to the other critical points, (x) and (y), raised by this appeal." Then answer the question briefly and move rapidly to (x) and (y). Then hope that this maneuver works.
Anthony J. Sirica, *Third Circuit*	Be patient. In most cases, there will be a break that will enable you to return to your argument. If time has run, ask the court for a few minutes to present your most compelling argument. Usually one judge on the panel will respond favorably.
Edward R. Becker, *Third Circuit* 1996–2003	Express appreciation for the questions of the wayward judge, but then pointedly ask the presider if he or she may have a few minutes to develop what he or she believes to be the critical issues.

Carolyn Dineen King, *Fifth Circuit*	The lawyer answers briefly and then says, respectfully, that he or she would like to make one or two additional points. The lawyer then returns to his or her argument.
Mary M. Schroeder, *Ninth Circui*	Briefly summarize the issue the judges' questions are concerned with, briefly state your position on that issue and then direct the court's attention to the "even more important issue" you wish to discuss.
Deanell Reece Tacha, *Tenth Circuit*	I counsel lawyers and students to have two or three central points that they simply must make in order to make sure that the judges understand their theory of the case. This limited number of points should be etched indelibly in the brain of the lawyer so that no matter how fast and furious the questioning is or how flustered the lawyer gets, the points will naturally be part of the responses to questions or the next point made after questions. I think perhaps the most useful advice that can be given to counsel is to view the oral argument as a conversation with the bench and treat it as the opportunity to organize a set of questions. In other words, the judge's questions will necessarily occupy a significant portion of the argument, but the organization and emphasis on specific points needs to be provided by the lawyer. The opportunity to provide this organization around a set of questions that may, at times, seem absolutely random is the challenge facing every oral advocate. It is, however, a challenge that must be met in order to present an effective and persuasive argument.

Douglas H. Ginsburg, *D.C. Circuit*	A lawyer cannot fail to answer a question posed by a judge. Nevertheless, in order to avoid getting too far off message, a lawyer should answer the question as succinctly and briefly as possible. Once an answer as been provided, the lawyer should immediately go back to his argument and continue with points he would like to address. While the judge may ask another question requiring an answer, the lawyer once again has to answer quickly and then change the topic.
Patricia Wald, Chief Judge Emeritus, *D.C. Circuit*	The only advice I can give is to ask at the end for a minute or two to sum up the key points you didn't get to make. Often the other judges will be sympathetic to your plight and let you have it. And, of course, you may never prophesy how a close case will come out by the way the judges act at argument. After all, that one week a month in court is the only recreation an appellate judge gets from the paperwork and she will likely act up, play devil's advocate, lead you down primrose paths, and pounce at the dead end. Later in conference she will say she was having some fun, testing the waters, and seeing how far you would actually go on a point.
Haldane Robert Mayer, *Federal Circuit*	If faced with a "hot court," before deciding that a judge is off on a frolic of his own, carefully analyze the questions that are being posed. A judge's frolic may suggest a lack of understanding of the issues, or perhaps the judge views the case from a perspective that you had not considered. In the early stages of preparing your appeal, write and rewrite until each issue and answer can be expressed in one succinct sentence. When a judge begins to go astray, answer the questions as succinctly as possible, always returning to one of your main points.

§ 24.7   The Appellee's Argument

Appellees' lawyers are always faced with two presentations—the one they prepare and the one they deliver. In preparing, you concentrate on those issues that will follow ruling case law of the appellate tribunal and will most effectively defend the action taken by the trial or intermediate court. Remember that the appellee simply defends, while the appellant must carry the burden of persuading the appellate court that the court below erred.

As stated in § 19.5, the appellee's brief both *confirms* your view of the applicable law and *refutes* the legal argument offered by the adversary. By the time oral argument rolls around, you have had the advantage of reading the appellant's reply brief (if one has been filed), and the preparation of your oral argument should include any new matter presented there. But your preparation should consist essentially of a mastery of all relevant law pertaining to the subject matter. You should not be content to rely on your brief. Why? Because the judges will not. The questions they will ask you and your adversary will probably range far beyond the contours of the briefs.

As you prepare, you will try to anticipate the points your adversary will argue. From experience in the lower courts and from the tenor of the appellant's brief, you already know the main thrust of your opponent's theory. Be prepared to meet it head-on.

Appellee's counsel should prepare a written outline of a possible argument, in broad terms covering points likely to be raised by the appellant. Preparing thoroughly and constructing a general outline are necessary; preparing a canned speech is not. Bring the outline to oral argument, and prepare your plan of attack by annotating the outline *during* the appellant's presentation. Use a magic marker to highlight the portions of your outline actually argued by the appellant. You will not have to divert your attention and dissipate your energies by writing feverishly during your opponent's performance. Your annotations should also reflect the dialogue between the judges and appellant's lawyer, which is even more important than the lawyer's presentation.

You must monitor all questions from the bench. This is critical because, first, the questions from the bench disclose the points that are troubling the court; they provide the strongest signal of the direction your answering argument *must* take. Second, the questions often reveal that the judges already know and understand, and possibly agree with, your strongest points; in this case, you need not belabor these points when you get up to speak. Often all you need say is, "As to point *A*, from the questions put to opposing counsel, it appears that the court understands our position. If the court has any additional questions to ask me on it, I will be pleased to oblige. If not, I will move to point *B*." Stick to your annotated outline. This guarantees that you will cover precisely the points raised by your adversary.

We have indicated that the appellant should begin with its strongest point. How should the appellee open? It depends. If the court's questions indicate an interest in the last point addressed by the appellant, it is probably advisable to continue the dialogue on that point. Because the issue is fresh in the judges' minds, leading off with it may put that issue to bed at the earliest opportunity.

At the very minimum, the appellee must weave into the argument the matters raised by the judges' questions. Frequently, it is helpful to turn to specific questions put to your adversary, and then provide corrected, or at least amplified, responses.

Statistics set forth chapter 1 disclose that the odds of prevailing on appeal are with the appellee. Although rules of court give the appellee argument time equal to that of the appellant, it has been my experience that in most cases the appellee does not need all the allotted time. The good appellee lawyers can sense when the court understands their arguments; indeed, they can often sense this during their adversaries' presentations. Under these circumstances, it is not necessary to pad the presentation to fill up the time allotted. Make your points, and then ask, "If the court please, I believe that the court understands our position. May I inquire if the court has any further questions to put to me?" If there are none, sit down.

"Never" is a very strong word, but I will use it here: if you have addressed your major points, *never* fill in the remaining time with answers to arguments contained in the appellant's brief but not presented in oral argument. If a point was not important enough for the appellant to argue, it is not important enough for you to answer. If the court desires you to respond to issues submitted on the appellant's brief, the judges will ask you to do so. If not, do not volunteer. Quit while you are ahead.

Paul Freund, for five decades the great Harvard constitutional law scholar, formerly served as a deputy United States Solicitor General. Once when he was arguing a case before the Supreme Court, the justices brought out in their questioning of the petitioner everything he had planned to say. Freund walked to the podium and said, "May it please the court, there is a typographical error on page 10 of our brief." He made the correction and then said, "If there are no questions, the government will rely on its brief." The court had no questions and government prevailed in an unanimous decision. For years afterwards, Justice Felix Frankfurter often would refer to Freund's performance and say: "Since I have been on the Court, I have heard learned arguments. I have heard powerful arguments. I have heard eloquent arguments. But I have only heard one *perfect* argument."

§ 24.8 The Rebuttal

My advice to appellants' lawyers: *Always* reserve some time for rebuttal, even if later it appears that you will not need it. The very act of reserving rebuttal time is an insurance policy to protect you against possible extravagant or unsubstantiated statements from the appellee. Protect yourself with the opportunity of having the last word to expose an exorbitant utterance. This alerts the appellee in advance that you are hanging back to enter the ring again if necessary. Whether you will also depends on what is said by your adversary, but the fact that you have reserved time is in itself a strategic ploy. The appellee knows that you may have the last word.

Strategy aside, keep in mind that rebuttal should be used sparingly. It is the opportunity to respond to the appellee's presentation, not to rehash your argument in chief. Generally speaking, appellate judges seem to be impatient with rebuttal speeches. To be effective, the argument should be very concise—"snappy" is the word some experienced lawyers use. Select only one or two major emphases, and cite the authority that most effectively rebuts any new dimension added to the case by your opponent and not already covered by you.

I consider rebuttal at oral argument the same as redirect examination if a witness at trial. You are limited to what was brought up in cross-examination. This is not the time to bore the judges with a repetition of what was said in your argument in chief. Its purpose is to respond to new matter—both facts and law—presented by the appellee.

Unless there has been some misrepresentation that deserves rejoinder, and you detect that the appellee's argument did not impress the judges, stand up with confidence and state, "Unless the court has questions, we waive rebuttal."

§ 24.9 Summing Up

All the foregoing represents contemporary advice. Yet, as early as 1851 the famed constitutional scholar and prolific legal writer, Joseph

Story, Justice of the U.S. Supreme Court and Dane Professor of Law at Harvard, encapsulated all of this in rhyme:

> You wish the court to hear, and listen too?
> Then speak with point, be brief, be close, be true.
> Cite well your cases; let them be in point;
> Not learned rubbish, dark, and out of joint;
> And be your reasoning clear, and closely made,
> Free from false taste, and verbiage, and parade.
> Stuff not your speech with every sort of law,
> Give us the grain, and throw away the straw.
> Whoe'er in law desires to win his cause,
> Must speak with point, not measure our "wise saws,"
> Must make his learning apt, his reasoning clear,
> Pregnant in manner, but in style severe;
> But never drawl, nor spin the thread so fine,
> That all becomes an evanescent line.[9]

---

9. Joseph Story, *Life and Letters II* , 89–90 (William Wetmore Story, Ed. 1851), *reprinted in* John M. Greaney, *Power of the Pen,* Trial 48, 54 (July 2002).9.

Part Five
CHECKLISTS

Chapter 25

TWO IMPORTANT CHECKLISTS: BRIEF WRITING AND ORAL ARGUMENT PREPARATION

§ 25.1 Brief Writing Checklist

When photocopied, the following may serve as a handy checklist in preparing an appellate brief. As each step is completed, indicate its performance with a check mark.

A. Follow a planned sequence of preparation.

☐ 1. *File a timely notice of appeal.* Examine the applicable statute or court rule.

☐ 2. *Learn the court rules.* Familiarize yourself with all rules relating to contents and filing of briefs.

☐ 3. *Ensure that the appellate court has jurisdiction.* Is the appeal from a final judgment or order of the trial tribunal? Have all the parties' claims been adjudicated? If it is not a final judgment, does the appeal qualify as an interlocutory appeal under the relevant statute or rule? If you are in federal court, did the district court have subject matter jurisdiction?

☐ 4. *Prepare a written statement of jurisdiction and timeliness of filing the appeal.* Save this for inclusion in the brief.

☐ 5. *Order the record.* Do not delay. You are faced with a tight briefing schedule. The clerk of court will not excuse a late brief because you have not ordered a timely transcript of the record.

☐ 6. *Know the record cold.* You must be totally familiar with the record before beginning your research and certainly before you start writing the brief.

☐ 7. *Make an informal list of issues.* Make an inventory of all possible points. Do not spend time phrasing the issues. This should be a gross listing of unrefined possibilities.

☐ 8. *Issue preservation.* Locate in the record where the issue has been preserved for review. Appellate determination of reversible error is based on the presence of three interrelated circumstances:

a. special rulings, acts, or omissions by the trial tribunal constituting trial error,

b. which follow an objection by counsel or the grant or denial of an oral or written motion or submission,

c. accompanied by a proper and appropriate course of action recommended by the appellant which was rejected by the tribunal.

If the issue has not been preserved at trial, consider the possibility of plain or fundamental error if your jurisdiction permits.

☐ 9. *Begin legal research.* Use the system you find most effective— yellow pad notes, file cards, or photocopies of leading cases. Highlight important passages and possible direct quotes for inclusion in the brief. Make lots of notes. Do not trust your memory. You do not want to let a good case get away because your memory failed. Do not start to write the brief. You are not ready yet.

☐ 10. *Weed out the issues (points) that will not persuade.* You have not written one word of your brief yet, but this process may be the most important part of brief "writing." What you exclude is as important as what you include. Avoid the shot-gun approach. Choose only those arguments that have a chance of prevailing. Do not fall in love with a pet issue. Look at a potential issue from the judge's viewpoint. The "final-ists" on your list must meet this test: *the issue more probably than not will attract the interest and serious consideration of the judges.*

☐ 11. *Limit your issues to three (possibly four) points.* Keep in mind the advice of all the judges in this book. Limit your discussion to a very small number of issues. When it comes to appellate advocacy, more is not better.

☐ 12. *Refine and intensify your legal research to focus on the chosen issues.* It is time to go back to the books again to determine whether additional research will be necessary.

☐ 13. *Standard of review.* Prepare a draft of the standard of review for each issue selected, including appropriate supporting authorities.

B. Writing the appellant's (or petitioner's) brief.

☐ 1. *Allow adequate time in your schedule.* Ideas need time to percolate. Crucial cases get overruled or reversed during the briefing process. Colleagues let you down on offers of vital help. Illness or emergency matters upset your schedule. All of your research is in the computer, and it crashes. If you arrange to have your brief ready for filing two or three days early, none of these events need concern you.

☐ 2. *Write the issues.* Rephrase with care the issues that you have selected for inclusion in your brief. Write each issue in the form of a simple declarative sentence to serve as the topic sentence of the point heading in the argument portion of your brief. The argument headings (points or issues) and their subparts must be full enough and clear enough for the judges to follow, and convincing enough for the court to accept. For those courts that require a statement of questions, recast each declarative sentence as an interrogatory.

☐ 3. *Express each issue as narrowly as possible to achieve your objective.* Be satisfied to have the court affirm or reverse. Do not insist that the court promulgate a holding broader than necessary.

☐ 4. *Look for a single dispositive issue.* Will the resolution of a single issue determine the outcome of the appeal? If yes, say so. That is the first issue to list. Indicate that other issues are alternatives only.

☐ 5. *Select the theme or equitable heart of the argument from your selected issues.* The theme should be the strongest point in your brief and the first one stated. *Your strongest point is that argument, objectively considered, based on precedent and the court's previously stated policy concerns, most calculated to persuade the court to your point of view.* Look back to this theme as you write. (You may, of course, have more than one theme.) It will help bring order and focus to your writing, as well as unity, logic and conciseness, but keep in mind that the organizing theme may need revision and refinement as the writing progresses.

☐ 6. *Organize.* Make an outline of your argument. It must include all the points selected and should serve as the framework of the argument portion of your brief. Remember these words of Henry M. Hart, Jr.: "Briefs on the merits need not only tell their story to one who takes the time to read all the way through them, but ought to be so organized that they can be used, like a book of reference, for quick illumination on any point of concern."

☐ 7. *Write the first draft summary of your argument.* Draft the argument summary from your outline. Keep this summary in front of you while you write the brief. You will find yourself rewriting the summary as you proceed.

☐ 8. *Write the statement of the case.* State briefly the nature of the case, the course of the proceedings and its disposition in the court below. Tell the appellate court "how you got here."

☐ 9. *Write the statement of facts.* Prepare a selective, economical, succinct exposition of the facts so that the reader can understand what follows.

   a. Do not begin writing until you have decided what issues you will raise. *Never, never* write the facts first.

   b. Master the record to glean the facts that support your issues and arguments.

   c. Tailor the narrative so that it fits the issues raised. Write as tersely as you can.

   d. Be accurate. Do not steal the facts. Set forth the findings in light of the verdict winner.

   e. Within the bounds of accuracy, however, state your facts in such a way that the judges will receive a favorable, lasting impression from your account of the facts.

   f. Unless the fact was uncontroverted, cite to the appendix or record for every assertion in the statement.

   g. Remember: be clear. It is not unconstitutional to be interesting. What you write must compete for attention in a mountain of other communications. Try to make it rise above the surrounding peaks.

☐ 10. *Write your argument, point by point.*

   a. Present a systematic discussion of the issues. Argument headings and subheadings must flow logically.

   b. Identify the flashpoint of controversy, and discuss only what is essential to the brief.

      i. If the law and its application are clear, your discussion should be short and to the point.

      ii. If the law is certain and the application alone is doubtful, explain how the law applies to the facts. Do not waste the judges' time justifying the choice of law.

      iii. If neither the rule of law nor its application is clear, discuss:

         • the choice, interpretation, and application of the legal precept, or

         • interpretation and application of the legal precept.

   c. Do not overwrite. Do not belabor or state the obvious.

   d. Follow the canons of logic.

      i. Is the choice of a major premise supported by applicable law?

      ii. Are you observing the rules of inductive and deductive reasoning? If analogizing, do you emphasize the resemblances and differences in the facts of the compared cases?

      iii. Have you violated any of the six rules of the categorical syllogism? If so, you are guilty of a formal fallacy. Is your argument free from material fallacies? If you are unsure of the canons of logic, refer to Ruggero J. Aldisert, *Logic for Lawyers: A Guide to Clear Legal Thinking* (3d Ed. 1997).

      iv. Does each thought follow from the previous one?

     v.   Is each thought explained or illuminated by the statements that follow?

     vi.   Are unobvious conclusions supported by citation or argument?

☐ 11. *Analyze the lower court's opinion.* The appellant must respond to every important authority relied upon by the lower court. If the flashpoint of controversy is the choice of a controlling legal precept, explain the reasons why your choice presents the better view. If the controversy is over interpretation, do the same. If the issue involves application of settled law to facts, explain factual resemblances and differences in the compared cases.

☐ 12. *The conclusion.* Tell the court exactly what relief you want— that is, reverse the judgment, affirm, or vacate and remand with a specific direction.

☐ 13. *The front cover.* Check the rules. Ascertain what information front covers should contain.

    a.   Cover color. Check the rules. The United States courts of appeals require that the cover of the appellant's brief be blue; appellee's brief, red; and the intervenor or amicus brief, green.

    b.   Multiple parties. When there are multiple appellants or appellees, identify the name of the party on the cover—for example, "Brief of the Appellant Harvey M. Tillman."

☐ 14. *Table of contents.* After the brief is in final form, prepare a detailed table of contents with accurate page references.

☐ 15. *Table of authorities.* Begin preparing the table of authorities as you write the brief. Do not wait until the last minute to start it. It is enough to wait until the argument is in final draft to insert the correct page references. After the brief is in final form, check the page references for accuracy and completeness. Avoid typos. Proofread carefully.

C. Proper use of authorities.

☐ 1. *Be accurate.* Do not miscite. Do not "trample on graves"—do not represent that a case stands for something that it does not.

☐ 2. *Distinguish between binding precedent (mandatory authority) and persuasive authority.* If it is from your jurisdiction, it is a precedent; if from another court, it is merely persuasive.

☐ 3. *Follow the* Bluebook *citation style.* Always identify the circuit when citing a court of appeals case. Give the year for every citation.

☐ 4. *Rely on primary authorities.* Cases and statutes are primary authorities. Secondary sources include *Corpus Juris Secundum, American Jurisprudence* and other legal treatises. These are properly cited as "*see* cases collected in . . . " A citation to a restatement is persuasive, but unless it has been adopted by the jurisdiction, it is not a primary authority.

☐ 5. *Do not overwrite when discussing a cited case.* You usually cite a case for its facts or its reasoning or its holding. Seldom do you cite for all three purposes. Always consider *why* you are citing it. If you limit the discussion to this purpose, you will not unduly pad the discussion. If appropriate, use a parenthetical to provide a paraphrase or direct quote.

☐ 6. *Do not use string citations.* Do not overcite if the most recent case says it all. But it is proper to use *multiple* citations to demonstrate that many courts follow a particular legal precept, or that the question is not settled.

☐ 7. *Shepardize and Insta-cite or Auto-cite.* Bring all citations up to date. Do not end up with egg on your face when you subsequently learn that your major authority has been overruled. Ascertain the most recent holdings. Do not show up at oral argument with supplementary citation lists that furnish the court with cases handed down months or years before the brief was written. They belong in your brief.

☐ 8. *Use pinpoint citations.* When referring to a particularstatement in a cited case, furnish the court with the page number where the statement appears.

☐ 9. *Cite adverse holdings in your jurisdiction.* Canons of ethics typically require lawyers to advise the court of controlling authorities adverse to their position.

☐ 10. *Respond to the unfavorable controlling case.* Do not "lie down." You should attempt to distinguish a case cited in the trial court's opinion or in your opponent's brief that seems to be on all fours against you. Do the best you can. Do not wait for oral argument to have a judge ask you about it the moment you open your mouth. If the case is against you, try to distinguish it. If you cannot, show why it should not be followed. Know what you are doing, and let the court know, too.

D. Preparing the appendix, excerpt of record, clerk's transcript, or reproduced record.

☐ 1. *Know the court rules.* Determine precisely what the court-tules require, because that's what the judges will expect. This is especially true in United States courts of appeals, where each circuit has its own idiosyncracies.

☐ 2. *Prepare an adequate appendix.* When in doubt, include, rather than exclude, material. The appendix or excerpt of record is designed for one purpose: to authenticate statements contained in your brief. The appendix will include trial court docket entries, the lower court's opinion, evidence adduced at trial, and relevant portions of pleadings, jury charge or findings, and pretrial and post-trial motions. If a portion of the record helps you authenticate a passage in your brief, be certain that it reaches the judges in their chambers; do not expect the judges to search through the files in the clerk's office. If the material is important enough to be cited in your brief, it is important enough to be included in the appendix and sent to all judges who will be reading the briefs.

☐ 3. *Use discretion in including materials.* Do not clutter the appendix with materials unnecessary to authenticate statements made in the brief. It is seldom necessary to furnish the entire trial testimony unless a serious question of sufficiency of evidence is presented.

☐ 4. *Paginate the appendix.* Regardless of what the letter of the court rule provides, paginate every page of an appendix or excerpt of record. Tabs are generally insufficient. Remember that you are always fighting time; make it as easy as possible for the judges.

☐ 5. *Table of contents.* Be certain to have a complete table of contents in your appendix or excerpt of record. If more than one trial court opinion appears in a proceeding, describe the subject matter and date of each opinion in the table. When reproducing a portion of testimony, be sure to identify the date, the witness, and the lawyers. In preparing the table, err on the side of detailed description rather than abridgment.

☐ 6. *Submit clean photocopies.* All is lost unless the judges can read each document. Do not supply fifth-generation photocopies of the originals. Use *photographic* prints of pictures, not *photocopies.* Color photos always impress. Where handwriting appears in the appendix, attach a scrupulously accurate, legible, typewritten version to it.

☐ 7. *Front cover.* Check rules to determine what the front cover should contain. Usually, the front cover of an appendix, if separately printed, is white.

E. Writing the appellee's (or respondent's) brief.

☐ 1. *You defend.* Your opponent has the burden. Show that the burden has not been met and that the lower court was correct.

☐ 2. *Follow the same basic procedure as suggested for the appellant.* Using the procedure outlined in Section *B* above, prepare a proper statement of issues, summary of the argument, enunciation of theme or focus, and point-by-point discussion. You may accept the appellant's statement of facts *in toto* or in part. Follow the same approach for preparing the front cover, table of contents, table of authorities, and conclusion.

☐ 3. *Confirm and refute.* In the style of the Greco-Roman rhetoricians, your argument must be a combination of *confutatio*, refuting your opponent's argument, and *confirmatio*, confirming the result reached by the court below.

☐ 4. *Analyze the trial court rationale.* Evaluate the reasons given by the trial court for its decision. You may either adopt them or offer alternative reasons to affirm.

☐ 5. *Statement of facts.* If you agree your with opponent's statement, say so (even if you are not happy with the literary style or length). If you disagree, accept it with some modifications of your own, or present your own statement.

☐ 6. *Controlling case omitted by opponent.* This is your big gun. Use it to blow your opponent away, but avoid *ad hominem* accusations.

☐ 7. *Answering cases.* As a rule of thumb, respond to every authority cited by the appellant, although the response need not be unduly prolix. Where the appellant has used irrelevant citations to pad the brief, use a footnote to dispose of them. Where the flashpoint of controversy is choice of law, give reasons to accept your choice; where the controversy is over interpretation, do the same. Where the issue involves an application of settled precept to facts, use canons of analogy to show factual resemblances or differences in the compared cases. Follow the suggestions for proper use of authorities set forth in Section *C* above.

☐ 8. *Identify formal or material fallacies.* Do not just say, "The appellant's reasoning is flawed." Note precisely what rule of syllogistic logic is being violated or which material fallacy is present.

☐ 9. *Defend any controlling case.* When you (and ostensibly, the lower court) insist that a certain case controls explain why.

F. Preparing the reply brief.

☐ 1. *Do not file a reply brief unless it is absolutely necessary.* A reply brief may antagonize the court if it simply rewrites the opening brief, restating what was said before.

☐ 2. *Proper use.* A reply brief is necessary only to (a) rebut cases cited by the appellee that are not covered in the opening brief, (b) expose an irrelevant argument, or (c) correct misstatements of fact. It may be used also to furnish the court with a discussion of relevant cases handed down since the opening brief was filed and which serve as proper rebuttal.

§ 25.2 Oral Argument Preparation Checklist

When photocopied, the following may serve as a handy checklist in preparing for oral argument before an appellate court. As each step is completed, indicate its performance with a check mark.

A. Follow a planned sequence of preparation.

☐ 1. *Know the court rules.* Some courts have specific rules governing oral argument.

☐ 2. *Reread your brief carefully.* Master it. Make notes regarding (a) the themes, (b) key facts in the case, and (c) key authorities.

☐ 3. *Reread the entire appendix (or excerpts of record).* Read this from cover to cover and make notes. Paper clip key pages on the top; tabs bend easily and fall off. For quick reference during argument, mark on the front cover of each appendix volume the key materials you may need during the argument. Use a felt-tip pen to note clearly the page numbers of, and a brief phrase describing, all key record citations. Do this even if a typed digest of key appendix references is available.

☐ 4. *Reread the adversary's brief(s).* Note the key points. Look for the weaknesses in your own case that the adversary has identified, and be prepared to respond to questions from the court about them.

☐ 5. *Reread the lower court opinion(s).* Appellant's counsel should reread and make notes concerning the opinion below. Can you identify any misstatements of fact or law? Errors of logic? Violations of the rules of the categorical syllogism (formal fallacies)? Material fallacies? How do any analogies stand up? Are cases miscited? Have appellate cases been decided subsequently that should change the result? What are the policy implications if the approach of the court below is upheld? How sound are the reasons supporting the opinion?

☐ 6. *Reread key cases.* Read thoroughly and understand the key cases upon which both sides rely. Be prepared for interrogation by the judges on the facts, reasoning, and holdings.

☐ 7. *Select your now-or-never points.* Select those points upon which you must prevail to win the appeal. Try to limit your argument to two points, and no more than three, even if given a full thirty minutes of argument. (You typically are allotted only fifteen minutes.) Be prepared to accept a narrower ruling than the one you advocate if that holding will achieve the results requested.

☐ 8. *Be prepared on other points.* Because the judges or your adversary may be interested in other points set forth in the brief, be prepared to discuss them as well.

☐ 9. *Plan a presentation taking one-third of allotted time.* Expect that questioning will consume at least two-thirds of the allotted time. Prepare a "fail-safe" presentation that permits you to deliver your points in the other third of the allotted time.

☐ 10. *Start your outline.* Prepare an outline based on your notes. Use those techniques with which you are comfortable. Many experienced lawyers use a plain sheet of 8½-by-11-inch white paper for each point of the argument. Others use index cards, but here you run the risk of the cards getting out of order or falling out of your file folder on the way to the lectern. The outline should be concise, but as long as necessary to include for each point, key themes, leading authorities and record citations to the briefs and appendix. To see better at the lectern, capitalize all letters and use large writing. Use a very short, key word approach. This is an *outline* to assist in preparation, not a *script* to be placed on the lectern. Some hints:

a. The purpose of this outline is to distill the essence of the case, not for use at the oral argument. It should be prepared at least one week before argument, studied every day, and revised constantly.

b. Wide margins should be left for revisions and notes.

c. Put the outline in a loose-leaf notebook (or file folder), along with excerpts from a few key authorities and important pages from the appendix.

d. For every case cited in the briefs, place in the notebook the names of the judges who sat on the panel. You may be appearing before a judge who wrote the opinion or who served on the panel.

☐ 11. *Refine your outline.* On the day before the oral argument, reduce the outline as much as possible, preferably to one page. Although the notebook and full outline will be available at oral argument should your mind go blank, try not to look at anything other than this final outline during argument. You must demonstrate courtroom presence. It is eyeball-to-eyeball time. Do not even give the appearance of reading your argument. The final outline serves only as a roadmap of points to be made when sidetracked by questions. By the day of argument, you must know your case well enough to talk about it, not just read notes.

☐ 12. *Final research.* One week before oral argument check current slip opinions, loose-leaf trade services, Westlaw and Lexis, or other computer law services for new authorities. Shepardize and Insta-Cite or Auto-Cite all authorities relied on by the parties. Repeat this process the day before the argument.

☐ 13. *Anticipate questions.* Think of questions the court may throw at you. Your adversary's brief will suggest most, but not all, of them.

B. Preparation by the appellee.

☐ 1. *Follow preparation steps for the appellant outlined in Section A above.* Do the detailed study and preparation required for the appellant, making appropriate adjustments.

☐ 2. *Scope of presentation.* To a large extent the appellee responds to the appellant, but your adversary should not determine the scope of your presentation. Make whatever points are necessary, even if the appellant chooses not to mention them. If the point is crucial, do not rely on your brief alone.

☐ 3. *Outline.* Always prepare an outline of key points. Do not trust your memory.

C. Office rehearsal.

☐ 1. *Mandatory office moot court.* If the case is important enough to appeal, it is important enough to rehearse the oral argument in your office. Enlist partners and associates (preferably those who are somewhat detached) to read the briefs and to assume the roles of judges and your adversary. Have them pepper you with questions. Rehearsing your argument is as important as any other billable hour. If you are a sole practitioner, enlist lawyer friends. Recall that in § 23.5, a Los Angeles firm that only handles appeals has a moot court rehearsal in EVERY case. And the only lawyers who do not follow this practice were highly experienced appellate lawyers. If enough money is in the case, bring in some top-flight appellate lawyers or retired appellate judges to sit on the moot court.

D. Reconnoiter the court and the courtroom.

☐ 1. *Discover who will hear your case.* Unless it is a full court (en banc), learn the names of the judges before whom you will appear. Most United States courts of appeals identify the panel a week before the argument. If your court does not, send someone to the court every day during the week before the argument to see who is on the panel. If a trial judge or judge from another court is sitting, use Westlaw or Lexis to determine whether that judge has written any opinions on the points involved in your appeal.

☐ 2. *Case the joint.* Familiarize yourself with the courtroom. Try to get to the court a day in advance to witness the judges in action. Learn their idiosyncracies. Find out where lawyers must report, how to reserve time for rebuttal, the arrangement of counsel tables, the size of the lectern for placement of materials, and how the court controls the length of argument. Get a feel for the acoustics. You do not want to shout at the judges, but you want to ensure that they can hear you.

APPENDIX

Appendix *A*

ISSUE PRESERVATION AND STANDARDS OF APPEAL

§ 5.9   Examples of Standards of Review

Some Good Ones

This court applies the clearly erroneous standard, Fed. R. Civ. P. 52(a), to a review of facts found by a judge. "It is the responsibility of an appellate court to accept the ultimate factual determination of the fact-finder unless that determination either (1) is completely devoid of minimum evidentiary support displaying some hue of credibility, or (2) bears no rational relationship to the supportive evidentiary data. Unless the reviewing court establishes the existence of either of these factors, it may not alter the facts found by the trial court." *Krasnov v. Dinan*, 465 F.2d 1298, 1302–03 (3d Cir. 1972).

[*Author's Comment*: Here the standard was not only stated but also defined. After checking the citation, the judge could lift this verbatim for inclusion in an opinion. Giving a citation is recommended because it not only authenticates the statement but also assists the court in pre and post-decision research.]

———————

This court's review of the grant of summary judgment is plenary. *Little v. MGIC Indemnity Corp.*, 836 F.2d 789, 792 (3d Cir. 1987). This court, like the district court, should consider only facts of record. *Harold Friedman, Inc. v. Thorofare Markets, Inc.*, 587 F.2d 127, 131 (3d Cir. 1978). Arguments of counsel alleging facts not supported by the record must be rejected. *Ness v. Marshall*, 660 F.2d 517, 519 (3d Cir. 1981).

This court should affirm if summary judgment could have been entered on any ground raised below. "A prevailing party can support a district court judgment on any ground, including ones overlooked or rejected by the trial court." *Cospito v. Heckler*, 742 F.2d 72, 78 n.8 (3d Cir. 1984), *cert. denied*, 471 U.S. 1131 (1985) (*quoting Washington Steel Corp. v. TW Corp.*, 602 F.2d 594, 600 (3d Cir. 1979)).

The standard of review over a district court's denial of qualified immunity is plenary. *Brown v. United States*, 851 F.2d 615, 617 (3d Cir. 1988); *Hynson v. City of Chester*, 827 F.2d 932, 934 (3d Cir. 1987), *cert. denied*, 108 S.Ct. 702 (1988).

This court reviews admission of evidence under Rule 404(b), Federal Rules of Evidence, under the abuse of discretion standard. *United States v. Lewis*, 837 F.2d 415, 418–19 (9th Cir. 1988). If the court concludes that the trial court abused its discretion in admitting the evidence, the conviction must be reversed unless the error was harmless. *United States v. Hodges*, 770 F.2d 1475, 1480 (9th Cir. 1984). The error was harmless if it is more probable than not that the erroneous admission of evidence did not affect the jury's verdict. *Id.*

———

The district court's judgments dismissing *Fleming* and *Diamond* present this court with purely legal issues for review in that they are based solely on the district court's authority to issue process under RICO and the Federal Rules of Civil Procedure. The error of the district court, being solely one of law, is subject to *de novo* review. *Pullman-Standard v. Swint*, 456 U.S. 273 (1982).

Some Not-so-Good Ones

Standard of Review:

Abuse of discretion.

[*Author's Comment*: Even if correct, this is no help to the court, because it is unsupported by the proper authorities.]

———

The standard of review for issues numbers 1 through 4 and 6 is whether the district court erred as a matter of law. This court has plenary review over issue number 5.

———

[*Author's Comment*: What is the difference between review of an error of law and plenary review? None, of course. Moreover, this is an example of "Let's give the court a little workout here. Make the judge flick back and forth in the brief to see what I'm talking about. Look, if this judge is going to help me out, he or she had better work for it. I'm not going to make it easy."]

———

ARGUMENT AND CITATIONS OF AUTHORITY

APPENDIX A

* * *

(iii) Statement of the standard or scope of review

ISSUE I

This court has held that a sentencing court's determination with respect to a defendant's acceptance of responsibility is entitled to great deference on review and should not be disturbed unless it is without foundation. *United States v. Spraggins*, 868 F.2d 1541, 1543 (11th Cir. 1989); *United States v. Davis*, 878 F.2d 1299 (11th Cir. 1989). Moreover, the court of appeals shall accept the findings of fact unless they are clearly erroneous. 18 U.S.C. 3742.

ISSUE II

This involves a question of fact. Questions of fact are judged under the clearly erroneous standard. 18 U.S.C. 3742.

[*Author's Comment*: This is excerpted from a brief filed not by a storefront lawyer but by a U.S. Attorney's office located in the eleventh circuit. The form of the brief leaves much to be desired. Note the statement of issues: "Issue I" and "Issue II." How does this help the judge? The standards of review are set forth on pages 5 and 6, but the statement of Issue I does not appear until page 8, and the statement of Issue II is on page 12. The statutory references should have been pinpointed to section 3742(d); the section contains five subsections with many subparts. Nor does the citation follow the *Bluebook*. It should properly have read: 18 U.S.C. § 3742(d).]

This court reviews findings of fact under the clearly erroneous standard. *In re Teichman*, 774 F.2d 1395, 1397 (9th Cir. 1985). When a case is submitted wholly on documents, less deference is accorded to the district court's findings of fact. *Bulls Corner Restaurant, Inc. v. Director of Federal Emergency Management Agency*, 759 F.2d 500, 502 (5th Cir. 1985).

[*Author's Comment*: This brief was filed in the 1990s. Note the reference to a 1985 case suggesting the distinction between written and oral evidence, a distinction that was wiped out by an amendment to Rule 52(a) effective August 1, 1985.]

Appendix *B*

THE BRIEF: STATING THE ISSUE(S)

§ 10.6 Examples of Issue Statements

An easy way to look at examples here is to compare how counsel framed the issues with what the court actually determined them to be. Usually the court is correct; in any event, it has the last word. Consider these examples from actual briefs and subsequent opinions. Note the large number beginning with "whether" or taking the form of an interrogatory. In your mind, restate the issue in a simple declaratory sentence favoring you.

Issue Formulation: Appellant, Appellee, and Court

Appellant:

> Whether the district court abused its discretion in denying the motion for reduction of sentence pursuant to Rule 35(b) of the Federal Rules of Criminal Procedure?

Appellee:

> Whether the district court's ruling denying the appellant's motion for reduction of sentence constituted an abuse of discretion?

Court:

> The sole question for decision is whether the district court abused its discretion in denying the motion of the appellant for a reduction of sentence pursuant to Rule 35(b) of the Federal Rules of Criminal Procedure.

Appellant:

> Whether the district court erred in sentencing the appellant to a term of imprisonment outside the applicable guideline range.

Appellee:

> Whether the district court erred in sentencing the defendant to a term of imprisonment that exceeded the maximum term allowable under the Sentencing Guidelines.

Court:

The question for decision in this appeal by the appellant is whether the sentence imposed by the district court is unreasonable under the provisions of the Sentencing Reform Act of 1984.

Appellant:

1. Did the district court lack jurisdiction to hear this case because the defendant was accused of engaging in conduct in violation of the Lacey Act, 16 U.S.C. § 3372(A) and 3373(d)(1)(b) that was not intended by Congress to be criminal?

2. Was the International Pacific Halibut Commission (IPHC) regulation, 50 C.F.R. § 30.9, promulgated in excess of the IPHC authority conferred on it by the Convention between the United States and Canada for the preservation of the halibut fishery of the North Pacific Ocean and Bering Sea and any amending protocols?

Appellee:

1. Did the district court err in concluding that the conduct alleged in this case constitutes a violation of the criminal provisions of the Lacey Act?

2. Did the district court err in concluding that the 20,000-pound trip limit regulation had not been promulgated within the IPHC's authority?

Court:

The question for decision is whether violating regulations of the International Halibut Commission is a proper basis for a criminal prosecution under the Lacey Act, 16 U.S.C. § 3372(a)(1), 3373(d)(1)(B). If so, we must then decide if promulgating a regulation limiting a day's catch to 20,000 pounds exceeded the commission's authority.

Appellant:

1. Whether the district court erred in failing to apply the proper standard relating to constructive discharge, and in injecting a "notice" requirement into that doctrine?

2. Whether the district court was clearly erroneous in holding that appellant was required to give additional notice to the president of the employer-corporation prior to resigning?

Appellee:

1. Whether the district court was clearly erroneous in finding that the employee's claim for gender discrimination by constructive discharge could not be sustained since the employee prematurely and precipitately resigned without informing her employer of the purportedly intolerable working conditions prior to her resignation?

2. Whether the district court was clearly erroneous in finding that the employee's resignation was premature and precipitate since she voluntarily chose to resign rather than inform her employer of the purportedly intolerable working conditions?

Court:

In the primary appeal at No. 89-3727 we must determine whether the district court erred as a matter of law in injecting a notice requirement into the doctrine of constructive discharge under Title VII of the Civil Rights Act of 1964, as amended, 42 U.S.C. §§ 2000e–2000h(6). Subsumed in this problem are two somewhat related but distinct subordinate inquiries: whether the existence of notice *vel non* is a question of fact, and if so, was the court clearly erroneous in finding no notice (a) on the basis of imputed notice to the employer based on actions of and notice to the employer, or (b) on the basis of inferred notice to the employer given the small size of the business enterprise and repeated unsuccessful efforts by the employee to reach the employer to complain about acts of gender discrimination.

Appellant:

1. Are there genuine issues of material fact as to the question of whether a contract was formed, or whether an enforceable contract was breached?

2. Did the district court err in granting defendant's motion for summary judgment?

Appellee:

1. Whether the entry of summary judgment by the lower court in favor of the appellee and against the appellant as to all claims asserted by the appellant was proper based upon the record presented to the court by the parties.

2. In defending the summary judgment motion in the court below, whether Automotive Management Systems, Incorporated failed to make a showing sufficient to establish the existence of an element essential to its case and on which it would bear the burden of proof at trial.

Court:

Presented for decision is a rather straightforward issue of contract law requiring us to decide whether there was an acceptance of an offer to sublease space in a shopping mall.

Appellant:

1. Whether the trial court erred in its conclusion of law that all defendants were part of a partnership under Pennsylvania law.

2. Whether the trial court erred as a matter of law in applying 59 Pa. C.S.A. § 328, holding all defendants, in the alternative, to be partners by estoppel in the absence of evidence that Rose Fantasia consented to representation as a partner and in the absence of evidence that plaintiff relied on representation that any appellant was a partner.

3. Whether the court erred in concluding that transfers of residential real estate between family members constitute wrongful acts of partners within the meaning of 59 Pa. C.S.A. § 325.

4. Whether the trial court erred in failing to apply the Statute of Frauds, 33 P.S. § 3.

5. Whether the trial court erred in failing to apply the Statute of Frauds of the Uniform Commercial Code, 13 Pa. C.S.A. § 2201.

6. Whether the trial court erred in failing to interpret the written credit application as a guaranty according to the expressed understanding of the parties.

7. Whether the trial court erred in failing to consider the defenses of fraud, or alternatively, mutual mistake in its interpretation of the credit application.

8. Whether the entry of judgment against Rose Fantasia in favor of Jeff Pozsonyi violates the due process clause of the Fifth Amendment of the United States Constitution, since Jeffrey Pozsonyi did not file any pleading against Rose Fantasia.

9. Whether the imposition of prejudgment interest in favor of Jeff Pozsonyi is inequitable.

10. Whether fact findings of the trial court are clearly erroneous.

Appellee:

I. Did the United States District Court err in its determination that appellee had established by a preponderance of the evidence presented at trial that appellants along with Amalia Fantasia and Fantasia Enterprises, Inc., were jointly and severally liable for the debt owed to appellee in the sum of $41,808.12.

(Appellee contends the answer is no.)

(Appellants contend the answer is yes.)

II. Did the United States District Court abuse its discretion in denying appellants' motion to alter or amend the judgment, or alternatively, to grant a new trial?

(Appellee contends the answer is no.)

(Appellants contend the answer is yes.)

Court:

The major question for decision is whether findings of fact made by the district court in a nonjury trial were clearly erroneous.

[*Author's Comment*: Do you get the feeling that the appellant lost the case the moment ten contentions were presented on appeal?]

———————

Appellant:

I. Appellant was convicted of offenses for which she was not charged by the grand jury, thus violating her right to due process as to counts 2 to 24.

II. The statement by the district court that it would give a requested instruction, but then did not, violated Rule 30 and appellant was prejudiced.

III. As a matter of law the appellant as an officer of a corporation cannot legally conspire with herself as an individual ,and the possibility of conviction on an impermissible legal theory requires reversal. Alternatively, the court erred in not giving the instruction requested by the defense (see preceding argument).

IV. Neither the mail fraud nor the wire fraud statute (18 U.S.C. §1341 and §1343) allows conviction where the person defrauded is not the person from whom the money or property is obtained.

V. The failure of the instructions to require the jury to find that the alleged mailings, wire communications, and falsities occurred on the dates alleged in the indictment requires reversal.

VI. The district court's failure to make a determination as to appellant's objection to the pre-sentence report is a violation of Rule 32 and requires remand for resentencing.

Appellee:

A. The instruction regarding the substantive offenses and the conviction of the substantive offenses were proper either because defendant directly participated, or because defendant was vicariously responsible for the acts of co-conspirators.

B. The court properly complied with Fed. R. Crim P. 30 and the defendant failed to properly object to the purported violation and such purported violation did not constitute plain error nor was the defendant prejudiced by it.

C. The remote possibility that the jury could have concluded that the defendant, as an officer of the corporation, conspired with herself does not require reversal.

D. The instruction concerning corporate responsibility was accurate and the defendant was not prejudiced by it.

E. The mail fraud and wire fraud convictions were proper in light of *McNally v. United States*, 483 U.S. 350 (1987).

F. The instructions accurately set forth the law regarding the requirement that the jury find that the crimes occurred on certain dates.

G. A hearing was held on defendant's objections to the presentence report and the court made findings regarding those objections.

Court:

The appellant presents many contentions on appeal, but her major argument is that the government made a basic change in its theory during trial to prove her culpability on the substantive counts. She argues that although she was prepared to defend the allegation that she directly participated in these offenses, she was not prepared when the government proceeded to rely also on the vicarious liability theory approved in *Pinkerton v. United States*, 328 U.S. 640 (1945), *reh'g denied*, 328 U.S. 818 (1946). *Pinkerton* teaches that a party to a conspiracy may be held responsible for a substantive offense committed by a co-conspirator in furtherance of the conspiracy even if that party did not participate in the substantive offense or have knowledge of it.

The appellant also argues that the trial court erred in its instructions to the jury, to wit: in instructing that she could be held culpable under the *Pinkerton* theory; in failing to deliver a requested instruction that she could not conspire with herself; in improperly describing corporate responsibility; and in failing to instruct that the jury must find that the crimes occurred on the exact dates alleged in the indictment. Additionally, she argues that the holding of *McNally v. United States*, 483 U.S. 350 (1987), precludes a mail or wire fraud conviction in her case and that the court violated the hearing requirements relating to presentence investigation matters as required by Fed. R. Crim. P. 32.

[*Author's Comment*: Until you read the excerpt from the court's opinion, did you have any idea of the appellant's major argument?]

Examples of Issues that Are Independent of Each Other

I. For the reasons that follow, appellant is requesting this court to reverse his conviction under the federal extortion statute, 18 U.S.C.§ 876. He contends that the statute is unconstitutional because it is overbroad and vague.

II. Should the court reject this challenge, appellant asks that the court vacate the judgment and order a new trial because the government, during its cross-examination of him, referred to statements made by appellant in a magistrate's pretrial inquiry regarding his eligibility for appointed counsel, and that this reference violated appellant's rights protected under the Fifth and Sixth Amendments.

I. The appellant's conviction must be reversed because there was no substantial evidence that he conspired with anyone else to defraud the United States in collection of revenue.

II. In the alternative, the district court committed reversible error in admitting evidence of the appellant's subsequent acts of uncharged misconduct, in admitting his tax returns, and in refusing his requested instruction regarding the failure of the United States to produce evidence regarding the Bahamian loan.

Appendix *C*

THE BRIEF: STATEMENT OF FACTS

§ 12.7 Examples of Statements of Facts

What follows is a random sampling of statements of facts. Are they clear? Readable? Could they have been shortened?

The Tucson Airport Authority (hereinafter "TAA") is a nonprofit Arizona corporation which operates the Tucson International Airport pursuant to A.R.S. §§ 2–311 and 2–312. The Airport exists for the purpose of movement of arriving and departing airline passengers, and all the streets surrounding the airport are private, nondedicated roadways constructed, maintained and operated exclusively with revenues derived from the use of Airport facilities without benefit of local tax dollars or highway user funds.

The TAA does not collect "taxes," nor does it get "tax" dollars fro the City of Tucson. It collects revenue from users of the Airport. All its users, including but not limited to the airlines, car rental agencies and facilities, the telephone company, banks with twenty-four-hour teller machines on the property, shoeshine establishments, gift shops, taxis, limousines, off-airport bus services, parking space users, insurance companies vending insurance policies through vending machines, concessionaires vending food and beverages from vending machines, restaurants, gift shops selling books and newspapers and other items, users of advertising space on the walls at the airport, pay rent or fees to the TAA. The rents and fees are calculated upon one or more negotiated formulae. These formulae may include total space occupied, total revenue generated per month, number of passengers using the airport, result of competitive bidding, and others.

The TAA Board of Directors authorized the collection of rental fees from newsracks by the Airport staff. The rental suggested for the newsracks at that time was an amount of $23.69 per month per newsrack, which reflects a space improvement charge and cost of custodial services, or 15 percent of gross sales, whichever is higher. Rental is routinely charged by other airports across the country and paid by newspaper publishers who vend newspapers through newsracks at airports. For example, *USA Today* pays $209 per rack, per year to the Denver airport, $60 per rack, per year to the Salt Lake City airport, $316 per rack, per year to the Dayton airport, and $1,165 per rack, per year to the Detroit airport.

Phoenix Newspapers, Inc. (hereinafter "PNI") is an Arizona corporation and publisher of an Arizona newspaper, and is vending newspapers through vending machines at the Airport. It delivers newspapers through a network of distributors and has very limited home deliveries in the Tucson area. In Tucson, the bulk of PNI's newspapers are distributed through gift shops, grocery stores, and convenience markets like Circle K and 7-Eleven. These various distributors, including the concessionaires at the Airport, get the daily papers from PNI at wholesale, or twenty cents each for dailies, and 53 cents each for Sunday papers. The distributors in turn sell those newspapers to the retailers at 29 cents each for dailies, and 89 cents for the Sunday papers, thereby making a profit of 9 cents each for the weekly papers and 36 cents each for the Sunday papers. The retailers in turn sell the dailies for 35 cents and the Sunday papers for one dollar, thereby making a 6-cent profit on the dailies and an 11-cent profit on the Sunday paper.

When the newspapers are sold through the newsracks instead of through gift shops, grocery stores, and convenience markets, the profit margin for the distributor goes up to 15 cents for the dailies and to 47 cents for the Sunday paper. This helps the newspapers meet the minimum $300 per month guaranteed to their distributors. It also directly competes with income derived from TAA from sale of newspapers sold through the newsstands. PNI does not sell newspapers through newsracks in front of or nearby convenience stores, gift shops, and grocery stores so that it does not compete.

The petitioner's conviction stems from her involvement with a narcotics distributor. The evidence at trial showed that from 1980 to 1986, the distributor controlled a large narcotics operation in Chicago, Illinois. He purchased cocaine and heroin from importers and (with the help of others) distributed it through several gambling establishments and lounges that he owned or controlled. He used the profits to purchase real and personal property, which he frequently placed in the names of other persons, including the petitioner and another codefendant.

In 1988, a grand jury returned a twenty-three-count indictment against the petitioner and others arising from the distributor's drug operation and his attempts to conceal assets and income. The indictment charged the distributor with managing a continuing criminal enterprise, and it charged the others with conspiracy to violate, and violation of, various narcotics statutes and related laws. Most pertinent to this case, Count 20 of the indictment alleged that the distributor, the petitioner and another co-defendant joined in a conspiracy to defraud the federal government, in violation of 18 U.S.C. § 371. Count 20 identified two objects of the conspiracy: (1) impairment of the efforts of the Internal Revenue Service to ascertain income taxes (the IRS object); and (2) impairment of the efforts of the Drug Enforcement Administration to ascertain forfeitable assets (the DEA object).

The evidence relevant to Count 20 showed that the distributor held and controlled assets in the names of both the petitioner and the other codefendant. He arranged for the codefendant to become (without capital contribution) the majority shareholder of Blacom Corporation, a company that he used to control various properties he acquired through his drug operation. He also placed real estate and a Mercedes Benz automobile that he used in the codefendant's name. Following the same modus operandi, he purchased a tavern and an adjoining building in the petitioner's name. The petitioner filed tax returns claiming the tavern as her own in order to conceal the distributor's ownership of the business and his underreporting of income. The distributor also purchased a $35,000 Jaguar automobile in the petitioner's name, and structured the payments on the car to evade federal reporting requirements for cash payments in excess of $10,000.

During the trial, the petitioner unsuccessfully moved for a severance, arguing that the government had failed to prove that she knew the distributor was a drug dealer or that she was aware of the DEA object of the conspiracy. At the close of trial, the petitioner proposed jury instructions that would have required the jury to find that she knew the object of the conspiracy was to impede the IRS in ascertaining the distributor's taxes. She also asked the court to require the jury to identify, through special interrogatories, whether the petitioner had knowledge of the IRS and DEA objects of the conspiracy. The court denied both the proposed jury instructions and the request for special interrogatories. The jury returned a general verdict of guilty against the defendants on Count 20.

For the period beginning November 19, 1987, and continuing until April 14, 1988, the plaintiff was an inmate at the Delaware County Prison. From the very beginning of this period, the defendants knew that the plaintiff had tested positive for HIV and was therefore a carrier of the virus. He was tested again as a matter of policy and the same results were obtained. The plaintiff was immediately administratively segregated from the rest of the prison population. He was placed in the infirmary. He had no physical manifestations of the virus, and was not ill. On April 5, 1988, the plaintiff was transferred to the new Special Medical Unit which was still segregated from the rest of the prison population.

In a letter to the court, which is dated before the plaintiff's *pro se* complaint, and seems to have been attached to it by the Clerk and/or the plaintiff, the plaintiff reported that "this prison singles us out as though we are contagious people and bringing charges against them for their inhuman treatment received they single you out when one speaks up about it they will try making trouble for a person who does." In his *pro se* complaint he described the conditions under which he lived: "We get no therapy. We get no proper medical attention. We are touch[ed] and searched with rubber gloves. We have no gym as all other inmates. We do not eat in chow hall as all other inmates etc. etc. We are locked in 24 hours a day etc. . . . [W]e are single[d] out because we are [kept] in yellow outfit from the women Veteran Administrator. . . ."

The medical staff did not maintain confidentiality; other inmates and prison officials were made aware of the plaintiff's condition. The plaintiff also did not receive proper treatment or monitoring for his specific condition because the doctors were not trained in treating infectious diseases.

The plaintiff's meals were served to him at his bed in the infirmary. While other prisoners were allowed six hours of exercise daily, the plaintiff was not allowed to participate. When the plaintiff was finally given the opportunity to use exercise equipment on April 5, 1988, he did so. He was not permitted to work, participate in religious activities, or have a television. The general prison population washed their clothes daily, while the plaintiff's clothing was laundered once a week until April 7, 1988. In addition to being constantly watched by nurses and guards, the plaintiff was continually on display for anyone in the area because the room to which he was confined had a large window.

Defendant Prison Health Services, Inc. denied many allegations but "admitted that [the plaintiff] was segregated from the general population because of his status as an AIDS carrier." The affidavits also admitted that the plaintiff was segregated solely because he tested positive for exposure to the virus (although he did not have AIDS) and that segregation was a blanket policy, regardless of individual circumstances.

Appendix *D*

THE BRIEF: SUMMARY OF THE ARGUMENT

§ 10.4.1   More Examples of Summaries of Arguments

Evaluate the following summaries of argument that I have chosen at random. They are not necessarily model summaries—some are good, some are rather pedestrian—but they do represent the summaries judges read in briefs today. Examine them through the judge's eyes and see if you can catch the "flavor" of the cases. Most of these summaries are too long.

Check to see if the orientation sentence or paragraph is adequate? Does the opening qualify as a dominant argument of maximum potency? Does it describe the equitable heart of the contention? Does it give the theme of the argument? Do the various statements or points support the contention? Do they furnish the issues the court must confront? Do they have enough punch to convince? Should they have been shortened? Expanded? Did the summary present a neat balance between the questions presented and a synopsis of the argument to come?

Summaries from Opposing Briefs

Appellant:

> Smith submits that the trial court erred in two respects. First, the Trial Court concluded that the mere fact that the filing used the unregistered trade name in and of itself rendered the Smith UCC-1 "seriously misleading" without regard to whether a reasonable searcher searching under the correct name would have found the UCC-1 filed by appellant. Second, the Trial Court gave undue emphasis to the fact that the UCC search under the correct name failed to disclose the Smith UCC-1 without determining whether a reasonable searcher searching under the correct name would have found the Smith UCC-1.
>
> Smith submits that the court must disregard the fact that a governmental employee conducted the search. Instead, the test is whether a reasonable searcher searching under the debtor's name would have come upon the index card for the Smith UCC-1 and been prompted by the information on it to inquire further.
>
> Under the uncontroverted facts here, Smith submits that the hypothetical searcher would have come upon the UCC-1 filed by it. Furthermore, the following information on that card would have

prompted further inquiry: the ethnicity of the name"Stebow," the use of the same address as for the debtor and the signature of one of debtor's officers.

Smith further submits that the outcome of a search conducted through the New Jersey Secretary of State's office is not relevant to the inquiry as a matter of law and is further flawed because it is the product of a procedure that is contrary to state law.

Appellee:

The Trustee is vested with the right to avoid the lien asserted by Smith under the provisions of the Bankruptcy Code, 11 U.S.C. § 544(a), which provides that a trustee in bankruptcy is vested with the status and powers of a lien creditor who extends credit to a debtor at the commencement of a case and at such time receives in exchange a judicial lien to secure the loan whether or not such creditor exists. A trustee with this lien creditor status may avoid an unperfected interest. 11 U.S.C. § 544(b).

Smith had to perfect its lien on assets described in the UCC-1 Financing Statement with the Secretary of State of New Jersey, in compliance with N.J.S.A. §§ 12A:9-401(1), 12A:9-402, 12A: 403(1)(4), 12A:9-407, whereby the name of the debtor must be stated, with allowance for a minor error which is not seriously misleading. N.J.S.A. § 12A:9-402(5) (in effect in 1980, the subsection was changed in 1981 by the renumbering of subparagraph (5) to (8)). The trial court properly found that the error by Smith in naming the debtor in the UCC-1 to be Stebow Excavating Co., Inc., was not a minor error and was seriously misleading, whereby the lien was avoided as against the Trustee.

The trial Court's determination, which was affirmed by the District Court, was correct in refusing to attach any weight or effect to Smith's attack upon the procedure followed by the Secretary of State of New Jersey in responding to a request for search of a particular lien debtor. The filing of the financing statement or security agreement by the filing clerk after "indexing" on a card the pertinent information of the names of the parties, which financing instrument was available for inspection by the parties or creditors, was proper. The search was not extended by the employee of the State Department beyond the name of the debtor for whom a search was requested.

Miscellaneous Summaries

The present decision, *Hernandez II*, incorrectly limits the power granted the district courts to dismiss a frivolous case under 28 U.S.C. § 1915(d), in that district courts within the Ninth Circuit must now base a section 1915(d) dismissal on facts subject to judicial notice under Rule 201 of the Federal Rules of Evidence. These facts must establish that a plaintiff's allegations are impossible. This is neither sound law nor consonant with this Court's 1989 remand of this case to the Ninth Circuit. *Hernandez II* does not comport with the intent of Congress in enacting section 1915(d) or the holdings in *Neitzke* and will adversely affect the ability of district courts to handle the growing problem of prisoner in propria litigation because, as a practical matter, it does not admit of any discretion in the District Court to dismiss a fantastic complaint as frivolous under section 1915(d).

Alabama Code § 8-1-1 (a) expresses the public policy of the State of Alabama that contracts in restraint of trade are disfavored. Paragraph 11 of the employment agreement is a total restraint of trade as to the employee. The district court, in reaching this determination as to paragraph 11 followed its previous decision in *Hudson v. Nationwide*, CV-86-AR-1375-M. The facts of the case at bar are identical to the *Hudson* case and the language of the employment agreement is exactly the same.

Alabama case law holds that an employment contract which creates a total restraint of trade is void. Paragraph 11 of the employment agreement totally restrains Cornutt from selling insurance within a twenty-five-mile radius of his office in Gadsden, Alabama.

It is clear that the district court followed Alabama law in this case by following both prior Alabama decisions and its previous decision in the *Hudson* case.

This is an individual sex discrimination action under Title IX in which a District Court has made findings of fact based on the evidence presented at trial. The most significant of those findings are as follows:

> Plaintiff was dismissed from her high school's National Honor Society solely because the Faculty Council members sincerely believed that Plaintiff's conduct of engaging in premarital sex was inconsistent with the honorary society's standards of leadership and character and *not* because of Plaintiff's gender or pregnancy;

> Plaintiff failed to prove she was treated differently than any male NHS member who engaged in premarital sex;

> Even if Plaintiff had met her burden of proof on the question of liability, she was not entitled to relief.

None of these findings was clearly erroneous. To the contrary, they were supported by the overwhelming weight of the evidence.

Plaintiff uses various contrived theories in an effort to divert attention from the trial court's findings that she failed to prove unlawful discrimination and that she would not be entitled to relief even if she had proved her case. Plaintiff ignores and mischaracterizes the District Court's dispositive findings of fact, distorts the record and the applicable legal standards and invokes various constitutional arguments which have no application to this case.

These attempts must fail. In this appeal after trial on the merits, the Court of Appeals is bound to apply the clearly erroneous standard of review. Under that standard, the District Court's determination in Defendants' favor should be affirmed.

This appeal presents the straightforward issue of whether the district court properly exercised its discretion by staying this case. It did. The stay order avoided the fundamental unfairness of forcing the Trust to choose between violating orders of the New York courts or having a default judgment entered against it in this case. It also fostered judicial efficiency and economy by allowing the district court and the parties to avoid the considerable time and expense of a trial while a class action, the settlement of which calls for the dismissal of the case below in favor of alternative dispute resolution, was proceeding in New York.

In their brief, the appellants attempt to divert the Court's focus from the discretion of the district court to various issues raised in the class action. In effect, appellants seek to appeal to this court issues which are appealable exclusively to the Second Circuit. Those issues are not properly before the court. Moreover, even were they somehow relevant to this appeal, the stay order still must be affirmed because appellants' arguments are without merit, as discussed below and in the New York court's exhaustive opinion certifying the class action and approving the settlement.

These appeals are much ado about nothing. Jurisdiction is absent in this Court as it was in the district court. The Kansas Supreme Court, applying governing Kansas law to these claims arising in Kansas between Kansas citizens, has affirmed final judgment in favor of Foulston Siefkin on all claims.

Miller's first appeal was filed more than thirty days after the Order dismissing his motion for lack of jurisdiction. The United States was not a party to the ancillary attorney's fee proceeding. In *Budinich v. Becton Dickinson & Co.*, 486 U.S. 196, 200 (1988), the Supreme Court held that a petition for attorney's fees is "an independent proceeding" for appeal purposes, so that a judgment on the merits is final and appealable when entered. An appeal filed within thirty days of a later fee order is thus not a timely appeal from the earlier merits judgment. Accordingly, since the United States was not "a party" to the independent fee proceeding, the 60-day appeal time under Rule 4(a)(1) is not applicable.

In denying Miller's motion to extend the appeal time for "excusable neglect or good cause" under Rule 4(a)(5), the district court correctly followed this Court's decisions holding that failure of the clerk to send a copy of the order to counsel is insufficient to permit the appeal time extension. *Gooch v. Skelly Oil Company*, 493 F.2d 366 (10th Cir. 1974), and other cases cited by the district court's June 10, 1988 Order.

Nor did the district court obtain ancillary jurisdiction, because the dispute did not arise from the same "operative facts" as those present in the principal case, and were not "logically dependent" on the outcome of the main claim. *Owen Equip. & Erection Co. v. Kroger*, 437 U.S. 365 (1978). In *Jenkins v. Weinshienk*, 670 F.2d 915, 918 (10th Cir. 1982), this Court limited ancillary jurisdiction to a claim by the lawyer for fees he earned in the main case, finding a lack of such jurisdiction over claims by the lawyer for fees earned in other legal matters. Miller's claims required litigation over his partnership relationship with Foulston Siefkin, including a written partnership agreement precluding his recovery of fees received by the firm years after his departure.

Even assuming ancillary jurisdiction, the district court plainly had discretion to decline it in light of the previously filed state court suit, as well as the delay and diversion of judicial energy into the partnership dispute. Miller's own motion, by alternatively asking for a stay in disbursement of the Foulston Siefkin fee award until disposition of the state court suit, recognized that the partnership dispute could be handled by the state courts.

Finally, the Kansas Supreme Court, in *Miller v. Foulston, Siefkin, Powers, etc.*, 246 Kan. 450, 790 P.2d 404 (1990), ruled that Foulston Siefkin's partnership agreement was valid, and that Miller's theories for avoiding the terms of that agreement filed November 30, 1987, almost five years after he left the firm, were barred by limitation. Under *Guaranty Trust Co. v. York*, 326 U.S. 99 (1945), a federal court sitting in Kansas must apply Kansas limitations law to a dispute arising in Kansas between Kansas citizens. It follows that the Kansas judgment is binding on the parties in any federal or state court in Kansas.

When a jury is confronted with testimony which describes a bizarre and clearly erratic behavior, together with highly technical expert testimony regarding the Defendant's mental disorders or defects, it is quite dangerous to assume that a jury would know how to apply that evidence to specific intent crimes.

The purpose of instructing the jury is to give the jury a guideline or road map on how to apply the facts to the rules of law in each case.

In this case, both the jury and the Defendant were deprived of an instruction that would have given the jury the legal connection between the mental disorder evidence and the specific intent elements of each crime; this prevented the Defendant from having a fair trial.

The trial court committed plain error in not instructing on the defense of diminished capacity and the Defendant's substantial rights were harmed. Defendant is entitled to a reversal of his conviction and a new trial.

TABLE OF AUTHORITIES
References are to chapters and footnotes.

Baldock, B., *What Appellate Advocates Seek from Appellate Judges and What Appellate Judges Seek from Appellate Advocates*, 31 N.M.L. Rev. 265 (2001), ch. 22 n. 1

Ball, D., *Theater Tips and Strategies for Jury Trial* (1994), ch. 12 n. 6

Barzun, J., *Behind the Blue Pencil*, 54 The Am. Scholar 385 (1985), ch. 17 n. 3

Bashman, H., *How Appealing*, at http://appellateblog.blogspot.com, ch. 23 n. 1

Bettinghaus, E., *Persuasive Communication* (3d ed. 1980), ch. 2 n. 2; ch. 3 n. 4

Boehm, D., *Clarity and Candor Are Vital in Appellate Advocacy*, N.Y. St. B.J., Sept./Oct 1999, ch. 17 n. 9

Boswell, J., *Life of Samuel Johnson* (1906), ch. 17 n. 19, n. 20

Bouvier, J., *Bouvier's Law Dictionary* (Rawle ed. 1914), ch. 5 n. 29

Bright, M., *Appellate Briefwriting: Some "Golden" Rules*, 17 Creighton L. Rev. 1069 (1983), ch. 10 n. 11

Bright, M., *The Ten Commandments of Oral Argument*, 67 A.B.A.J. 1136 (1981), ch. 3 n. 7, n. 8; ch. 24 n. 6

Cardozo, B., *Growth of the Law* (1924), ch. 17 n. 17

Cardozo, B., *Law and Literature*, 14 Yale L.J. 705 (1925), reprinted in *Selected Writings of Benjamin Nathan Cardozo* (M. Hall ed. 1967), ch. 13 n. 2, n. 6

Cardozo, B., *The Nature of the Judicial Process* (1921), ch. 8 n. 6; ch. 15 n. 1; ch. 16 n. 15; ch. 17 n. 16; ch.19 n. 8, n. 13

Cherrick, J., *Issues, Facts, and Appellate Strategy*, 16 Litig. 15 (1990), ch. 9 n. 1; ch.10 n. 8, n. 13

Coffin, F., *The Ways of a Judge: Reflections from the Federal Appellate Bench* (1980), ch. 3 n. 2; ch. 13 n. 6

Creighton, R., *An Introductory Logic* (1898), ch. 20 n. 1

Cripe, N., *Fundamentals of Persuasive Oral Argument*, 20 Forum 342 (1985), ch. 2 n. 3, n. 4, n. 12; ch. 3 n. 3, n. 11

Currier, T., *Time and Change in Judge-Made Law: Prospective Overruling*, 51 Va. L. Rev. 20 (1965), ch. 8 n. 15

Davis, J., *The Argument of an Appeal*, 26 A.B.A.J. 895 (1940), ch. 1 n. 1; ch. 2 n. 11; ch. 17 n. 8; ch. 24 n. 5, n. 7

Davis, K., *Administrative Law* (1958 & Supp. 1970), ch. 5 n. 22

Denning, A., *The Closing Chapter* (1983), ch. 17 n. 5

Devlin, P., *The Judge* (1979), ch. 17 n. 18

Dewey, J., *How We Think* (1933), ch. 2 n. 6; ch. 16 n. 5, n. 8, n. 9; ch. 20 n. 6, n. 7

Douglas, W., *Stare Decisis*, 49 Colum. L. Rev. 735 (1949), ch. 15 n. 8

Dworkin, R., *The Model of Rules*, 35 U. Chi. L. Rev. 14 (1967), ch. 5 n. 34

Dworkin, R., *Taking Rights Seriously* (1977), ch. 5 n. 31

Dworsky, A., *The Little Book on Oral Argument* (2000), ch. 24 n. 4

Eaton, R., *General Logic* (1931), ch. 20 n. 2

Foley, B., & Robbins, R., *Fiction 101: A Primer for Lawyers on How to Use Fiction Writing Techniques to Write Persuasive Fact Sessions*, 32 Rutgers L. Rev. 459 (2001), ch. 12 n. 7

Friendly, H., *Reactions of a Lawyer—Newly Become Judge*, 71 Yale L.J. 218 (1961), ch. 17 n. 17

Gabriel, H., *Preparation and Delivery or Oral Argument in Appellate Courts*, 22 Am. J. Trial Advoc. 571 (1999), ch. 14 n. 1, n. 2

Haggard, T., *Writing the Reply Brief*, Scrivener, Mar./Apr. 2001, ch. 19 n. 12

Hart, H., & Sacks, A., *The Legal Process* (tent. ed. 1958), ch. 5 n. 30

6

Highet, G., *The Scholarly Life*, 41 The Am. Scholar 522 (1972), ch. 21 n. 1

Hoffman, A., *Corralling Constitutional Fact: De Novo Fact Review in the Federal Appellate Courts*, 50 Duke L.J. 1427 (2001), ch. 5 n. 11

Holmes, O.W., *The Common Law* (1881), ch. 16 n. 1

Holmes, O.W., *The Path of the Law*, 10 Harv. L. Rev. 457 (1897), ch. 8 n. 7, n. 14

Jackson, R., *Advocacy Before the United States Supreme Court*, 37 Cornell L.Q. 1 (1951), ch. 3 n. 10; ch. 9 n. 10; ch. 24 n. 2, n. 3

Jackson, R., *Decisional Law and Stare Decisis*, 30 A.B.A.J. 334 (1944), ch. 19 n. 3

Jones, H., *An Invitation to Jurisprudence*, 74 Colum. L. Rev. 1023 (1974), ch. 5 n. 45; ch. 16 n. 3

Kant, I., *Groundwork of the Metaphysics of Morals* (Paton trans. 1964), ch. 15 n. 2

Kozinski, A., *How You Too Can...Lose Your Appeal*, Mont. Law., 5 (Oct. 1997), ch. 12 n. 2

Lasky, M., *A Return to the Observatory Below the Bench*, 19 Sw. L.J. 679 (1965), ch. 12 n. 11

Lee, E., *Principled Decision Making and the Proper Role of Federal Appellate Courts: The Mixed Questions Conflict*, 64 S. Cal. L. Rev. 235 (1991), ch. 5 n. 11

Levi, E., *An Introduction to Legal Reasoning*, 15 U. Chi. L. Rev. 501 (1948), ch. 12 n. 4

Llewellyn, K., *The Bramble Bush* (7th prtg. 1981), ch. 15 n. 5

Lloyd, D., *Reason and Logic in the Common Law*, 64 L.Q. Rev. 468 (1948), ch. 8 n. 3

Lucero, C., *What Appellate Advocates Seek from Appellate Judges and What Appellate Judges Seek from Appellate Advocates*, 31 N.M.L. Rev. 265 (2001), ch. 22 n. 1

MacCormick, N., *Legal Reasoning and Legal Theory* (1978), ch. 14 n. 3; ch. 15 n. 3, n. 4

McCormick, M., *Selecting and Framing the Issues on Appeal: A Powerful Persuasive Tool*, 90 Ill. B.J. 203 (2002), ch. 9 n.

MacEachern, K., Manager, West Group, Letter to Ruggero J. Aldisert, (Nov. 15, 2002), ch. 1 n. 4

Mandell-King, V., *What Appellate Advocates Seek from Appellate Judges and What Appellate Judges Seek from Appellate Advocates*, 31 N.M.L. Rev. 265 (2001), ch. 22 n. 1

Martineau, R., *Appellate Justice in England and the United States: A Comparative Analysis* (1990), ch. 2 n. 8, n. 9

Mikva, A., *Counsel Lack Selectivity in Appellate Advocacy, Legal Times* (Nov. 15, 1982), ch. 9 n. 12

Mill, J., *A System of Logic Ratiocinative and Inductive* (8th ed. 1916), ch. 16 n. 14

Miller, A., *Death of a Salesman* (1949), ch. 1 n. 2

Miner, R., *Professional Responsibility in Appellate Practice: A View from the Bench*, 19 Pace L. Rev. 323 (1999), ch. 1 n. 5; ch. 9 n. 7

Moore, J., *Moore's Federal Practice* (2d ed. 1989), ch. 4 n. 42

Morris, *Oral Arguments and Written Briefs—DCA Judges Comment*, 62 Fla. B.J. 23 (1988), ch. 6 n. 25

Ottensen, S.E., *Effective Brief-Writing for California Appellate Courts*, 21 San Diego L. Rev. 371 (1984), ch. 6 n. 23; ch. 10 n. 6

Parker, F., *Appellate Advocacy and Practice in the Second Circuit*, 64 Brook L. Rev. 457 (1998), ch. 9 n. 12

Pierce, L., *Appellate Advocacy: Some Reflections from the Bench*, 61 Fordham L. Rev. 829 (1993), ch. 9 n. 13

Pound, R., *The Causes of Popular Dissatisfaction with the Administration of Justice, in The Pound Conference: Perspectives in Justice in the Future* (A. Leo Levin & Russell R. Wheeler eds. 1979), ch. 8 n. 8

Pound, R., *Hierarchy of Sources and Forms in Different Systems of Law*, 7 Tul. L. Rev. 475 (1933), ch. 12 n. 3, n. 9; ch. 16 n. 7; ch. 19 n. 7

Pound, R., *Interpretations of Legal History* (1923), ch. 8 n. 10

Pound, R., *Mechanical Jurisprudence*, 8 Colum. L. Rev. 605 (1908), ch. 8 n. 9

Pregerson, H., *The Seven Sins of Appellate Brief Writing and Other Transgressions*, 34 UCLA L. Rev. 431 (1986), ch. 9 n. 3, n. 4; ch. 15 n. 10

Price, H., *Belief and Will*, in 28 Proceeding of the Aristotelian Society (1954), ch. 6 n. 16

Re, E., *Brief Writing and Oral Argument* (6th ed. 1987), ch. 12 n. 1

Rehnquist, W., *Oral Advocacy*, 27 S.. Tex. L.J. 289 (1986), ch. 3 n. 1

Robbins, R., *Fiction 101: A Primer for Lawyers on How to Use Fiction Writing Techniques to Write Persuasive Fact Sessions*, 32 Rutgers L. Rev. 459 (2001), ch. 12 n. 7

Robertson, J., *From the Bench: Reality on Appeal*, 17 Litig. 3 (1990), ch. 9 n. 6; ch. 13 n. 1

Rodell, C., *Goodbye to Law Reviews*, 23 Va. L. Rev. 38 (1936), ch. 17 n. 1, n. 4

Rosenberg, M., *Appellate Review of Trial Court Discretion*, Federal Judicial Center Publication FJC-ETS-77-3 (1975), ch. 5 n. 38

Rosenberg, M., *Judicial Discretion of the Trial Court, Viewed from Above*, 22 Syracuse L. Rev. 635 (1971), ch. 5 n. 35

Sacks, A., & Hart H., *The Legal Process* (tent. ed. 1958), ch. 5 n. 30

Sahakian, W. & M., *Ideas of the Great Philosophers* (1966), ch. 20 n. 5

Sasso, G., *Anatomy of the Written Argument*, 15 Litig. 30 (1989), ch. 10 n. 15

Sasso, G., *Appellate Oral Argument*, 20 Litig. 27 (1994), ch. 23 n. 2

Schaefer, W., *Precedent and Policy*, 34 U. Chi. L. Rev. 3 (1966), ch. 8 n. 4, n. 10; ch. 19 n. 3, n. 4

Shakespeare, W., *King Lear*, act 4, sc. 6, ch. 24 n. 1

Shapiro, S., *Oral Argument in the United States Supreme Court*, 33 Cath. U. L. Rev. 529 (1984), ch. 3 n. 5, n. 6, n. 9

Stebbing, L., *A Modern Introduction to Logic* (6th ed. 1961), ch. 16 n. 12, n. 13

Story, Joseph, *Life and Letters II* (William Wetmore Store, Ed. 1851) reprinted in John M. Greaney, Power of the Pen, Trial 48 (July 2002), ch. 24, n. 9

Tuchman, B., *An Author's Mail*, 54 The Am. Scholar 313 (1985), ch. 17 n. 2

Tuchman, B., *Practicing History* (1981), ch. 12 n. 5

Von Jhering, R., *Der Geist Des Rominischen Rechts* (1887), ch. 16 n. 2

Waxman, S., *In the Shadow of Daniel Webster: Arguing Appeals in the Twenty-First Century*, 3 J. App. Prac. Process 521 (2001), ch. 23 n. 3

Weber, M., *Value Judgements in Social Science, in Weber Selections* (W. Runciman ed. 1987), ch. 15 n. 7

Wigmore, J., *Evidence in Trials at Common Law* (1983), ch. 9 n. 15; ch. 17 n. 21

Witkin, B., *Manual on Appellate Court Opinions* (1977), ch. 12 n. 10

Wright, C., *The Doubtful Omniscience of Appellate Courts*, 41 Minn. L. Rev. 751 (1957), ch. 5 n. 20

Wright, C., Foreword to Bryan Garner, *The Elements of Legal Style* viii (1991), ch. 17 n. 6

INDEX
References are to section numbers.

—A—

Accident, fallacy of
defined, 20.3.2
**Accuracy, importance of
cover page, 6.9.2**
statement of facts, 12.6
table of contents, 6.9.3
table of authorities, 6.9.4
Acronyms
use, 12.1
Administrative agencies
fact-finding by, 5.5.2
nomenclature, 6.1
Administrative appeals
odds of winning appeal, 1.3
Admiralty cases
28 U.S.C. § 1292(a), 4.3.4.1
Advice, a Compendium,
chapter 21
Aldisert, Ruggero J., 1.1,
1.2, 2.2, 2.4, 5.6, 7.3, 8.2,
8.4.3, 12.3.2, 12.8, 13.2,
15.6, 19.1–19.3, 20.2, 24.4.3,
24.6.1
**Alter or amend judgment,
motion to**
tolling, 4.7, 4.7.1
Amendment
Rule 52(a), Fed. R. Civ. Pro.,
5.5.1
Rule 28(a), Fed. R. Civ. Pro.,
13.1
statutes, 7.3

**Amend or make additional
finding of fact, motion to**
tolling, 4.7.1
Amphibology, fallacy of
defined, 20.3.3
Analogies
at oral argument, 3.2, 22.7,
22.8, 24.6.3.1
defined, 16.5.2
effective use, 7.3, 8.2, 15.4,
19.3, 19.4
material facts, 12.8, 19.3
***Anders* briefs**
generally, 21.4
Andersen, Kenneth, 2.1
Appellate advocacy
trial advocacy
distinguished,
1.1, 2.1, 3.3, 5.4, 5.4.2, 9.8,
12.4, 15.9.2, 16.6, 19.1
Appellate judges, federal,
see **United States circuit
judges**
Appellate judges, state,
see **state appellate
judges**
Appellate lawyers,
see **Lawyers, appellate**
**Appellate Lawyers, How
Top-Flight Prepare for
Oral Argument**,
chapter 23
**Appellate Review: A
Panorama**, chapter 1